BREAKING AND MAKING MODELS

Cultural Inquiry

EDITED BY CHRISTOPH F. E. HOLZHEY
AND MANUELE GRAGNOLATI

The series 'Cultural Inquiry' is dedicated to exploring how diverse cultures can be brought into fruitful rather than pernicious confrontation. Taking culture in a deliberately broad sense that also includes different discourses and disciplines, it aims to open up spaces of inquiry, experimentation, and intervention. Its emphasis lies in critical reflection and in identifying and highlighting contemporary issues and concerns, even in publications with a historical orientation. Following a decidedly cross-disciplinary approach, it seeks to enact and provoke transfers among the humanities, the natural and social sciences, and the arts. The series includes a plurality of methodologies and approaches, binding them through the tension of mutual confrontation and negotiation rather than through homogenization or exclusion.

Christoph F. E. Holzhey is the Founding Director of the ICI Berlin Institute for Cultural Inquiry. Manuele Gragnolati is Professor of Italian Literature at the Sorbonne Université in Paris and Associate Director of the ICI Berlin.

BREAKING AND MAKING MODELS

EDITED BY
CHRISTOPH F. E. HOLZHEY
MARIETTA KESTING
CLAUDIA PEPPEL

ISBN (Hardcover): 978-3-96558-084-8
ISBN (Paperback): 978-3-96558-085-5
ISBN (PDF): 978-3-96558-086-2
ISBN (EPUB): 978-3-96558-087-9

Cultural Inquiry, 33
ISSN (Print): 2627-728X
ISSN (Online): 2627-731X

Bibliographical Information of the German National Library
The German National Library lists this publication in the Deutsche Nationalbibliografie
(German National Bibliography); detailed bibliographic information is available online at
http://dnb.d-nb.de.

Cover design: Studio Bens

In Europe, volumes are printed by Lightning Source UK Ltd., Milton Keynes, UK. See the
final page for further details.

Digital editions can be viewed and downloaded freely at: https://doi.org/10.37050/ci-33.

ICI Berlin Press is an imprint of
ICI gemeinnütziges Institut für Cultural Inquiry Berlin GmbH
Christinenstr. 18/19, Haus 8
D-10119 Berlin
publishing@ici-berlin.org
www.ici-berlin.org

Contents

MODELLING AT THE MARGINS

Introduction

CHRISTOPH F. E. HOLZHEY, MARIETTA KESTING,

AND CLAUDIA PEPPEL

A model can be an object of admiration, a miniature or prototype, an abstracted phenomenon or applied theory, a literary text — practically anything, from a human body on a catwalk to a mathematical description of a system. It can elicit desire, provide understanding, guide action or thought. Despite the polysemy of the term, models across disciplines and fields share a fundamental characteristic: their effect depends on a specific relational quality. A model is always a model of or for something else, and the relation is reductive insofar as it is selective and considers only certain aspects of both object and model. The literary examples of maps made to the scale of a territory, described by Lewis Carroll and Jorge Luis Borges, humorously point to the absurdity of thinking that models keep improving by becoming less reductive until they eventually coincide with their target.[1]

Critical discussions of models often revolve around their restrictive function. Such critiques can draw on the notion of scientific paradigms, referring to accepted models that cohere in totalizing,

---

1 See Lewis Carroll, *Sylvie and Bruno Concluded*, in *The Complete Works of Lewis Carroll* (New York: Vintage Books, 1976), pp. 509–749 (pp. 616–17); and Jorge Luis Borges, 'Of Exactitude in Science', in Borges, *A Universal History of Infamy*, trans. by Norman Thomas di Giovanni (New York: Dutton, 1972), p. 139.

self-reinforcing worldviews, presenting models *of* reality and at the same time serving as models *for* the development of further models.[2] Paradigms articulate problems and solutions deemed exemplary by a community of scientists, thereby rendering alternative approaches increasingly implausible and marginal. Feminist, queer, and decolonial approaches have put forth powerful critiques of the oppressive function of identity models. In recent debates about the wider consequences of data-driven technologies, artificial intelligence is again and again found to reproduce entrenched biases, and its predictive models are said to flatten history into a pre-stabilized present.

And yet models are less prescriptive or definitive and more ambiguous than codified rules or norms. In the sciences, they are usually considered more modest, tentative, and local than theories, which are more expansive and aspire to universality.[3] Models can indeed be considered as intermediaries between theories and the worlds they help constitute — as creative, partially autonomous tools for understanding and as media of theorizing and worlding.[4] Toy models in physics and

---

2   The allusions here are to Thomas S. Kuhn's *The Structure of Scientific Revolutions*, intro. by Ian Hacking (Chicago: University of Chicago Press, 2012), for the association of models, paradigms, and self-reinforcing worldviews; and to Clifford Geertz, 'Religion as a Cultural System', in Geertz, *The Interpretation of Cultures: Selected Essays* (New York: Basic Books, 1973), pp. 87–125 (especially pp. 93–94), for the influential distinction between 'model of' and 'model for'.

3   See, for example, Roman Frigg and Stephan Hartmann, 'Models in Science', *The Stanford Encyclopedia of Philosophy* (Fall 2024 edition), ed. by Edward N. Zalta and Uri Nodelman <https://plato.stanford.edu/archives/fall2024/entries/models-science/> [accessed 10 December 2024]. The fourth section, titled 'Models and Theory', notes that philosophers of science have found it difficult to systematize such a distinction and outlines the various ways in which the relationship between theory and models has been conceptualized. At one end of the spectrum the encyclopedia entry places the 'syntactic view' of theories as axiomatic systems, which models merely interpret, and at the other end the 'semantic view' of theories as 'families of models'.

4   Borrowing from *Models as Mediators: Perspectives on Natural and Social Sciences*, ed. by Mary S. Morgan and Margaret Morrison (Cambridge: Cambridge University Press, 1999) <https://doi.org/10.1017/CBO9780511660108>, this sentence already gestures beyond a purely cognitive approach to models — focused on representing and learning about theories and the world — towards their role in making not only theories but also worlds. The vocabulary of 'worlding' is partially inspired by the ICI Berlin's collaboration with the transnational project Worlding Public Cultures (WPC, see https://www.worldingcultures.org/). This collaboration, which is still ongoing through the WPC chapbook series published by ICI Berlin Press, included a workshop examining the multiple understandings of the concept of 'worlding'. Organized by Birgit Hopfener and Ming Tiampo in collaboration with Annette Bhagwati and Alexandra Chang, the

economics form an intriguing extreme in their deliberately simplistic and arguably non-representational character. At the other end of the spectrum, some models are so complex and messy that they cannot be understood, do not even aim at explanation, and instead promise accurate prediction through (computer) simulation. Somewhere in between are models coordinating several heterogeneous, even mutually incompatible theories in a pragmatically efficacious manner.

What is the role of reduction in modelling practices, and what are its critical potentials? When artists emulate other artists, for example, they do not copy works so much as they model the aesthetic principle that generated those works. This process is by necessity selective and introduces a divergence in the artists' own artistic output. At least since modernity, the tendency has been not to correct but to amplify this divergence in work after work, thus differentiating an 'individual style'. In view of histories of camp or drag and associated theories of performativity, one could ask whether oppressive norms based on gender or race can similarly be seen as the basis for divergence. At the same time, such performative practices highlight the precarity of such balancing acts between ironic distancing and affirmation, and raise the question of how subversive or transformative they can ultimately be.

The reductiveness of models facilitates their travelling across historical, disciplinary, cultural, and other boundaries. This may encourage homogenization but can also generate new perspectives, unpredictable transformations, and complex entanglements. One can trace the transfer of evolutionary and morphological models between biology and art history, and one could even extend this analysis to the discourse on memes. If abstract painting has long been discredited for its universalist claims, this stance has recently been re-evaluated with regard to Black abstraction, queer abstraction, and Indigenous abstraction, which may be seen to counter the pressure to represent otherness within an art market that is still largely dominated by the West.[5] Technical media such as the phonograph and the telephone

---

workshop took place within the symposium 'Co-Constituting the Global: Ethical Challenges and Implications' at the ICI Berlin on 22 June 2018 as part of GAX 2018 <https://doi.org/10.25620/e180622>.

5   David J. Getsy contributed to the first instantiation of the core project 'Reduction' with the talk 'Reduction as Expansion: The Queer Capacities of Abstract Art', ICI Ber-

provided models of the 'psychic apparatus' and its functioning that were foundational to psychoanalysis.

Donna J. Haraway's cyborgs and feminist science fictions demonstrate how models change with their transposition to different domains and transform these fields in turn, giving rise to new questions and approaches. Such transformations are far from uncontroversial. The digital humanities, for example, have often claimed to do away with the humanities' reductive focus on canons by importing computational models that allow for scaling up the analysis to encompass discourses in their entire breadth. Conversely, this purely quantitative 'fix' to the problem of reduction has in turn been criticized as the ultimate reductionism — one that replaces theoretical models, aesthetic categories, and deliberate prioritizations with mere statistics, providing excessively detailed answers to simplistic questions. Eschewing such reciprocal accusations of reduction, one may rather highlight the wide spectrum of possible reductions and their specific affordances and generative potentials. From big data to the moves towards inclusivity encapsulated in terms such as *LGBTQIA2S+*, attempts to counter the reductiveness of models through an accumulation of details, cases, and data abound. Debates over theoretical turns or the notion of conceptual personae in philosophy may provide examples at the deliberately reduced end of the spectrum, while diffractive or intersectional models that coordinate the cooperation of different or even mutually exclusive approaches lie somewhere in the middle.

---

lin, 1 February 2021. The video recording is available at <https://doi.org/10.25620/e210201>. See also his book *Abstract Bodies: Sixties Sculpture in the Expanded Field of Gender* (New Haven, CT: Yale University Press, 2015); and his essay 'Ten Queer Theses on Abstraction', in *Queer Abstraction*, ed. by Jared Ledesma (Des Moines, IA: Des Moines Art Center, 2019), pp. 65–75. On Black abstraction, see, for example, Margo Natalie Crawford, 'The Politics of Abstraction', in Crawford, *Black Post-Blackness: The Black Arts Movement and Twenty-First-Century Aesthetics* (Champaign: University of Illinois Press, 2017), pp. 42–81 <https://doi.org/10.5406/illinois/9780252041006.003.0003>; and on Indigenous abstraction, see Jason Baerg, 'Indigenous Abstraction: A Vehicle for Visioning', in *The Routledge Companion to Indigenous Art Histories in the United States and Canada*, ed. by Heather Igloliorte and Carla Taunton (New York: Routledge, 2022) <https://doi.org/10.4324/9781003014256>; and the exhibition *Action/Abstraction Redefined: Modern Native Art, 1945–1975* at the Westmoreland Museum of American Art, 26 February–28 May 2023 <https://thewestmoreland.org/blog/action-abstraction-redefined-modern-native-art-1945-1975> [accessed 10 December 2024].

What is the critical purchase of models and how does their generative potential relate to their constitutive reduction? What are the stakes in decreasing, increasing, altering, or proliferating the reductiveness of models? How can one work with and on models in a creative, productive manner without disavowing power asymmetries and their exclusionary or limiting effects?

MODEL FOCUS AT THE ICI BERLIN

These questions concluded the project description that the ICI Berlin circulated in the call for its 2022–24 fellowship programme.[6] Eleven fellows were appointed across several disciplines, including anthropology; creative writing and poetry; history of science; literary, film, and media studies; law and critical race theory; psychoanalytic theory; sociology; economics; philosophy; and queer and gender studies. During the two years of their fellowship, they dedicated themselves not only to their individual projects, but also to a joint research project, which took shape through a weekly research colloquium and a lecture series, as well as numerous workshops, symposia, and conferences usually conceptualized by smaller subgroups of fellows.

The project description formed the starting point for the common project, and discussion of the rich literature on models in the philosophy and history of science helped develop a common vocabulary for the multidisciplinary group.[7] Questions of representation — the roles of idealization and abstraction, analogy and fiction, etc. — have resonated for most contributors, and so have propositions to move beyond a focus on representation towards a more performative dimension. Mary S. Morgan and Margaret Morrison, for instance, regard models as 'autonomous agents' and 'mediators', and Tarja Knuuttila's artefactual account considers models as 'tools'.[8] However, the performative dimension of models here remains limited to 'tools of understanding'

---

6 'Models: ICI Focus 2022–24 of the Core Project "Reduction"', ICI Berlin, 13 November 2021 <https://www.ici-berlin.org/projects/models/> [accessed 20 August 2024]. Special thanks go to Jakob Schillinger, who was then research coordinator of the ICI Core Project Reduction, for significantly contributing to the project description.

7 See Frigg and Hartmann, 'Models in Science', and references therein.

8 *Models as Mediators*, ed. by Morgan and Morrison; Tarja Knuuttila, 'Modelling and Representing: An Artefactual Approach to Model-Based Representation', *Studies in*

or other 'cognitive functions'.[9] Philosophers of science indeed tend to take it for granted that models have an 'epistemic value' and worry about its possibility when modelling involves deliberate simplifications and distortions. By contrast, while adopting quite quickly the shift of emphasis from what and how models represent to what they do and enable, the fellowship cohort organized their discussions in three clusters focused on three other kinds of values or functions, namely the political and aesthetic values of models as well as their worldmaking function.

The political value of modelling was explored in contexts ranging from the politics of recognition to the right-wing instrumentalization of genetic studies, and the aesthetic value in contexts ranging from the philosophy of science and language to architecture, installation art, and music therapy. The third cluster explored manifold models of worldmaking in relation to image operations, practices of extraction and archiving, and conditions of war, surveillance, and environmental violence. In a sense, the first two strands came together in the exploration of the worldmaking value or function of models insofar as the politics cluster already involved discussion of how a discipline like economics 'makes its world',[10] and the aesthetic cluster included an excerpt from José Esteban Muñoz's *Cruising Utopia: The Then and There of Queer Futurity*.[11] Muñoz's take on Nelson Goodman's classic, *Ways of Worldmaking*, proved particularly inspiring in giving the notion of worldmaking a 'performative as opposed to epistemological energy', that is, in shifting, again, the emphasis from representation and cognition to a more material sense of worldmaking — of making inhabitable worlds, especially for 'minoritarian people'.[12] With such

---

History and Philosophy of Science Part A, 42.2 (2011), pp. 262–71 <https://doi.org/10.1016/j.shpsa.2010.11.034>.

9   See the section 'Epistemology: The Cognitive Functions of Models' in Frigg and Hartmann, 'Models in Science'.

10   Timothy Mitchell, 'The Work of Economics: How a Discipline Makes its World', *European Journal of Sociology*, 46.2 (2005), pp. 297–320 <https://doi.org/10.1017/S000397560500010X>.

11   José Esteban Muñoz, *Cruising Utopia: The Then and There of Queer Futurity* [2009], 10th anniversary edn (New York: New York University Press, 2019).

12   José Esteban Muñoz, *Disidentifications: Queers of Color and the Performance of Politics* (Minneapolis: University of Minnesota Press, 1999), pp. 195–96.

a performative and situated take, the function of 'worldmaking' furthermore approaches the notion of 'worlding' that the initial project description evoked, especially when it is understood along the lines of the transnational Worlding Public Cultures (WPC) project.[13]

The Models lecture series provided further inspiration for the collective project.[14] It included philosophers of science Knuuttila and Morgan but also explored non-epistemic values and non-cognitive functions of models. Teresa Fankhänel, for instance, presented models in architecture as a powerful tool for testing, constructing, and selling novel architectural ideas. Leigh Raiford showcased how Black Panther Party communications secretary Kathleen Neal Cleaver used photography to make 'home' abroad. Nadia Yala Kisukidi's talk dealt with questions of the Black archive and dreams as necessary to arrive at a model for independence in Congo. These and other topics in the lecture series have not all found their way into this volume; some were dealt with in separate workshops or symposia,[15] others are echoed as tacit knowledge, but they all inspired the individual contributions as well as the entire project.

In autumn 2023, the fellowship cohort held a workshop titled 'Making and Breaking Models', which focused on how the meaning of models changes as it travels between different domains, and on how a given model is constructed and broken depending on how tightly it

---

13   The WPC project draws on Martin Heidegger's 'The Origin of the Work of Art' [1950], in Heidegger, *Poetry, Language, Thought*, trans. by Albert Hofstadter (New York: HarperCollins Modern Classics, 2001), pp. 15–86; but also Gayatri Chakravorty Spivak, 'The Rani of Sirmur: An Essay in Reading the Archives', *History and Theory*, 24.3 (1985), pp. 247–72 <https://doi.org/10.2307/2505169>; Sarah Hunt, 'Ontologies of Indigeneity: The Politics of Embodying a Concept', *Cultural Geographies*, 21.1 (2014), pp. 27–34; and Pheng Cheah, *What Is a World? On Postcolonial Literature as World Literature* (Durham, NC: Duke University Press, 2016) <https://doi.org/10.1515/9780822374534>. See Birgit Hopfener and Ming Tiampo, 'Worlding Global Art Histories', *Texte zur Kunst*, 128 (2022), pp. 146–51; as well as their introduction to *Worlding the Global: The Arts in the Age of Decolonization*, and the volume *Worlding Concepts*, ed. by Paul Goodwin and Ming Tiampo, both forthcoming within the WPC book series at ICI Berlin Press.

14   All the talks in the Models lecture series are available as video recordings. They are listed and linked on the ICI Berlin website at <https://www.ici-berlin.org/series/models-lecture-series-2022-23/> and <https://www.ici-berlin.org/series/models-lecture-series-2023-24/>.

15   See the ICI Berlin website for an overview of events related to the Models focus: <https://www.ici-berlin.org/projects/models/>.

is bound to its reference. Opposing the idea that models are mere representations, contributions inquired into their generative properties: to make a model involves abstractions and idealizations that can have very real effects on the target system. Likewise, to break a model often leads to novel theoretical insights, revealing hidden presuppositions and opening up the possibility of making, and breaking, again.[16] In the workshop, each paper was followed by a short response from the preceding presenter, creating a circle of interlaced calls and responses — a form meant to evoke, in an experimental and playful manner, the endless iteration of making and breaking, over and over and over again.[17]

Emerging from this workshop as the second publication within the core project 'Reduction',[18] the present volume inverts the title to become *Breaking and Making Models* in order to highlight that 'breaking' is part of any process of model building insofar as one always already lives, works, and thinks with models not of one's own making. In a sense, it thereby extends to modelling Muñoz's emphasis on 'disidentification' and 'reiteration',[19] which in turn gives performative energy to Goodman's insistence that 'worldmaking as we know it always starts from worlds already on hand; the making is a remaking'.[20] It also resonates with WPC's emphasis on the ongoing processuality of worlding and of continuous world-opening through deworlding and

---

16   See 'Making and Breaking Models', workshop, ICI Berlin, 16–17 October 2023 <https://doi.org/10.25620/e231016>.

17   In this sense the workshop and its form resonate with those leading to the publications of *Re-: An Errant Glossary*, ed. by Christoph F. E. Holzhey and Arnd Wedemeyer, Cultural Inquiry, 15 (Berlin: ICI Berlin Press, 2019) <https://doi.org/10.25620/ci-15>; and *Over and Over and Over Again: Reenactment Strategies in Contemporary Arts and Theory*, ed. by Cristina Baldacci, Clio Nicastro, and Arianna Sforzini, Cultural Inquiry, 21 (Berlin: ICI Berlin Press, 2022) <https://doi.org/10.37050/ci-21>.

18   See the ICI Website for the description of the core project 'Reduction' <https://www.ici-berlin.org/projects/reduction/>. See also *The Case for Reduction*, ed. by Christoph F. E. Holzhey and Jakob Schillinger, Cultural Inquiry, 25 (Berlin: ICI Berlin Press, 2022) <https://doi.org/10.37050/ci-25>.

19   Cf. Muñoz, *Disidentifications*, p. 196: 'Disidentificatory performance's performativity is manifest through strategies of iteration and *reiteration*. Disidentificatory performances are performative acts of conjuring that deform and re-form the world. *This reiteration builds worlds*' (emphasis in the original).

20   Nelson Goodman, *Ways of Worldmaking* (Hassocks: The Harvester Press, 1978), pp. 6 and 7 <https://doi.org/10.5040/9781350928558>.

reworlding.[21] The volume furthermore retains the workshop's circular form and has longer papers interrupted by short responses that are intended to be experimental and associative, bridging topics or acting as new starting points, in order to invite readers to explore new ways of thinking about, and with, models. Further openings and interventions are provided by Marietta Kesting, the research coordinator; Orit Halpern, who took part in the lecture series; and ICI associate member Astrid Deuber-Mankowsky, who was a keynote speaker at the conference 'Models', organized by World Picture in cooperation with the ICI Berlin.[22]

TRANSFERRING MODELS BETWEEN THE ARTS AND THE SCIENCES

The volume opens with a contribution by Astrid Deuber-Mankowsky that reads the initial project description of the ICI Berlin together with one of its implicit references, the distinction between 'model of' and 'model for' in Clifford Geertz's 'Religion as a Cultural System'. It does so in order to distinguish different models of modelling, worlding, or worldmaking: one where models belong to symbol systems that are totalizing and self-reinforcing, and in which 'the model's being *for* and *of* coincide'; and one where models are 'deliberately reductive, experimental, playful, and modest', and function as media for non-exclusive worlding. Moving to concrete examples, the essay 'Models as Media of Worlding in Sadie Benning and Fernand Deligny' explores how this tension between different concepts of models informs practices of worlding in two very different cases: Sadie Benning's artistic and experimental video practice and Fernand Deligny's extended cinematic life-art experiments with 'autistic' children. Both make use of the camera as a tool for (self-)investigation, both aim 'to change the existing worldviews, which are emotionally and affectively firmly anchored in certain normalizing models', but neither is against the use of models as such. On the contrary, 'models play a crucial role for both in their explorations of different forms of worlding', as Deuber-

---

21 See Hopfener and Tiampo, 'Introduction', in *Worlding the Global*.
22 See 'Models: World Picture Conference', ICI Berlin, 17–18 November 2023 <https://doi.org/10.25620/e231117>.

Mankowsky shows in her analysis of their practices, which are very different but equally reliant on forms of reduction and abstraction: Benning's Fisher-Price PixelVision camera, for instance, recorded a reduced black-and-white image and was meant to be a toy for children, whereas Deligny and his colleagues used a 16 mm camera — sometimes even without film — that became a silent companion and presence in their daily practice of living together in the mountains.

Julia Sánchez-Dorado proposes 'Abstraction as Strategy for Worldmaking' in practices of scientific modelling as much as in aesthetic practices. Her essay begins with the common emphasis on the epistemic and representational function of scientific models and the dilemma of misrepresentation — of how scientific models can be trusted to guide actions if they are known to simplify and distort. It then questions the way in which contemporary philosophy of science typically characterizes abstraction by contrasting it to idealization, understanding it as the epistemologically uninteresting and innocuous 'omission' of irrelevant features of a phenomenon represented, rather than as the addition of idealized, deliberately false features. Taking an example from oceanography — Marie Tharp's map of the ocean floor showing mountainous rifts but no water — and drawing on theorizations of abstract art, Sánchez-Dorado unsettles the opposition between abstraction and idealization and emphasizes the worldmaking potential of abstraction, insofar as it involves — notwithstanding its reductiveness — a creative act of ordering and establishing previously unseen connections between relevant features of the world.

Ross Shields's contribution moves in the opposite direction, from scientific models to the possibility and challenges of making their insights experienceable through literature. Titled 'From Climate Model to Climate Fiction', it focuses on Kim Stanley Robinson's *The Ministry for the Future*, which narrates global warming over the next thirty-odd years. Referencing the theoretical work and interpretive schemas of Walter Benjamin and Fredric Jameson, Shields argues that Robinson's novel exerts an 'operative function' by means of its formal treatment of three themes taken from climate science and climate politics: the feedback loop between climate scenarios and human behaviour, the impossibility of perceiving global warming as a unified phenomenon, and the difficulty of speaking for non-human actors. Climate fiction not only draws from but extends the work of climate models, inasmuch as it bridges the gap between statistical abstraction and concrete reality via the fictional representation of a hypothetical world.

Questions of understanding and learning from non-human actors — taking them as models and modelling them upon humans — are likewise key to Maria Dębińska's essay. Further intertwining scientific and aesthetic modelling practices, it evokes the dizzying possibilities of reciprocal modelling. Dębińska focuses on the slime mould *Physarum polycephalum* as a model organism whose networks have been the object of interdisciplinary studies and artistic interventions for more than two decades. Using Tim Ingold's typology of lines, she considers different experimental and speculative practices of abstracting and modelling lines of movement traced by humans and slime moulds into networks. She thereby investigates how *Physarum* is used to model and explore human patterns of movement and vice versa. Exploring how *Physarum* has functioned as 'a catalyst for new narratives and imaginaries of the social', Dębińska argues that, far from anthropomorphizing the slime mould, the effect of these experiments is instead a slimy rendering of the human. This striking reversal draws attention to what the previous two chapters together already suggested, namely the difficulty of fixing *what*, in a modelling relationship, functions as a model for, or of, *what*.

PERFORMING MODELS

The relationality that is essential to modelling is arguably inherently unstable and requires a narrative framing in order to make intelligible both the terms of the relationship and the sense in which they are related. This means in particular that the normative power that is often attributed to models and that is of central concern in the following contributions has less to do with the models themselves than with the narratives in which they are embedded. Model narratives, in turn, succeed in setting norms — or unsettling them — to the extent that they are able to mobilize established narrative models.

In their chapter 'Persistence: Model Asylum Narratives and a Recognizable "Transgenderness"', B Camminga engages with the persistent narrative model of the 'trans travel narrative'. This model, which involves the trope of 'being trapped in the wrong body' — a journey on which the body gets 'corrected', marking a 'safe return' home in both a metaphorical and geographic sense — was established in early trans autobiographical writings in order to make trans existence culturally intelligible, recognizable, and respectable. There have been concerted efforts to break with this model on account of its perpetuation of a pathologizing perspective and normative gender binary, which forecloses other possibilities, such as taking the risk of non-teleological experiments with indeterminacy. Yet, Camminga shows its partial resurgence in recent autobiographical narratives by transgender migrants and refugees from Africa, such as Farah Abdi's *Never Arrive* (Somalia/Kenya), Neo L. Sandja's *Right Mind, Wrong Body* (Democratic Republic of Congo), and Rizi Xavier Timane's *An Unspoken Compromise* (Nigeria). Adhering to the more recent model of the asylum narrative, these texts cannot dispense with the recognizability, legibility, and intelligibility of the wrong body narrative as their protagonists seek to convince refugee determination officers of their asylum claims. At the same time, they break with the 'safe return' model to produce what Camminga terms the 'unsafe return': highlighting 'home in exile', this model is structured on indeterminacy and is only made possible through the risky exploit, the daring journey to freedom, that undergirds trans becoming.

Shifting to the role of anthropological race-making in the history of biology, Ben Woodard explores the complex ways in which competing modelling schemes in biology align with different politics and ethics. More specifically, he asks to what extent the importation of statistical modelling into biology in the 1930s, where it contributed to establishing the modern synthesis of evolutionary theory while shifting focus from the study of model organisms to populations, remains tethered to the then-pervasive eugenical thinking. Titled 'The Statistical Cloud of Race: Lancelot Hogben's Anti-Eugenics between Populations and Organisms', this essay interlaces an account of Hogben's scientific work with biographical elements of his political fight against eugenics in the first half of the twentieth century, showing how the kind of knowledge that he mobilized has become even more relevant in recent efforts to decolonize biological and statistical knowledge. While Woodard notes that statistical models are neither useless nor inherently normative, malicious, and politically bankrupt, he stresses that their use in a racist science cannot be reduced to personal bias or an ideological misappropriation. Rather, he highlights how Hogben mistrusts scientific claims to neutrality while retaining it as a goal, and how he sought to 'clean' statistical concepts and research through careful distinctions and attention to their subtle functions, such as their use in justifying political authority by helping to confirm preconceptions, cloaking them in apparent neutrality, and making them immune to revision.

Alina-Sandra Cucu highlights the performativity of statistical models that fail to describe reality but help bring about the conditions of their applicability. Providing a case study on 'Articulations of the Romanian Labour Market in the Long 1990s', her essay 'Crises in Modelling' shows how labour market models were rather useless in illustrating what was happening during the transition in post-socialist Romania from a centrally planned economy to a market economy, but nonetheless succeeded in working performatively, as promissory utterances, insofar as they were instrumental in bringing about the reality they were supposed to depict. While Western econometrics takes the timeless figure of *Homo economicus* — the self-interested, fully informed, rational agent of neoclassical economics — as its reference point, Cucu amplifies the views of economists who have highlighted that such agents can only emerge in relation to a fully functional market and that such a market, in turn, far from being a natural order of things, is a historically contingent, institutionally created arrangement. While one might speak of normativity inhering in neoclassical economic models, Cucu concludes by stressing that models are not performative by themselves but come with their own stories and are 'narrative in nature'. Their success relies on a number of actors — which in her case study includes the surprising role of trade unions in pushing for privatization — and 'depends upon the outcome of political struggles' that include 'the politics of knowledge production within the field of economics'.

That models do not merely represent the world but create it, and, more specifically, that 'models make markets' is also stressed in Orit Halpern's contribution. Moving to New York City, the world's financial centre, her essay 'Models, Markets, and Artificial Intelligence' sketches

'A Brief History of our Speculative Present'. It also emphasizes the push towards free market models against any form of state planning but characterizes the model agent rather differently. The reconfiguration of human agency and decision-making that Halpern identifies and associates with a longer neoliberal tradition involves breaking with the model of the conscious, well-informed, rational agent privileged since the democratic revolutions of the eighteenth century and — we might add — underlying neoclassical economics. The new model reimagines human intelligence as machinic and networked, takes for granted that any individual has limited information and is incapable of making reasoned, objective decisions, and relies instead on the rationality and self-regulation of algorithms and markets to coordinate dispersed information and embody a superior networked intelligence. Halpern's essay traces this development to the neoliberal economist Friedrich Hayek, who inherited his idea of environmental intelligence from psychologist Donald O. Hebb's neural network model, and links it, by way of a joint background in cybernetics and engagement with the learning models of psychologist Frank Rosenblatt, to the development of machine learning and AI. It concludes by highlighting the disavowal of the possibility of representation and the work it takes to maintain a belief in markets as quasi-divine forces of nature with unlimited possibilities of evolution through chance and emergence, provided that they are not constrained by consciousness, planning, or calls for justice and equity.

Marietta Kesting's essay discusses some aspects of large language models (LLMs) in 2023 that use a type of machine learning called 'deep learning', and that model human speech and text in English. Her essay problematizes operations of learning, 'parroting', and mimicry. Kesting points out analogies and differences between modelling language in current AI applications and learning processes in children, as they play out in discussions of human versus machine intelligence and creativity and their translation into popular discourses. LLMs were often described by human authors in 2023 as comparable to human intelligence, but only to that of a small child. These descriptions were evidence of the human commentators projecting qualities of human understanding and learning into the language models. Kesting suggests that the anthropomorphizing perspective often employed in these debates is the legacy of Turing's model of machine intelligence, which had suggested that the simulation of human intelligence by a machine is key and sufficient for it to pass as intelligent, as described in his well-known 'Turing Test'. Current debates about AI creativity and learning are haunted by these reductive models of education and schooling, as well as postcolonial power asymmetries and the question of 'proper' language use versus local variations or accents, the written versus the oral, and the notion that animals, formerly colonized people, and machines supposedly only imitate 'correct' language.

MODELLING AT THE MARGINS

While problematizing the normative performativity of models that have become dominant, the preceding contributions already imply the possibility of making alternative models that break with the dominant ones. The final contributions are more focused on the possibilities of creative and precarious processes of minor modelling at the margins of normative models. They analyse unique instances of the remaking of models that thereby challenge pre-existing standards or the status quo. While each contribution draws from a specific and separate field, they share an insistence on disturbing dominant models, especially heteronormative and anthropocentric ones, as well as an attention to the ambiguous power of language and an emphasis on the world-making performativity of non-hegemonic models, whether in judicial institutions, the literary canon, psychoanalytic theory and art, or in the (re)naming of queer identities in South Africa.

Natascia Tosel's contribution focuses on the possibility of remaking normative models within institutions. Titled 'Modelling Institutions, Instituting Models: The Juridification of Politics and the Performative Power of Naming', it starts from Gilles Deleuze's claim that institutions perform a social activity of constituting and imposing models of conduct on both bodies and minds. The essay analyses three main paradigms in which this modelling activity has been conceptualized in political theory. The first is a 'sovereign' performativity that attributes the efficacy of institutional language entirely to the authority and legitimacy of the speaking subject. The second is a 'subversive' performativity that, drawing on Judith Butler's analysis of the iterability of speech acts, opens legal and institutional discourse to the possibility of resignification, namely a reclaiming of the name through which a group is traditionally stigmatized or excluded from power. The third is a properly 'instituting' performativity that, following Pierre Bourdieu's analyses in *The Force of Law*, identifies the power of naming with a power of form. This entails a 'calling into being' of both a name and the vision of the world that it implies. Tosel argues that this instituting performativity, wherein models are construed as previsions of the world, enables a better understanding of the current relationship between law and politics. Indeed, she interprets the increasing use of legal language to address political issues — referred to as the 'juridification of politics' — as a symptom of intensified worldmaking activity *within* institutions, rather than its neutralization.

The ambiguous position of language in relation to repressive models of the human is the subject of Marta Aleksandrowicz's essay, titled 'Aesthetic Modelling at the Limit of the Human Montage'. Exploring the psychoanalytic work of Willy Apollon and the creative work of the artist Lygia Clark and the writer Clarice Lispector to rethink the human through an aesthetic lens, Aleksandrowicz shows how all three oppose the dominant anthropocentric, individualistic, and self-enclosed model of the human established by what Apollon and Lispector respectively call the 'cultural montage' and 'human montage'. While Apollon locates the human *outside* the cultural montage that controls and represses unconscious desire and creativity, Clark's sculpture series *Bichos* and Lispector's novel *The Passion According to G.H.* model the human as a different, transindividual kind of montage. This transindividual montage is supported through the aesthetic practice of breaking prevailing models of language, subjectivity, and sculpture; it not only disrupts the anthropocentric, individualistic model of the human, but also problematizes other models that risk arresting the human on either side of the historically, culturally, socially, or economically predetermined subject/object, oppressor/victim binary. Aleksandrowicz concludes by noting that the two kinds of montages discussed — the cultural/human and the transindividual — correspond to different conceptions not only of the human but also of the model, and suggests that the transindividual model of modelling would not be possible without the aesthetic.

Mark Anthony Cayanan's contribution engages with Jahan Ramazani's contemporary model of the lyric, which is 'intergeneric, transnational, [and] translingual'. Situating the discussion within the context of the author's own creative practice and, more broadly, Philippine
anglophone literary production, the essay analyses how Ramazani's
model accommodates — and is indeed affirmed by — exophony, that
is, the practice of literature written in a language that is not the author's native tongue. The intergeneric and transnational qualities of the
contemporary lyric emerge in its exophonic iteration through the communion of various traditions: the transplanted tradition of the lyric
and one drawn from vernacular poetics. Scrutiny of Cayanan's own
creative production also exhibits how the 'compressed heteroglossia'
located within the lyric — the paradoxical fusion of multiple voices
and registers into an ostensibly singular enunciatory phenomenon —
may be deployed to signify cultural irreconcilabilities. Finally, sample
poems from the author's work in progress supplement the essay's preoccupation with articulating a poetics of the exophonic lyric.

The volume's final chapter, Ruth Ramsden-Karelse's 'Towards a
Genealogy of *Moffie:* Troubling the Binary Model of Understanding
either Homosexuality or Homophobia as Un-African', historicizes the
Southern African word *moffie*, which was customarily used as a pejorative marker for individuals read as effeminate men. Over the past
few decades, the term has been somewhat reclaimed as a defiant self-
descriptor. Foregrounding the word's predominance in relation to
communities that were legally classified 'coloured' under apartheid,
Ramsden-Karelse begins to advance an alternate genealogy of *moffie*,
sketched in relation to two 'scenes': first, *moffie's* use in the 1990s
by academic researchers seeking historical precedent for newly articulated claims to gay rights; second, print media's mid-twentieth-century
constitution of 'Cape Moffies' as a distinct social class onto which
political anxieties were projected. Considered together, these scenes
reveal complex and non-linear formational processes of descent and
emergence that importantly underscore the misleading nature of the
debate about what is 'un-African'. While the terms of this debate have
limited the possible answers to the alternative of homosexuality or
homophobia, a critical genealogy of *moffie* points to an underlying
sexualization of racialization and highlights its specific contingencies.

The chapter thereby presents one more example of the many ways in which inherited models of representation and understanding may be broken and the possibility opened to make them — and thus the world — anew.

TRANSFERRING MODELS BETWEEN
THE ARTS AND THE SCIENCES

Models as Media of Worlding in Sadie Benning and Fernand Deligny

ASTRID DEUBER-MANKOWSKY

INVENTING NEW AESTHETIC PRACTICES

Sadie Benning grew up with a single mother in Milwaukee. They were fifteen years old and had dropped out of high school because of homophobia when their father, Los Angeles-based avant-garde artist James Benning, gave them a Fisher-Price PKL-2000 camera, also called 'Pixelvision', for Christmas in 1988. It was a toy, a camera for children that ran on batteries and produced pixelated black-and-white images on standard cassette tapes that did not allow reels longer than four minutes. Although Benning says they were disappointed that it was only a child's camera and not a camcorder, they very soon began experimenting with it, and invented a new video aesthetic. In a 1992 interview, they recalled how they began shooting their first video, *A New Year* (1989): 'I just set the camera down and it didn't judge me. It just listened. I used it to get things out that I couldn't tell anybody yet.'[1]

---

1   Kim Masters, 'Auteur of Adolescence', *The Washington Post*, 17 October 1992 <https://www.washingtonpost.com/archive/lifestyle/1992/10/17/auteur-of-adolescence/bad908d9-02b0-4a56-a336-8d0cd1b78b31/> [accessed 20 August 2024].

Fig. 1. Screenshot from the film *A New Year* (1989), dir. by Sadie
Benning (03:15). Image copyright of the artist, courtesy of Video Data
Bank, School of the Art Institute of Chicago.

They recorded TV images and their body in their bedroom, combining performance, close-ups of their face, handwriting and text,
snippets of newspapers, music from the underground feminist punk
movement that was just emerging, as well as hip hop and jazz, and
experimental narrative to critically explore gender, sexuality, racism,
homophobia, and the 'normal' violence of their social environment
(Figure 1).

Benning showed their first four short films to their father, who
immediately recognized the artistic value and expressiveness of these
videos. He screened them in his class at the California Institute of
the Arts, and, from there, their reputation quickly spread to the art
world and to a queer public. Benning's Pixelvision videos were shown
at the Museum of Modern Art in New York City in 1991, at the 1993

Whitney Biennial, and at all relevant independent film festivals. They established a new aesthetic and helped found New Queer Cinema.[2]

Fernand Deligny was not an artist; his work was not exhibited. But he was similarly interested in questions of perception and technology's potential to change the way we see the world. Deligny's focus was on sharing the world with children and young people who did not conform to the model of normality. In 1949, he created the network La Grande Cordeé, dedicated to the attempt to free psychotic and delinquent youths from institutions and to take care of them 'in an independent therapy'.[3] Nine years later, together with the psychoanalyst and free thinker Josée Manenti, a few companions, and the children entrusted to his care, he moved to the Cévennes countryside. They used the camera to collaborate on a project that focused not on language but on the universe of gestures in which the children lived.[4] The presence of the camera opened a space for play that allowed new encounters and the forging of new relationships among the participants, including the landscape and the recording equipment.[5] Between 1962 and 1964, Deligny, Manenti — who operated the 16 mm camera — and their companions spent days with the children in the landscape, shooting footage for a film to come. The film material was only edited by Jean-Pierre Daniel five years later, becoming the famous experimental film *Le Moindre Geste* (Figure 2), shown in a first version at the Cannes Film Festival in 1971. The final 35 mm version was completed with the help of Chris Marker, but was not released until 2004.[6]

---

2   On the emergence and history of New Queer Cinema, see Ruby Rich, *New Queer Cinema: The Director's Cut* (Durham, NC: Duke University Press, 2013) <https://doi.org/10.1215/9780822399698>.

3   Sandra Alvarez de Toledo, 'Fernand Deligny: Repères cinèbiographiques', in *Le Cinéma de Fernand Deligny* (Paris: Editions Montparnasse et les auteurs, 2007), pp. 3–8 (p. 4; my translation).

4   See Jean-Pierre Daniel, 'Josée Manenti, la force de l'amitié. *Le Moindre Geste*, ou filmer l'enfant psychotique', *Le Coq-Héron*, 209 (2012), pp. 65–70 <https://doi.org/10.3917/cohe.209.0065>.

5   See, in this regard, Astrid Deuber-Mankowsky, 'The Space of Appearance in Deep Underground: *A Film Is Being Made* and the Documentary Gesture', *MLN*, 137.3 (2022), pp. 443–65 <https://doi.org/10.1353/mln.2022.0034>.

6   On the circuitous and by no means conflict-free production history of *Le Moindre Geste*, see Daniel, 'Josée Manenti, la force de l'amitié'.

FIG. 2. Poster for the film *Le Moindre Geste* (1971)
<https://www.imdb.com/title/tt0431917/mediaviewer/rm1588603136/>
[accessed 20 August 2024].

After working for two years at the Clinique de la Borde with Jean Oury and Félix Guattari, Deligny returned to the Cévennes in 1967 to undertake a new *tentative*. A *tentative*, for Deligny, was more of an experience or experimentation than an experiment. In his words, it was 'a small ensemble, a small, very flexible network that weaves itself into reality as it is, in circumstances as they are, even encountering rather rare events that cannot be created arbitrarily'.[7] 'La tentative des Cévennes', also called 'the network of Cévennes', existed from 1969 until 1986. It denotes a certain form of cohabitation of Deligny and his companions — he called them 'presences proches' — with up to twelve 'autistic' children in the countryside. Autism, at that time, meant to Deligny in the first place that the children were mute, without any relation to symbolic language. At the centre of the group was Janmari, who had been placed in Deligny's care by his mother in 1966 as a twelve-year-old boy, diagnosed by the Salpêtrière Hospital with incurable, profound brain damage. This boy, who lived in the group all the time, changed his behaviour in astonishing ways, participating in common activities such as baking bread, fetching water, chopping wood, and so forth, but did not speak a word in all these years. During all this time, the camera was almost always present. For Deligny, as he explained in the 1975 documentary *Ce gamin, là*, these children lived at 'the other pole of our existence',[8] and for him it could not be a question of the children adapting to our point of view, but that we must learn to live with them, their gestures, and their 'point de voir' ('point of view'). In the course of this reversal of perspective, which was at the same time a radical change of perspective towards what Deligny called the 'common body of the human species', Deligny and his adult companions drew more than two hundred maps, on which they marked their own journeys and then, on tracing paper, the children's 'lignes d'erre', their 'wander lines'.[9]

---

7   Fernand Deligny, *Oeuvres*, ed. by Sandra Alvarez de Toledo (Paris: L'Arachnéen, 2007), p. 705; my translation.

8   Fernand Deligny, in *Ce gamin, là (Radeaux dans la montagne)*, dir. by Renaud Victor (France, 1975) (03:47–03:49).

9   See Fernand Deligny, Sandra Alvarez de Toledo, and Cyril Le Roy, *Cartes et lignes d'erre / Maps and Wander Lines: Traces du réseau de Fernand Deligny, 1969–1979* (Paris: L'Arachnéen, 2013).

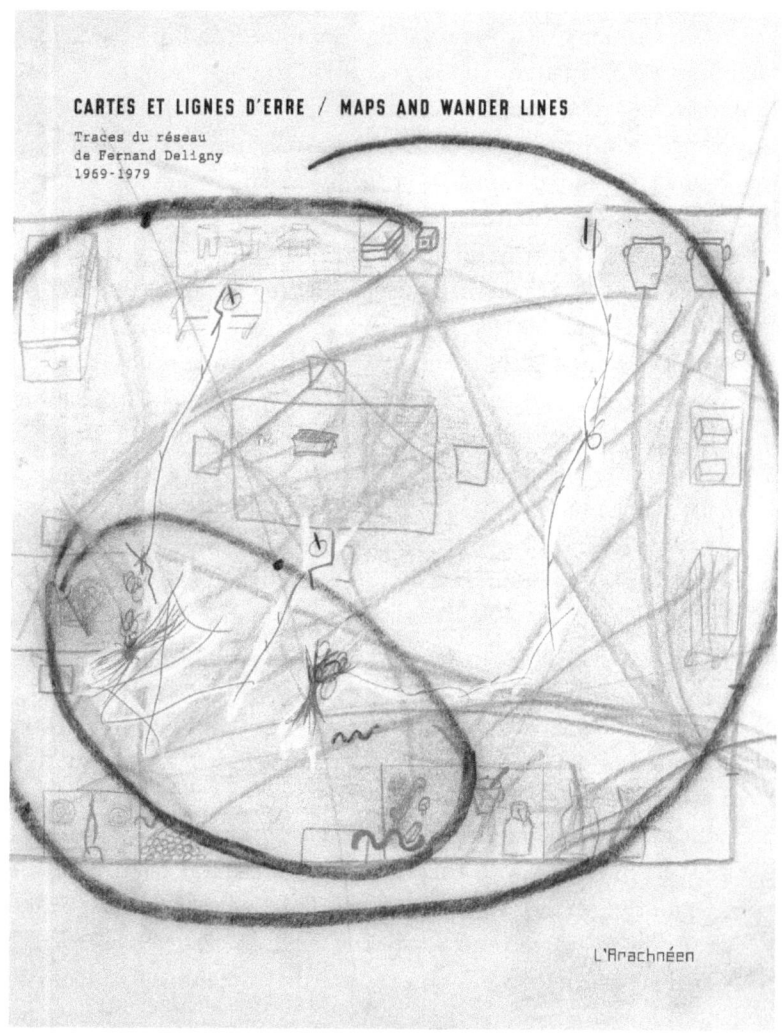

FIG. 3. Fernand Deligny, Sandra Alvarez de Toledo, and Cyril Le Roy, *Cartes et lignes d'erre/Maps and Wander Lines: Traces du réseau de Fernand Deligny, 1969–1979* (Paris: L'Arachnéen, 2013) <https://www.editions-arachneen.fr/catalogue/cartes-et-lignes-derretraces-du-reseau-de-fernand-deligny-1969-1979/> [accessed 6 December 2024].

This practice became famous under the name 'mapping the wander lines' (see Figure 3). The goal of these maps was to locate places where encounters took place while the adults were mainly engaged in everyday tasks, such as making a fire, washing dishes, or feeding animals, and while the children were also outside, near them, following their own ways and rhythms. Deleuze and Guattari derived their method of cartography and the notion of the rhizome in *A Thousand Plateaus* in part from Deligny's practices.

WHAT MODEL?

Yet, what do Sadie Benning's Pixelvision videos and Deligny's *tentative* have in common, and what connects them to the question of models? Both criticize existing models and decidedly do not wish to create new models. The French scholar Igor Krtolica, for example, emphasizes that Deligny's *tentative* does not follow any model and does not represent a model that could be followed: the network of Deligny, he writes, has 'no monopolistic pretensions: it is not a model to follow'.[10] Even clearer: 'The word "tentative" should therefore be taken literally: as an experimentation that has no model and does not pretend to become one.'[11] From Sadie Benning comes the related statement: 'I want to be free to try things that don't make sense yet.'[12] And: 'As a transgender queer youth without access at that time to images or language that affirmed my reality, I saw it as urgent to make my own images.'[13]

Both Benning and Deligny want to change existing worldviews, which are emotionally and affectively firmly anchored in certain normalizing models. Moreover, both build on the singularity and contingency of the present to initiate a practice of world exploration that is less exclusive and less violent. This approach is not geared towards new models that serve to normalize and subjectivize.

---

10   Igor Krtolica, 'La "Tentative" des Cévennes. Deligny et la question de l'institution', *Chimères*, 72 (2010), pp. 73–97 (p. 85).

11   Ibid.

12   Sadie Benning, in 'Sadie Benning, American, born 1973', Museum of Modern Art, n.d. <https://www.moma.org/artists/34902> [accessed 20 August 2024].

13   Sadie Benning, in Diana Solway, 'Transgender Artist Sadie Benning Is Not Afraid', *W*, 13 May 2016 <https://www.wmagazine.com/story/sadie-benning-artist-mary-boone-callicoon-fine-arts> [accessed 20 August 2024].

And yet, models play a crucial role for both in their explorations of different forms of worlding. The two hundred maps of wander lines that Deligny and his team produced can undoubtedly be described as models of a kind. Benning also plays with models in her videos when she disguises herself and uses gestures, moves, movements, songs, and utterances from the subculture to queer and rearrange the world. The question is, of course, what one means by 'model'. I shall now explore this question in more detail.

A well-known, indeed almost canonical, definition of 'model' in the fields of anthropology and cultural studies goes back to Clifford Geertz and his 1966 essay 'Religion as Cultural System'.[14] Here, Geertz introduces his concept of the model to explain how the processes he calls 'culturally programmed' should be understood. His text concerns the analysis of religion, which he defines as follows:

> (1) a system of symbols which acts to (2) establish powerful, pervasive, and long-lasting moods and motivations in men by (3) formulating conceptions of a general order of existence and (4) clothing these conceptions with such an aura of factuality that (5) the moods and motivations seem uniquely realistic.[15]

As Geertz argues, by analogy with genetics, the way religion reproduces itself as a cultural pattern can be understood as a cultural programme. He introduces the concept of the model to explain how the teachings of religions, which are linked to moods and motivations, rituals and melodies, are passed on. As with the term 'programming', Geertz borrows the term 'model' from the sciences and defines cultural patterns as models in the sense that they are 'sets of symbols whose relations to one another "model" relations among entities, processes or what-have-you in physical, organic, social, or psychological systems by "paralleling", "imitating", or "simulating" them'.[16] He makes no distinction as to whether these systems, of which the entities are components, are physical, organic, mental, or social. However, he emphasizes that the two aspects inherent in the model, as being both *of* (reality) and

---

14   Clifford Geertz, 'Religion as a Cultural System', in Geertz, *The Interpretation of Cultures: Selected Essays* (London: Fontana Press, 1993), pp. 86–125.

15   Ibid., p. 90.

16   Ibid.

for (reality), respectively, make the model the medium and executive organ of doctrines and rites in the field of religion, whereas in the sciences models remain bound to theory. That is, for anthropology, the model is an analytical tool to explain how it is that religion and similar authoritative value systems function like cultural programmes to create realities. In contrast, the model in the sciences is not so much tied to doctrines, rites, moods, and motivations but to theories and concepts. This means that only models as cultural patterns are normative in the sense that they 'give meaning, that is, objective conceptual form, to social and psychological reality both by shaping themselves to it and by shaping it to themselves'.[17]

The connection Geertz draws between models and religion — as a 'system of symbols which acts to establish powerful, pervasive, and long-lasting moods and motivations in men by formulating conceptions of a general order of existence and clothing these conceptions with such an aura of factuality that the moods and motivations seem uniquely realistic' — explains the violent effect that models, as cultural patterns, can have on people, and especially on those who do not fit into a given cultural system. Models in this sense are intrinsically normative. This also explains why Benning and Deligny neither follow models nor wish to create models to follow. Instead, they are interested in analysing and criticizing the power of these models and exploring the frameworks in which they are so powerful. At the same time, through alternative forms of expression, they seek practices of worlding or world-making that are non-exclusionary and non-violent. However, they work with models for this as well.

My thesis is that the models Benning and Deligny relate to, as the media of worlding, differ significantly from those Geertz describes so accurately: Benning's and Deligny's models are neither normative nor oriented towards a totalizing view of the world. They are local, playful, and experimental. I base my argument on the decisive questions posed in the ICI Focus 'Models' statement. Christoph Holzhey and his co-authors here assume, first, that all models share the fundamental characteristic that their effect depends on a specific relational quality.

---

17   Ibid., p. 93.

Second, they underscore that this relation is 'reductive insofar as it is selective and considers only certain aspects of both object and model'.[18]

Unlike Geertz, the 'Models' statement emphasizes less the performative aspect of the model than the difference between the model and its referent. In this regard, it cites Lewis Carroll and Jorge Luis Borges, both of whom humorously point out 'the absurdity of thinking that models keep improving by becoming less reductive until they eventually coincide with their target'.[19] The ICI's statement points out that models have often been criticized precisely because of this restrictive function:

> Such critiques can draw on the notion of scientific paradigms, referring to accepted models that cohere in totalizing, self-reinforcing worldviews, presenting models *of* reality, and at the same time serving as models *for* the development of further models.[20]

Now, it is striking that Holzhey and his co-authors link the self-referentiality of models to their restrictive function and cite this as the reason for totalizing, self-reinforcing worldviews, while Geertz identifies in this very fact the central potentiality of the model qua cultural pattern for religions as systems of symbols. These different perspectives on models are related to the fact that the ICI's statement starts from the differences between models in various disciplines. While Geertz points out that models in the sciences refer to theories and not to doctrines and melodies, but draws no conclusion from this, Holzhey and his co-authors emphasize this very fact. They state: 'In the sciences, they are usually considered more modest, tentative, and local than theories, which are more expansive and aspire to universality'.[21] They highlight, furthermore, that models are 'less prescriptive or definitive and more ambiguous than codified rules', and conclude that models

---

18   'Models: ICI Focus 2022–24 of the Core Project "Reduction", ICI Berlin, 13 November 2021 <https://www.ici-berlin.org/projects/models/> [accessed 20 August 2024], quoting from the introduction of this volume, p. 1.

19   Ibid.

20   Ibid., pp. 1–2.

21   Ibid., p. 2.

can be considered 'as creative, partially autonomous tools for under-standing and as media of theorizing and worlding'.[22]

So, we have two models of models that belong to different forms of worlding: one belongs to symbol systems that are totalizing and self-reinforcing. In this, the aspects of the model's being *for* and *of* coincide. The other model is tentative, deliberately reductive, local, experimental, playful, and modest. It is a medium for a non-exclusive, local, and tentative worlding.

In what follows, I will move from the tension between these two different concepts of models to concrete examples, to examine the ways in which Sadie Benning, in her early Pixelvision videos, and Fernand Deligny, in his 'tentative des Cévennes', draw on models as media of a more inclusive and less violent exploration of the world. In this way, I hope both to sharpen the understanding of the concept of the model and to contribute to the understanding of the artistic practices of Benning and Deligny.

SADIE BENNING: FREE TO TRY THINGS THAT DON'T MAKE SENSE YET

The first tapes Benning shot with her Fisher-Price toy camera in 1989 are raw. The black-and-white images are heavily pixelated and sur-rounded by a thick black border. The sound is overlaid with a strong hiss. The videos address the violence of the Reagan era in the US and the violence Benning experienced as a teenager who described them-selves as being 'as queer as can be'.[23]

Benning filmed the first tapes enclosed in the safety of their bed-room and from this position observed the influences of US culture on their queerness and lesbian identity through the camera lens and video screen. The compressed spatial format of the Fisher-Price PKL-2000 camera images reflects the limited space of Benning's bedroom: the image quality of these videos is low, the images' relationship to the subject is weak, their combination with music and sound is tentative, and the use of Benning's own body is experimental. They oppose the normative model that is part of a totalizing and self-reinforcing symbol

---

22   Ibid.
23   Masters, 'Auteur of Adolescence'.

Fig. 4 and 5. Screenshots from the film *A New Year* (1989), dir. by Sadie Benning (00:10 and 00:41). Image copyright of the artist, courtesy of Video Data Bank, School of the Art Institute of Chicago.

system. That is, Benning analyses in and with their videos the patterns of a culture based on exclusion and violence, and thus the very models that Geertz identifies as the executive organ of doctrines and rites.

A New Year (1989) starts with a Pixelvision-recorded sample of the television game show *The Price is Right*, in which contestants compete by guessing the prices of merchandise to win cash and prizes (Figure 4). The camera then moves to pan across a hand-scrawled sentence: 'I realized how crazy everyone is and I realized what a small part I played in it' (00:39–01:09; Figure 5). Following this, the camera pans over newspaper headlines while 'I Shot the Sheriff' can be heard on the soundtrack. No music is heard while the camera scans Benning's handwritten lines — only the noise of the camera. Following this, Benning laconically, yet precisely, describes the everyday violence of her immediate surroundings ('A girl I know got hit by a drunk driver. Her leg was broken & twisted like puddy', 01:39–02:09). In contrast, there are pictures of a snow globe in which Mary and Joseph can be seen fleeing with the baby Jesus (Figure 6).

The video analyses the sinister dynamic in which poverty, sexism, homophobia, and racism intertwine ('A friend of mine got raped by a Black man. Now she's a racist Nazi skinhead', 03:09–03.55; Figure 1),

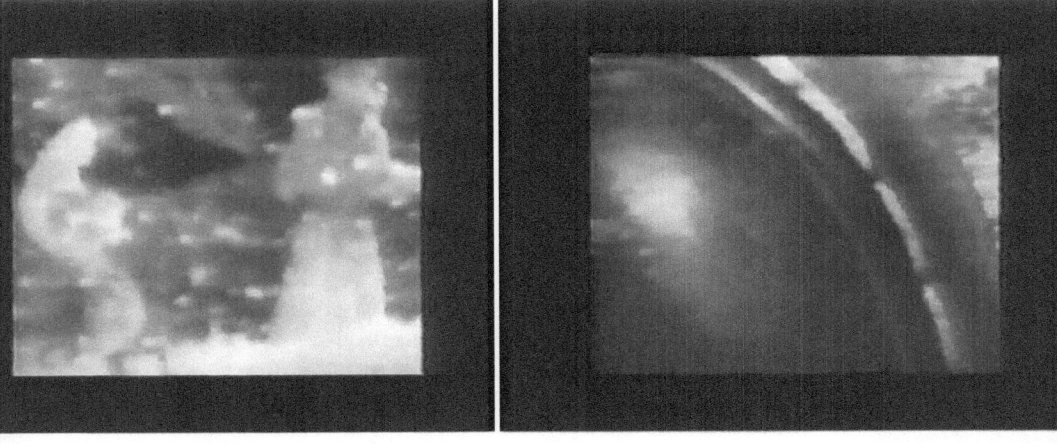

FIG. 6 and 7. Screenshots from the film *A New Year* (1989), dir. by Sadie
Benning (02:19 and 04:40). Image copyright of the artist, courtesy of
Video Data Bank, School of the Art Institute of Chicago.

and explores the relation between addictions ('My neighboor [*sic*] is
selling crack', 04:52–05:06) and capitalism ('But our nation is addicted
to a more harmful drug, money', 05:30–05:50). Between these statements, there are close-ups of her own body, an eye, a shoe (Figure 7)
— real, yet at the same time monstrous and powerful.

In her seminal 1998 essay about Benning's early videos, Mia Carter
succinctly summarizes:

> Benning associates the persecution of sexually different bodies
> with the histories of racism and imperialism, thereby tran-
> scending the boundaries of both the personal and the histor-
> ical.[24]

These histories of racism, imperialism, and homophobia are based precisely on those cultural models that are at the centre of a 'system of
symbols' which, according to Geertz, 'acts to establish powerful, pervasive, and long-lasting moods and motivations in men by formulating
conceptions of a general order of existence and clothing these concep-

---

24   Mia Carter, 'The Politics of Pleasure: Cross-Cultural Autobiographic Performance in
      the Video Works of Sadie Benning', *Signs*, 23.3 (1998), pp. 745–76 (p. 751) <https://
      doi.org/10.1086/495287>.

tions with such an aura of factuality that the moods and motivations seem uniquely realistic'.[25]

The closeness of Benning's works to the form of the diary meant that they were quickly perceived as 'video diaries'. Benning, however, was critical of this reception. In an interview ten years later, responding to the question 'would you call your first works video diaries?', they stated:

> They were, in a way, forerunners to YouTube videos. I was young and aware of the diary as a format, but I was more conscious that the videos were experimental and performance based — my concern with the word diary is that it highlights the confessional and is less about the imaginative and abstract qualities that I associate with those videos.[26]

I propose to connect the imaginative and abstract qualities of the videos with the very qualities that Holzhey and his co-authors attribute to these models, which can be considered 'as creative, partially autonomous tools for understanding and as media of theorizing and worlding'.[27] The restriction to their bedroom; the limitations of the Pixelvision camera; the concentration on their own person, their body, and the known environment; the use of the objects; and the performances in front of and with the camera can be interpreted as rules that create a place, limited in time and space — a 'room-for-play', in which new worlds and new models can be designed. It is a way of modelling that, as Annabel Jane Wharton points out, can be thought of as play: '"Play", at least if it is understood in terms of its definition by the Dutch historian Johan Huizinga, is a productive way to understand models and their manipulation'.[28]

From this perspective, the sound and the music, Benning's body, the clothes, the caps, and all the other parts, like the sentences scribbled on paper, the voice-overs, the drawings, puppets, newspapers,

25   Geertz, 'Religion as a Cultural System', p. 90.

26   Sadie Benning, in Solway, 'Transgender Artist Sadie Benning Is Not Afraid.'

27   'Models: ICI Focus 2022–24', quoted in this volume on p. 2.

28   Annabel Jane Wharton, 'Defining Models', in *Modelwork: The Material Culture of Making and Knowing*, ed. by Martin Brückner, Sandy Isenstadt, and Sarah Wasserman (Minneapolis: University of Minnesota Press, 2021), pp. 3–20 (p. 10) <https://doi.org/10.5749/j.ctv1z9n20d.4>.

 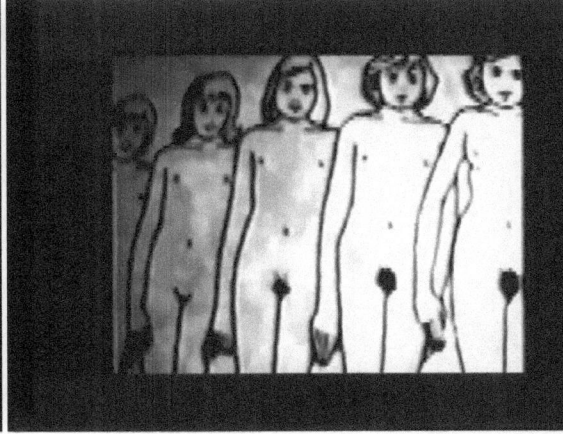

FIG. 8 and 9. Screenshots from the film *Girl Power (Part 1)* (1992), dir.
by Sadie Benning (00:13 and 00:20). Image copyright of the artist,
courtesy of Video Data Bank, School of the Art Institute of Chicago.

television pictures, and found footage, appear as elements of a game in
which the camera plays a privileged role. The camera simultaneously
sets the rules, plays along, and records the game. The camera thus
becomes an active agent in Benning's practice of modelling. It does
not function as a tool to achieve a specific purpose or a specific result;
rather, its presence and materiality open up the possibility of a different
form of worlding. The videos irritate the viewer, inviting them to think
and to play along with them.

The way Benning carefully and deliberately assembles the various
elements into a local and provisional model is evident in the way she
relates to music:

> I think music is a place where you can challenge social conven-
> tions because rhythm is so personal. It makes you feel things.
> I think that musical influences and the experience of creating
> music is in everything I do. It's like a heartbeat.[29]

This brings me to the fourteen-minute video *Girl Power (Part I)*, of
1992, featuring the underground feminist Riot Grrrl punk band Bikini
Kill, and the underground rock band Sonic Youth, as elements of

---

29   Benning, in Solway, 'Transgender Artist Sadie Benning Is Not Afraid'.

FIG. 10 and 11. Screenshot from the film *Girl Power (Part 1)* (1992), dir. by Sadie Benning (00:38 and 00:41). Image copyright of the artist, courtesy of Video Data Bank, School of the Art Institute of Chicago.

the counterculture in which Benning grounds their new model for worlding. The video begins with a scene in which sound and image are woven into a single rhythm. We hear a sample of the song 'Shoot' by Sonic Youth and move with the Pixelvision camera from a drawn portrait of a woman (Figure 8) to a series of drawings of naked girls' bodies (Figure 9) over which the camera moves in time with the music, and after a cut we finally see a profile view of an older woman pointing a gun at a model of a male torso and shooting (Figures 10 and 11).

This subtle deconstruction of the prevailing normative models through which a totalizing heteronormative order is reproduced and reinforced runs through the entire fourteen-minute video.

Using video technology and playing with the mediality of moving images, Benning creates a kind of equality between the close-ups of their own body and the various models through which the heteronormative order inscribes itself as a 'cultural programme' in the hearts and minds of its subjects, similar to that which Geertz describes for religion. The close-ups make their body appear both more unfitting and more powerful. Benning is repeatedly seen dancing wildly, and, in some scenes, we see home videos of them as a small child, dreaming of riding a motorcycle like actor Erik Estrada, even in those early days.

Fig. 12, 13, and 14. Screenshots from the film *Girl Power (Part 1)*
(1992), dir. by Sadie Benning (03:15, 03:20, and 03:22). Image
copyright of the artist, courtesy of Video Data Bank, School of the Art
Institute of Chicago.

The video plays with scientific and medical models that confirm gender
and generational order. Benning contrasts these with the desire for
a different, more open, less violent world, in which models are not
performative but invite us to play. Particularly beautiful and famous
is the scene in which Benning remembers how they imagined themself
as Matt Dillon in front of the mirror as a child, imagining themself to
be just as sexy as the star (Figures 12, 13, and 14).

'So I built my own world [...] made my own rules.' These voice-over statements, spoken by Benning themself, show that the refusal to conform to the harmful normative ideals of society is accompanied by a different worlding. Just as the models Benning designs as media for theorizing and worlding are playful, local, humble, and experimental, so the imaginary world they design is open to change.

FERNAND DELIGNY: A RAFT IN THE MOUNTAINS

The camera plays an important and active role not only in Sadie Benning's modelling practices, but also in Fernand Deligny's *tentatives*. The 16 mm camera was there from the beginning of Deligny's work with delinquent and behaviourally conspicuous children. Initially thought of as a pedagogical tool, the camera became for Deligny a medium for thinking differently about language, image, communication, gestures, landscape, technology, and human community — even the human species.[30] Deligny, a philosophical poet and cinephile, was well versed in the history of experimental film and not only experimented with the camera himself, but also developed an original theory about it.[31] He coined the term *camérer* to denote a method of being-with the camera, distinguishing this from the more familiar result-oriented, purposeful uses of the camera, which he called *scénarier*. Unfortunately, due to space constraints, I cannot go into more detail about Deligny's concept of *camérer*, but I would like to point out that the presence of the camera is embedded in the philosophy of media and aesthetics that the concept entails. The 16 mm camera was present during all the years of the 'tentative des Cévennes' and was part of the method and practices of modelling that became known as 'mapping the wander lines'. Deligny documented this method and the 'tentative des Cévennes' in the 1975 film *Ce gamin, là (Radeaux dans la montagne)*.

Deligny wrote the script for the documentary together with director and cinematographer Renaud Victor. Victor lived for several years in Monoblet, participating in daily life with Deligny, the other 'presences proches', and the 'autistic' children, before the film was

---

30   See Deuber-Mankowsky, 'The Space of Appearance in Deep Underground', p. 473.
31   See Marlon Miguel, *Camering: Fernand Deligny on Cinema and the Image* (Leiden: Leiden University Press, 2022) <https://doi.org/10.1017/9789400604308>.

realized. One can interpret this as an aspect of Deligny's practice of modelling, by which he sets himself apart from those models that he associates with the 'conventional arsenal' — the equipment, personnel, and instruments that go into the making of a conventional film. Deligny reminds us that 'arsenal' means 'a facility where everything necessary for the construction, repair and equipping of warships is brought together', while 'conventional' means 'conforming to social conventions; unnatural, insincere'.[32] He then counters this model of the conventional arsenal with his own way of modelling, which he calls 'construire un radeau': building a raft. He summarizes pointedly: 'To escape the conventional and the arsenal that goes with it, you have to build a raft.'[33]

Right at the start, *Ce gamin, là (Radeaux dans la montagne)* impressively shows what it means to follow the model of the conventional arsenal and the difference that it makes to 'construct a raft in the mountain'. First, we see a written document that certifies that Janmari, the boy living in Deligny's care, has severe brain damage. Words fall: 'uncurable', 'unbearable', 'unlivable'. The document is contrasted with a photograph of Janmari in a free environment, playing with a clay ball hanging from a string (Figure 15), while Deligny's voice-over explains what the psychiatrists say about the boy. This leads to the next image, a bird's-eye view of a closed psychiatric hospital from the turn of the twentieth century (Figure 16). It is almost a model for a model that is part of a symbol system that is totalizing and self-reinforcing.

The architecture itself ensures that the anticipated future of the child — incurable, unlivable, unbearable — will arrive, with its walls, closed doors, and windows that are not windows providing nothing but monotony, sameness, and immobility. Deligny's voice-over then leads back to the photograph of the boy playing with the clay ball, telling us that the photograph was taken 'here', in Monoblet, 'away from those predicted places, built on purpose, on the other pole' (03:46). While the camera zooms slowly into the image, Deligny interprets the clay ball and the child's play as an indication that the world may need

---

32   Fernand Deligny, 'Les Fossiles ont la vie dure', in *Fernand Deligny: Camérer. A propos d'images*, ed. by Sandra Alvarez de Toledo and others (Paris: L'Arachnéen, 2021), pp. 142–49 (p. 143).

33   Ibid.

FIG. 15. Screenshot from the film *Ce gamin, là (Radeaux dans la montagne)* (1975), dir. by Renaud Victor (00:45).

to turn differently: that 'autistic' children should not be forced to adapt to our world and judged from our perspective, but that we must go in search of their world, which is not the world of language.

The change of perspective is accompanied by a change of model and modelling. Instead of following the model of the 'conventional arsenal', rafts have to be built in the mountains. Indeed, right after the scene described above, the film shows in a very condensed way how this is to be done. At the same time, it becomes clear that 'building

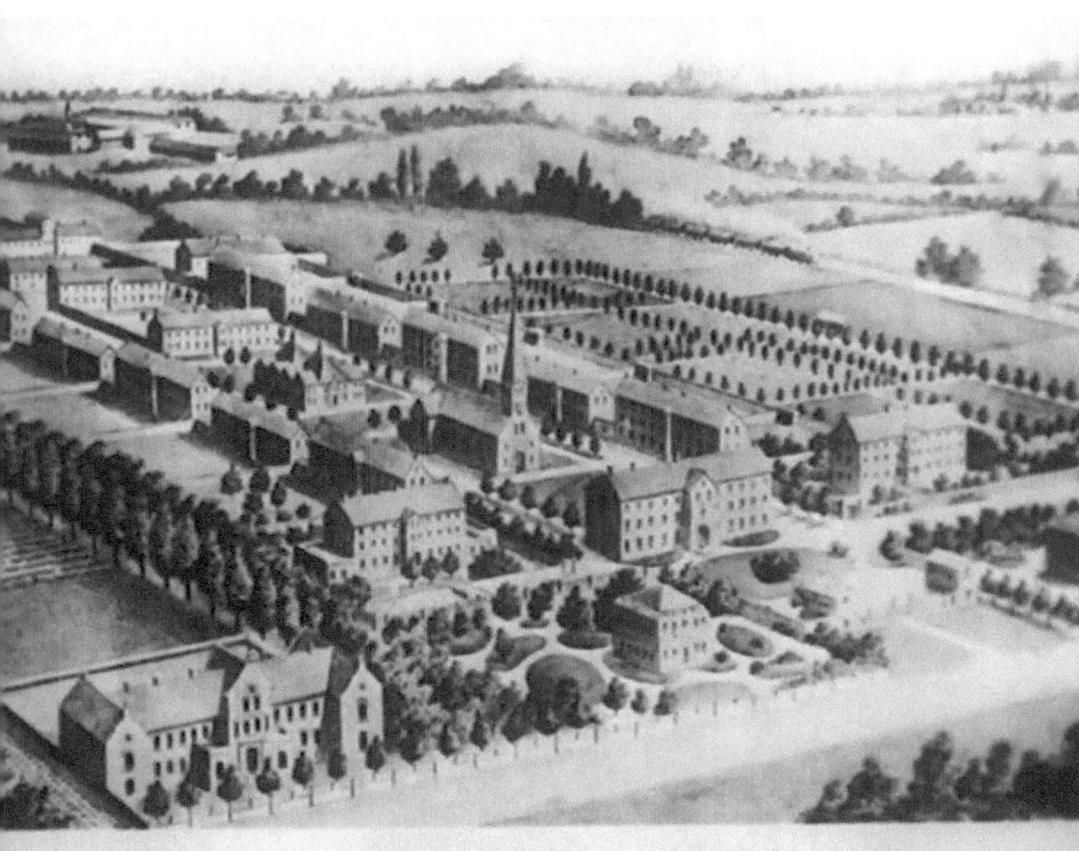

L'Hôpital Psychiatrique Autonome avant les destructions de 1914-1918

FIG. 16. Screenshot from the film *Ce gamin, là (Radeaux dans la montagne)* (1975), dir. by Renaud Victor (02:07).

a raft' refers to the construction of those models that are tentative, deliberately reductive, local, experimental, playful, and modest. We see an open house in the mountains — a ruin, without windows or a roof, ready to be converted and rebuilt in a new form (Figure 17). The camera zooms out and opens up a bird's eye view of the landscape (Figure 18).

The rafts are the overlapping crosses on the map (Figure 19). They indicate the places where the adults, Deligny, his companions, and the

FIG. 17. Screenshot from the film *Ce gamin, là (Radeaux dans la montagne)* (1975), dir. by Renaud Victor (04:55).

children meet in their everyday tasks — washing dishes, baking bread, boiling water, fetching water, taking the goats out to pasture — where the rhythm of the water, the glitter and flicker of the fire count more than the purpose. All without language, but full of gestures, images, movement, and life.

As we have seen, Benning and Deligny differ in many respects. They deal with different topics at different times and in different places. However, there are moments that connect their works *methodologic-*

FIG. 18. Screenshot from the film *Ce gamin, là (Radeaux dans la montagne)* (1975), dir. by Renaud Victor (05:05).

ally. The early video works of Benning and the *tentatives* of Deligny each carry their own spatiotemporal limitations as an inner condition and neither is explicitly intended to serve as a model. 'Model' refers here to the normative, cultural model that Geertz so aptly describes as a 'system of symbols which acts to establish powerful, pervasive, and long-lasting moods and motivations in men'. While Benning and Deligny criticize the dominance of these normative models, their respective methodological procedures can be compared and contrasted

FIG. 19. Screenshot from the film *Ce gamin, là (Radeaux dans la montagne)* (1975), dir. by Renaud Victor (05:31).

with the integration of the modelling in a methodological procedure that Holzhey and co-authors characterize as deliberately reductive, local, and playful.

I would like to conclude with the question of what it might mean today to deal with the early video works of Benning and the *tentatives* of Deligny. Both figures insist on the transience of their practices of worlding. I agree with Igor Krtolica: a *tentative*, an experimentation, invents new living possibilities. Thus, it is the art of innovation that is transferred — the transference of an experience: 'So there's no contradiction in Deligny's simultaneous assertion that the attempt has no monopolistic pretensions, but proposes to swarm, that it hasn't validated a paradigm, but invites other networks to be woven.'[34]

Deligny and Benning both build on the singularity and contingency of the present to initiate a practice of world exploration that is less exclusive and less violent. To this end, they break with those models that, in the sense of Clifford Geertz, are part of a self-reinforcing and tendentially totalizing view of the world. They invent aesthetic practices that incorporate a playful, experimental approach to local and constantly changing models. In this way, cultural models are transformed, in the sense of Holzhey and his co-authors, into creative 'media of theorizing and worlding'.

---

34   Krtolica, 'La "Tentative" des Cévennes', p. 93.

Abstraction as Strategy for Worldmaking

JULIA SÁNCHEZ-DORADO

1. INTRODUCTION

Contemporary scientists are invested in the study of a range of highly complex natural phenomena. One of the most pervasive investigative tools they exploit to learn about those phenomena are models. Scientific models, despite their variety in form, style, and materiality, seem to share a fundamental epistemic function, namely, they are representational devices, designed to stand for and depict the behaviour of specific target systems in the world.[1] However, the conception of models as representations has given rise to a dilemma in recent philosophy of science: on the one hand, partly thanks to the role played

---

1   The conception of models as representations gained predominance in the second half of the twentieth century, under the semantic view within the philosophy of science. Classic semantic view works include: Patrick Suppes, 'A Comparison of the Meaning and Uses of Models in Mathematics and the Empirical Sciences', *Synthese*, 12 (1960), pp. 287–301 <https://doi.org/10.1007/BF00485107>; Bas C. van Fraassen, *The Scientific Image* (Oxford: Oxford University Press, 1980) <https://doi.org/10.1093/0198244274.001.0001>; and Ronald Giere, *Explaining Science: A Cognitive Approach* (Chicago: University of Chicago Press, 1988) <https://doi.org/10.7208/chicago/9780226292038.001.0001>. Following these works, in the 1990s and 2000s, more pragmatic approaches to the understanding of scientific models were advanced, such as the 'models as mediators' perspective, according to which models are still treated as representational devices, but more attention is given to the plurality of epistemic functions that they serve in practice. See *Models as Mediators*, ed. by Mary S. Morgan and Margaret Morrison (Cambridge: Cambridge University Press, 1999) <https://

by models, contemporary science has achieved numerous accurate descriptions of nature which, in turn, have facilitated effective world interventions. On the other hand, as soon as one approaches the study of scientific models with an analytic eye, one notices that models are notorious for their partial, simplifying, and distorting character, with respect to the very same objects they aim to represent. So, if models misrepresent (that is, simplify and distort) the objects they attempt to bring to light, how can one assert that they provide accurate descriptions of them? Even more pressing is the question of whether it is justified to implement certain policies and practical interventions based on model results, given the kinds of misrepresentation they entail. Responding to these questions involves more than solving an epistemological conundrum; it goes to the heart of the role that philosophers, especially in collaboration with historians of science, can aspire to play in informing scientists' practices, by making manifest and assessing the epistemic and social consequences of the insertion of misrepresentations in their modelling work.[2]

This essay is dedicated to discussing one specific cognitive strategy that scientists make use of in their modelling practices, namely abstraction, and the implications it has for the dilemma of misrepresentation. Abstractions, this essay argues, can be enormously useful in the construction of epistemically successful models, even if, at the same time, they are a form of misrepresentation, insofar as abstracting involves the selection and isolation of presumably relevant features of the natural phenomenon studied, and the imaginative superimposition of relationships connecting those features to form a coherent whole (that

---

doi.org/10.1017/CBO9780511660108>. In recent years, the imbricate relationship between models and representation has been openly challenged by scholars. See, for instance, Tarja Knuuttila, 'Epistemic Artifacts and the Modal Dimension of Modeling', *European Journal for Philosophy of Science*, 11.65 (2021) <https://doi.org/10.1007/s13194-021-00374-5>; and Guilherme Sanches de Oliveira, 'Representationalism Is a Dead End', *Synthese*, 198 (2018), pp. 209–35 <https://doi.org/10.1007/s11229-018-01995-9>, who emphasize above all the 'artefactual' nature of models.

2   For a discussion on the role that historians and philosophers of science can play in informing scientists' practices, see Hasok Chang's account of 'complementary science', that is, the practice of knowledge production based on the systematic historical and philosophical re-examination of scientific questions that are excluded from current specialist science. See Hasok Chang, *Inventing Temperature: Measurement and Scientific Progress* (Oxford: Oxford University Press, 2004), chapter 6, pp. 235–50 <https://doi.org/10.1093/0195171276.003.0006>.

is, a functioning model). Section two introduces the most common characterization of abstraction in the contemporary modelling literature in philosophy of science, which identifies it with the 'omission' of certain features of the phenomenon represented. This characterization is then partially criticized, in sections three and four, using an illustrative example taken from oceanography, namely, Marie Tharp's practice of abstraction during the construction of her physiographic maps of the ocean floor. The aim is to highlight the (insufficiently recognized) creative potential of abstractions in science. To do so, section five incorporates some insights from the philosophy and history of art, fields where there is a longer and richer tradition of discussion about the creative roles of abstraction. Finally, to tackle the dilemma of misrepresentation for the specific case of abstraction, section six suggests that one needs to think of modelling practices not only as practices of representing but also as practices of worldmaking. In his 1978 book *Ways of Worldmaking*, Nelson Goodman identified several ways in which cognitive agents engage in practices of worldmaking through the manipulation of their symbol systems.[3] Among these, Goodman hinted at, but did not explicitly talk about, abstraction. Thus, this essay concludes by suggesting that we should think of abstraction as a worldmaking strategy as well, as much in science as in art, but that we should also reflect on the potential consequences, including the possible epistemic and social harms, that its worldmaking capacity might entail.

2. ABSTRACTION AS OMISSION

The two most common strategies that philosophers of science have identified as introducing misrepresentations in modelling practices are abstractions and idealizations. Typical definitions of abstraction in recent modelling debates state that abstracting is the act of omitting those aspects of a natural system that are deemed irrelevant during the process of constructing a model. Meanwhile, idealization is the purposeful introduction of falsehoods, such as when economists work with models that assume subjects to be perfectly rational, when ecolo-

---

3   Nelson Goodman, *Ways of Worldmaking* (Hassocks: The Harvester Press, 1978) <https://doi.org/10.5040/9781350928558>.

gists include an infinite population in their mathematical simulations, or when physicists resort to frictionless planes in their modelling. An abstract model, then, presents an incomplete, detail-poor image of a target, while an idealized model offers a partially false image of that target. This distinction can be found, among other places, in the works of Nancy Cartwright, Martin Jones, Hans Radder, Peter Godfrey-Smith, and Arnon Levy.[4] Abstraction, Jones says, 'is a matter of complete silence' about the features of a certain target that are left out of the model.[5] Similarly, Godfrey-Smith argues that an abstract model entails the 'description of a system [that] leaves out a lot', 'but [...] is not intended to say things that are literally false'. Meanwhile, an idealized model 'fictionalizes in the service of simplification', and so is not a literally true description of an aspect of the world.[6]

While abstraction remains scarcely discussed in current debates in philosophy of science, there is an extensive and growing literature on idealized models.[7] This seems motivated by the thought that, if abstracting only means omitting the irrelevant features of a target system, then there is not much of epistemological interest to be said about it, beyond the observation that it requires researchers to leave out unnecessary details when creating their representations. In contrast, idealizations would pose particularly interesting and challenging

---

4   See Nancy Cartwright, *The Dappled World: A Study of the Boundaries of Science* (Cambridge: Cambridge University Press, 1999) <https://doi.org/10.1017/CBO9781139167093>; Martin Jones, 'Idealization and Abstraction: A Framework', in *Idealization XII: Correcting the Model; Idealization and Abstraction in the Sciences*, ed. by Nancy Cartwright and Martin Jones (Amsterdam: Rodopi, 2005), pp. 173–217 <https://doi.org/10.1163/9789401202732_010>; Hans Radder, *The World Observed/The World Conceived* (Pittsburgh: Pittsburgh University Press, 2006) <https://doi.org/10.2307/j.ctt6wrcvz>; Peter Godfrey-Smith, 'Abstractions, Idealizations, and Evolutionary Biology', in *Mapping the Future of Biology: Evolving Concepts and Theories*, ed. by Thomas Pradeu and others (Dordrecht: Springer Netherlands, 2009), pp. 47–56 <https://doi.org/10.1007/978-1-4020-9636-5>; and Arnon Levy, 'Idealization and Abstraction: Refining the Distinction', *Synthese*, 198 (2018), pp. 5855–72 <https://doi.org/10.1007/s11229-018-1721-z>.

5   Jones, 'Idealization and Abstraction', p. 175.

6   Godfrey-Smith, 'Abstractions, Idealizations, and Evolutionary Biology', p. 48.

7   Two insightful accounts of idealization in the current literature in philosophy of science are Angela Potochnik, *Idealization and the Aims of Science* (Chicago: University of Chicago Press, 2017) <https://doi.org/10.7208/chicago/9780226507194.001.0001>; and Collin Rice, *Leveraging Distortions: Explanation, Idealization, and Universality in Science* (Cambridge, MA: MIT Press, 2021) <https://doi.org/10.7551/mitpress/13784.001.0001>.

questions, insofar as they demand that philosophers make sense of how falsehoods can be dealt with or their epistemic value explained. In fact, it seems that the motivation of some scholars to maintain the idealization–abstraction distinction might consist in their attempt to find a strategy to minimize the dilemma of misrepresentation, by making abstraction an innocuous form of misrepresentation that does not really obstruct accurate representation. Thus, the dilemma would be channelled exclusively into the effects of idealization.[8]

However, a closer look at actual modelling practices reveals that to account for the epistemic value of abstractions requires revising and going beyond the standard definition of abstraction as 'omission'. In a recent article, Natalia Carrillo and Sergio Martínez precisely criticize the understanding of abstraction as omission, which has become the 'orthodox view' in the modelling debate, with the unfortunate consequence of turning abstraction into a mere issue concerning the 'level of detail' with which a target system is described.[9] Similar critiques are found in an essay by Sergio Gallegos Ordorica, and in a recent collective volume on abstraction edited by Chiara Ambrosio and myself.[10] But, if not exclusively in terms of omission, how should one conceptualize the activity of abstracting in modelling practices? I will briefly introduce a historical case in oceanography to exemplify how scientists can fruitfully employ abstractions in their work. This example shows that omission is one of the aspects involved in practices of abstraction. At the same time, however, a creative ordering process is fundamentally entailed in the very same practices.[11]

---

8   This reading of the motivations for sustaining the idealization–abstraction distinction in current philosophy of science, as well as a critique of the idea that models can be de-idealized, can be found in Rice, *Leveraging Distortions*, pp. 120–21.

9   Natalia Carrillo and Sergio Martínez, 'Scientific Inquiry: From Metaphors to Abstraction', Perspectives on Science, 31.2 (2023), pp. 233–61 (p. 237) <https://doi.org/10.1162/posc_a_00571>.

10   See Sergio Armando Gallegos Ordorica, 'The Explanatory Role of Abstraction Processes in Models: The Case of Aggregations', *Studies in History and Philosophy of Science Part A*, 56 (2016), pp. 161–67 <https://doi.org/10.1016/j.shpsa.2015.10.002>; and *Abstraction in Science and Art: Philosophical Perspectives*, ed. by Chiara Ambrosio and Julia Sánchez-Dorado (London: Routledge, 2024).

11   Similar views on abstractions have been previously defended by Gallegos Ordorica, who refers to a form of 'aggregative abstraction' to indicate that this practice is not just about omitting features but about adding new elements to the process as well. See Gallegos Ordorica, 'The Explanatory Role of Abstraction Processes in Models', p.

3. MARIE THARP: ABSTRACTING THE OCEAN FLOOR[12]

In the 1950s, oceanographer and geologist Marie Tharp (1920–2006), together with her colleague Bruce Heezen (1924–1977), postulated the existence of the Mid-Atlantic Ridge, a mountain chain that divides the Atlantic seafloor from the north of Iceland to the Antarctic. After centuries of considering the seafloor *terra incognita*, Tharp took a fundamental step in exposing its mountainous landscape formations in a clear and innovative visual manner. With the assistance of new data gathered from sonar technology (specifically, deep sea echo sounders) developed during World War II, as well as with data regarding earthquake epicentres in the ocean, Tharp constructed a series of graphs, diagrams, maps, and even some 3-D analogues of the globe, which in conjunction worked as models to help uncover the structure of the ridge. Moreover, Tharp's models showed remarkable continuities between the Mid-Atlantic Ridge and the mountain chains on the Pa-

---

162. Michael Stuart and Anatolii Kozlov, similarly, talk about a form of 'generative abstraction' in contrast to a mere 'subtractive abstraction'. See Michael Stuart and Anatolii Kozlov, 'Moving Targets and Models of Nothing: A New Sense of Abstraction for Philosophy of Science', in *Abstraction in Science and Art*, ed. by Ambrosio and Sánchez-Dorado, pp. 118–42 (p. 121).

12 This section substantially builds on the rich work that Rasmus Winther has developed on Marie Tharp's practice of map-making, as well as the role that abstraction played in the production of her physiographic diagrams. My intention is to use this case, largely following Winther, to develop some points of his analysis that could be further spelt out, such as on the roles of omission and creative ordering, as well as on the world-making capacity of abstractions. I particularly draw on Rasmus Winther, 'Mapping the Deep Blue Oceans', in *The Philosophy of GIS*, ed. by Timothy Tambassi (Cham, CH: Springer Geography, 2019), pp. 99–124 <https://doi.org/10.1007/978-3-030-16829-2>; and Rasmus Winther and Marie Raffn, 'What If?', in *Abstraction in Science and Art*, ed. by Ambrosio and Sánchez-Dorado, pp. 217–49. Additional sources consulted for this section are: Bruce Heezen, Marie Tharp, and Maurice Ewing, *The Floors of the Oceans: I. The North Atlantic; Text to Accompany the Physiographic Diagram of the North Atlantic*, Special Paper 65 (New York: The Geological Society of America, 1959) <https://doi.org/10.1130/SPE65-p1>; Marie Tharp, 'Connect the Dots: Mapping the Seafloor and Discovering the Mid-Ocean Ridge', in *Lamont-Doherty Earth Observatory: Twelve Perspectives on the First Fifty Years, 1949–1999*, ed. by Laurence Lippsett (Palisades, NY: Lamont-Doherty Earth Observatory of Columbia University, 1999), pp. 31–37; reproduced as 'Marie Tharp's Adventures in Mapping the Seafloor, in her Own Words', 24 July 2020 <https://news.climate.columbia.edu/2020/07/24/marie-tharp-connecting-dots/> [accessed January 2024]; Hali Felt, *Soundings: The Story of the Remarkable Woman Who Mapped the Ocean Floor* (New York: Picador, 2012); and Andrew K. Knoll, *A Brief History of the Earth* (New York: Mariner, 2021).

cific and Indian ocean floors, indicating the presence of a global ridge system.[13]

The recent works of Rasmus Winther and Hali Felt offer helpful readings of the practices through which Tharp's models led to one of the most important discoveries in twentieth-century geoscience. Near the crest of the mid-ocean ridge, Tharp observed that there was a 'deep notch' or rift valley.[14] The existence of a V-shaped rift, Tharp and Heezen knew, suggested continental drift, a hypothesis originally proposed by Alfred Wegener in the 1920s, which stated that the Earth's surface was formed by plates that had gradually moved throughout geological time, pushing continents apart. However, continental drift was not a widely accepted theory in the 1950s. In fact, it remained scientific 'heresy' for some,[15] so Tharp's findings were vehemently rejected at first, and even Heezen dismissed them at one point as 'girl talk'.[16] Eventually, Tharp's graphs and maps, where the rift valley was clearly visible, became central to the exploration of the mechanisms of continental drift and the subsequent acceptance of the theory of plate tectonics by the international geoscientific community.[17]

Among the various visual artefacts that Tharp produced, the physiographic diagrams of the Mid-Atlantic Ridge became the most well-known outcomes of her exploratory work (see Figure 1).[18] A physiographic diagram is a type of map that represents the topographical features of an area, not just by applying simple strokes to outline the location of mountains and valleys, but, as Felt describes, by using 'intricate nests of black lines that made the crags and ridges on the ocean floor look three-dimensional'.[19] Tharp stated that this technique helped her to represent a terrain as if viewed 'from a low flying plane',

---

13   See Winther and Raffn, 'What If?', pp. 219–23; Knoll, *A Brief History of the Earth*, p. 45; and Heezen, Tharp, and Ewing, *The Floors of the Oceans*.

14   Tharp, quoted in Felt, *Soundings*, p. 99.

15   Felt, *Soundings*, p. 100.

16   See Tharp, 'Connect the Dots'; Winther, 'Mapping the Deep Blue Oceans', p. 110; Felt, *Soundings*, p. 99.

17   Knoll, *A Brief History of the Earth*, pp. 45–47.

18   For a review of the variety of scientific maps that Tharp produced, beyond the physiographic diagrams, see Winther and Raffn, 'What If?', pp. 221–22.

19   Felt, *Soundings*, p. 104.

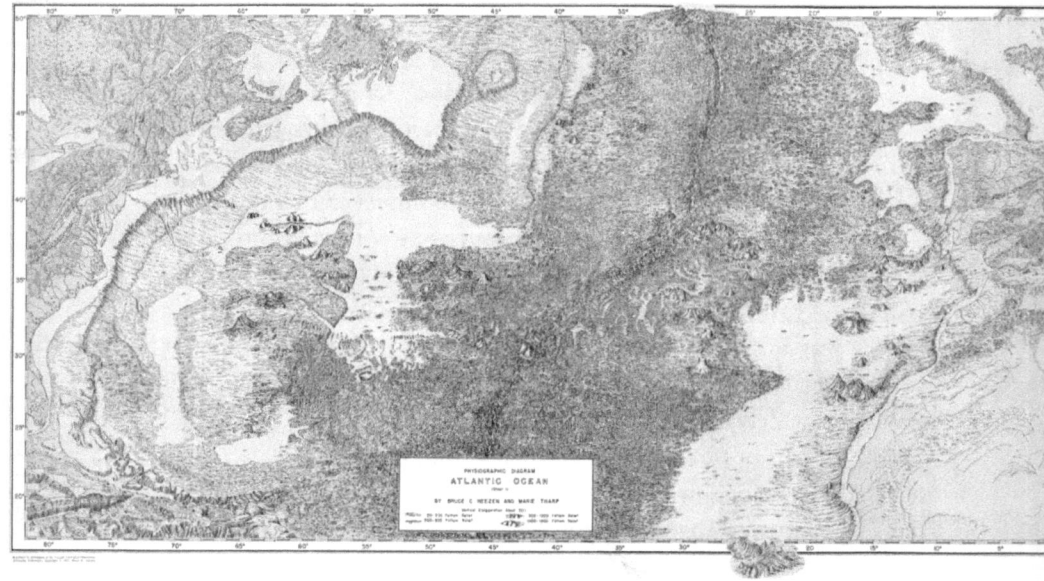

FIG. 1a. Physiographic Diagram: Atlantic Ocean, 1959. Source: Bruce Heezen,
Marie Tharp, and Maurice Ewing (1959), *The Floors of the Oceans*, Sheet 1
(Plate 1). Mid-Atlantic Ridge map. Reproduced with the kind permission of the
Columbia Climate School, Lamont-Doherty Earth Observatory.

adopting a forty-five-degree angle.[20] The physiographic technique was
developed by Armin Kohl Lobeck, a Columbia professor of geomorph-
ology who aimed to produce vivid and accessible sketches of territories
that could be easily read without any specialized knowledge in geology
or cartography. At the Lamont-Doherty Earth Observatory, also based
at Columbia University, Tharp and Heezen adopted this technique in
their work, similarly motivated by the goal of producing accessible,
readable representations of the vast, hitherto mysterious seafloor.[21]

Abstraction, understood as omission, was indeed a key strategy
employed in the production of Tharp's physiographic diagrams. Winther has made this point with regard to the 'simplifications' required
to streamline the most valuable information necessary to produce a

---

20   Tharp, quoted in ibid., p. 104.
21   Felt, *Soundings*, pp. 104, 108.

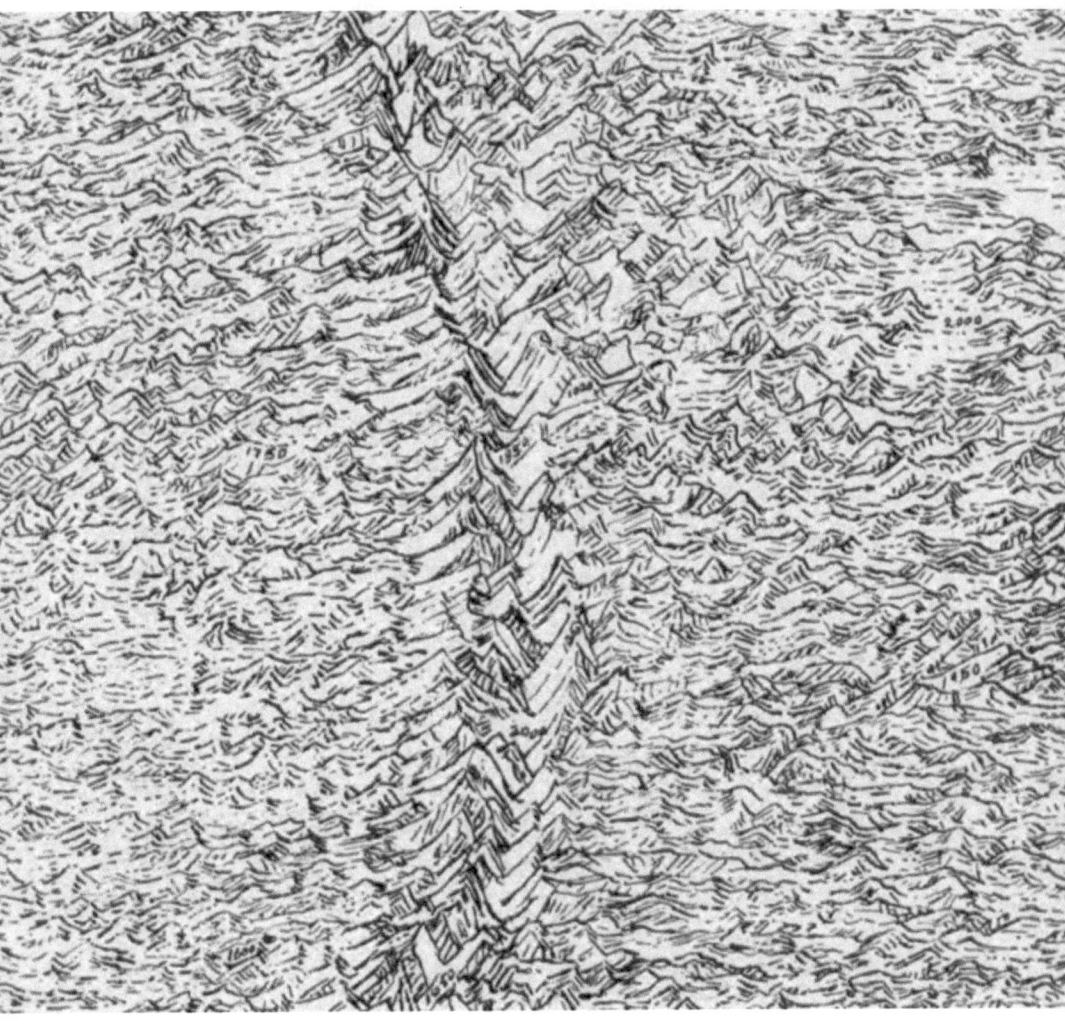

FIG. 1b. Physiographic Diagram: Atlantic Ocean, 1959. Source: Bruce Heezen,
Marie Tharp, and Maurice Ewing (1959), *The Floors of the Oceans*, Sheet 1
(Plate 1). Detail of map, with visible V-shaped rift. Reproduced with the kind
permission of the Columbia Climate School, Lamont-Doherty Earth Observatory.

readable map of the ocean floor.[22] Many features were omitted in the
representation of the Mid-Atlantic Ridge, since, from the overwhelm-
ing amount of data collected during ocean sounding expeditions and
brought to the laboratory, Tharp left out all that which did not appear
directly relevant to the study of the morphology of the landscape formations postulated, such as the V-shape valley profile of the ridge.[23]
Yet, the omission of one notable feature is especially conspicuous in
her maps: the Atlantic ridge is depicted as if the water in the ocean
basin was completely subtracted from it. As Tharp remarked: 'There is
only one proper way to sketch or to contour the ocean floor and that
is to present it as it actually exists as it would be seen if all the water
were drained away.'[24] Once water was omitted, Tharp could depict the
seafloor as viewed from above, employing shading in her drawing to
indicate the different heights of the mountains, as if the sun was projecting their shadows onto the ground.[25] She used a type of sketching
called *hachuring*, consisting in the accumulation of (thin or thick) lines
to indicate the orientation and length of the slopes, while emphasizing
the flatness of the abyssal plains.[26] Also, Tharp and Heezen decided
that the vertical scale used to represent the ridge profile needed to be
exaggerated, in order to facilitate the recognition of the rift running
along it. They used a strong geometric distortion of 40:1; that is, the
mountain height was reduced by considerably less — by a factor of
forty — in the scaling process than the ocean width and length (hori-
zontal scales). Winther explains how 'she had to do this in order to
show the Mid-Atlantic Ridge profile in a meaningful and memorable
way. Otherwise, the profile would have nearly disappeared into a solid
line barely crawling along the ocean bottom.'[27]

---

22 Winther, 'Mapping the Deep Blue Oceans', p. 106. Here I try to further spell out
    Winther's point about omission in the physiographic diagrams.
23 Ibid., p. 110.
24 Marie Tharp, 'Mapping the Ocean Floor: 1947–1977', in *The Ocean Floor: Bruce Heezen
    Commemorative Volume*, ed. by R. A. Scrutton and M. Talwani (New York: Wiley,
    1982), quoted in Winther and Raffn, 'What If?', p. 219.
25 Winther, 'Mapping the Deep Blue Oceans', pp. 107, 116.
26 Felt, *Soundings*, p. 109.
27 Winther, 'Mapping the Deep Blue Oceans', p. 107. See also Felt, *Soundings*, p. 97.

Two observations regarding abstraction can be made from this case, developing points already hinted at by Winther.[28] Firstly, Tharp's practice of abstraction, understood as the omission of either irrelevant or obstructing features (such as the ocean water), was central to her construction of memorable maps. At the same time, one can see that Tharp's omissions and her parallel acts of exaggerating the profiles of the mountains and introducing fictional shading are hardly separable from one another. That is, the omission of features permitted the insertion of idealizations, while the possibility of idealizing the look of the ridge in a fertile manner motivated the omission of certain features of the ocean instead of others.

Secondly, Tharp's practice of abstraction involved more than omission, not only in the sense that idealizations were intertwined with the omissions she introduced, as I have just pointed out, but in a stronger sense. Abstraction here involved ordering and the establishment of connections between features in order to impose a pattern onto previously disjointed sets of data. As I will develop in section five, this entailed an imaginative, creative activity. In their 1959 article, Tharp, together with Heezen and Maurice Ewing, commented on how preparing a marine physiographic diagram 'requires the author to *postulate the patterns and trends of the relief* on the basis of cross sections and then to portray this interpretation in the diagram'.[29] Patterns on the ocean floor that were previously unseen are now brought to the fore by the practice of abstraction, facilitating the production of diagrams that could advance hypotheses about the morphology of the ocean floor and, in turn, help examine its implications for the theory of continental drift.

More specifically, Tharp and her colleagues had to proceed through a series of steps to produce the physiographic diagrams (see Figure 2). These successive steps exemplify how abstraction here involved ordering, together with omission, and the establishment of

28   Winther also makes additional points about Marie Tharp's practice of abstraction that I do not address here, regarding, for instance, the role of her selection of scale and projection in the production of her maps, and the types of modal reasoning ('what-if thinking') that abstraction allowed Tharp to perform. See Winther, 'Mapping the Deep Blue Oceans', pp. 103–05; and Winther and Raffn, 'What If?', p. 223.

29   Heezen, Tharp, and Ewing, *The Floors of the Oceans*, p. 3, my emphasis. See also Winther, 'Mapping the Deep Blue Oceans', p. 4.

connections between features to form a coherent, readable map.[30] First, they produced simple, flat diagrams with the plotted lines of soundings, using data collected from ships tracking across the ocean with fathometers (labelled 'b' in Figure 2). Here the vertical scale distortion was already inserted, in order to help visualize the location of the V-shaped rift. These first diagrams were then transformed into sketches of the mountain profiles of the seafloor, highlighting the succession of peaks and valleys observed ('c'). Then, using these scattered sketches, Tharp drew the mountains onto the maps with a three-dimensional appearance, in such a way that the 'entire pattern' of the ocean would appear to the eye.[31] Tharp, Heezen, and Ewing filled the areas for which no sounding data was available by way of extrapolation from nearby areas and interpolation from general trends inferred ('d'). 'In other words', they explained, 'we made educated guesses to fill in the dataless gaps.'[32] Abstraction, understood as a dynamic combination of omission and the imaginative, resourceful ordering of previously disconnected features as an intelligible whole, was a fundamental part of the process required to move from diagrams to profile drawings, and then to three-dimensional maps. As Tharp stated, the study of the succession of peaks and valleys in the profiles plotted during the preparation of the physiographic diagram 'revealed the existence of morphological features and morphological provinces not previously delineated.'[33] These newly revealed structures were then accentuated and vividly displayed by the three-dimensional drawings on the maps. Winther comments that Tharp 'possessed powerful capacities to see all the parts of a system in a holistic, dynamic, and interactive manner', skills that went hand in hand with her mastery of abstraction in the drafting practice here illustrated.[34]

This historical episode suggests that, on the one hand, abstraction as omission is important for modelling practices, as it concerns the

---

30   The following description of these steps is taken from Heezen, Tharp, and Ewing, *The Floors of the Oceans*, p. 3; Tharp, 'Connect the Dots'; Felt, *Soundings*; and Winther and Raffn, 'What If?'.

31   Felt, *Soundings*, p. 97.

32   Heezen, Tharp, and Ewing, *The Floors of the Oceans*, p. 3; Tharp, 'Connect the Dots'.

33   Heezen, Tharp, and Ewing, *The Floors of the Oceans*, p. 3.

34   Winther, 'Mapping the Deep Blue Oceans', p. 109.

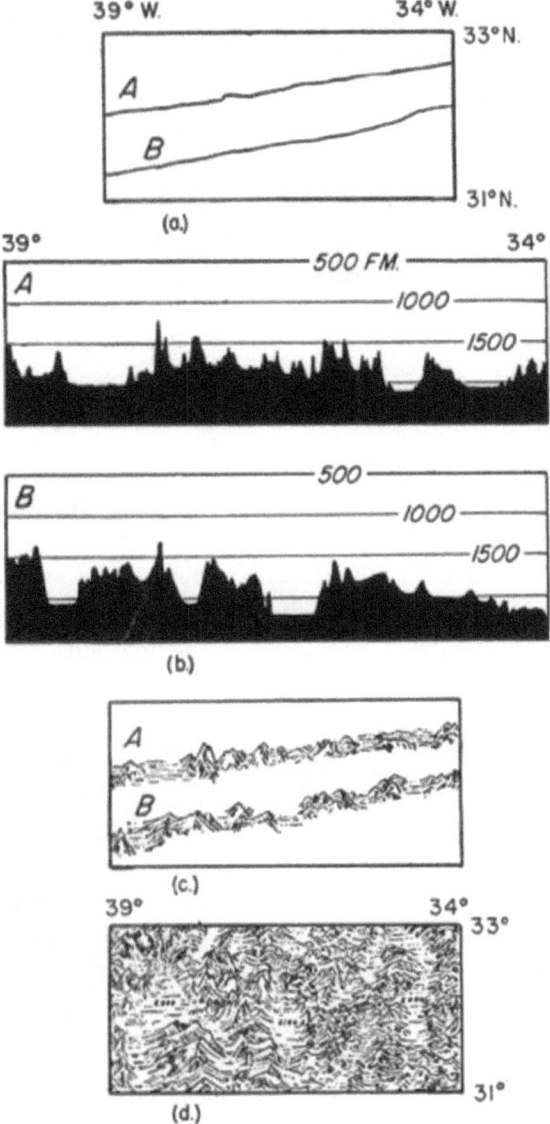

FIG. 2. Method of preparation of physiographic diagram. (a) Positions of sounding lines (A, B) are plotted on chart; (b) Soundings are plotted as profiles (A, B) with a 40:1 vertical scale exaggeration; (c) Features shown on profiles (A, B) are sketched on chart along tracks; (d) After all available sounding profiles are sketched, the remaining unsounded areas are filled in by extrapolating and interpolating trends observed in a succession of profiles. Source: Heezen, Tharp, and Ewing, *The Floors of the Oceans*, Figure 1, p. 4. Reproduced with the kind permission of the Columbia Climate School, Lamont-Doherty Earth Observatory.

fundamental activity of singling out, simplifying, and distinguishing the relevant from irrelevant features of a represented target system. On the other hand, a closer look at the process of abstraction in Tharp's mapmaking practices reveals that more than omission is required in order to account for the value of abstraction as a cognitive strategy; that is, this demands the inclusion of an element of ordering and the imaginative superimposition of connections between the features included in the representation.

4. THREE CRITICISMS OF ACCOUNTS OF ABSTRACTION AS OMISSION

Based on the foregoing analysis, three specific criticisms of traditional accounts of abstraction as mere omission can be formulated. A first criticism points to the difficulty of drawing a clean distinction between abstraction and idealization in practice. When Tharp removed the water from the representation of the ocean basin, she inevitably had to idealize the look of the seafloor, for instance by including fictional shading, since the visual depiction of the mountain chains, for which only sounding data was available, required her to imagine their appearance, as well as how shadows would be projected, in analogy with visible mountains above sea level. More generally, abstractions and idealizations are not easily distinguishable from one another because there are often causal dependencies between the different features constituting a system, so that by omitting some of them, the relations between the features included in the representation and those left out become lost. Collin Rice has recently argued that 'the abstraction of certain features would almost always insert distortions with respect to other features. For instance, leaving out environmental features distorts how genetics contributes to development.'[35] Leif Hancox-Li agrees that there is

---

35 Rice, *Leveraging Distortions*, p. 4. The example Rice uses is taken from Helen Longino, *Studying Human Behavior: How Scientists Investigate Aggression and Sexuality* (Chicago: Chicago University Press, 2013) <https://doi.org/10.7208/chicago/9780226921822.001.0001>. The difficulties of distinguishing idealization from abstraction are also discussed in Uskali Mäki, 'Isolation, Idealization and Truth in Economics', in *Idealization VI: Idealization in Economics*, ed. by Bert Hamminga and Neil B. De Marchi, Poznań Studies in the Philosophy of the Sciences and the Humanities, 38 (Amsterdam: Rodopi, 1994), pp. 147–68 <https://doi.org/10.1163/9789004457379_010>; and Leif Hancox-Li, 'Idealization and Abstraction in Models

no general way of unambiguously distinguishing between abstractions (understood as omission) and idealizations, unless one determines in advance that if the form of the omission one introduces is 'harmless' for the goals of the modelling, then it is an abstraction, whereas if it distorts, for instance by omitting a difference-maker or key feature in the identification of a mechanism, then it is an idealization.[36] But, of course, whether an omission is harmless or not will depend on the particular purposes of the model and on what scientists believe to be the main features of the phenomenon under investigation at the beginning of the activity.

A possible consequence of this first criticism might be the rejection of the terminological distinction between idealization and abstraction altogether. It remains to be seen whether this conclusion must necessarily be reached, or whether it might remain a useful distinction to be drawn, in order to identify different aspects of practices of misrepresentation that are not exactly equivalent. Introducing this first criticism here has the more limited aim of calling attention to the fact that, in actual modelling practices, omitting certain features of the target under investigation most often elicits the introduction of either intentional or unintentional distortions, enriching and complementing one another.

A second criticism of accounts of abstraction as mere omission is that such accounts imply that scientists omit certain features of a target because they know from the beginning of their practice which features of the system being investigated are relevant and which are not. However, determining which features are relevant is often the result of a process of modelling with abstractions, and not the starting point. Tharp inferred certain trends from the profile diagrams that she and Heezen produced based on sounding data, and then projected those trends onto the map in the form of conspicuous visual patterns, by making 'educated guesses' to fill the data gaps. They wished to find out how things would look, and how things would be structured, if certain peak and valley successions were imposed on wide areas of the seafloor.

---

of Injustice', *Hypathia*, 32.2 (2017), pp. 329–46 <https://doi.org/10.1111/hypa. 12317>.

36   Hancox-Li, 'Idealization and Abstraction in Models of Injustice', p. 6.

They did not know with certainty, in advance, what the central aspects were of the morphology of the system they were studying. The process of abstracting facilitated the visualization of noteworthy relationships that had until then remained occluded.

A third criticism of accounts of abstraction as omission follows from the previous two. It has been frequently assumed in these accounts that abstraction is 'harmless', in the sense that it does not hamper accurate representation.[37] This is a questionable claim not only because something's being harmless or not will depend on the particular modelling goals set in advance, as discussed above, but also because if we take abstraction to be harmless in general, then the contribution of abstraction to modelling will be 'strictly passive', that is, it will not do any serious explanatory or exploratory work.[38] To the contrary, what Tharp's case makes manifest is that the abstractions employed were neither passive nor innocuous. They were in fact highly creative, in the sense that they demanded scientists to engage in an active practice of ordering and establishing connections between the scattered data they possessed concerning the morphological features of the ocean floor, in conceptually and visually imaginative ways, until noteworthy patterns emerged. In a recollection of their research in the 1950s, Heezen remarked that the physiographic maps drawn by Tharp afforded an 'abstract view of the sea floor [… which] can be seen in no other way but in the mind's eye'.[39] The mind's eye was required to imagine the content of as-yet-unexplored areas of the deep ocean and to transform that content into a unifying material representation in the form of a map. Creativity and the systematic exercise of the imagination were fundamental to carrying out this task. An anecdote recalled by Tharp, concerning the final step of the production of the physiographic map of the Atlantic, affirms and nicely illustrates abstraction as a creative practice. At the bottom of the map, she located a large white legend (see Figure 1), partly for the purpose of covering up an area of the ocean about which almost no sounding data was available, but also — as Tharp playfully suggested to Heezen — so as to 'include

---

37   Ibid.

38   Rice, *Leveraging Distortions*, pp. 120–21.

39   Bruce Heezen and Charles D. Hollister, *The Face of the Deep* (Oxford: Oxford University Press, 1971), p. 7, quoted in Winther and Raffn, 'What If?', p. 221.

mermaids and shipwrecks' next to it, to surreptitiously imply, 'like the cartographers of old', that acts of guesswork about unknown areas were fundamental to the process of constructing the map. Unfortunately, 'Bruce [Heezen] would have none of it.'[40]

5. CREATIVE ABSTRACTION IN THE ARTS

Taking into account the three foregoing criticisms of the orthodox view of abstraction as omission, what could an alternative, revised account of abstraction in science be? Much has been advanced already, as the key seems to be to incorporate the fact that abstraction is an active, creative practice through which epistemic agents gain access to important patterns concerning the relationships between (morphological, structural, mechanistic) features operating in a system of interest. In attempting to spell out the implications of a creative account of abstraction, this section incorporates some insights from the arts, given the longer and more sophisticated tradition of discussion about the aesthetic and epistemic potential of abstraction in this field.[41] In the writings of early twentieth-century modernist artists, for instance, one finds multiple reflections on abstraction as a highly creative activity.[42] In the theoretical as well as more practice-oriented writings of artists like Wassily Kandinsky, Hilma af Klint, Paul Klee, Piet Mondrian, Anni Albers, and Kazimir Malevich, abstract composition is rarely understood as a matter of pure omission or of the elimination of details

---

40 Tharp, 'Connect the Dots'; Winther and Raffn, 'What If?'.

41 One might ask to what extent this leap of argumentation, and move from the discussion of abstraction in science to abstraction in art, is justified. If one adopts a framework that accepts that the sciences and the arts are domains that share the epistemic aim of advancing understanding of the world, as, for instance, Nelson Goodman and Catherine Elgin each do, then the leap may not be that difficult to bridge. Still, even from a more traditional conception of the separation between the two domains, according to which the sciences are understood as the enterprise of producing new knowledge, while the arts are a purely aesthetic domain with no genuinely epistemic function, one could nevertheless accept that a dialogue with the arts, where the notion of abstraction has been problematized thoroughly, might yet serve as an inspiring resource for philosophers of science to examine unexplored aspects of the debate on abstraction in science. See Nelson Goodman, *Languages of Art: An Approach to a Theory of Symbols* (Indianapolis: The Bobbs-Merrill Company, 1968); and Catherine Elgin, *True Enough* (Cambridge, MA: MIT Press, 2017) <https://doi.org/10.7551/mitpress/9780262036535.001.0001>.

42 Anna Moszynska, *Abstract Art*, 2nd edn (London: Thames and Hudson, 2020).

from an initially realistic pictorial form. Here, abstraction also involves adding and supplementing, in such a way that the artist creates connections in the world that have not been seen before. Thus, abstraction is for modernist artists a 'creative' practice in the literal sense of the word.

More specifically, Wassily Kandinsky describes the practice of producing an abstract composition as occurring in successive steps. '[O]ne of the first steps into the realm of abstraction', he writes, is the 'rejection of the third dimension', the perspectival core of figurative representation, to the point that the identification of everyday objects on the surface of the canvas is no longer possible.[43] Until this point, the process he describes seems to coincide with the conception of abstraction as the omission of features, as discussed earlier, which in this case primarily entails the omission of spatial perspective and of recognizable three-dimensional objects. Yet the key for Kandinsky is the subsequent step, in which the artist, in their continued work towards abstract composition, creates 'an ideal surface', with its own internal organization, existing independently of the original scene or experience that motivated the artistic creation.[44] This new ideal plane, despite being non-figurative, is still three-dimensional for Kandinsky, since lines, shapes, and colours are here superimposed, creating the impression of depth, with some forms appearing closer to the viewer than others. Viewers are then to examine the internal configurations of the ideal plane on the canvas, and to cultivate an aptitude for the detection of relevant relationships existing among those lines, shapes, and colours.

Anni Albers, student and then teacher and workshop director at the Bauhaus school in Dessau, has a comparable creative conception of abstract composition. Weaving, Albers asserts, is an art form that uses material resources such as thread and loom operations to produce genuine abstractions (Figure 3).[45] Her own 'pictorial weavings' are acts of creating independent abstract planes on two-dimensional textile surfaces: 'let threads be articulate again and find a form themselves

---

43   Wassily Kandinsky, *On the Spiritual in Art* [1911], ed. and trans. by Hilla Rebay (New York: Solomon R. Guggenheim Foundation, 1946), p. 77.

44   Ibid., p. 77.

45   Ann Coxon, Briony Fer, and Maria Müller-Schareck, *Anni Albers* (London: Yale University Press and Tate, 2018).

to no other end than their own orchestration.'[46] This internal orchestration of the composition is not only the product of a practice of omission, by which figurative form is left out and only essential geometric shapes kept in, but also of a practice of creative ordering, implemented 'out of dots, out of lines, out of a structure built of those elemental elements' which compose the organized abstract plane in textile form.[47]

It is not only modernist visual artists that have highlighted the creative nature of abstract composition. In contemporary aesthetics, one can also find illuminating philosophical reflections on how abstraction constitutes a creative practice. Kendall Walton, whose work on make-believe has been as crucial for philosophers of science as for philosophers of art in describing the epistemic functions of fictions, explains the role of abstraction in terms of the 'imagined seeing' of connections that it affords.[48] When viewers encounter an abstract artwork and recognize the various elements present in the composition (lines, shapes, colours), they can imagine seeing relationships between them and, in turn, make inferences about further relationships occurring between objects and features in the world outside of the plane, in light of the learning process that the abstract work facilitated.[49] In comparable terms, Michael Newall has more recently referred to the 'non-veridical perception' that takes place in our encounters with visual abstractions.[50] This is because abstract space is a 'space other to that of our everyday experience', where the 'planes, lines and strokes of paint that do inhabit it appear to be ruled by different laws to those of gravity and mechanics'. As in a liberated territory, relationships between features can occur more freely, 'according to some alternative, pictorial mechanics'.[51] Abstractions, understood in this way, help us

---

46   Ibid., p. 13.

47   Ibid., p. 21.

48   Kendall Walton, *Mimesis as Make-Believe: On the Foundations of the Representational Arts* (Cambridge, MA: Harvard University Press, 1990).

49   Richard Wollheim, 'Seeing-as, Seeing-in and Pictorial Representation', in Wollheim, *Art and its Objects*, 2nd edn [1980] (Cambridge: Cambridge University Press, 2015), pp. 137–51 <https://doi.org/10.1017/CBO9781316286777.009>.

50   Michael Newall, *What Is a Picture? Depiction, Realism, Abstraction* (Basingstoke: Palgrave Macmillan, 2011) <https://doi.org/10.1057/9780230297531>.

51   Ibid., p. 194.

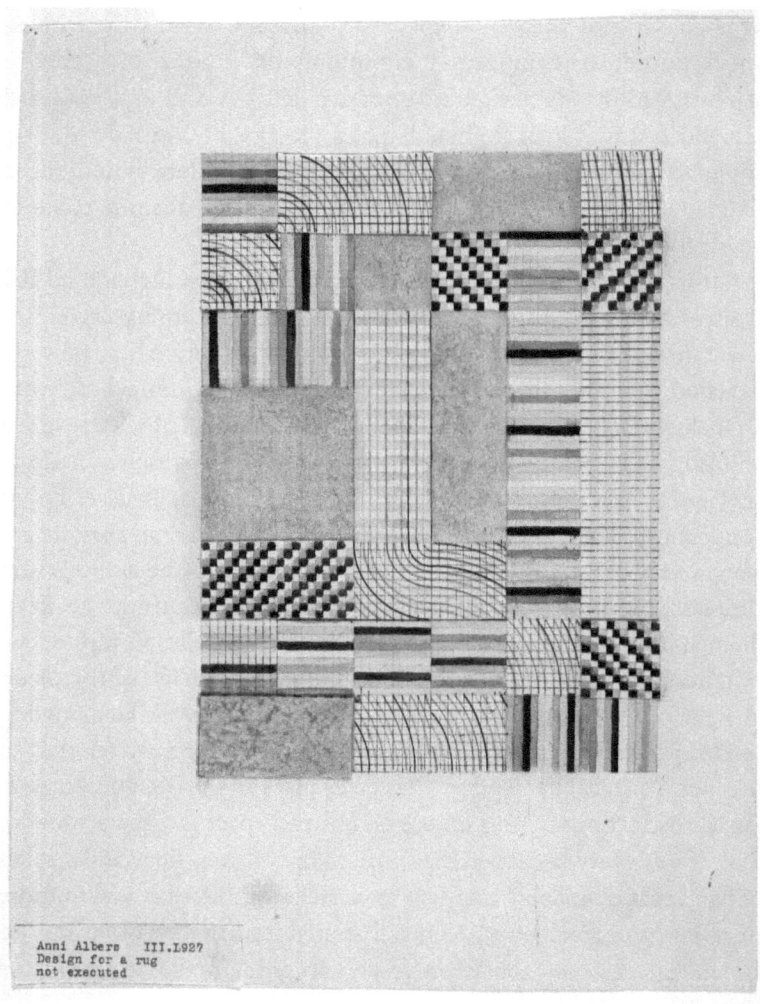

Anni Albers   III.1927
Design for a rug
not executed

FIG. 3. Anni Albers, *Design for a Rug*, 1927, black ink and watercolour over graphite with drawn and cut paper additions on off-white woven paper. Image: 21 × 15.6 cm; Sheet: 32.1 × 25.1 cm. Harvard Art Museums, Cambridge, Massachusetts. © The Josef and Anni Albers Foundation / VG Bild-Kunst, Bonn 2024. Reproduced with the kind permission of VG Bild-Kunst.

to freely explore and imagine possibilities within the abstract space thus created, and to eventually transfer some of the formal, visual, or material relationships perceived within the autonomous space of the artwork to aspects of the world existing outside of it.

The ideas concerning artistic abstraction succinctly collected here can inform the debate on the epistemic value of abstraction in scientific modelling. What we seem to find in debates in the arts is a general tendency to consider the omission of irrelevant features at best the first step, and not the goal, of abstract composition. Artistic abstraction is primarily conceived as an imaginative, creative act, which produces autonomous spaces for the exploration of forms, materials, and structures, and foregrounds relevant relationships recognized between these components. Scientific modelling practices, such as the production of Tharp's physiographic maps, should be understood as an analogous type of creative act. Thanks to abstraction, insightful relationships between previously disconnected features of a natural system, such as the ocean floor, can be brought to the fore and organized in a coherent, unifying manner. If philosophers of science were to adopt more creative conceptions of abstraction in the current modelling debate, the supposed differences between abstraction and idealization would to some extent vanish, since the two strategies would wear their active, imaginative character on their sleeves. That is to say, idealization would remain an active practice of inserting (potentially fruitful) falsehoods in a model, while abstraction would stand now as an active practice of omitting and creatively ordering features until a cogent, insightful pattern emerges.

6. ABSTRACTION AS STRATEGY FOR WORLDMAKING

So far, the sense of abstraction sketched here builds on omission but adds an aspect of creative ordering to it. Yet one could take this proposal a step further and admit that if abstraction has a creative nature, then abstract representations can be generative too. That is, the strongest consequence of the present account is that abstraction can be understood as a strategy for worldmaking. In *Ways of Worldmaking*, Nelson Goodman argues that worlds are constantly made from other worlds, which we already have at hand, through the manipulation of symbol systems.[52] His thesis is that what there is in the world depends on our conceptual schemes and representational systems. As he states: 'recognizing patterns is very much a matter of inventing and imposing them.'[53] And abstraction, as we have seen, is especially helpful for uncovering/establishing trends and patterns in modelling practices. Goodman specifically enumerates 'deletion', 'weighting', 'composition', 'decomposition', 'ordering', and 'deformation' as strategies commonly used to build world versions, to which we could add abstraction, understood in the rich, creative sense described here (or perhaps as a systematic combination of several of the strategies listed by Goodman).[54]

The worldmaking capacity of abstraction was in fact already hinted at in early abstractionist thought. Kandinsky produced a series of prints, entitled *Kleine Welten* (*Small Worlds*), which stands as an intriguing example of the new, independent worlds that abstraction helps create.[55] More explicitly, Paul Klee held that 'art does not reproduce the visible; rather, it makes visible', so that 'out of abstract elements a formal cosmos is ultimately created'.[56] If the omission of irrelevant features of a target system were, at best, the first step in the practice of abstracting, 'creating a cosmos' would be its final, most ambitious step, that which exposes its incredibly generative potential. Not surprisingly, Winther also identifies this worldmaking potential in Marie Tharp's work. The oceanographic community initially received the publication of her first physiographic map of the Mid-Atlantic Ridge in 1957 with scepticism, but progressively '*Tharp's maps became the world*'.[57]

Of course, some philosophers committed to metaphysical realism might be dissatisfied with the idea of taking the term *worldmaking* too

---

52 Goodman, *Ways of Worldmaking*.

53 Ibid., p. 22.

54 Ibid., pp. 7–16.

55 I thank Ross Shields for the lead to these artworks. The twelve prints of the portfolio *Small Worlds* (*Kleine Welten*) by Kandinsky, from 1922, can be seen as part of the Museum of Modern Art's digitalized collection. See <https://www.moma.org/collection/works/portfolios/143911> [accessed December 2023].

56 Paul Klee, 'Creative Confession' [1920], in Klee, *Creative Confessions and Other Writings*, ed. by Matthew Gale, trans. by Norbert Guterman (London: Tate, 2013), pp. 7–14 (p. 7).

57 Winther, 'Mapping the Deep Blue Oceans', p. 109, italics in the original.

literally. They may wish to contest that nothing is really created in the practice of using abstractions in representation.[58] Did Tharp's maps, Kandinsky's and Klee's paintings, and Albers's fabrics really make a world? Even Goodman asked himself, rather rhetorically: 'shouldn't we now return to sanity from all this mad proliferation of worlds?'[59] In a sense, the relationships foregrounded by practices of abstraction, and the patterns made visible through them, are not really brought into existence by the abstractions: they were there all along, waiting to be organized and unified by the scientist or artist in question.[60] This is true but trivial, argues the philosopher of science and art Catherine Elgin, in line with Goodman, since we have little reason to care about the many potential relationships that exist outside of our representational practices in a non-meaningful way.[61] Intentionally employing the resource of abstraction is an act of creating meaningful relationships, by discriminating between the myriad features that agents encounter and drawing lines (also literally in the cases of Tharp, Kandinsky, and Albers) between some of them. The novel relationships highlighted by our best artistic and scientific representations have the potential to transform our vision of the world as we conceive it. So, both for Goodman and Elgin, the prospect of an alternative metaphysical position, which rejects the worldmaking capacity of strategies like abstraction, and tries instead to search for a neutral, underlying version of the world that is not explained through our representational systems, is desolating. Such a world would be a 'world without kinds or order [...] or patterns — a world not worth fighting for or against'.[62]

Leaving metaphysical worries aside, do we have reasons to be concerned about the potential of abstraction for worldmaking? It was mentioned earlier that those who support accounts of abstraction as omission assume not only that abstraction is passive but also that it is harmless. In clear contrast, to adopt a creative view on abstraction means to acknowledge that abstraction has the potential to be both a positively fruitful and a harmful cognitive strategy, insofar as it is

---

58   Elgin, *True Enough*, p. 257.
59   Goodman, *Ways of Worldmaking*, p. 20.
60   This is a modified version of the argument made in Elgin, *True Enough*, p. 257.
61   Ibid., p. 257.
62   Goodman, *Ways of Worldmaking*, p. 20.

a tool to make, remake, and transform the world. Abstraction can produce epistemic fruits as well as epistemic harms, so one should be wary of the epistemic and pragmatic consequences of adopting dubious abstractions. Pragmatist philosophers such as John Dewey and William James referred to the dangers of 'vicious abstractionism' with precisely this worry in mind. Winther reads the warnings of pragmatists as pointing to the effects of the 'pernicious reification' that abstractions can lead to.[63] Roughly put, pernicious reification happens when cognitive agents endorse the knowledge that results from an abstract concept or abstract visual representation but ignore the particular function that the abstraction was supposed to play, overlooking the historical conditions of the emergence of the abstraction, and disregarding its appropriate domain of application.[64] When such aspects are not considered, the products of the abstraction are inappropriately universalized and ontologized, thus failing to operate in real life.[65]

Other types of warnings about the risks of abstraction have come from political theory and feminist critique in recent decades. A claim commonly found in these fields is that there are no such things as value-free abstractions, as when abstract formal models of justice[66] or general ethical principles[67] are proposed, or when the consequences of adopting certain abstract scientific representations are uncritically endorsed.[68] The political philosopher Onora O'Neill

---

63 Rasmus Winther, 'James and Dewey on Abstraction', *The Pluralist*, 9.2 (2014), pp. 1–28 (p. 1) <https://doi.org/10.5406/pluralist.9.2.0001>. Winther applies the notion of 'pernicious reification' in his reading of different pragmatist works, including William James, *Pragmatism* [1907] (Cambridge, MA: Harvard University Press, 1979); and John Dewey, *Human Nature and Conduct, 1922*, ed. by Jo Ann Boydston, The Middle Works, 1899–1924, 14 (Carbondale: Southern Illinois University Press, 1983).

64 In comparable terms, Alfred North Whitehead calls this the 'fallacy of misplaced concreteness'. See Alfred North Whitehead, *Science and the Modern World* [1925] (New York: The Free Press, 1967), p. 51; and Alfred North Whitehead, *Process and Reality: An Essay in Cosmology* [1929] (New York: The Free Press, 1978), p. 93.

65 Winther, 'James and Dewey on Abstraction', pp. 1, 9.

66 Lisa H. Schwartzman, 'Abstraction, Idealization, and Oppression', *Metaphilosophy*, 37.5 (2006), pp. 565–88 <https://doi.org/10.1111/j.1467-9973.2006.00457.x>.

67 Onora O'Neill, 'Abstraction, Idealization and Ideology in Ethics', *Royal Institute of Philosophy Supplements*, 22 (1987), pp. 55–69 <https://doi.org/10.1017/S0957042X00003667>.

68 On the presence of social and other non-epistemic values in science, see Helen Longino, *Science as Social Knowledge* (Princeton, NJ: Princeton University Press, 1990); Heather Douglas, *Science, Policy, and the Value-Free Ideal* (Pittsburgh: Univer-

has, for instance, highlighted that idealized as much as abstract theory, in aiming towards generality, can ignore the distinctive experiences of the oppressed, because the abstractions such theories entail are value-charged in ways that often exclude the social and historical features that are constitutive of human agency.[69] Lisa Schwartzman also points out that 'methods of abstraction often involve the bracketing of information that is crucial to understanding the nature and sources of oppression', adding that 'many allegedly abstract theories actually assume a male norm'.[70] Although the conceptualization of abstraction in the work of these feminist scholars matches the definition of abstraction-as-omission more closely than the creative definition of abstraction that is endorsed here, their critical assessments reflect the attribution of a generative, worldmaking potential to abstractions, hence their critiques still hold strongly here.

Importantly, Schwartzman avers, the solution to the potential harms of abstraction 'is not simply to do away with all abstraction' and focus on the particularities of specific situations and individuals. The best way to approach the problem 'may be to pay attention to the kinds of abstraction' that a given representation employs and to disallow those that perpetuate forms of oppression.[71] The reason why the possibility of eliminating abstractions from our representations should be rejected in general is that it would be both unfeasible and unproductive: 'abstraction is unavoidable in all reasoning',[72] since abstract models and images help us to navigate among concrete descriptions of situations. 'It is only when we see situations *of that sort* as requiring action *of this type*', O'Neill says, 'that knowledge of some description becomes action guiding.'[73] Critical race theorist Charles Mills adds, similarly, that rejecting abstraction 'deprives one of the apparatus necessary for making general theoretical statements', and indeed hampers the pos-

sity of Pittsburgh Press, 2009) <https://doi.org/10.2307/j.ctt6wrc78>; and Potochnik, *Idealization and the Aims of Science*.

69   O'Neill, 'Abstraction, Idealization and Ideology in Ethics', pp. 56–64.

70   Schwartzman, 'Abstraction, Idealization, and Oppression', p. 567.

71   Ibid., p. 575.

72   O'Neill, 'Abstraction, Idealization and Ideology in Ethics', p. 55.

73   Ibid., p. 64, emphasis in the original.

sibility of 'critiquing those same hegemonic misleading abstractions' that one observes in certain forms of representation.[74]

These last remarks about the potential harms of abstraction have a much broader scope than the specific case of scientific modelling with which this chapter began. I end with them to stimulate further reflections on how the worldmaking abilities of scientists, artists, and social agents more generally, should also remind us of the limits, constraints, and risks that abstractions, among other (mis)representational strategies, impose. Amia Srinivasan has perceptively noted that 'successful representational interventions have a Janus-faced structure': they picture an aspect of the world 'as it is currently constituted, and yet also picture it anew', striking 'a fine balance between familiarity and departure'.[75] It is precisely in this sense that abstract representations are creative acts. They afford understanding of a familiar, yet not fully known world, and, at the same time, they describe it in a manner that has never been thought of before. Like Tharp's map-making world interventions, they find a balance between depicting a part of the world as it is, accurately, and constructing it anew.

---

74   Charles Mills, 'Ideal Theory as Ideology', *Hypatia*, 20.3 (2005), pp. 165–83 (p. 173) <https://doi.org/10.1111/j.1527-2001.2005.tb00493.x>.

75   Amia Srinivasan, 'VII — Genealogy, Epistemology and Worldmaking', *Proceedings of the Aristotelian Society*, 119.2 (2019), pp. 127–56 (p. 150) <https://doi.org/10.1093/arisoc/aoz009>.

Gertrude Stein begins her biography of Pablo Picasso with a claim
that is equal parts provocation and banality: 'In the nineteenth century
painters discovered the need of always having a model in front of them,
in the twentieth century they discovered that they must never look at
a model.'[76] The point is not, as the art-historical cliché would have
it, that early twentieth-century painters had stopped emulating past
works. Rather, Stein is referring to models in the sense of real people,
in various stages of undress, who provided painters with a real-world
referent and object of representation. Of course, Stein sat for Picasso.
But she recalls that her portrait could only be finished after the sessions
had concluded:

> I posed for him all that winter, eighty times and in the end
> he painted out the head, he told me that he could not look
> at me any more and then he left once more for Spain. It was
> the first time since the blue period and immediately upon his
> return from Spain he painted in the head without having seen
> me again and he gave me the picture and I was and I still am
> satisfied with my portrait, for me, it is I, and it is the only
> reproduction of me which is always I, for me.[77]

Counterintuitively, the representational success of Picasso's painting
depended on the absence of the physical presence of a model. For Stein,
this is more than a mere anecdote, in that it illustrates a redefinition
of truth in relation to visual experience: namely, that 'the truth that
the things seen with the eyes are the only real things, had lost its sig-
nificance.'[78] Painters, in other words, had ceased to represent models
because models — at least in the sense defined above — had ceased to
represent reality.

In 'Abstraction as Strategy for Worldmaking', Julia Sánchez-
Dorado makes a convincing case for how the abstractive character
of scientific models can be better understood by looking to the

---

76 Gertrude Stein, *Picasso* (New York: Dover, 1984), p. 1. Stein is obviously exaggerating,
    as is clear from the sentence that precedes this one: 'Painting in the nineteenth century
    was only done in France and by Frenchmen [...].' Ibid.

77 Ibid., p. 8.

78 Ibid., p. 10.

twentieth-century tradition of painterly abstraction. In this short
response, I will suggest that this tradition of painterly abstraction, as
characterized by Stein and others, can itself be better understood by
looking to the nineteenth-century tradition of scientific modelling.
Prominent strands of both art and science, I will argue, define the
model not as a positive object of visual experience, but as a relational
construction that, as Paul Klee said of art, 'makes visual' (*sichtbar
macht*).[79]

Ludwig Boltzmann summarizes the nineteenth-century view in
his 1902 entry on 'Model' for the *Encyclopaedia Britannica*. Referring
to the psychophysiological observations of Hermann von Helmholtz
and Ernst Mach, he writes:

> [W]e can know but little of the resemblance of our thoughts to
> the things to which we attach them. What resemblance there is
> lies principally in the nature of the connexion, the correlation
> being analogous to that which obtains between thought and
> language, language and writing, the notes on the stave and
> musical sounds, &c.[80]

Referencing the work of Johannes Müller, Helmholtz had observed
that sensations relate to physical stimuli in a manner that is both arbitrary and fixed, involving no more similarity than a printed note has
to the tone expressed by a violin. In one of his favourite examples, the
optic nerve produces a visual sensation of light regardless of whether
it is stimulated by an actual photon or by the pressure of a finger on
the eyeball. However, while there is no similarity between a given
sensation and a given stimulus, Helmholtz admitted a 'trace of a similarity' between a sequence of sensations and a sequence of stimuli,
just as a sequence of printed notes bears the trace of a similarity to
the musical phrase it represents, moving up and down on the staff to

---

79   Paul Klee, 'Klee', in *Schöpferische Konfession*, ed. by Kasimir Edschmid (Berlin: Erich
     Reiss, 1920), pp. 26–40 (p. 28).
80   Ludwig Boltzmann, 'Model', in *Theoretical Physics and Philosophical Problems*, ed. by
     Brian McGuinnes (Dordrecht: D. Reidel, 1974), pp. 213–20 (p. 214) <https://doi.
     org/10.1007/978-94-010-2091-6_16>.

indicate higher and lower pitch.[81] For both Helmholtz and Boltzmann, scientific models — like visual perception — depend on a correlation between the 'connexion' of the elements within the model and the 'connexion' of the features within its referent.

Helmholtz's influence on the development of early twentieth-century painting is difficult to overstate. The Impressionists' reception of his writings on optics is well documented, and his insistence on the arbitrariness of sensation is literally manifested in the Fauves' radical use of colour.[82] But it was his concept of modelling, as summarized in Boltzmann's article, that impacted the formal innovations of abstract painters like Wassily Kandinsky.[83] For Kandinsky, abstraction does not imply a complete absence of object or reference. Instead, it signals a shift in emphasis from the realistic representation of details to a presentation of a 'connexion' between forms and colours. This is evident in the Bauhaus exercises to which Sánchez-Dorado refers in her article, in which a still life is reduced to the abstract relations among its elements, which then cease to be identifiable as such. It is also on display in Kandinsky's reworkings of traditional compositions, which render the original scene unrecognizable.[84] But modelling becomes an object of theoretical reflection in his 1910 essay on 'Content and Form'. Here Kandinsky observes that '[m]an is continuously bombarded with the effects [of the world on his senses]. He continuously collects experiences, which first accumulate in him unconsciously, and

81   Hermann von Helmholtz, 'The Facts in Perception', in Helmholtz, *Science and Culture: Popular and Philosophical Essays*, ed. by David Cahan (Chicago: University of Chicago Press, 1995), pp. 342–80 (p. 347). The musical example is from Boltzmann, 'Model', p. 214.

82   See Martin Kemp, 'The Impressionists' Bible', *Nature*, 453.37 (2008) <https://doi.org/10.1038/453037a>.

83   I develop this argument in my dissertation, Ross Shields, 'Hanging-Together: Goethe, Kant, and the Theory of Aesthetic Modernism' (unpublished doctoral thesis, Columbia University, 2019) <https://doi.org/10.7916/D8475TVQ>. See Lynn Edward Bowland, 'A Culture of Dissonance: Wassily Kandinsky, Atonality, and Abstraction' (unpublished doctoral thesis, University of Texas at Austin, 2014), pp. 90–130 <https://hdl.handle.net/2152/30323> [accessed 1 August 2024]. Clark V. Poling, *Kandinsky: Russian and Bauhaus Years, 1915–1933* (New York: Solomon R. Guggenheim Foundation, 1983), p. 59.

84   See Paul Weber, 'Kandinskys Pädagogik aus der Perspektive seiner Theorie der Verschiebung', in *Wassily Kandinsky: Lehrer am Bauhaus*, ed. by Magdalena Droste (Berlin: Baushaus-Archiv, 2014), pp. 150–75.

are subsequently sought out consciously.'[85] As he goes on to argue, scientists differ from artists insofar as the former classify and systematize experiences that have been sought out consciously, while the latter classify and systematize those subtler impressions that sensations make on our *Geist* — our 'spirit' or 'mind' or even 'intellect' — which tend to be ignored in everyday perception.

An abstract painting might lack a model in the traditional sense, meaning that its complex of brushstrokes does not refer to any particular physical body, sitting in the artist's studio. But it could also be said that painterly abstraction constitutes a model of perception itself, which, according to the insights of late nineteenth-century psychophysiology, involves far more than that which is 'seen with the eye'. Kandinsky reaches a similar conclusion in his book *On the Spiritual in Art* (*Über das Geistige in der Kunst*), which argues that the 'inner sound' of a painting — whether abstract or representational — is perceived not by the eye but by the *Geist*.[86] Statements like these are often attributed to Kandinsky's fleeting interest in theosophy, which he shared with a number of early twentieth-century artists. But I propose that they have more to do with the epistemology of models introduced by Helmholtz and his colleagues, which emphasized structural analogy over positive sensation. The inner sound of an abstract painting could then be defined as the complex 'connexion' that inheres among its elements, and that takes on value to the extent that it can be transferred, as Sánchez-Dorado writes, from the 'autonomous space of the artwork to the world existing beyond the aesthetic plane'. This value is immediately aesthetic, to the extent that it involves a preconscious intuition of law-likeness (*Gesetzmäßigkeit*). But it is also proto-scientific, at least according to Helmholtz, for whom all scientific theories originate 'in an analogous way to artistic intuition, as a presentiment of a new law-likeness'.[87]

---

85   Wassily Kandinsky, 'Inhalt und Form' [1910], in Kandinsky, *Gesammelte Schriften 1889–1916*, ed. by Helmut Friedel (Munich: Prestel, 2007), p. 400; my translation.

86   Wassily Kandinsky, *Über das Geistige in der Kunst* [1911] (Bern: Benteli, 2009), p. 72; my translation.

87   Hermann von Helmholtz, 'Goethe's Presentiments of Coming Scientific Ideas', in Helmholtz, *Science and Culture*, ed. by Cahan, pp. 393–412 (p. 401).

Picasso's portrait of Stein represents a transitional moment from his blue and rose periods to Analytic Cubism, in which the model dissolves into abstract compositions of lines and forms that frustrate any immediate object recognition. But it already contains a hint of the later style, insofar as the left and right sides of the face are depicted from distinct and clashing perspectives.[88] Although this is most obvious in the eyes, its effect on the mouth is no less striking, insofar as the latter is effectively doubled, featuring three peaks on the upper lip that together form two cupid's bows. On the one hand, this is a fitting portrait of a poet who tended to double herself, as a 'me which is always I, for me'. On the other hand, it reminds us that all perception is constructed from multiple distinct aspects, as in the experience of the child who beholds the face of its mother but only knows, as Stein puts it, 'one feature and not another, one side and not the other'.[89]

---

88   See Pablo Picasso, *Gertrude Stein*, 1905–06, oil on canvas, 100 × 81.3 cm, Metropolitan Museum of Art, New York City <https://www.metmuseum.org/toah/works-of-art/47.106> [accessed 16 December 24].

89   Stein, *Picasso*, p. 15.

From Climate Model to Climate Fiction

Kim Stanley Robinson's *The Ministry for the Future* as Operative Literature

ROSS SHIELDS

'FOR FREDRIC JAMESON'

I begin with the dedication of Kim Stanley Robinson's *The Ministry for the Future* (2020) as a way of motivating the title of this essay, which will enquire into the operative function of climate fiction (and in particular climate/science fiction) with respect to the political discourse and practice surrounding climate change.[1] This discourse and practice is not restricted to, but increasingly involves, a Marxist critique of capitalism, such as Fredric Jameson has sought to articulate in relation to literature, in the tradition of Sergei Tretyakov, Bertolt Brecht, and Walter Benjamin.[2] *The Ministry for the Future*, a cli/sci-fi novel written by an author versed in Jameson's ideas, will thus serve as a case study for

---

1   Kim Stanley Robinson, *The Ministry for the Future* (New York: Orbit, 2020), dedication.

2   On the question of whether climate fiction constitutes a literary genre, see Alison Sperling, 'Climate Fictions: Introduction', *Paradoxa*, 31 (2019), pp. 7–21 <https://paradoxa.com/no-30-climate-fictions-2020/> [accessed 4 August 2024]; and Derek Woods, 'Genre at Earth Magnitude: A Theory of Climate Fiction', *New Literary History*, 54.2 (2023), pp. 1143–67 <https://doi.org/10.1353/nlh.2023.a907162>.

understanding how the environmental humanities have both inherited and modified the political stakes of critical literary theory.

Having studied under Jameson at UC San Diego in the 1970s, it is no great surprise that Robinson would make use of the Brechtian strategy of defamiliarization (*Verfremdung*), going so far as to end a chapter on the redistribution of wealth by breaking the literary fourth wall: 'Arranging this situation is left as an exercise for the reader.'[3] And yet, despite its author's politics and education, *The Ministry for the Future* cannot be said to promote an explicitly Marxist agenda. As a work of fiction narrating the next thirty-odd years of global warming, its 'organizational usefulness' is in no way restricted to its 'value as propaganda', and its overall political tendency is ambiguous to say the least.[4] I will argue that the novel nevertheless exerts a clear set of operative functions, which manifest themselves in the relation between its ecological theme and the literary techniques with which that theme is presented.

Until recently, Marxist criticism has been distanced from ecological or environmental concerns on account of its purported 'Prometheanism' (that is, its uncritical embrace of technologies of environmental exploitation). However, a growing number of ecosocialist philosophers and critics, including John Bellamy Foster (*Marx's Ecology*, 2000), Nancy Fraser (*Cannibal Capitalism*, 2021), and Kohei Saito (*Marx in the Anthropocene*, 2023), have made the convincing case that capital both disavows and hits against the intractable limits imposed by the natural world on economic growth.[5] Drawing on Marx's critique

---

3   Robinson, *The Ministry for the Future*, p. 41. For Jameson's reading of Brecht, see Fredric Jameson, *Brecht and Method* (London: Verso, 1998), especially pp. 35–42. Note that, when I say that Robinson breaks the fourth wall, I am identifying the author of the book with his narrative persona, at least in some of the theoretical chapters. This is justified by the fact that sections of the theoretical chapters are repeated by Robinson in real-world interviews, and ultimately contributes to the book's heteroglossic character. See note 30, below.

4   Walter Benjamin, 'The Author as Producer', trans. by Edmund Jephcott, in *Selected Writings*, ed. by Michael Jennings and others, 4 vols (Cambridge, MA: Harvard University Press, 2004–06), II.2: *1931–1934*, ed. by Michael W. Jennings, Howard Eiland, and Gary Smith (2005), pp. 768–82 (p. 777).

5   John Bellamy Foster, *Marx's Ecology: Materialism and Nature* (New York: Monthly Review Press, 2000); Nancy Fraser, *Cannibal Capitalism: How Our System Is Devouring Democracy, Care, and the Planet — and What We Can Do about It* (London: Verso, 2022); Kohei Saito, *Marx in the Anthropocene: Towards the Idea of Degrowth Com-

of industrial agriculture, these thinkers have pointed to a fundamental discrepancy — or 'metabolic rift' — between capital's potentially infinite process of self-valorization and the finite conditions of its existence on Earth.[6] The result of this discrepancy is literal disaster, albeit with unequally distributed consequences: global warming, widespread species extinction, and the increasingly futile attempt to 'shift' ecological burdens from the Global North to the Global South, and from present to future generations.[7]

It is in response to these crises that scholars in the humanities have rallied around the banner of ecocriticism, which, in distinction from many twentieth-century literary-theoretical movements, wears its political tendency on its sleeves.[8] To be sure, not all environmental humanists are Marxist or even Marxian.[9] Nevertheless, I would argue that the task of ecocriticism is clear enough: to develop and employ narrative and imaginative strategies that work against the efforts of capital to disguise or shift its negative impact on the globe. But how

munism (Cambridge: Cambridge University Press, 2023) <https://doi.org/10.1017/9781108933544>. See also Jason W. Moore, *Capitalism in the Web of Life: Ecology and the Accumulation of Capital* (New York: Verso, 2015); and Drew Pendergrass and Troy Vettesse, *Half-Earth Socialism* (New York: Verso, 2022).

6   Saito, *Marx in the Anthropocene*, pp. 23–28.

7   Ibid., pp. 29–34.

8   As Stephanie Foote and Jeffrey Jerome Cohen write in their introduction to the *Cambridge Companion to Environmental Humanities*: '[I]f anything anchors the diversity of E[nvironmental]H[umanities] projects within its wider discipline of the Humanities, [...] it is a commitment to the world-making power of narrative, and especially its commitment to how stories mediate different registers of power.' Stephanie Foote and Jeffrey Jerome Cohen, 'Introduction: Climate Change/Changing Climates', in *The Cambridge Companion to Environmental Humanities*, ed. by Jeffrey Jerome Cohen and Stephanie Foote (Cambridge: Cambridge University Press, 2021), pp. 1–10 <https://doi.org/10.1017/9781009039369.002>. See Hannes Bergthaller, 'Cli-Fi and Petrofiction: Questioning Genre in the Anthropocene', *Amerikastudien/American Studies*, 62.1 (2017), pp. 120–25 <https://amst.winter-verlag.de/article/AMST/2017/1/10> [accessed 4 August 2024]; Stephanie LeMenager, 'Climate Change and the Struggle for Genre', in *Anthropocene Reading: Literary History in Geologic Times*, ed. by Tobias Menely and Jesse Oak Taylor (University Park: Penn State University Press, 2017), pp. 220–38 <https://doi.org/10.5325/jj.22247044.15>; and Matthew Schneider-Mayerson, 'Climate-Change Fiction', in *American Literature in Transition, 2000–2010*, ed. by Rachel Greenwald Smith (New York: Cambridge University Press, 2017), pp. 309–21 <https://doi.org/10.1017/9781316569290.021>.

9   See Timothy Clark, 'Liberalism and Green Moralism', in *The Cambridge Introduction to Literature and the Environment* (Cambridge: Cambridge University Press, 2011), pp. 102–10 <https://doi.org/10.1017/CBO9780511976261>.

is this task to be realized? Can literature really 'save the planet' (a hyperbolic cliché often employed in discussions of cli-fi)?[10] How do literary models relate to scientific models of climate change? And what is their function with respect to extra-literary and non-representational forces?

As a way of approaching these questions, I propose to re-examine the early twentieth-century category of 'operative literature', a term coined by Tretyakov and developed in Benjamin's essay on 'The Author as Producer'.[11] There is an obvious sense in which the contemporary political situation differs from that of 1934, when Benjamin wrote his posthumously published piece, and it is not my intention to resume the question of political tendency and aesthetic autonomy as it played out in early twentieth-century Western-Marxist circles. Rather, it is my hope that the framework developed in Benjamin's essay will be of use in defining the role of the contemporary (environmental) humanities with respect to a set of present-day political concerns — concerns that provide the concepts of 'literary tendency' and 'formally progressive technique' with a new meaning in relation to a new, albeit negative, telos; in other words, a progress and tendency determined by neither providence nor spirit nor dialectical materialism (although it has everything to do with the contradictions of capital).

My essay will unfold in five sections. In the first, I develop the concept of operative literature, focusing on its relevance for climate fiction and abstracting it from its Marxist origins. Sections two through

---

10   See David Holmes, '"Cli-Fi": Could a Literary Genre Help Save the Planet?', *The Conversation*, 20 February 2014 <https://theconversation.com/cli-fi-could-a-literary-genre-help-save-the-planet-23478> [accessed 3 January 2024]; J. K. Ullrich, 'Climate Fiction: Can Books Save the Planet?', *The Atlantic*, 14 August 2015 <https://www.theatlantic.com/entertainment/archive/2015/08/climate-fiction-margaret-atwood-literature/400112/> [accessed January 3 2024].

11   For a Jamesonian reading of operative literature, see Hunter Bivens, 'Revisiting German Proletarian-Revolutionary Literature', in *Working-Class Literature(s): Historical and International Perspectives*, ed. by John Lennon and Magnus Nilsson, 2 vols (Stockholm: Stockholm University Press, 2017–20), II, pp. 83–113 <https://doi.org/10.16993/bbf>. See Soo Hwan Kim, 'Sergei Tretyakov Revisited: The Cases of Walter Benjamin and Hito Steyerl', *e-flux*, 104 (2019) <https://www.e-flux.com/journal/104/298121/sergei-tretyakov-revisited-the-cases-of-walter-benjamin-and-hito-steyerl/> [accessed 3 January 2024]. My reading focuses on Benjamin's use of Tretyakov's concept, abstracting from Tretyakov's argument, although I do return to Tretyakov in the penultimate section.

four define three operative functions that *The Ministry for the Future* takes on with respect to the discourse and politics of global warming. A concluding section addresses the ecological content and form of Robinson's novel as a whole, bringing it into relation to contemporary ecosocialist ideas, and making use of the Greimas square, a tool of semantic analysis and cognitive mapping that Jameson brings into proximity to his concept of ideology — a concept that also plays a no less prominent role in Robinson's novel.

CLIMATE FICTION AS OPERATIVE LITERATURE

In 'The Author as Producer', Benjamin takes up Tretyakov's notion of operative literature by resuming what he calls the 'unfruitful debate on the relationship between tendency and quality in literature'.[12] Instead of asserting an antagonism or priority of one against the other, Benjamin divides the concept of tendency into two parts, one literary and one political. He argues that the political tendency of a novel (for example) necessarily includes its literary tendency, which in turn constitutes its literary quality, concluding that '[t]he correct political tendency of a work thus includes its literary quality because it includes its literary tendency'.[13] This formulation has two consequences. First, it implies that mere propaganda, that is, writing that is not 'literarily correct', also lacks a 'correct political tendency'.[14] In Benjamin's example, the New Objectivity movement (*Neue Sachlichkeit*) has, due to its lack of formal innovation, effected little more than the 'transformation of the political struggle from a call-to-decision into an object of contemplative enjoyment, from a means of production into a consumer article'.[15] The movement may take class struggle as its object, but does little or nothing to promote class struggle as an agenda.

The second consequence of Benjamin's argument is the contrapositive of the first, namely, the insight that every work displaying a correct political tendency is also literarily correct, meaning that it involves a degree of 'progressive literary technique' that in turn

---

12   Benjamin, 'Author as Producer', p. 769.
13   Ibid.
14   Ibid.
15   Ibid., p. 776.

constitutes its literary quality.[16] Benjamin's examples of progressive literary technique fall into two main categories. The first, drawn directly from Tretyakov, involves the democratization of the means of literary production, for example, when the Soviet press 'revises even the distinction between author and reader'.[17] In the age of Facebook, X (Twitter), and Mastodon, the question of whether the democratization of media necessarily supports democratic politics has become fraught, and it is not my intention to contribute to the already substantial body of work devoted to this topic.[18] But Benjamin illustrates a second type of progressive artistic technique that is more germane to the issue at hand, namely, the artistic technique of Brecht's epic theatre, which routinely interrupts its own plot in a way that 'compels the listener to adopt an attitude vis-à-vis the process'.[19] By breaking off the contemplative enjoyment of the play's plot, the public is estranged 'in an enduring way, through thinking, from the conditions in which it lives'.[20] This is a good thing.

There is an obvious sense in which Kim Stanley Robinson's *The Ministry for the Future* enacts a Brechtian gesture of estrangement. I have already mentioned the didactic essays that interrupt the novel's plot, quite literally demanding the reader, like the author, 'to think, to reflect on his position in the process of production'.[21] But I do not believe that Brechtian moments like this account for the full scope of *The Ministry for the Future*'s operative function. On the contrary, as Benjamin remarks on the music of Hanns Eisler, a correct artistic tendency involves the elimination of two antitheses: 'first, between performers and listeners and, second, *between technique and content*'.[22] To speak of formal innovation in abstraction from content (whether that content is politically progressive or not) is therefore insufficient.

---

16   Ibid., p. 770. Note that this does not imply that a work's literary tendency entails its political tendency.

17   Ibid., p. 772.

18   See, for example, the essays collected in *Marx in the Age of Digital Capitalism*, ed. by Christian Fuchs and Vincent Mosco (Leiden: Brill, 2015) <https://doi.org/10.1163/9789004291393>.

19   Benjamin, 'Author as Producer', p. 778.

20   Ibid., p. 779.

21   Ibid.

22   Ibid., pp. 775–76, my emphasis.

Instead, progressive literary technique — if the term is to have any meaning for contemporary literary theory — will involve a necessary connection to its content, which, in the case of Kim Stanley Robinson's work of climate fiction, involves three issues: first, that climate scenarios both determine and are determined by human behaviour; second, that global warming defies our all-too-human perception; and finally, that any attempt to act or speak on behalf of the environment risks enforcing an anthropocentric worldview that has been, at least historically, part of the problem.

I will now argue that these three questions of content, correlated with three formal techniques, yield three distinct operative functions. Following this, I will address the relation of these operative functions to the modalities of metabolic shift conceptualized by Saito, before considering their interdependency in Robinson's novel as a whole.

PROBLEM 1: CLIMATE MODELS ARE NOT WEATHER FORECASTS

The Ministry for the Future has a plot; one, moreover, that is both linear and coherent. Although this can hardly be considered a 'progressive literary technique' in its own right, it plays an important function with respect to the specific requirements of a work of climate/science fiction — namely, to flesh out a future that already exists in the projections of climate scientists. A distanced glance at the novel reveals 106 chapters distributed between the years 2025 and 2053. The plot begins in the wake of the UNFCCC COP29 (the twenty-ninth Conference of the Parties of the United Nations Framework Convention on Climate Change), which has led to the creation of what has become known as the 'Ministry for the Future', a subsidiary body for the implementation of the Paris Agreement following the general failure of the world's nations to hit their 2023 targets. The plot ends just after COP58, when a 'turning point' is reached and the 'birth of a good Anthropocene' is announced.[23] But the road to this happy ending is anything but easy, involving a series of horrific climate disasters, a mounting sense of collective frustration, and the drastic measures taken by various groups in response thereto.

---

23   Robinson, *The Ministry for the Future*, p. 475.

By sketching a possible future, beginning in the near present, Robinson's novel fills in the abstract scenarios described by climate scientists with a copious amount of fictitious detail. In 2025 a heat wave kills twenty million people in India.[24] The Arctic Ocean's ice cover melts in 2032.[25] The year 2034 yields Crash Day, when clouds of small drones bring down sixty passenger jets, murdering thousands of civilians.[26] Some of these events are described through first-hand accounts, others through historical reports, but all are believable, and all force the reader to consider what our future has in store.

Keeping pace with this litany of dates is a second series, no less regular, and of greater importance for the novel's pacing, namely, the progression of CO_2 concentrations in the atmosphere. As shown in Figure 1, the numbers and facts strewn throughout Robinson's novel trace an all-too-believable projection for greenhouse gas emissions over the next fifty years. In fact, the fictional numbers supplied by Robinson closely match — at least at first — the *450 Core* climate projection published by the OECD in 2012, a real-world scenario in which the global concentration of greenhouse gases stabilizes at around 450 parts per million.[27] But while the OECD scenario gradually levels off, the parts per million recorded in Robinson's novel plunge from 475 to 451 after a combination of political unrest and extreme weather events finally leads to a change in global political consciousness.[28] This draws attention to one of the most striking similarities between climate/science fiction and the science of climate change, namely, the necessity of predicting a future that is anything but fixed. The problem is not that the

---

24   Ibid., p. 24.

25   Ibid., p. 147.

26   Ibid., p. 228.

27   OECD, 'Concentration Pathways for the Four Outlook Scenarios Including All Climate Forcers, 2010–2100', in *OECD Environmental Outlook to 2050: The Consequences of Inaction* (Paris: OECD Publishing, 2012) <https://doi.org/10.1787/env_outlook-2012-graph38-en> [accessed 4 August 2024]. See Robinson, *The Ministry for the Future*, chapters 36, 56, 69, 75, 89, and especially 94. The 2036 data point assumes that the 463 ppm reading was taken approximately two years after crash day; the 2040 data point assumes that the American heat wave occurred in 2040. Note that, on the basis of this graph and the Mauna Kea measurement of 447 ppm mentioned in chapter 25, it is possible to date Mary's kidnapping to 19 February 2030. Robinson, *The Ministry for the Future*, p. 90.

28   Ibid., p. 445.

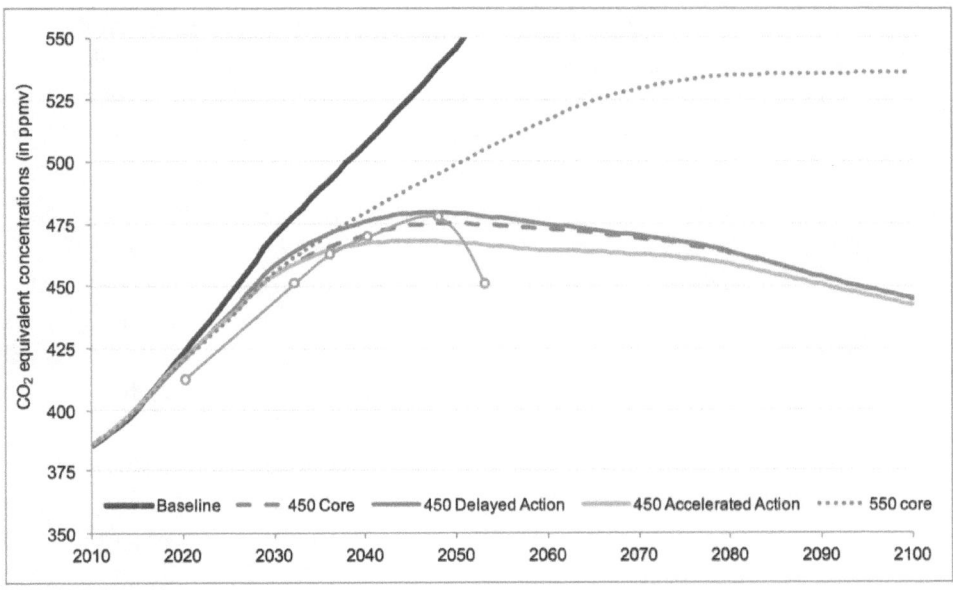

FIG. 1. CO_2 concentrations mentioned in *The Ministry for the Future* (with circles representing data points) superimposed on OECD projection.

models used by climate scientists are uncertain; on the contrary, if things continue as they are now (as represented in the baseline of the OECD graph), there is little doubt about what will happen: greenhouse gases will continue to increase, the 2 °C goal will be crossed, the seas will continue to rise, species will continue to go extinct, extreme weather events will increase in frequency and strength, and so on.

The problem is that the predictions of climate scientists, if they are effective in modifying our behaviour, end up proving themselves wrong. A good model is one that invalidates the scenario it describes — this constitutes its performative, as opposed to merely representative, function.[29] I propose that the operative function of climate/science

---

29   The performativity of climate models can be compared to illocutionary uses of language, as described in John L. Austin, *How to Do Things with Words* [1962] (Oxford: Oxford University Press, 1976), lectures 8 and 9 <https://doi.org/10.1093/acprof:oso/9780198245537.003.0008>. On the performativity of scientific models, see Donal Khosrowi, 'Managing Performative Models', *Philosophy of the Social Sciences*, 53.5 (2023), pp. 371–95 <https://doi.org/10.1177/00483931231172455>.

fiction can be understood in similar terms, insofar as its presentation of a hypothetical future works against the realization of that hypothesis.[30] It is for this reason that the coherent linear plot of *The Ministry for the Future*, although it may amount to a literary regression with respect to comparable works like David Mitchell's *Cloud Atlas* (2004) or even Robinson's own *The Years of Rice and Salt* (2002), contributes to one of the novel's principal operative functions. It concretizes and dramatizes climate models, showing that the future is both foreseeable, insofar as it follows the predictions of scientific scenarios, and subject to change, insofar as the possible future represented in those scenarios can be averted through transformations of behaviour, policy, and law, albeit at high costs.

The CO_2 curve drawn from the work of real-world climate scientists supplies Robinson's novel with a rising action, climax, and falling action that recalls Gustav Freytag's Aristotelian model of a tragic plot. However, unlike a traditional tragedy, which concludes with the recognition and submission to fate, it is precisely the fate modelled in the *450 Core* scenario that is ultimately averted in the novel's denouement, as a consequence of the collective response of the world's agents. This further clarifies the operative function of the Brechtian moments that interrupt the plot, which encourage us, as readers, to reflect on the inevitability of our fate in much the same way that the characters portrayed in the novel reflect on the inevitability of their own.

PROBLEM 2: REPRESENTING GLOBAL WARMING

Global warming takes place on spatial and temporal scales that overwhelm our powers of comprehension. Timothy Morton has referred to it as a *hyperobject*: something that is too big for us to perceive, but

---

30   Woods makes a similar observation: 'If the genre fulfills its goal by contributing to the equilibrium of the climate, then its verisimilitude will diminish.' Woods, 'Genre at Earth Magnitude', p. 1144. Or as Robinson himself suggests in an interview from 2021: 'as prophecy, SF is always wrong'. See James Bradley , 'It's Science over Capitalism: Kim Stanley Robinson and the Imperative of Hope', in *Tomorrow's Parties: Life in the Anthropocene*, ed. by Jonathan Strahan (Cambridge, MA: MIT Press, 2022), pp. 1–10 (p. 3) <https://doi.org/10.7551/mitpress/14384.003.0003>. Robinson continues, echoing his definition of ideology: 'The impetus comes from ideology, from one's invented imaginary relationship to the real situation. Here the discursive battle is paramount. The stories we tell each other will make the difference.' Ibid.

with which we must nevertheless contend.[31] Hence, while it may be possible to gain an abstract understanding of climate change as the statistical object of climate science, the climate in itself remains imperceptible, presenting very different aspects depending on the local conditions in which it appears as weather. The question — and this is very much a narrative question — is how to connect local perspectives in a way that does justice to their plurality without losing sight of their global cause.

This problematic is addressed in one of *The Ministry for the Future*'s first didactic essays, which provides the following definition of ideology: 'Ideology, n. An imaginary relationship to a real situation.'[32] Although Robinson observes that the 'common usage' of the term tends to refer pejoratively to 'what the other person has', he immediately recognizes a more fundamental meaning, indeed, one that recalls the theory outlined in Jameson's *Allegory and Ideology*, which is itself dedicated to Robinson (as Robinson's novel is dedicated to Jameson):

> But it seems to us that an ideology is a necessary feature of cognition, and if anyone were to lack one, which we doubt, they would be badly disabled. There is a real situation, that can't be denied, but it is too big for any individual to know in full, and so we must create our understanding by way of an act of the imagination.[33]

According to Robinson's definition, ideologies are 'imaginary' in the Lacanian sense of the term: far from comprising mere epiphenomena (or, for that matter, materialist superstructure), they play a constitutive role in the development and function of objectivity. This is clear from Jameson's definition of ideology in *Postmodernism*, which in turn stems from Louis Althusser's Lacanian-Marxist definition as 'the representation of the subject's *Imaginary* relationship to his or her *Real* conditions

---

31   Timothy Morton, *Hyperobjects: Philosophy and Ecology after the End of the World* (Minneapolis: University of Minnesota Press, 2013), p. 3. See also Amitav Ghosh, *The Great Derangement: Climate Change and the Unthinkable* (Chicago: University of Chicago Press, 2016), p. 62 <https://doi.org/10.7208/chicago/9780226323176.001.0001>.

32   Robinson, *The Ministry for the Future*, p. 41.

33   Ibid., p. 41. See, for example, Fredric Jameson, *Allegory and Ideology* (London: Verso, 2019), p. 240.

of existence'.[34] But while Robinson agrees with Jameson and Althusser that ideology is synonymous with '[w]orldview, philosophy, religion', he goes a step further in asserting that science, too, is an ideology, albeit 'the different one, the special one, by way of its perpetual cross-checking with reality tests of all kinds, and its continuous sharpening of focus'.[35]

Robinson's recognition that science, qua ideology, is an 'imaginary relationship to a real situation' is in no way intended to promote a sceptical argument. On the contrary, his position agrees with theories of scientific modelling developed by recent philosophers, who argue that all models are 'imaginary' or 'fictional', in that they always involve a degree of distortion and/or abstraction with respect to their target systems.[36] But here again a distinction can be made. Unlike these authors, whose concerns are limited to the accurate description of scientific representation, Robinson takes up the questions of ideology and science from the unique perspective of an author of climate/science fiction. He is ultimately concerned not with science as such, but with the central role that science plays for a 'most interesting project', namely, 'to invent, improve, and put to use an ideology that explains in a coherent and useful way as much of the blooming buzzy inrush of the world as possible. What one would hope for in an ideology is clarity and explanatory breadth, and power'.[37]

---

34   Louis Althusser, 'Ideological State Apparatuses', in Althusser, *Lenin and Philosophy and Other Essays*, trans. by Ben Brewter (New York: Monthly Review Press, 1972), quoted in Frederic Jameson, *Postmodernism, or, The Cultural Logic of Late Capitalism* (Durham, NC: Duke University Press, 1991), p. 51, emphasis in the original <https://doi.org/10.1215/9780822378419>. See also Jameson, *The Political Unconscious* (London: Routledge, 1981), p. 15.

35   Robinson, *The Ministry for the Future*, p. 41.

36   See Fiora Salis, 'The New Fiction View of Models', *British Journal for the Philosophy of Science*, 72.3 (2021), pp. 717–42 <https://doi.org/10.1093/bjps/axz015>; and Roman Frigg and James Nguyen, 'The Fiction View of Models Reloaded', *The Monist*, 99.3 (2016), pp. 225–42 <https://doi.org/10.1093/monist/onw002>. Frigg and Nguyen are not concerned with the relation of scientific representation to the imaginative representations of narrative fiction. For an account that is, see Catherine Elgin, *True Enough* (Cambridge, MA: MIT Press, 2017) <https://doi.org/10.7551/mitpress/9780262036535.001.0001>. See also Adam Toon, *Models as Make-Believe: Imagination, Fiction and Scientific Representation* (London: Palgrave Macmillian, 2012) <https://doi.org/10.1057/9781137292230>.

37   Robinson, *The Ministry for the Future*, p. 41.

What could such a project be? Not any of the particular sciences, which, despite their success in bringing certain facts into sharp focus, are ill-suited for providing a clear picture of how those distinct sets of facts interrelate. Nor can it be science as such, which is said to be 'central' to this new ideology, not identical to it. I propose that Robinson's project is the one that he sets himself, as a writer of climate/science fiction: to construct an imaginary relationship to the real situation of the warming planet that would have clarity and explanatory breadth, and power, in order to facilitate an understanding of what is too big for any individual to know in full. Not a fictional scientific model, in the sense defined above, but a science-fictional model that can assist us in coming to terms with the hyperobject of global warming. In confirmation of this interpretation, and continuing the above quotation, Robinson again breaks the novelistic fourth wall: 'We leave the proof of this as an exercise for the reader.'[38]

This brings me to the second formal characteristic of Robinson's novel: namely, its fragmented narrative. Although the plot itself is linear and coherent, the narrative through which it unfolds is anything but, voiced by a diversity of actors in chapters that are distributed across the world, and that can be distinguished into five rough categories (see Figure 2). First there are the chapters dealing with personal narratives: we have Frank May, the 'firangi' survivor of the Indian heat wave, who seeks to cope with his PTSD by attempting to join the group of climate activists (some say climate terrorists) known as the 'Children of Kali'; and then there is Mary Murphy, the head of the eponymous Ministry, whom Frank kidnaps and eventually befriends.[39] A second category consists of group narratives, which tell the story of the Ministry, of a group of scientists working in the Antarctic, of climate refugees, activists, and many others. Most of these chapters are narrated in the first-person plural 'we', which is not always defined, but is generally understood to be locally situated and to change from chapter to chapter. The third category of chapters takes a global perspective, describing the events of the coming decades from

---

38 Ibid.
39 One chapter, something of an exception, focuses on Mary's second-in-command Badim Bahadur (although he is not actually named as such, and there is some uncertainty regarding this identification), who runs the Ministry's 'black wing'.

No.	Category	No.	Category	No.	Category	No.	Category
1	Frank	27	Mary	53	non-human actor	79	Frank
2	non-human actor	28	didactic essay	54	Mary	80	"we" (other)
3	the ministry	29	"we" (Antarctica)	55	"we" (other)	81	the ministry
4	Mary	30	didactic essay	56	Mary	82	global perspective
5	"we" (other)	31	"we" (other)	57	"we" (Antarctica)	83	the ministry
6	global perspective	32	"we" (other)	58	"we" (other)	84	Mary
7	Frank	33	"we" (other)	59	"we" (other)	85	"we" (collective)
8	global perspective	34	the ministry	60	Mary	86	Mary
9	Mary	35	"we" (refugees)	61	didactic essay	87	"we" (other)
10	"we" (other)	36	"we" (Antarctica)	62	"we" (other)	88	non-human actor
11	didactic essay	37	"we" (refugees)	63	Mary	89	Mary
12	global perspective	38	dialogic argument	64	didactic essay	90	dialogic argument
13	Frank	39	"we" (other)	65	"we" (other)	91	Mary
14	"we" (other)	40	didactic essay	66	non-human actor	92	"we" (refugees)
15	the ministry	41	"we" (other)	67	didactic essay	93	"we" (Antarctica)
16	dialogic argument	42	the ministry	68	the ministry	94	Mary
17	dialogic argument	43	non-human actor	69	global perspective	95	non-human actor
18	Frank	44	"we" (Antarctica)	70	global perspective	96	Mary
19	"we" (other)	45	Mary	71	the ministry	97	global perspective
20	didactic essay	46	non-human actor	72	"we" (other)	98	the ministry
21	"we" (other)	47	Frank	73	didactic essay	99	dialogic argument
22	"we" (Antarctica)	48	"we" (refugees)	74	Frank	100	Mary
23	Frank	49	didactic essay	75	global perspective	101	"we" (other)
24	didactic essay	50	Mary	76	"we" (other)	102	Mary
25	Mary	51	global perspective	77	non-human actor	103	"we" (other)
26	Frank	52	"we" (other)	78	Badim	104	Mary
						105	"we" (refugees)
						106	Mary

Individual narrative: 31
- Mary: 21
- Frank: 9
- Badim: 1

Group narrative: 42
- the ministry: 9
- "we" (Antarctica): 6
- "we" (refugees): 5
- "we" (other): 21
- "we" (collective): 1

Global perspective: 9

Theory: 16
- didactic essay: 12
- dialogic argument: 4

Non-human actor: 8

FIG. 2. Chapters from *The Ministry for the Future* sorted into five narratological categories.

the abstracting perspective of world history. These first three categories, which together comprise the novel's plot, are supplemented by two additional categories that I will consider in more detail in the next two sections: the theoretical interruptions already mentioned, and the perspectives of non-human actors.

Although *The Ministry for the Future* may be the product of a single biographical author, it is strongly heteroglossic: a 'hybrid construction' that incorporates multiple perspectives into a fiction of multi-perspectivalism.[40] Hence, by switching back and forth between

---

40   Mikhail Bakhtin, 'Discourse in the Novel', in Bakhtin, *The Dialogic Imagination: Four Essays*, ed. by Michael Holquist, trans. by Caryl Emerson and Michael Holquist (Austin, TX: University of Texas Press, 1981), pp. 259–422 (pp. 304–05). Keeping in mind that every text is to some extent co-authored, I would like to use this opportunity to thank my colleagues at the ICI Berlin Institute for Cultural Inquiry for their comments, criticisms, and suggestions on drafts of the present essay, especially Alina-Sandra Cucu, Maria Dębińska, Julia Sánchez-Dorado, and Christoph Holzhey, to whom I owe the phrase 'fiction of multi-perspectivalism'.

individual, local, and global scales, and by incorporating both literary and theoretical genres, it yields a model — Robinson would say
'ideology' — of a phenomenon that exceeds any particular point of
view.[41] The global perspective, as informative as it may be, involves dry
abstractions that both defy our imagination and overwhelm our sense
of agency. The individual perspective, though it anchors the reader's
understanding in a concrete narrative, is blind to the structural conditions that shape it. The local perspective avoids some of the pitfalls
of the other two, and it effectively combats the illusion that the 'An-
thropos' of the Anthropocene can be taken as a monolithic whole.[42]
It remains, however, irreducibly partial, and therefore inadequate to
the situation in its fullest scope. By including multiple perspectives at
various scales, Robinson does not so much supply the reader with a
positive ideology, in the sense that he communicates a unitary worldview, philosophy, or religion, as he does present the construction of
such an ideology as an 'exercise for the reader': to think the individual
and collective activities portrayed in the novel in relation to each other.

It is fitting that Frank, who is arguably the closest thing that
the novel has to a protagonist, mediates between the various levels
sketched above: having suffered his own death, symbolically if not literally, during the Indian heat wave, he becomes a wanderer, travelling
to Scotland, Kenya, Antarctica, India, and then Switzerland, where he
abducts Mary on her way home from a Ministry social event.[43] Indeed,
it is Frank who first formulates the problem of individual agency in
relation to global problems, drawing inspiration from the microscopic
milieu with respect to which his body takes on a planetary scale:

> One person had one-eight-billionth of the power that human-
> ity had. This assumed everyone had an equal amount of power,
> which wasn't true, but it was serviceable for this kind of think-

---

41   The novel presents, in other words, a planetary perspective opposed to the global nar-
      rative that the collective scale can alone supply. For the globe/planet distinction with
      regard to climate fiction, see Jennifer Wenzel, *The Disposition of Nature: Environmental
      Crisis and World Literature* (New York: Fordham University Press, 2020) <https://doi.
      org/10.1515/9780823286805>.

42   See Bruno Latour, *Facing Gaia: Eight Lectures on the New Climatic Regime*, trans. by
      Catherine Porter (Cambridge: Polity Press, 2017), p. 121.

43   'I did die, but for some reason my body lived on after my death. And here I am, still
      trying to do things.' Robinson, *The Ministry for the Future*, pp. 101–02.

ing. One-eight-billionth wasn't a very big fraction, but then
again there were poisons that work in the parts-per-billion
range, so it wasn't entirely unprecedented for such a small agent
to change things.[44]

And while Frank can hardly be considered a hero, his questionable act
of taking Mary hostage convinces her, as she in turn convinces the Ministry, of the necessity of pursuing more drastic measures, including the
establishment of the clandestine 'black wing' that — she is informed to
her chagrin — already exists. Ultimately, Frank's agency is more akin
to that of a virus than a poison: having himself become 'sick' during the
deadly heat wave, his sense of desperate urgency infects others, starting
with Mary, who reflects on her brief kidnapping in terms that recall his
own trauma: 'Words like fists to the face. Paper bullets of the brain. It
was enough to make her heart hammer all over again. Her face burned
with the memory.'[45]

PROBLEM 3: DECENTRING THE HUMAN(ITIES)

This figure of viral agency brings me to my third and final problem,
which concerns the role of non-human actors in the environmental
humanities. A related question makes up one of the novel's central
concerns; after all, it is the ministry's appointed purpose to represent
the 'interests of generations to come. And the interests of those entities
that can never speak for themselves, like animals and watersheds.'[46]
Ignoring, for the moment, the question of whether the intra-diegetic
ministry succeeds, one can pose an analogous question to the novel,
and, by extension, to the critical scholarship done under the banner of
ecocriticism and the environmental humanities: How is it possible to
represent the interests of those not yet born? Of non-human entities
incapable of speech? Of non-living things not typically defined as
agents?

   Regarding the first question, at least, one can draw a lesson from
Frank: having lived through his own death, he cannot help but adopt

---

44   Ibid., p. 65.
45   Ibid., p. 107. Mary becomes conscious of the extent to which Frank has influenced
     her during a meeting with a group of Swiss officials: 'She almost laughed as she heard
     herself doing a version of what Frank had done to her that night.' Ibid., p. 316.
46   Ibid., p. 98.

the perspective of the future. Not absolutely, in the time-travelling sense of some of Robinson's other work, but relatively, in terms of the multiple temporalities that intersect in his person. Consider his first discussion with Mary, who is well aware of the scientific limits of her foresight: "'We can only model scenarios,' she said. "We track what has happened, and graph trajectories in things we can measure, and then we postulate that the things we can measure will either stay the same, or grow, or shrink.""[47] From Mary's perspective — the global view of a politician versed in climate science — various scenarios are possible, many of which involve climate disasters, and a few that don't, but all of which, as mere possibilities, have only a limited ability to inspire change in the present. By contrast, from Frank's perspective the future is all too real: 'There are about a hundred people walking this Earth, who if you judge from the angle of the future like you're supposed to do, they are mass murderers.'[48]

By relating Frank's experience of the Indian heat wave in vivid detail, Robinson compels the reader, as Frank compels Mary, to judge from the angle of the future. But what about non-human and non-living agents? How is it possible to speak on behalf of things without committing the twin fallacies of anthropomorphism and anthropocentrism? Jane Bennett, drawing on Bruno Latour's actor-network theory, has argued that a dose of the former is helpful in resisting the latter: by adopting a self-consciously anthropomorphic view of things, attributing to them agency and interests, one can come to a better understanding of the assemblages of humans and non-human agents that condition our capacity to introduce change into the world, thereby resisting the anthropocentric tendency that attributes dominion over the Earth to 'man'.[49] But this is not the position taken by Robinson's novel, which at one point in a dialogue between unnamed characters — presumably members of the ministry — suggests that such a position would be short-sighted:

47   Ibid., p. 96.
48   Ibid., p. 99.
49   Jane Bennett, *Vibrant Matter: A Political Ecology of Things* (Durham, NC: Duke University Press, 2010), pp. 98–100 <https://doi.org/10.1215/9780822391623>.

> – Yes, but it's an actor network. Some of the actors in an actor
> network aren't human.
>
> – Balderdash.
>
> – What, you don't believe in actor networks?
>
> – There are actor networks, but it's the actors with agency who
> can choose to do things differently.[50]

In *The Progress of This Storm*, Andreas Malm has argued that intellectual
currents like actor-network theory and new materialism culminate in
a 'determinism of the crudest variety' that mitigates if not eliminates
the culpability of the individuals and corporations that are responsible
for climate change.[51] That the Ministry should adopt a similar critique
makes a degree of sense, given that the culpability of individuals and
corporations is precisely their concern. But what about the novel? If
the intra-diegetic Ministry seeks to maintain the distinction between
human society and nature that Latour and Bennett work so hard to
trouble, then why does Robinson include not one but eight chapters
that give voice to non-human actors?

Answering this question leads to the third and final literary tendency that I have chosen to analyse, namely, the attribution of voice
to non-human agents. The majority of chapters, including all of those
devoted to individual and collective narratives, are written in the third
person. Supplementing these is a collection of approximately thirty
chapters written in the first-person singular 'we', which describe the
various responses to the warming planet by non-Ministry groups mentioned in the previous section. Indeed, much of the force of the 'we'
chapters consists in Robinson's use of the first-person pronoun, which
decentres the novel's plot away from the UN Ministry and towards
the geopolitical periphery: from globe to planet. But 'we' is not yet
'I', and the first-person singular is, with a few exceptions, reserved for
those chapters that adopt the perspectives of non-human agents.[52]
Although one might expect that the use of the first person would an-

---

50   Robinson, *The Ministry for the Future*, p. 60.

51   Andreas Malm, *The Progress of This Storm: Nature and Society in a Warming World*
     (New York: Verso, 2017), p. 110.

52   Chapter thirty-eight, though it is centred on non-human agents, uses 'we' instead of 'I'
     — but this is motivated by the assertion of the collective subjects' affinity with humans:
     'we are all the great herd animals of Earth, among whom you should count yourselves.'

thropomorphize these agents, bringing them closer to human affairs and problematizing the distinction between humans and non-humans, a short survey reveals that the situation is considerably more complex:

- The first and shortest of the 'I' chapters, chapter two, follows upon the horrific description of the Indian heat wave with the paradoxical announcement: 'I am a god and I am not a god. Either way, you are my creatures. I keep you alive.'[53] As slowly becomes clear over the course of three short paragraphs, the subject of this chapter is the sun: although it is clearly represented as an agent — 'I keep you alive', 'at my touch you burn' — it is an agent that is both unaffected by our greenhouse gas emissions and supremely indifferent to its impact on the Earth.[54]

- The strangeness of non-human agents is reinforced by the chapters chronicling the adventures of a photon and a carbon atom, in chapters fifty-three and sixty-six respectively, which (who?) experience the world at a spatio-temporal scale that defies our human perception, referring, for example, to the journey from the sun to the Earth as 'zipping off', or to the emergence and disappearance of a new landmass with the flippant remark 'they go away pretty fast'.[55]

- Even social constructions like 'the market' and 'history', which are given voice in chapters forty-six and seventy-seven, are presented at a remove from human concerns through the use of natural metaphors: 'I grew so large that I ate the world and all the blood in the world is mine'; 'I am the tide running under the

---

Robinson, *The Ministry for the Future*, p. 88. Other instances of the first person include dialogue in the various Ministry chapters, as well as occasional moments when a single voice emerges from the 'we' chapters, including an Angeleno's description of an atmospheric river, Sibilla Schmidt's report on Mary Murphy's security, an unnamed sailor's memoir of her time with the US Navy, an anecdote told by a farmer, and, most notably, a list of delegates from nations across the world introducing their efforts to reverse global warming. Robinson, *The Ministry for the Future*, pp. 275, 299, 381, 399, 425–28.

53   Ibid., pp. 12–13.
54   Ibid.
55   Ibid., p. 327.

world that no one sees or feels.'[56] Likewise, chapter forty-three, devoted to 'code' (and 'blockchain' — this was 2020 after all), insists that '[y]ou don't know me, you don't understand me.'[57]

– The last chapter to adopt a non-human perspective is the most mysterious. Since it is important for my reading, I will quote it in full:

> I am a thing. I am alive and I am dead. I am conscious and unconscious. Sentient but not. A multiplicity and a whole. A polity of some sextillions of citizens.
>
> I spiral a god that is not a god, and I am not a god. I am not a mother, though I am many mothers. I keep you alive. I will kill you someday, or I won't and something else will, and then, either way, I will take you in. Someday soon.
>
> You know what I am. Now find me out.[58]

If the subject of this chapter is not clear, one need only refer back to the prior definition of the sun as a 'god and not a god' to realize that it concerns the Earth, 'spiralling' the gigantic nuclear furnace in its four-dimensional movement through space-time. Unlike the other 'things' to which Robinson gives voice — sun, code, market, photon, carbon, history — the Earth includes humanity in a material sense: alongside a few sextillion microbes, slime moulds, fungi, plants, and animals, we humans are citizens in its polity. But while we may be included in the person of the Earth, we are also singled out and distanced by the use of the second person 'you', which ambiguously addresses either the reader or humanity as such. We know what the Earth is because we are a vital part of it, but it is precisely that relation of inclusion that we continually overlook and must therefore 'find out'.

Each of the seven 'I' chapters is written in the form of a 'What Am I?' riddle, even if it is only the seventh and last that poses any real challenge. And while Robinson's use of such riddles does not in itself qualify as a progressive literary technique, it takes on an operative function in the context of the distribution of personhood (both

56   Ibid., pp. 192, 385.
57   Ibid., p. 177.
58   Ibid., p. 491.

grammatical and otherwise) in the novel as a whole, which subverts the conventional gaze dynamics of human subject and non-human object. To better understand in what this function consists, it is useful to recall Jameson's foreword to Andre Jolles's *Simple Forms*, a work of literary analysis whose brilliance is marred by its author's Nazi affiliation. Jameson, in his consideration of the politics of Jolles's theory of verbal gestures, compares and contrasts the small form of the riddle with the estranging gesture of Brecht's epic theatre:

> Here Jolles offers an interesting parallel to Brechtian usage, where the *gestus* is a whole unity of situation and reaction captured as a unique act. But where, in Brecht, such a unity (ideological, political, even philosophical) is an act to be captured on stage by the enlightened play of actors trained in the *Verfremdungseffekt* — or 'estrangement effect' — in Jolles what results is a proto-literary form, which I would designate as narrative (despite its embodiments in such things as riddles and sayings).[59]

On the basis of Jameson's reading of Jolles, it can be argued that *The Ministry for the Future* imbues the narrative form of the riddle with a Brechtian (or even Schklovskian) capacity to estrange. This is achieved by the uneasy combination of the most intimate narrative gesture — 'I' addressing 'you' — with a subject that is radically indifferent to our concerns as a species, but on which our existence as a species depends. To be sure, Robinson is quick to recognize the 'material agency or effectivity of nonhuman [...] things'.[60] But he does so in a way that forecloses any possibility of identifying our concerns with theirs, framing our human relation to nature (qua thing) as one of intimate exteriority or 'extimacy'.[61]

As Tretyakov observed in 1929: 'Books such as *The Forest, Bread, Coal, Iron, Flax, Cotton, Paper, The Locomotive*, and *The Factory* have not been written. We need them, and it is only through the "biography

---

59   Fredric Jameson, foreword to Andre Jolles, *Simple Forms*, trans. by Peter J. Schwartz (London: Verso, 2017), pp. vii–xviii (p. x).

60   Bennett, *Vibrant Matter*, p. ix.

61   Jacques Lacan, *The Seminar of Jacques Lacan*, ed. by Jacques-Alain Miller (New York: Norton, 1988–), VII: *The Ethics of Psychoanalysis, 1959–1960*, trans. by Dennis Porter (1997), p. 139.

of the thing" that they can be adequately realized.'[62] To be sure, the things of Tretyakov's hypothetical biographies have been selected for their role in the production process. By narrating their existence, the proletarian author decentres the bourgeois hero from their central role in the novel, which thereby attains an operative function with respect to the ends of class struggle. By contrast, Robinson's novel gives voice to another kind of thing, narrating the lives of photons, carbon atoms, the market, the sun, and so forth, and with the aim of decentring the human subject towards a different, though related, end. Nevertheless, Tretyakov's words still apply, *mutatis mutandis*:

> Thus: not the individual person moving through a system of things, but the thing proceeding through the system of people — for literature this is the methodological device that seems to us more progressive than those of classical belles lettres.'[63]

The effect, as Tretyakov writes, is that the novel's human characters cease to imagine themselves as sovereign rulers of the things around them — as 'promethean' subjugators of nature by technology — but instead recognize their own activity as 'conditioned by these things and influences'.[64]

CLIMATE FICTION AND ECOLOGY

Climate fiction becomes disaster porn when it transforms its object — global warming — into an object of contemplative enjoyment. Over the course of this essay, I have considered three operative functions that, recalling Benjamin's reflections on operative literature, raise *The Ministry for the Future* above this suspicion, and that together constitute its literary and political tendency. First, the linear plot of Robinson's novel both concretizes and dramatizes climate models, which are thereby augmented in their capacity to impact our behaviour. Second, the novel's fragmentary narrative compels us to construct a

---

62   Sergei Tretyakov, 'The Biography of the Object', *October*, 118 (2006), pp. 57–62 (p. 62), translation modified <https://doi.org/10.1162/octo.2006.118.1.57>. Tretyakov's ideas bear fruitful comparison to the writings of Francis Ponge. See Francis Ponge, *Partisan of Things*, trans. by Joshua Corey and Jean-Luc Garneau (Berkeley, CA: Kenning Editions, 2016).

63   Tretyakov, 'The Biography of the Object', translation modified, p. 62.

64   Ibid., p. 60, translation modified.

non-totalizing representation of global warming as a planetary phenomenon, thereby enabling us to 'face Gaia', as Latour might say.[65]
Finally, its use of first-person riddles challenges us to 'find out' our
extimate relation to the planet, avoiding the pitfalls of both anthropocentric hierarchies (which place humans 'above' non-human actors)
and flat ontologies (which risk mitigating the responsibilities of certain
human actors). Together, these three functions constitute what Robinson might call the novel's ideological force, which aims to reconfigure
the reading subject in relation to the challenges of the coming decades.
They also clarify the extent to which Robinson's novel, as a work of
climate/science fiction, can be considered a model in its own right,
in the performative sense defined by Donal Khosrowi: 'A model is
performative if and only if it has the capacity to causally affect an aspect
of the world that it is intended to represent.'[66]

Although I take the terms of my analysis from Benjamin — operative literature, literary and political tendency, progressive literary
technique — I do not want to suggest that they should be understood
in the classical sense of Western Marxism, which, at least in its general
thrust, had a more positive concept of the ends of progress than I am
able to envision. The end that I am able to envision is wholly negative,
in the sense that it consists in avoiding the ongoing catastrophe of the
status quo.[67] Nevertheless, I would like to point out that these three
operative functions respond to the three ways in which capital works
to 'shift' the environmental 'rifts' it has opened in the metabolic interaction between capitalist society and the rest of nature, as analysed by
Kohei Saito. By tracing a fictional plot through a possible future, the
novel counteracts the 'temporal shift' that invites us to ignore the long-
term consequences of short-term economic gain.[68] By representing

---

65   Latour, *Facing Gaia*.

66   Khosrowi, 'Managing Performative Models', p. 374.

67   I draw this formulation from Benjamin's late writings, which reject the notion of
      progress assumed in his earlier 'Author as Producer': 'The concept of progress must
      be grounded in the idea of catastrophe. That things are "status quo" *is* the catastrophe.
      It is not an ever-present possibility but what in each case is given.' Walter Benjamin,
      The Arcades Project, trans. by Howard Eiland and Kevin McLaughlin (Cambridge, MA:
      Belknap Press, 1999), p. 473.

68   'Since capital reflects the voice of current shareholders, but not that of future generations,
      the costs are shifted onto the latter. As a result, future generations suffer from conse-
      quences for which they are not responsible.' Saito, *Marx in the Anthropocene*, p. 33.

the effects of and responses to global warming from disparate perspectives across the planet, it works against the 'spatial shift' through
which the ecological burden of climate change is displaced onto the
Global South.[69] By leading us to reflect critically on our extimate relation to nature, it resists the 'technological shift' that represents human
ingenuity as capable of transcending the natural limits of capital accumulation.[70]

Having begun this essay with Robinson's dedication to Jameson, I
conclude by applying Jameson's favourite method of literary analysis to
Robinson's novel: namely, the Greimas square, a tool that is useful for
both discerning and summarizing the semantic structure of a literary
text (see Figure 3).[71] In the case of *The Ministry for the Future*, an
initial pair of 'contrary' terms is provided by the *plot* and the *narrative*
through which that plot is presented. These are then complemented
by two 'contradictory' terms, in this case, the *non-plot* represented
by a nature that is indifferent to our activities, and the *non-narrative*
core of all climate fiction: the actually existing extra-diegetic world.
By arranging these abstract terms in a square, it becomes possible to
correlate the chapters of Robinson's novel with the concrete moments
at which those terms intersect, here represented by the corners of the
outer diamond.

At the top we discover the individual and group narratives through
which the novel's plot is presented: these include all of the Frank and
Mary chapters, along with the 'we' chapters and those focusing on the
intra-diegetic Ministry. An abridged version of *The Ministry for the Future*, like those editions of *Moby Dick* that remove all of the tangents and
digressions, would consist in this corner alone, and so lose any claim to

---

69   'By constantly shifting the ecological rifts and making them invisible to the capitalist
      centre, the current capitalist order of society appears attractive and comfortable for
      a wide range of social groups in the Global North. It thus facilitates a general social
      consensus, while its real costs are imposed upon other social groups in the Global
      South.' Saito, *Marx in the Anthropocene*, p. 33.

70   '[M]etabolic shift creates externalities with the aid of new technologies. [...] In other
      words, nature's biological systems are not mere obstacles or barriers for capital but their
      degradation creates new sources of profit.' Saito, *Marx in the Anthropocene*, pp. 30–31.

71   For one of Jameson's many Greimas squares, see Jameson, *The Political Unconscious*, p.
      267. See Algirdas Julien Greimas, 'The Interaction of Semiotic Constraints', in Greimas,
      On Meaning: Selected Writings in Semiotic Theory, trans. by Paul J. Perron and Frank H.
      Collins (Minneapolis: University of Minnesota Press, 1987), pp. 48–62.

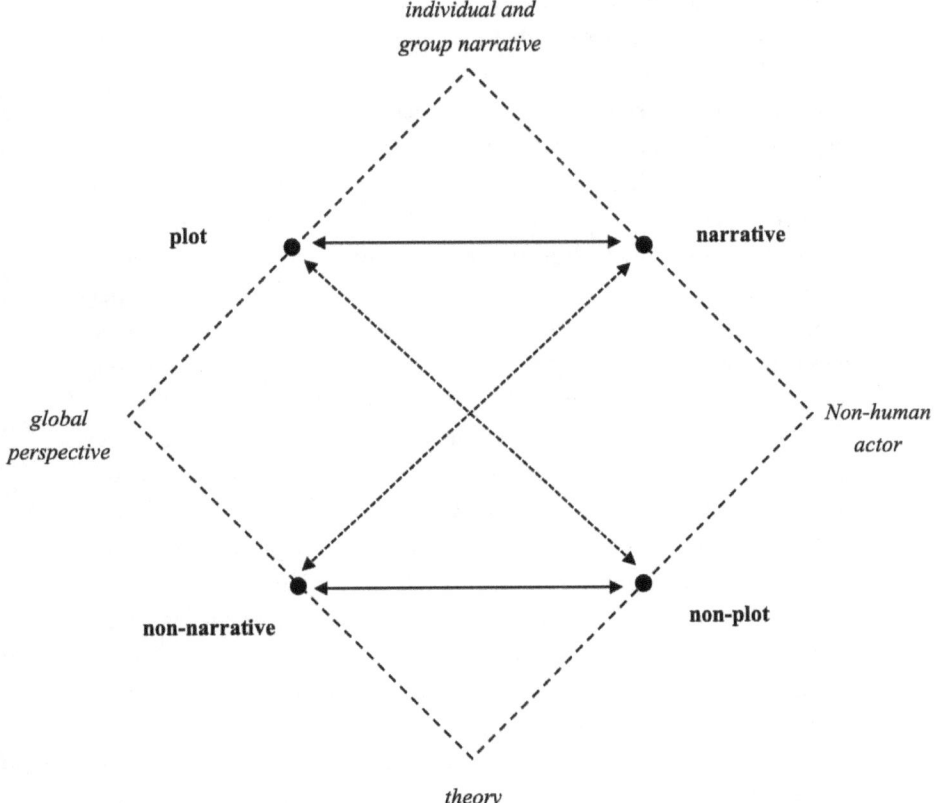

FIG. 3. Greimas square of *The Ministry for the Future*.

possess a literary or political tendency. But this is not the case. Instead, the Greimas square reveals what one might call a *model* of the novel's fictional ecology, in which the operative functions that I have analysed in isolation can be seen to depend on each other. Hence, the operative function of the novel's plot depends on Robinson's inclusion of a global perspective (left), which lends it a reference to real-world climate science. Likewise, the operative function of the novel's fragmented narrative is sustained by Robinson's inclusion of the various non-human actor chapters (right), which remind us that the sum of human perspectives can only add up to a partial representation of the problem at hand. These latter chapters, if isolated from the others, would comprise no more than a series of vaguely entertaining riddles: the small forms that Jolles is content to analyse, but that lack the estranging power of a Brechtian gesture. And the theory chapters (bottom), abstracted from the novel's plot and narrative, would amount to just that: theory, another form of ideology, more or less effective in its political tendency, but beyond the purview of an essay on climate/science fiction.

Greimas squares facilitate 'cognitive mapping', or what Jameson defines as the 'situational representation on the part of the individual subject to that vaster and properly unrepresentable totality which is the ensemble of society's structures as a whole'.[72] As such, they are intimately connected with the Althusserian definition of ideology that is taken up in both Jameson's theory and Robinson's novel: 'the subject's *Imaginary* relationship to his or her *Real* conditions of existence'.[73] Given these definitions, but adding an ecocritical inflection to Jameson's words, the above square can be characterized as my own situational representation of Robinson's situational representation of that vaster and properly unrepresentable totality that exceeds society while including it, and that constitutes the real conditions of my own existence. But I leave the proof of this as an exercise for the reader.

---

72   Jameson, *Postmodernism*, p. 51. See Özgün Eylül İşcen, 'Black Box Allegories of Gulf Futurism: The Irreducible Other of Computational Capital', in *The Case for Reduction*, ed. by Christoph F. E. Holzhey and Jakob Schillinger, Cultural Inquiry, 25 (Berlin: ICI Berlin Press, 2022), pp. 91–115 (pp. 101–03) <https://doi.org/10.37050/ci-25_05>.

73   See note 34.

Ross Shields provides an elegant analysis of the political and literary tendencies of Kim Stanley Robinson's *The Ministry for the Future*. He identifies the major problems in representing global warming in mainstream political discourses, namely, the difficulties of including non-humans, collectives, and the future, and demonstrates that Robinson's novel is a successful attempt to address them. What strikes me most in his account are the distinctions and relations between different types of fiction, with their distinct temporal orientations, which get tangled and blurred when they come into contact with global warming.

Amitav Ghosh, in *The Great Derangement* (2016), describes a writer's struggle with the uncanny qualities of climate change and attributes them to the fact that the genre of the modern novel has been designed to exclude descriptions of rare and improbable events, as it is defined by the 'grid of literary forms and conventions that came to shape the narrative imagination in precisely that period when the accumulation of carbon in the atmosphere was rewriting the destiny of the earth'.[74] Those forms and conventions are what the bourgeois novel and modern science have in common, favouring probability and the average over the extraordinary and miraculous, and rendering 'nature' as a stable background to human affairs. According to Ghosh, 'the mere mention of the subject [of global warming] is often enough to relegate a novel or a short story to the genre of science fiction';[75] climate change is a matter of science not literature, even though, despite their nineteenth-century separation, they operate within the same 'narrative imagination'. Not surprisingly, then, climate fiction is seen as a subgenre of science fiction, even though it is based on the current state of scientific knowledge and not on speculation about its future development, and belongs to the realm of averages and probabilities — after all, it is only through statistics that we can attribute freak storms and monster floods to an abstract entity we call 'global warming'.

The Ministry of the Future can be interpreted as an attempt to unify science and fiction; Shields observes that '[t]he CO_2 curve drawn from

---

74   Ghosh, *The Great Derangement*, p. 7.
75   Ibid.

the work of real-world climate scientists supplies Robinson's novel with a rising action, climax, and falling action that recalls Gustav Freytag's Aristotelian model of a tragic plot'. The curve is based on the assumption that at some point carbon emissions will fall. It is thus a political fiction written by climate scientists that serves as the timeline of the novel; its science is real and its politics is speculative. It could also be argued, however, that linear time itself becomes a political fiction in the face of global warming, anchoring the novel within the humanist narrative imagination. As William Gibson famously declared, the future is not evenly distributed; global warming presents us with the challenge not just of mapping the future but also of readjusting our modernist conception of time to include the delayed effects of carbon concentration in the atmosphere and their acceleration through feedback loops, which makes it difficult to establish what has already happened and what has yet to happen. History, for Robinson, is the 'nightmare from which we cannot wake', but so is the future.

This leads me to the uncanny aspect of climate change, underscored by Ghosh but conspicuously absent in Robinson. Shields engages Sergei Tretyakov's attempt to free the novel from the constraints of bourgeois individualism in order to show the social system of production and the process by which the world is made, through objects that cease to shimmer in the background as an 'immense collection of commodities' (what John Holloway calls the 'horrific world of political economy',[76] uncanny in its own sense), and instead acquire their own biographies. According to Shields, a similar strategy can be identified in Robinson's novel, which, in an attempt to decentre the narrative, brings to the foreground multiple human and non-human points of view. However, even though the sun, the Earth, and other non-human elements speak in their own voices, what they have to say is mostly didactic. Robinson uses the form of the riddle to render them unfamiliar, but the moment the riddle is solved, there is no mystery left. In that, and in choosing 'science' as the driving force of the narrative, he represents a modernist tendency that is similar to Tretyakov's. How

---

76   John Holloway, 'Read Capital: The First Sentence: Or, Capital Starts with Wealth, not with the Commodity', *Historical Materialism*, 23.3 (2015), pp. 3–26 (p. 3) <https://doi.org/10.1163/1569206X-12341420>.

stark a contrast with Ghosh's comparison of climate change to the Sundarban tigers, which are everywhere and nowhere, but by which, one can be sure, one is always being observed.[77]

---

77   Ghosh, *The Great Derangement*, p. 28.

The Slime Mould's Many Bodies, or Modelling Networks with *Physarum polycephalum*

MARIA DĘBIŃSKA

> The shining path of humanity is only ever the
> verminous-like trail of our own oozing across
> time and space — the trace and proof of our
> complete sliminess through and through.
>
> Ben Woodard, *Slime Dynamics*[1]

Physarum polycephalum is a chimeric creature combining characteristics of fungi and animals, which at a certain stage of its life cycle forms a yellow blob that crawls around forming complex networks, captivating scientists and lay people alike. The simplicity of its structure and simultaneous complexity of its behaviour invite experimentation and have inspired investigations into the nature and origins of intelligence, memory, learning, and sociality. The peculiarity of this organism, a

*   This paper is based on research funded by the National Science Centre (Poland), grant no. 2019/33/B/HS3/02332.

1   Ben Woodard, *Slime Dynamics: Generation, Mutation, and the Creep of Life* (Winchester: Zero Books, 2012), p. 67.

pulsating bag of slime that can perform complicated tasks, turns it into a productive 'epistemic thing', an instrument to think with.[2]

In the laboratory context *Physarum* is most commonly used as a model organism by biologists and biophysicists in numerous areas of research, such as basal cognition,[3] cell ageing,[4] cell aggregation, and the emergence of collective behaviours,[5] to name just a few. However, due to the fact that it is relatively easy and safe to cultivate (it does not demand sterile conditions and its favourite food is common oats), *Physarum* also lends itself as a model for sociocultural phenomena, especially human-made networks and emergent social processes. In the projects discussed in this chapter, *Physarum*'s function as a model expands to new territories of art, mathematics, and computer science; the slime mould retains some of the characteristics of a model organism,[6] but also acquires new ones, which turn it into a speculative device, a catalyst for new narratives and imaginaries of the social.

The focus of this paper is experiments mapping human-made networks of movement and transportation, since this is the area in which comparisons between the slime mould and humans impose themselves most forcefully and in which the analogies are most pronounced. In the preface to a collected volume devoted exclusively to recreating human transportation systems with *Physarum*, Andrew Adamatzky recalls his first encounter with the slime mould:

---

2   Hans-Jörg Rheinberger, *Toward a History of Epistemic Things: Synthesizing Proteins in the Test Tube* (Stanford, CA: Stanford University Press, 1997).

3   Pamela Lyon and others, 'Reframing Cognition: Getting Down to Biological Basics', *Philosophical Transactions of the Royal Society B*, 376 (2021) <https://doi.org/10.1098/rstb.2019.0750>.

4   Angèle Rolland and others, 'Behavioural Changes in Slime Moulds over Time', *Philosophical Transactions of the Royal Society B*, 378 (2023) <https://doi.org/10.1098/rstb.2022.0063>.

5   Sheryl Hsu and Laura Schaposnik, 'Cell Fusion through Slime Mould Network Dynamics', *Journal of The Royal Society Interface*, 19 (2022) <https://doi.org/10.1098/rsif.2022.0054>.

6   An overview of the characteristics and functions of model organisms, as well as the forms of social organization of research they generate, can be found in Rachel A. Ankeny and Sabina Leonelli, *Model Organisms* (Cambridge: Cambridge University Press, 2021) <https://doi.org/10.1017/9781108593014>.

On the next day I saw that the oat flakes were spanned with a net-work of protoplasmic tubes. The tubes looked like roads. 'What if we cut a piece of filter paper in the shape of some island and place oat flakes where cities are? Will the protoplasmic network match the existing roads?', I thought. There is only one way to find out. I have chosen the Isle of Wight as my first 'Physarum-land'. Results were intriguing yet inconclusive. Some roads were matched by the slime mould, others not. 'Minor roads are too messy. Let us try to imitate UK motorways', I thought. First experiments showed that I hit a gold mine. I placed oat flakes in major urban areas of the United Kingdom and inoculated the slime mould in London. The slime mould grew the motorways in a couple of days. The match was almost perfect.[7]

In the following sections I discuss certain artistic and scientific experi-ments that engage *Physarum* as a model for human-made transporta-tion systems or for collective human behaviours, and focus on how they conceptualize the relations between the slimy and the human. I investigate how these are mediated via different patterns of movement and network creation. In the first section, I discuss the properties of the slime mould that make for its weird appeal and openness to interdis-ciplinary applications. I then introduce Tim Ingold's typology of lines, which will serve as a means of analysis of chosen *Physarum* network experiments. Finally, I compare two types of experiments and trace how they draw their connections between the human and the slime.

BLACK BOX

Physarum polycephalum belongs to a large and diverse group of slime moulds: eukaryotic organisms that resist classification as either fungi, plants, or animals. They have been assigned to the kingdom of Protists, created to accommodate a variety of organisms that taxonomists could not fit anywhere else, and to the phylum of Myxomycetes.[8] *Physarum* lives on forest floors in most parts of the world, feeding on bacteria, fungi spores, and decaying plant matter. At a certain point of its life

---

7   Andrew Adamatzky, 'Preface', in *Bioevaluation of World Transport Networks*, ed. by Andrew Adamatzky (Singapore: World Scientific, 2012), pp. v–vi (p. v) <https://doi.org/10.1142/8482>.

8   See *Myxomycetes: Biology, Systematics, Biogeography, and Ecology*, ed. by Carlos Rojas and Steven L. Stephenson (London: Elsevier, 2017).

cycle it forms a giant cell called a *plasmodium*, which is an aggregate of single-celled amoebae that can extend over tens of centimetres and contains millions of nuclei. When food sources are abundant it grows and moves at a relatively fast rate: its mass can double every few hours and it moves with the speed of approximately one centimetre per hour.

Even though *plasmodium* has a very basic internal structure, it forms a network of protoplasmic tubes that create an efficient system for transportation of nutrients within the cell. It is capable of simple forms of learning, such as habituation,[9] and anticipates regularly occurring stimuli. The biophysical mechanisms behind these processes remain largely unknown, since at the molecular level the slime mould becomes an unstable and thus unwieldy research subject, due to its large number of nuclei and fast growth rate. Therefore, researchers so far have mostly focused on behavioural experiments, while the relations between behaviour and its underlying molecular mechanisms remain obscure. The way *Physarum* transforms environmental inputs into behavioural outputs is not controllable but is predictable. Arguably, in network recreation experiments it plays a role similar to a cybernetic black box. This resonates with Alexander Galloway's observations on invisibility as an anarchist political strategy and on the emergence of a new kind of opacity that is not a form of subversion but a function of a social system in which politics is replaced by management, and which conceives of biological, physical, and social behaviour as programmed and programmable.[10] Galloway notes that 'the behaviourist subject is a black-boxed subject'[11] — that is, it is not necessary to understand its internal workings to be able to manipulate it. Therefore, 'it is no longer a question of illuminating the black box by decoding it, but rather that of functionalizing the black box by programming it.'[12]

---

9   Manon Ternois and others, 'Slime Molds Response to Carbon Nanotubes Exposure: From Internalization to Behavior', *Nanotoxicology*, 15.4 (2021), pp. 511–26 <https://doi.org/10.1080/17435390.2021.1894615>; Aurèle Boussard and others, 'Adaptive Behaviour and Learning in Slime Moulds: The Role of Oscillations', *Philosophical Transactions of the Royal Society B*, 376 (2021) <https://doi.org/10.1098/rstb.2019.0757>.

10   Alexander Galloway, '"Black Box, Black Bloc"', lecture delivered at the New School, New York City, 12 April 2010 <http://cultureandcommunication.org/galloway/pdf/Galloway_Black_Box_Black_Bloc.pdf> [accessed 25 March 2024].

11   Ibid.

12   Ibid.

The formation of plasmodium happens through aggregation of single-celled amoebae and is used as a model in studies of emergence and self-organization.[13] Its internal structure is the product of a complex oscillatory system and metamorphoses at different stages of its movement under the influence of external factors, such as attractants and repellents encountered in its environment.[14] Its shape transforms in the process of foraging and transporting nutrients, at a certain point contracting into a clear-cut web of tubes connecting food sources. There is ongoing research on slime mould's internal mechanisms,[15] but in the network experiments discussed below it is treated as a black box, which reveals more about the pervasiveness of the idea of the social as a cybernetic system than about the slime mould itself.

While the black box metaphor is meant to capture the mechanistic aspects of *Physarum*'s behaviour, it does not exhaust its meanings and effects on the observer. The patterns and fluctuations of *Physarum*'s movements cannot be discerned with the naked eye, but are easily captured by means of time-lapse photography. The slime mould operates in a temporality adjacent to our own; it is just slightly too slow for its movements to be perceptible in real time by a human eye, but fast enough to surprise us with sudden expansions or attempts to escape from its Petri dish. It leaves us with the uncanny feeling that it only moves when we look the other way. It exists in the sphere just beyond our intuitive grasp, which David Roden postulates as the object of a dark phenomenology: '[a] feature of conscious experience is intuition-transcendent or "dark" if it confers no explicit or implicit understanding of its nature on the experiencer.'[16] Even though it can-

---

13   Bernd Meyer, Cedrick Ansorge, and Toshiyoku Nakagaki, 'The Role of Noise in Self-Organized Decision Making by the True Slime Mold *Physarum polycephalum*', *PLoS ONE*, 12.3 (2017) <https://doi.org/10.1371/journal.pone.0172933>; Philipp Fleig and others, 'Emergence of Behaviour in a Self-Organized Living Matter Network', *eLife*, published online 21 January 2022 <https://doi.org/10.7554/eLife.62863>.

14   Boussard and others, 'Adaptive Behaviour'.

15   See, for example, Richard Mayne, Andrew Adamatzky, and Jeff Jones, 'On the Role of the Plasmodial Cytoskeleton in Facilitating Intelligent Behavior in Slime Mold *Physarum polycephalum*', *Communicative and Integrative Biology*, 8.4 (2015) <https://doi.org/10.1080/19420889.2015.1059007>.

16   David Roden, 'Nature's Dark Domain: An Argument for a Naturalized Phenomenology', in *Phenomenology and Naturalism: Examining the Relationship Between Human Experience and Nature*, ed. by Havi Carel and Darian Meacham, special issue of *Royal*

not be directly made sense of, '[a] dark phenomenon could influence the dispositions, feelings or actions of the experiencer without improving her capacity to describe them. [...] Our access to the dark side would thus be as theoretically and technically mediated as our access to the humanly unobservable universe.'[17] One of Roden's dark examples is time, as the thing that we perceive without being able to grasp; slime mould's slow movements could be one of the instantiations of a phenomenon to which we only have mediated access due to its peculiar temporal characteristics, but so would be the internal mechanisms of slime mould's behaviour.

Slime mould's movements are perceptible only when mediated by time-lapse photography (or registered on video); the gaps between the snapshots are cut out, the representation of slime mould's movement is assembled from them and leaves out most of its activity. However, the human eye can perceive its shape at all times; its changes escape us not because they are invisible, but because they are too fine-grained for us to grasp. This constitutes another area of obscurity; the time-lapse is a technique of modulating the movements of *Physarum* (by setting up different snapshot intervals, different images are obtained) as much as representing them. It captures the fluctuations of the slime mould's internal cytoplasmic streams and reveals the stunning diversity of its morphology, inviting a human observer to interpret these movements as moments of hesitation, grasping, climbing, waving, pulsating, and forming different types of meshes. The time-lapse renders the slime mould alive and capable of making its own decisions, providing a fertile ground for scientific and artistic investigations into the non-human and distributed nature of cognition, intelligence, and emergent behaviour.

THREADS AND TRACES

Physarum's ability to create efficient nutrient transportation systems by finding the shortest path between food sources has been used in a number of experiments that have employed it to model different types of human-made networks. The first and most famous of these

---

Institute of Philosophy Supplement, 72 (2013), pp. 169–88 (p. 173) <https://doi.org/10.1017/S135824611300009X>.

17   Ibid.

were performed by Toshiyoku Nakagaki and his team at Hokkaido University. In 2000, they discovered that the slime mould could find the shortest way out of a maze, and in 2010 they demonstrated that it could recreate the suburban railway network around Tokyo with stunning precision.[18] In both cases the time-lapses show a wave-like expansion of plasmodium covering a plane, followed by a contraction into a network of protoplasmic tubes. In the Tokyo experiment, suburban towns are represented by oat flakes located on a Petri dish covered by agar gel — these are given in advance, while *Physarum*'s task is to connect them in the most efficient way. The oat flakes constitute nodes in the network formed by *Physarum*'s tubes. Even though this and other similar experiments are usually claimed to recreate 'roads', 'railways', or 'routes', what they do is recreate the particular elements of modern maps that are reducible to networks.

However, before they are rendered as connections between points on a surface and abstracted into networks, *Physarum* tubes are just lines that emerge from its bodily movement, and it seems necessary to examine their qualities as lines before analysing the practices of network modelling in which they are involved. Tim Ingold proposes a typology of lines that consists of two basic classes: threads and traces. 'A thread is a filament of some kind, which may be entangled with other threads or suspended between points in three-dimensional space.'[19] A fungal mycelium or the synapses of a nervous system fall into this category. A trace, in turn, is 'any enduring mark left in or on a solid surface by a continuous movement'.[20] Ingold also mentions ghostly lines, such as the ones that we imagine connect stars into constellations: 'lines of this sort may of course appear on maps and charts as traces drawn with pen and ink, using a ruler and compass. But they have no physical counterpart in the world that is represented on these maps.'[21]

---

18 Toshiyoku Nakagaki, Hiroyasu Yamada, and Ágota Tóth, 'Maze-Solving by an Amoeboid Organism', *Nature*, 407 (2000) <https://doi.org/10.1038/35035159>; Atsushi Tero and others, 'Rules for Biologically Inspired Adaptive Network Design', *Science*, 327 (2010), pp. 439–42 <https://doi.org/10.1126/science.1177894>.

19 Tim Ingold, *Lines: A Brief History* (New York: Routledge, 2007), p. 41 <https://doi.org/10.4324/9780203961155>.

20 Ibid., p. 42.

21 Ibid., p. 49. The fourth type of line, which features less prominently in his taxonomy and which does not interest me here, comprises cuts, cracks, and creases.

Ghostly lines are imagined but may have real and tangible effects, which I will discuss in the following sections.

According to Ingold, 'It is through the transformation of threads into traces, [...] that surfaces are brought into being. And conversely, it is through the transformation of traces into threads that surfaces are dissolved.'[22] It follows from Ingold's argument that relations between lines and surfaces are determined by perspective; a thread enables orientation in a three-dimensional space, while a trace is made on a two-dimensional surface and is visible from a vantage point above that surface. Ingold uses the example of a maze as an illustration of this difference, referring, among other examples, to the labyrinth in which Theseus found his way thanks to Ariadne's thread, the Chukchee representations of the world of the dead that is also an underground maze, and the protective patterns drawn by women in Tamil Nadu on the thresholds of houses and temples, called *kampi kōlam*. In his polemic with Alfred Gell's claim that mazes are apotropaic patterns used for protection against evil forces, Ingold proposes another explanation of the maze, pointing out that Gell's argument 'assumes from the outset a kind of "demon's eye view" — an aerial perspective from which the overall layout of the maze may be surveyed and represented in a pattern-like form'.[23] The evil spirit is confronted with a riddle, which is supposed to stop it from entering the protected space. Contra Gell, Ingold argues that

> [t]he entrance to the maze marks the point not at which [the traveller] touches down upon the surface, but at which he goes underground. Now as an interface between earth and air, the ground is a kind of surface that is visible from above, but not from below. It does not have another side. Thus at the very moment of going underground, of entering the labyrinth, the surface itself disappears from sight. [...] Thenceforth — and quite unlike Gell's demon which, caught in the contemplation of an apotropaic pattern, is glued to a surface — the ghostly traveller finds himself in a world without any surface at all. Every path is now a thread rather than a trace.[24]

---

22   Ibid., p. 52.
23   Ibid., p. 56.
24   Ibid.

Ingold suggests that the function of mazes is to catch stray wanderers inside rather than present them with a riddle:

> Rather than ambushing demons with an insoluble speculative conundrum, as Gell suggests, and causing them to get stuck in their attempts to figure out from the completed pattern the principles of its construction, the *kampi kōlam* more likely exercises its protective functions by catching them in the labyrinth, from which they can no more escape than ghosts in the world of the dead.[25]

Both Gell's and Ingold's claims are of course highly speculative, but they illustrate a productive tension between the notions of the maze as a two-dimensional pattern and a three-dimensional space of wandering and getting lost, which characterizes the *Physarum* maze experiment as well. Its body is coextensive with its paths, which means its tubes can be characterized as both threads and traces: threads that transport nutrients in three-dimensional space, and traces on the two-dimensional surface of the agar gel. In Nakagaki's experiment, the slime mould enters the labyrinth and, after wandering along its paths, creates the shortest connection between the oat flakes located at its two entrances. The time-lapse allows us to observe it from 'the demon's eye view' and turn the tactile process of wandering and exploration into an intellectual puzzle.

Ingold's argument is built on the juxtaposition between the image of a maze drawn on a surface and the actual maze that requires a descent under the surface. It could be argued, though, that any maze is simultaneously both of these things. This is quite apparent when the slime mould gets caught in the maze but manages to escape by weaving a thread that is at the same time the solution to the 'speculative conundrum', a pattern visible from above. *Physarum*'s morphology requires some surface for it to crawl, just as Ingold's underground traveller has to walk on something; however, those surfaces do not constitute geometrical planes on which patterns can be drawn. Such a surface exists and is visible only from one side; from the other, the traces dissolve into a three-dimensional tangle of threads.

---

25   Ibid., p. 57.

Ingold's aim is to uncover the material history of lines and the gradual process of their geometrical abstraction. Just as 'surfaces are dissolved through the transformation of traces into threads', threads in turn can be weaved into surfaces. However, Ingold distinguishes two types of surfaces: those woven from threads and those created by connecting points into geometrical shapes; the former material and textured, the latter smooth and abstract. As he writes, 'Lines that join dots mark the outlines of a mosaic of shapes. Such lines are not only drawn on a surface; they actually *define* that surface as a geometrical plane.'[26] Only after a thread is transformed into a trace on a surface can it be abstracted into a geometrical pattern. The Tokyo railway network experiment performs an analogical task by transforming the agar jelly in a Petri dish into an abstract geometrical surface on which a map can be drawn. Thus we arrive at another important distinction which Ingold takes from Paul Klee: between active and static lines. For Klee, lines that are traces of a physical gesture are active and 'go for a walk', as opposed to 'static' lines that connect predetermined spots:

> Another kind of line, however, is in a hurry. It wants to get from one location to another, and then to another, but has little time to do so. The appearance of this line, says Klee, is 'more like a series of appointments than a walk'. It goes from point to point, in sequence, as quickly as possible, and in principle in no time at all, for every successive destination is already fixed prior to setting out, and each segment of the line is pre-determined by the points it connects. [...] If the former takes us on a journey that has no obvious beginning or end, the latter presents us with an array of interconnected destinations that can, as on a route-map, be viewed all at once.[27]

According to Ingold, this transformation of the line from a trace on a surface to an assemblage of abstract points is characteristic of modernity:

> Once the trace of a continuous gesture, the line has been fragmented — under the sway of modernity — into a succession of points or dots. This fragmentation [...] has taken place in the related fields of *travel*, where wayfaring is replaced by destination-oriented transport, *mapping*, where the drawn

---

26   Ibid., emphasis in the original.
27   Ibid., p. 73.

sketch is replaced by the route-plan, and *textuality*, where storytelling is replaced by the pre-composed plot. It has also transformed our understanding of *place*: once a knot tied from multiple and interlaced strands of movement and growth, it now figures as a node in a static network of connectors.[28]

The fragmentation of lines replaces wayfaring with transportation — while wayfaring is for Ingold a form of inhabiting the world and weaving it from threads (lives, paths, stories), transport is a function of the imperial occupation of space. The lines that form the tissue of the habitable world are tangled and irregular, in contrast to the straight lines imposed by empires:

> [I]n the course of history, however, imperial powers have sought to occupy the inhabited world, throwing a network of connections across what appears, in their eyes, to be not a tissue of trails but a blank surface. These connections are lines of occupation. They facilitate the outward passage of personnel and equipment to sites of settlement and extraction, and the return of the riches drawn therefrom. Unlike paths formed through the practices of wayfaring, such lines are surveyed and built in advance of the traffic that comes to pass up and down them. They are typically straight and regular, and intersect only at nodal points of power.[29]

What to the wayfarer appears as a world weaved from crisscrossing threads is, in the imperial optics, a blank surface, or what the European lawyers defined as *terra nullius*, waiting for the imposition of a network of connections that will make it legible and governable by the empire.

Ingold's analysis shows that the word *network* is itself a homonym, meaning both a system of connections between nodes and a web of entangled threads, which are products of two different modes of movement and being in space: one based on the production of a surface, the other on its dissolution; one occupying a single viewpoint situated above the surface, the other taking on a wayfarer's perspective. The origin of the word *network* itself comes from fishing nets — tools for catching things, that is, performing a function analogical to Ingold's

---

28   Ibid., p. 75, emphases in the original.
29   Ibid., p. 81.

mazes. The threads and nodes of such a net have no meaning themselves, since what matters is the catch. Networks in the sense of systems
of connections have the opposite function of leaving out all that is not
part of the network. In *Physarum* network experiments, the lines drawn
by the slime mould are simultaneously three-dimensional threads and
two-dimensional traces, depending on perspective: from the slime
mould's perspective, they are products of wayfaring and subsequently
getting caught in a pattern of oats; from the researcher's perspective,
they recreate imperial lines of occupation and extraction. Since they
are given the nodes of the network, *Physarum* lines tend towards fragmentation, but after connecting the nodes they remain alive and keep
moving, never exactly repeating the same pattern.

SLIME CARTOGRAPHIES

Nakagaki's widely publicized experiments spawned a number of similar attempts at recreating human-made transportation systems with the
help of *Physarum*. One of the most prolific experimenters has been Andrew Adamatzky, head of the Unconventional Computing Laboratory
at the University of the West of England in Bristol, who has engaged
the slime mould in a wide variety of enterprises, from constructing
Boolean logic gates to creating a biological microchip.[30] Adamatzky
has cooperated with artists and urbanists in a number of interdisciplinary projects that have resulted in a large corpus of publications as
well as exhibitions and art projects exploring *Physarum*'s uncanny abilities.[31] The projects that interest me here investigate analogies between
human and slime mould networks by means of recreating large-scale
transportation systems, most of which have been documented in a
volume entitled *Bioevaluation of World Transport Networks*.[32]

---

30   See Andrew Adamatzky, *Physarum Machines: Computers from Slime Mould* (Singapore:
     World Scientific, 2010) <https://doi.org/10.1142/7968>; and *Advances in Physarum
     Machines: Sensing and Computing with Slime Mould*, ed. by Andrew Adamatzky (Cham,
     CH: Springer, 2016).

31   Andrew Adamatzky and others, 'On Creativity of Slime Mould', *International Journal of
     General Systems*, 42.5 (2013), pp. 441–57 <https://doi.org/10.1080/03081079.2013.
     776206>.

32   See *Bioevaluation of World Transport Networks*, ed. by Andrew Adamatzky (Singapore:
     World Scientific, 2012) <https://doi.org/10.1142/8482>.

Adamatzky's first success in the faithful recreation of British motorways with *Physarum* prompted him to perform a large number of similar experiments aiming to 'uncover analogies between biological and man-made [*sic*] transport networks'.[33] *Physarum* very efficiently approximates the lines of imperial occupation described by Ingold, because they too are designed to connect population centres via the shortest possible paths. The slime mould is placed at the centre of a system of political and spatial domination, given the points at which resources can be extracted, and faithfully recreates the transportation network that connects the nodes in the most efficient way. What is left out from the descriptions of these experiments is the fact that the capture of a network pattern is a temporal state, after which the slime mould continues to explore the Petri dish to create new patterns, which with time become more and more dense and tangled. Adamatzky's experiments followed the slime mould until the point at which all oats were connected, presenting this particular moment as an overall result, and imposing on the slime mould their own teleology. All experiments were repeated several times and the results were represented as graphs that captured the average shape of *Physarum* networks; the transformation of threads into traces was followed by the transformation of traces into what Ingold calls 'ghostly lines', by further straightening them out.

Ostensibly, the aim of the experiments was the 'bio-optimisation' of global transport networks by *Physarum*. The results were presented as numbered 'findings'. The experiments not only aspired to measure the precision with which *Physarum* can imitate modern transportation networks and to compare their efficiency, but also explored hypothetical catastrophic scenarios such as nuclear disasters. Using repellents such as sodium chloride to disrupt slime mould networks, they tested the networks' resilience and modelled their possible reorganization. For example, 'Finding 83' refers to a possible scenario of chemical or nuclear pollution in Malaysia and its impact on the transportation system:

> If the epicentre of contamination is located in Kuantan and the speed of propagating contamination is about 100 miles per 24h, transport functionality will be significantly diminished in X14, X3 and X63 roads; a substantial increase in traffic will be

---

33   Ibid., p. 8.

observed between the Kota Bahru and the Alor Star, Sungai
Petani and Kulim areas; a significant increase in migration and
economic activity would also be observed in Kedah and north
Perak and Kelantan states.[34]

The predictive value of Finding 83 is impossible to estimate, but the
narrative is compelling because it invokes a popular genre of apocalyptic fiction. Even though the ostensible aim of the book is to uncover
analogies between large-scale transportation systems and *Physarum*
networks, the experiments cross the boundaries between art and science and engage in speculation on the catastrophic scenarios built into
the imperial lines of occupation. Some experiments model hypothetical disasters such as the malfunction of nuclear facilities, while other
scenarios include the simulation of drug trafficking routes in Mexico or
the colonization of Germany. That the apocalyptic storytelling is an important, albeit unstated, aim of the experiments is reflected in some of
the chapter titles, such as 'Germany colonised' or 'Physarum narcotrafi-
cum'. Other experiments conducted by Adamatzky have speculated on
possible human migration routes between Mexico and the USA,[35] provided scenarios of future world colonization beginning in China,[36] and
projected the colonization of the Moon.[37] All of these use *Physarum*
for modelling what Ingold understands as lines of imperial occupation
and control.

The slime mould is used as a model for the effective regeneration
and recreation of connectivity after a network is disrupted, but at
the same time the procedure is one of colonization, which here denotes both the colonization of an agar plate by the slime mould and
the colonization processes that resulted in the emergence of global
transportation systems. *Physarum* colonizes the Petri dish by covering it with its slimy body and imposing on it a map of protoplasmic

---

34   Ibid., p. 192.
35   Andrew Adamatzky, and Genaro J. Martinez, 'Bio-Imitation of Mexican Migration
     Routes to the USA with Slime Mould on 3D Terrains', *Journal of Bionic Engineering*,
     10 (2013), pp. 242–50 <https://doi.org/10.1016/S1672-6529(13)60220-6>.
36   Andrew Adamatzky, 'The World's Colonisation and Trade Routes Formation as Imi-
     tated by Slime Mould', *International Journal of Bifurcation and Chaos*, 22.8 (2012)
     <https://doi.org/10.1142/S0218127412300285>.
37   Andrew Adamatzky and others, 'Slime Mould Analogue Models of Space Exploration
     and Planet Colonisation', *Journal of the British Interplanetary Society*, 67 (2014), pp.
     290–304.

tubes, thus turning it into a geometrical plane. By recreating large-scale transportation systems with *Physarum*, Adamatzky's experiments at the same time retell the history of imperial expansion that led to their creation.

The properties of *Physarum* graphs — such as average edge length, average shortest path, diameter, and cohesion — are compared with the actual transportation networks that were the basis for the experiments. The final chapter of *Bioevaluation of World Transport Networks*, titled 'Bio-rationality of Motorways', summarizes the analogies found between motorways and *Physarum* networks. The fact that the comparison is made between graphs — one representing the actual transportation network and the other its recreation by *Physarum* — can be missed, because the narrative that accompanies and explicates them conflates the graphs with *Physarum* itself. The analogy becomes lost and enters the realm of fiction when the authors suggest that the comparison is not between two graphs based on a particular map, but between slime mould's behaviour and socio-political phenomena, such as the colonization of particular countries, the building of roads, or the smuggling of drugs. In the narratives of Adamatzky and his collaborators, *Physarum* metamorphoses from a biomechanical device that can effectively connect oat flakes on an agar plate into an entity that roams the earth, connecting population centres with its protoplasmic tubes and extracting their resources, as reflected in paper titles such as 'Road Planning with Slime Mould: If *Physarum* Built Motorways It Would Route M6/M74 through Newcastle'.[38]

Staying within the narrative style of *Physarum* experiments, one could say that the slime mould has a taste for dystopia, in which the flows of human masses and the flows of capital are treated as emergent phenomena that can be modelled, predicted, and optimized but not problematized in any way. *Physarum* confers onto them the black box logic that makes the experiments possible in the first place; the scope of its networks and the processes they are meant to represent are limited by what is already given. The network experiments are elaborately

---

38   Andrew Adamatzky and Jeff Jones, 'Road Planning with Slime Mould: If Physarum Built Motorways It Would Route M6/M74 through Newcastle', *International Journal of Bifurcation and Chaos*, 20.10 (2010), pp. 3065–84 <https://doi.org/10.1142/S0218127410027568>.

staged to imitate the process of colonization; agar plates provide a *terra nullius*, an uninhabited space for expansion,[39] while the nodes of the network given in advance are literally resources ready for extraction. The experiments result in the emergence of a system of ghostly lines that approximate cellular expansion and historical colonization. The scale of the maps is never mentioned because the scenarios have no predictive value; rather, they are an exercise in imaginary worldmaking. They serve to reproduce a map of the colonized world, staging the act of imperial occupation through the capture of *Physarum*'s threads and their transformation into straight lines and abstract networks.

LIVED ABSTRACTION

The performances collectively entitled *Being Slime Mould*, alongside other projects by the London-based artist Heather Barnett, operate within the same conceptual coordinates as the network experiments discussed above, but here the relations between threads and traces, slime and human behaviours, and maps and movements are in various ways shifted, reverted, or displaced.[40] Barnett invites participants in her experiments to form a collective body that acts according to the same rules as the slime mould; for this purpose *Physarum*'s behaviour is reduced to a simple algorithm that the participants are asked to follow.[41] The experiment is a comparative procedure in which human behaviour approximates the slime mould's by means of embodied practice. The rules of movement and aggregation are given in advance, and by following them participants create patterns of connection that can be abstracted into networks. However, this is not the point of

---

39   Such an argument, in the context of microbiology in general, is made in Georgina Tuari Stewart and others, 'Colonization of All Forms', *Educational Philosophy and Theory*, 56.11 (2024), pp. 1039–43 (p. 1040) <https://doi.org/10.1080/00131857. 2022.2040482>.

40   For an overview of Barnett's artistic engagement with *Physarum*, see Heather Barnett, 'Many-Headed: Co-Creating with the Collective', in *Slime Mould in Arts and Architecture*, ed. by Andrew Adamatzky (Gistrup, DK: River Publishers, 2019), pp. 13–37 <https://doi.org/10.1201/9781003339540-3>.

41   The algorithm imitates the process of aggregation of slime mould amoebae and consists of three or four steps, such as: 1. Move around, maintaining equal distance from others; 2. When you find a resource, stop; 3. When you bump into a person connected to a resource, make a link; 4. If you bump into a person connected to another person, make a link.

the performance. Rather, its aim is to stage the process of emergence of a collective body and to provide the participants with a different experience of collectivity, one that emerges from bodily movements, unmediated by symbolic communication. The results are connection patterns but also ethnographic observations, as every group behaves differently, making different use of their bodies and interpreting the rules in different ways. The collective performances allow the artist to investigate how different human bodies relate to other bodies and to space. As Barnett's title suggests, *Being Slime Mould* is about approximating the slime mould's perspective and exploring the environment as a slime mould would — its form of engagement is that of the embodied perception of a wayfarer rather than of the totalizing imperial eye. The rules of behaviour are abstracted from the observation of slime mould's movement and are analogous to cellular automata, but their implementation creates a space for exploring embodied connections and collective movement. At the moment when the algorithm is implemented by humans in a three-dimensional space, it becomes a method of inquiry into this space and the threads and connections that sustain it.

The process of embodied inquiry can then be abstracted back into a two-dimensional pattern of lines, as in the project *Swarm/Cell/City* (2017), a cooperation between Barnett and Art Laboratory Berlin, which aimed to explore 'collective communication, cooperation and navigation at different scales [...] in slime mould and in humans' by means of 'participatory art and performance practices'.[42] The experiment was designed to investigate 'the creative potential for bio/social models' and to create a collective 'system of enquiry'.[43] The human slime mould evolved from a performance into a method of collective research: Barnett's experiment provides an opportunity for self-inquiry that starts with wayfaring rather than occupation. The participants in the *Swarm/Cell/City* project explored a neighbourhood of Berlin's Pankow district by leaving and tracking traces, weaving a surface from the threads of individual movements and creating maps that emerged

---

42 'NONHUMAN AGENTS: Swarm | Cell | City', artlaboratory-berlin.org, n.d. <https://artlaboratory-berlin.org/events/swarm-cell-city/> [accessed 26 July 2024].

43 Ibid.

in the process of collective exploration of urban space. This collective wandering was tracked and transferred onto a map, producing abstract images that captured the contingencies and convergences between individual lines, revealing a pattern of collective movement. As in the network experiments, the wayfaring experience was transformed into a pattern of traces on a two-dimensional map, but there were no pre-given nodes of the network and no imperative to find the shortest paths between them. The emerging image was a projection of the tangled threads onto a two-dimensional plane, consisting of lines literally going for a walk.

In important ways, Barnett's performances are the antithesis of Adamatzky's experiments: the slime mould is used to model human collective wayfaring instead of modern transportation; the lines of movement are continuous and not broken; the lines that emerge are threads and not traces; and the patterns of aggregation are investigated in their uniqueness and not in the average. Nonetheless, they are haunted by the abstract body of the slime mould and the ghostly lines that are drawn from it. The slime mould appears to have a double body — the material blob and the abstract network — and to oscillate continuously between wayfaring and transporting, creating threads and leaving traces, meandering and straightening its lines to find the shortest path between the oats, and between getting caught up in a three-dimensional space and revealing patterns on a surface. The attempts at approximating human-made and *Physarum* lines and networks produce effects that go far beyond their stated aims: as has been demonstrated above, the comparison between slime mould and humans is made possible through a multilayered process of abstracting their behaviour into networks; at the same time, the lines that those networks are made of are revealed to be complex processes.

COMPARING THE INCOMMENSURABLE

In a paper based on sociological research among biologists working with *Physarum*'s cognitive capacities, Jacqueline Dalziell asks: 'Could it be that within the microbiological we might find humanity's self-inquiry, a form of self-reflection yet one whose refracted involvements do not return us to anthropocentrism in any straightforward way?'.[44] This question leads me to Eduardo Viveiros de Castro's account of Amerindian perspectivism, which assumes that all living entities are persons and thus occupy a point of view. Those points of view are often as incommensurable as the bodies they are located in, but they nonetheless have to be imagined as inhabitable if any form of communication and understanding is to be possible. The method for doing so, according to de Castro, would be a 'controlled equivocation', taking the incommensurability as its premise and vantage point. 'Only the incommensurate is worth comparing',[45] claims de Castro; the experiments described in this paper are based on a similar premise, as the homonymy between webs and networks, as well as the interchange between lines as threads and lines as traces, constitutes their operating mechanism. The slime mould's two bodies converge in lines and networks that oscillate between materiality and abstraction in a process analogous to de Castro's controlled equivocation, in which both the slimy and the human are mediated by a tangle of material and abstract lines. De Castro invokes Patrice Maniglier, claiming that any anthropology worth its name 'returns to us an image in which we are unrecognizable to ourselves'.[46] Recreating human networks with *Physarum* achieves a similar effect: far from anthropomorphizing the slime mould, it renders the human slimy, modelling its patterns of movement in a way that is at the same time material and abstract, and distinctively non-human.

---

44 Jacqueline Dalziell, 'Microbiology as Sociology: The Strange Sociality of Slime', in *What If Culture Was Nature All Along?*, ed. by Vicki Kirby (Edinburgh: Edinburgh University Press, 2017), pp. 153–78 (p. 154) <https://doi.org/10.1515/9781474419307-010>.

45 Eduardo Viveiros de Castro, *Cannibal Metaphysics: For a Post-Structuralist Anthropology* (Minneapolis: University of Minnesota Press, 2014), p. 90.

46 Ibid., p. 41. Quote from Patrice Maniglier, 'La Parenté des autres. À propos de Maurice Godelier', *Critique*, 701 (2005), pp. 758–74 <https://doi.org/10.3917/criti.701.0758>.

To better understand the *Physarum polycephalum*, also known as *slime mould*, I watched the 1958 'schlock' sci-fi classic *The Blob*. The film not only marked a breakthrough for Steve McQueen but is often referenced in discussions of the single-celled organism as one of its few cinematic depictions. The accompanying theme tune, with its lyrics 'Beware of The Blob, it creeps and leaps and glides and slides', introduces the organism as a mischievous trickster (think *The Addams Family*, 1991). However, as the story unfolds, the audience is offered the image of a slowly metastasizing and all-consuming terror. In *The Blob*, humans are the oat flakes. We are the resource to be extracted. Turning up the fear with the much shorter tagline 'Terror has no shape', *The Blob* was remade in 1988. To my surprise, though, aside from *The Blob*, one or two short stories, and Philip K. Dick's *Clans of the Alphane Moon* (1964), which features a telepathic slime mould named 'Lord Running Clam', the slime mould's eerie vibe and alien-like qualities have not attracted as much attention from sci-fi writers and filmmakers as one might expect. Of course, there is the recent appearance of *Physarum* in the 2023 hit TV series *The Last of Us*. However, in the show, *Physarum* plays stunt double to the main character, Mycelium, and for the most part, the audience is unaware that one is substituting for the other.

Science fiction, then, has perhaps not yet fully tapped into the potential of *Physarum*; the 1958 film poster indeed billed the organism as 'indescribable'. Yet, as Maria Dębińska's chapter suggests, slime mould, or, more precisely, the narratives of slime mould experiments, have certainly leaned into the science fiction subgenre of 'apocalyptic fiction'. As Dębińska explains: 'Staying within the narrative style of *Physarum* experiments, one could say that the slime mould has a taste for dystopia.'

The narrative descriptions of experiments unmistakably portray slime mould as mysterious, otherworldly, and alien. One of the startling outcomes in Dębińska's chapter is a difference in the narrative between slime mould modelling and modelling slime mould. When slime mould is modelled, as in the Andrew Adamatzky experiments, it is imbued with nefarious intent: it is extractive, imperial, and almost single-mindedly colonialist. However, when humans model slime mould, as with Heather Barnett's artistic experiment, imperial imageries and colonial metaphors and descriptors are conspicuously absent. Instead, the focus is on connection, engagement, exploration, and embodied movement.

The desire to describe what the slime mould does in colonialist terms is a surprising difference in the models the chapter presents, revealing more about humans than about slime mould, as Dębińska makes clear. While the experiments may 'render the human slimy', perhaps they also accentuate the slimy or unpleasant propensities in humans themselves. Indeed, Noah Berlatsky argues that the 'colonial experience remains more tightly bound up with our political life and public culture than we sometimes like to think'.[47] In placing Adamatzky alongside Barnett, these 'exercise[s] in imaginary world making' reveal the limits of those worlds. Whether as dystopic projections onto experiments in modelling slime, or as engagements with slime as a harmless algorithmic model for experimental human connection, they reveal, to follow Berlatsky, 'the extent to which dreams of what we'll do remain captive to the things we've already done'.[48]

47   Noah Berlatsky, 'Why Sci-Fi Keeps Imagining the Subjugation of White People', *The Atlantic*, 25 April 2014 <https://www.theatlantic.com/entertainment/archive/2014/04/why-sci-fi-keeps-imagining-the-enslavement-of-white-people/361173/> [accessed 14 April 2024].

48   Ibid.

PERFORMING MODELS

Persistence
Model Asylum Narratives and a Recognizable 'Transgenderness'

B CAMMINGA

Replete with geographical and geo-oriented vocabulary, the contours and substance of the term *transgender*[1] are defined by movement, mobility, borders, and migration. Not only is it a term that travels and morphs as it does so, but encoded in its very meaning is the perception that a body might have to migrate, both metaphorically and physically, to enter into possibility — a journey from point A to point B, along the shortest route. This journeying has perhaps been most famously described by Jay Prosser in *Second Skins: The Body Narratives of Transsexuality* (1998) as 'coming home', either to oneself or to the body that always should have been.[2] Thus, *transgender* often travels in the company of companions like *from* and *to*. Transitioning is often denoted, as Aren Aizura explains, as 'a one-way trajectory across a terrain in which the stuff of sex is divided into male and female territories, divided by the border or no man's land in between.'[3] There is, as Aizura further

---

1   I use *trans* and *transgender* interchangeably throughout this chapter.

2   Jay Prosser, *Second Skins: The Body Narratives of Transsexuality* (New York: Columbia University Press, 1998), p. 83.

3   Aren Z. Aizura, 'The Persistence of Transgender Travel Narratives', in *Transgender Migrations: The Bodies, Borders, and Politics of Transition*, ed. by Trystan T. Cotten (New York: Routledge, 2012), pp. 139–56 (p. 140) <https://doi.org/10.4324/9780203808269>.

describes, an unyielding 'persistence' to this 'trans travel narrative' and its migratory metaphors.[4]

Although, in his initial analysis, Prosser was addressing transsexuality and the narrative of being 'trapped in the wrong body', there has been some slippage between what was termed *transsexuality* and what is more often now referred to as *transgender*. Autobiography has proven to be a key genre for the representation of transgender journeys, especially in relation to narratives of medical transition, where home in oneself is to be achieved through a process of leaving, or journeying out, and return. For Prosser, the 'metaphoric territorializing of gender and literal territorializations of physical space have often gone hand in hand' in trans narratives.[5] Early exemplars of this form include Lili Elbe's *Man into Woman: An Authentic Record of a Sex Change* (1933), often referred to as the first trans autobiography; Christine Jorgensen's *A Personal Autobiography* (1967), which followed some years later; and Jan Morris's *Conundrum* (1974). Travelling to Germany, Denmark, and Morocco, respectively, to rectify the wrong body, before returning to their countries of origin, is a narrative model that Lucas Crawford critiques.[6] Crawford characterizes the trans travel narrative as revolving around 'the safe return',[7] which aligns 'the metaphorical return to the protagonist's gendered home with an account of their arrival at their literal home'.[8] According to Crawford, this narrative model, invested in binary understandings of gender and an ontologically stable conceptualization of transness, closes off the potential for transition to be seen as 'a risky exploit or experiment in embodied selfhood'.[9] These narratives predominantly align with the established form and structure of medical case histories.

The medical case history is a coherent narrative of gender incongruence that has, until very recently, remained the prerequisite for

---

4   Ibid.
5   Prosser, *Second Skins*, p. 101.
6   Lucas Cassidy Crawford, 'Transgender without Organs?: Mobilizing a Geo-Affective Theory of Gender Modification', *Women's Studies Quarterly*, 36.3–4 (2008), pp. 127–43 <https://doi.org/10.1353/wsq.0.0092>.
7   Ibid., p. 128.
8   Aizura, 'The Persistence of Transgender Travel Narratives', p. 142.
9   Crawford, 'Transgender without Organs?', p. 128.

access to affirming healthcare. Initially, it functioned as the evidence or truth that a trans person would be required to present in order to verify and validate their trans identity. This evidence was to be presented in the form of a narrative or autobiography. Medical professionals thus functioned as the first audience at the heart of early trans narrative production. For Prosser, the autobiographical act is intrinsic to trans identity, and the initial autobiographical act is that which occurs in the 'clinician's office'.[10] The archetypal structure of this model fulfils a particular narrative organization of consecutive stages: 'suffering and confusion; the epiphany of self-discovery; corporeal and social transformation/conversion; and finally the arrival "home" — reassignment'.[11]

Appealing to trans and non-trans audiences alike, although perhaps for different reasons, these life stories have come to form a particular literary canon. Starting in the 2000s, however, a concerted effort has been made to move away from the constraints of early trans writing. Evan Vipond suggests that in contemporary texts, trans writers may 're-linquish their intelligibility' in order to 'allow for new understandings of trans identities, subjectivities, and embodiments', thus troubling the genre.[12] Of course, more recent narratives have also turned the gaze on the medical establishment, highlighting how it perpetuates pathologization. This critique has framed the trope of the wrong body as the outcome of having to explain trans life to cisgender audiences. Texts such as Paul B. Preciado's *Testo Junkie* (2013) and Julia Serano's *Whipping Girl* (2007) are perhaps the most salient examples of this turn. However, the ability to relinquish intelligibility that we see in such texts may only be accessible, as Sarah Ray Rondot points out, to individuals who are 'privileged by other identity vectors'.[13] These might include documentation or citizenship status, as well as white-

---

10   Ibid.
11   Ibid.
12   Evan Vipond, 'Becoming Culturally (Un)Intelligible: Exploring the Terrain of Trans Life Writing', *a/b: Auto/Biography Studies*, 34.1 (2019), pp. 19–43 (p. 4) <https://doi.org/10.1080/08989575.2019.1542813>.
13   Sarah Ray Rondot, '"Bear Witness" and "Build Legacies": Twentieth- and Twenty-First-Century Trans* Autobiography', *a/b: Auto/Biography Studies*, 31.3 (2016), pp. 527–51 (p. 537) <https://doi.org/10.1080/08989575.2016.1183339>.

ness, which has been extensively critiqued in the broader transgender studies literature.[14]

In the last decade, a series of trans autobiographies by African authors have emerged, potentially offering a new lens through which to consider the trans travel narrative. In this chapter, I focus on three such texts: Farah Abdullah Abdi's *Never Arrive* (2015); Neo L. Sandja's *Right Mind, Wrong Body* (2016); and Rizi Xavier Timane's *An Unspoken Compromise* (2017), recently republished as *Love Wins Out: My Journey as an African Transman* (*sic*) (2021).[15] Though not the first trans autobiographies to be published by authors from the African continent, each represents a first for their country of origin — Somalia/Kenya, the Democratic Republic of Congo, and Nigeria. I argue that these texts adhere more closely to a more recent narrative model that, since the early 90s,[16] has emerged as a secondary space of trans narrative rendition — the asylum claim.[17] In what follows, I

---

14   See Katrina Roen, 'Transgender Theory and Embodiment: The Risk of Racial Marginalisation', *Journal of Gender Studies*, 10.3 (2001), pp. 253–63 <https://doi.org/10.1080/09589230120086467>; Emily Skidmore, 'Constructing the "Good Transsexual": Christine Jorgensen, Whiteness, and Heteronormativity in the Mid-Twentieth-Century Press', *Feminist Studies*, 37.2 (2011), pp. 270–300 <https://doi.org/10.1353/fem.2011.0043>; Salvador Vidal-Ortiz, 'Whiteness', *TSQ: Transgender Studies Quarterly*, 1.1–2 (2014), pp. 264–66 <https://doi.org/10.1215/23289252-2400217>; B Camminga, 'Where's Your Umbrella? Decolonialisation and Transgender Studies in South Africa', *Postamble*, 10.1 (2017), pp. 61–77.

15   Xavier chooses to use *transman* as a single term. It is widely accepted that there should be a space between *trans* and *man*, indicating that *trans* is an adjective used to further specify the noun *man*. See B Camminga, 'What Is Private about "Private Parts"? On Navigating the Violence of the Digital African Trans Refugee Archive', in *Queer and Trans African Mobilities: Migration, Asylum and Diaspora*, ed. by B Camminga and John Marnell (London: Bloomsbury Academic, 2022), pp. 153–69 <https://doi.org/10.5040/9780755639021.ch-8>.

16   In 1995, a transgender woman from Algeria, known by the case name 'Ourbih', sought asylum in France. This is widely considered to have been one of the first claims to asylum made by a trans person. Since Ourbih there has been a growing global recognition of claims to asylum made on the basis of persecution due to gender identity and/or expression. See B Camminga, 'Ourbih's Legacy: Transgender Forced Displacement, Legal Boundaries, Lived Realities, and the Struggle for Recognition', in *Oxford Handbook of Intersectional Approaches to Migration, Gender, and Sexuality*, ed. by Gökce Yurdakul and others (Oxford: Oxford University Press, 2025).

17   Fadi Saleh, 'Transgender as a Humanitarian Category: The Case of Syrian Queer and Gender-Variant Refugees in Turkey', *TSQ: Transgender Studies Quarterly*, 7.1 (2020), pp. 37–55 <https://doi.org/10.1215/23289252-7914500>; Martha Balaguera, 'Trans-Migrations: Agency and Confinement at the Limits of Sovereignty', *Signs*, 43.4 (2018), pp. 641–64 <https://doi.org/10.1086/695302>; Jhana Bach, 'Assessing

outline the relatively recent emergence of published trans autobiographies by African authors and what distinguishes these three texts
from this emergent canon. Drawing from the literature in migration
studies, I discuss the contours and expectations of the asylum narrative
for trans people. With a specific focus on how this is visible in the
geographical investments of these texts and the resurgence of the trope
of the wrong body — expressing within asylum what Leticia Sabsay
calls 'a recognisable form of [...] transgenderness'[18] — I suggest that
the trans asylum narrative is the trans travel narrative in the absence of
the safe return, a phenomenon I term the 'unsafe return'.

AFRICAN TRANS AUTOBIOGRAPHIES

There are only a handful of published book-length trans autobiographies by African authors, with the majority commercially published in
English in South Africa. Published in 1998, Ugandan trans and intersex
activist Julius Kaggwa's *From Juliet to Julius: In Search of My True Gender
Identity* follows the author's early childhood, the discovery of his intersex variation, his transition, and his journey to acceptance in Uganda.[19]
Though not an exclusively trans text — Kaggwa defines himself as 'an
intersex man who went through a trans experience'[20] — it is read and
considered as part of an African trans canon. The first exclusively trans
text was an oral history project featuring archival material, images, body
maps, and interviews documenting the lives of trans people in South
Africa: *Trans: Transgender Life Stories from South Africa* (2009). Quite
possibly the African continent's first trans autobiography, centring on
the life of a singular person, was the Algerian publication *Mouzakarat*

Transgender Asylum Claims', *Forced Migration Review*, 42 (2013), pp. 34–36; Fatima
Mohyuddin, 'United States Asylum Law in the Context of Sexual Orientation and
Gender Identity: Justice of the Transgendered?', *Hastings Women's Law Journal*, 12.2
(2001), pp. 387–410.

18   Leticia Sabsay, 'The Emergence of the Other Sexual Citizen: Orientalism and the
Modernisation of Sexuality', *Citizenship Studies*, 16.5–6 (2012), pp. 605–23 (p. 611)
<https://doi.org/10.1080/13621025.2012.698484>.

19   Julius Kaggwa, *From Juliet to Julius: In Search of My True Identity* (Kampala: Fountain
Publishers, 1998).

20   Caroline Ausserrer, 'Portrait of Julius Kaggwa, Intersex Activist from Uganda',
blog.lsvd.de, 24 February 2022 <https://blog.lsvd.de/portrait-of-julius-kaggwa-
intersex-activist-from-uganda/> [accessed 9 April 2024].

Randa Al-Trans, or The Memoirs of Randa the Trans (2010). Available in Arabic and co-authored with Lebanese journalist Hazem Saghieh, the book follows the life of Algerian activist Randa.[21]

These were followed by a run of trans autobiographies from South Africa, including Liberty Matthyse's self-published *A Darling's Journey to Liberty* (2016) and the first text by a Black trans man, Landa Mabenge's *Becoming Him: A Trans Memoir of Triumph* (2019).[22] A series of publications by white South Africans were also published during this period. These include Anastacia Tomson's *Always Anastacia: A Transgender Life in South Africa* (2016), Robert Hamblin's *Robert: A Queer & Crooked Memoir for the Not so Straight & Narrow* (2021), and Elise Bishop's *Twee Lewens (Two Lives)* (2022).[23] Following the life of Elise Bishop, who transitioned in the mid-1970s in South Africa, *Twee Lewens* is the first to be published in Afrikaans and documents the earliest life story thus far. Finally, in 2021, famed Nigerian author Akwaeke Emezi published *Dear Senthuran: A Black Spirit Memoir.*[24] Emezi, though they use the terms *non-binary* and *transgender*, considers themself to be an ogbanje, or 'an Igbo spirit that's born into a human body'.[25]

The three texts that are the focus of this chapter, though they form part of this canon, are distinct from the above in that they are all self-published, single-authored English language texts written from a diasporic perspective.[26] Initially published in 2017 as *An Unspoken*

---

21   Hazem Saghieh, *Mouzakarat Randa Al-Trans, or The Memoirs of Randa the Trans* (Beirut: Dar al-Saqi, 2010).

22   See Liberty Matthyse, *A Darling's Journey to Liberty* (Cape Town: self-published, 2016); and Landa Mabenge, *Becoming Him: A Trans Memoir of Triumph* (Johannesburg: Jacana Media, 2019).

23   See Anastacia Tomson, *Always Anastacia: A Transgender Life in South Africa* (Johannesburg: Jonathan Ball, 2016); Robert Hamblin, *Robert: A Queer and Crooked Memoir for the Not so Straight or Narrow* (Cape Town: Melinda Ferguson, 2021); and Elise Bishop, *Twee Lewens* (Hermanus, SA: Hemel & See, 2022). Tomson's memoir has been mistakenly referred to as the 'the first transgender memoir to come out of Africa'. See Germaine de Larch, 'Transgender Identity: The Context and Intersectionality of Identity', *Gender Questions*, 5.1 (2017), pp. 1–4 (p. 2).

24   Akwaeke Emezi, *Dear Senthuran: A Black Spirit Memoir* (London: Riverhead Books, 2021).

25   Ibid., p. 11.

26   On the digital emergence of an African transgender refugee diaspora, see B Camminga, 'When the Homo Deamon Went Digital: Writing Africa's Transgender Refugee Dias-

Compromise, Timane's 2021 republication of his autobiography under the new name *Love Wins Out: My Journey as an African Transman* (sic) adds an extra chapter addressing the healing of his relationship with his parents. Born into a profoundly Christian family, headed by a widely respected and well-known Nigerian military leader, Timane moved to the US to escape his family and their desires for him to marry and become a 'normal woman'.[27] The book follows Timane through his discomfort in childhood and the realization that he was a boy, but with no language to explain this to his parents, who made several attempts to exorcize what they understood to be his 'demon of homosexuality'.

Published a year before *Unspoken Compromise*, Neo L. Sandja's *Right Mind, Wrong Body* (2016) carries several similar themes to Timane's. Tracing the author's childhood in the Democratic Republic of Congo (DRC) and his eventual 'escape' to the US in 2004 after also enduring an exorcism at the hands of his family, the narrative highlights his struggles and resilience. The book tells a similar journey of his self-discovery, trans manhood, relationship to spirituality, and living as an undocumented migrant.

The final text, Farah Abdullah Abdi's *Never Arrive* (2015), diverges from the other two in several ways, not least because Abdi is a trans woman and a recognized refugee. Abdi, born in Somalia, was also a minor when she journeyed from Kenya via Uganda, South Sudan, Sudan, and Libya to Malta. Abdi's text reads as an unfinished autobiography, ending with her arrival in Malta. Though she had already begun transitioning by the time the text was published, the book itself largely refers to her sexuality, albeit broadly conceived. In interviews, at book launches, and in her subsequent written work, Abdi refers to her leaving as a result of her gender identity.[28] She has also read her trans identity back into her book on public platforms, reiterating that the book is, in fact, about her journey as a trans woman.[29] Most regularly,

pora', *Communication, Culture and Critique*, 17.3 (2024), pp. 213–16 <https://doi.org/10.1093/ccc/tcae007>.

27   Rizi Xavier Timane, *An Unspoken Compromise: My Story of Gender and Spiritual Transition* (n.p.: self-published, 2017), p. 29.

28   *Faarax Xuseen Cabdi Ama Kim Abdi*, dir. by sspamediacom, online video recording, YouTube, 25 March 2020 <https://www.youtube.com/watch?v=agjsTjRBTkg> [accessed 7 October 2023].

29   Ibid.

she reads the following excerpt from *Never Arrive*, substituting in 'trans woman': 'I have been told many times by family, friends, colleagues and strangers that I am a black, African, refugee, Muslim, *trans woman*; that I am outside the norms accepted by society.'[30] As with Timane's second edition, which repeats the first but adds two new chapters covering his reconciliation with his parents and the birth of his daughter, and substitutes 'Transman' (*sic*) into the title, I read Abdi's autobiography, written at sixteen and published at nineteen, as only the beginning of her story.

RIGHT GEOGRAPHY

Asylum is a complex, bureaucratic, and often lengthy process. For transgender people, it is a process distinctively constructed on narrative. The 1951 United Nations Convention Relating to the Status of Refugees provides a singular, universally applicable definition of a refugee. The Convention, offering five grounds on which a person may claim asylum, defines a refugee as follows:

> Any person who [...] owing to well-founded fear of being persecuted for reasons of race, religion, nationality, membership of a particular social group or political opinion, is outside the country of his nationality and is unable to, or owing to such fear, is unwilling to avail himself of the protection of that country.

When a refugee status determination officer[31] engages with an applicant who makes a claim on the basis of gender identity, the officer tries to determine whether that applicant belongs to a particular social group — in this case, transgender people — and whether, on this basis, they have a well-founded fear of being persecuted in their country of origin. As Laurie Berg and Jenni Millbank make clear, refugee claims based upon any of the other five grounds 'will more commonly have some form of independent verification of group membership'.[32] In contrast, claims to belong to a particular social group are far more difficult

---

30   Farah Abdullah Abdi, *Never Arrive* (Malta: self-published, 2015), p. 17, my emphasis.

31   This position might also be termed *asylum officer* or *asylum official*.

32   Laurie Berg and Jenni Millbank, 'Constructing the Personal Narratives of Lesbian, Gay and Bisexual Asylum Claimants', *Journal of Refugee Studies*, 22.2 (2009), pp. 195–223 (p. 196) <https://doi.org/10.1093/jrs/fep010>.

to prove and depend upon the presentation, through narrative, 'of a very internal form of self-identity'.[33]

In this narrative process, claimants relive trauma as part of a truth-telling exercise. However, there are very few ways to evidence this truth offered through narrative. The audience for the narrative holds the power over its narrative schema. The power dynamics of asylum 'dictate that the construction of the applicant's life story cannot challenge foundational tenets of the decision-maker's understanding of the world'.[34] Stephanie Hsu reminds us that the asylum narrative has two audiences. The first is the nation state, represented by the refugee status determination officer, which elicits the official account. Indeed, Sudeep Dasgupta frames the interpretation of these accounts by the law as a form of 'reading'.[35] The second is the community or public into which a transgender person desires to assimilate. This public also demands a narrative that explains the applicant's presence.[36] There are two critical elements to this narrative. First, it must follow a linear path of identity development from persecution and repression in the country of origin to freedom and liberation in the country of arrival. Second, it must fit within the audience's available knowledge frameworks or, more succinctly, be culturally intelligible to a largely non-trans audience.

This linear trajectory is evident in these three texts through the types of social proof used to validate these narratives, emphasizing the specific geographic investments of asylum and the authority of the countries of arrival in the first few pages. Early trans autobiographies often carried endorsements from doctors or clinicians involved in treatment. For example, the preface for Elbe's *Man into Woman: An Authentic Record of a Sex Change* (1933) is provided by medical doctor and sexologist Norman Haire, while Jorgensen's *A Personal Autobiog-*

---

33 Ibid.

34 Ibid., p. 197.

35 Sudeep Dasgupta, 'Sexual and Gender-Based Asylum and the Queering of Global Space: Reading Desire, Writing Identity and the Unconventionality of the Law', in *Refugee Imaginaries: Research Across the Humanities*, ed. by Emma Cox and others (Edinburgh: Edinburgh University Press, 2019), pp. 86–103 (p. 87) <https://doi.org/10.1515/9781474443210-009>.

36 Stephanie Hsu, 'Exotic Spectacle in *Tara's Crossing*, a Transgender Asylum Narrative', in *Queer Exoticism*, ed. by David Powell and Tamara Powell (Newcastle: Cambridge Scholars Publishing, 2010), pp. 81–91.

raphy (1967) carries a foreword by Harry Benjamin. Abdi's foreword is provided by Cecile Malmström, who in 2015 was the European Commissioner for Trade at the European Commission. Sandja's book is endorsed by Blackfoot/Latinx American writer Max Wolf Velario, author of *The Testosterone Files* (2006), widely considered the first published autobiography by a 'trans Indigenous person'. Finally, *An Unspoken Compromise* is endorsed by US-based social justice and independent reporting non-profit *Truthout*. While doctors or clinicians may have provided social proof (as endorsements do) of early autobiographies, we might cumulatively read the endorsements of a European Commissioner, an Indigenous US-based trans man, and a US-based media non-profit as indexing a different kind of social proof, one which links intelligibility to belonging, in the absence of the safe return.

Relatedly, regarding geographic investment, a stark contrast exists between the framing of countries of origin and countries of arrival. This appears most explicitly in Timane and Sandja, but it is also visible to a lesser degree in Abdi. Asylum narratives must emphasize the impossibility of the return and the probability of persecution if this happens. As a result, the key to these narratives is the repudiation of the country of origin and the espousal of a sense of gratitude for the possibility of safety in the new country. David Murray describes this phenomenon as the 'migration to liberation nation narrative',[37] emphasizing the contrast between the gift of freedom and the progress of rights in countries of arrival, and the perceived backwardness of (post)colonial national cultures in countries of origin.

All three texts frame countries of arrival as spaces of freedom or potential freedom, contrasting them with countries of origin as backward in various respects, particularly in Timane and Sandja's narratives. Abdi, reflecting on Kenya, states, 'I clearly knew that what was home for everybody else would never be home for me.'[38] However, while Abdi hints at the complexities of Kenya and Somalia, where survival seemed impossible, and describes her journey as a choice between freedom and death, Timane and Sandja predominantly refer to 'Africa' rather

---

37   David Murray, 'The (Not so) Straight Story: Queering Migration Narratives of Sexual Orientation and Gendered Identity Refugee Claimants', *Sexualities*, 17.4 (2014), pp. 451–71 <https://doi.org/10.1177/1363460714524767>.

38   Abdi, *Never Arrive*, p. 37.

than their specific countries of origin. Africa, for Timane and Sandja, is portrayed as a space of 'corrective rape', 'religious fundamentalism', and as a place where the perpetrators of crimes, 'via the police and courts [...] go unpunished.'[39] For both Sandja and Timane, Africa signifies backwardness, lack of acceptance, and harshness, and as with Abdi, it is a space of unfreedom. Foregrounding his arrival in America as necessary to escape expectations that he be 'a normal woman', Timane explains his relief at arriving in the US, a place that 'was very, very, very far away'.[40] For Sandja, not only is the US some distance from Africa, but it is a space of possibility where he might find himself and find healing. Referring to his exorcisms, Sandja explains: 'If the church couldn't do it, hopefully, the American doctors could.'[41] Thus, not only are these geographical spaces of freedom distinct from an Africa where the church, closed mindedness, and gendered expectations hold sway, but they are also invested with particular medical possibilities. It is to these medical possibilities or the trope of the wrong body that I turn to in the next section.

WRONG BODY

In the early years, trans authors like Elbe, Jorgenson, and Morris were called on to explain themselves in ways culturally intelligible to a larger non-trans public.[42] Centring the voices of white trans women[43] for whom surgery, travel, and publication were attainable possibilities, texts forming the early canon of trans autobiography narrativized their authors' lives through the limiting pathological rhetoric available.[44] At the time, cultural intelligibility was crucial to establishing the humanity of these authors. Thus, it was of the utmost importance to finesse

---

39   Timane, *An Unspoken Compromise*, p. 179.

40   Ibid., p. 45.

41   Neo L. Sandja, *Right Mind, Wrong Body: The Ultimate Trans Guide to Being Complete and Living a Fulfilled Life* (n.p.: Light Publishers, 2016), p. 26.

42   Sasha Kruger and Sayantani DasGupta, 'Embodiment in [Critical] Auto|biography Studies', *a/b: Auto/Biography Studies*, 33.2 (2018), pp. 483–87 (p. 485) <https://doi.org/10.1080/08989575.2018.1445608>.

43   Heath Fogg Davis, 'Sex-Classification Policies as Transgender Discrimination: An Intersectional Critique', *Perspectives on Politics*, 12.1 (2014), pp. 45–60 <https://doi.org/10.1017/S1537592713003708>.

44   Rondot, '"Bear Witness" and "Build Legacies"', p. 532.

the narrative away from constructions of 'freak' or 'pervert' to 'diagnos-able', 'treatable', and 'respectable'.[45]

Such narratives became 'legible and legitimate through their con-tinued repetition',[46] creating what Prosser describes as a 'narrative map' that others might follow.[47] These early texts were constructed around a set of 'recognizable clichés and conventions'.[48] Among these was the notion of being 'born in the wrong body', alongside childhood stories of consistent and confusing cross-gender identification. Clare Hemmings refers to these as 'technologies' of the genre, so consist-ently 'reproduced that they are understood to "speak for themselves" without further elaboration'.[49] These autobiographies and their wrong bodies became the framework through which trans existence became culturally intelligible.

The power (and persistence) of the wrong body narrative lies in its recognizability, legibility, and cultural intelligibility, perhaps all the more so in a system like asylum, which relies on narrative to ascertain truth. As migration scholars make clear, only those individuals who can adapt to 'Western-style identities and narratives' can cross or find refuge.[50] Thus, it should be unsurprising that the wrong body, inter-twined with medicalization, plays a central role in these narratives of refuge written from the position of diaspora. This centrality is high-lighted by Sandja's choice of title, *Right Mind, Wrong Body*. Addressing potential controversy, Sandja clarifies his choice of the title, explaining it's 'not because I believe I am a defect of humanity, but because it does describe a medical condition. I have been diagnosed with gender dysphoria and have taken the medical steps necessary to align my body to my correct gender.' [51]

45   Vipond, 'Becoming Culturally (Un)intelligible', p. 11.

46   Ibid., p. 4.

47   Prosser, *Second Skins*, p. 140.

48   Juliet Jacques, 'Forms of Resistance: Uses of Memoir, Theory, and Fiction in Trans Life Writing', *Life Writing*, 14.3 (2017), pp. 357–70 (p. 359) <https://doi.org/10.1080/14484528.2017.1328301>.

49   Clare Hemmings, 'Telling Feminist Stories', *Feminist Theory*, 6.2 (2005), pp. 115–39 <https://doi.org/10.1177/1464700105053690>.

50   Alexander Dhoest, 'Learning to Be Gay: LGBTQ Forced Migrant Identities and Nar-ratives in Belgium', *Journal of Ethnic and Migration Studies*, 45.7 (2019), pp. 1075–89 <https://doi.org/10.1080/1369183X.2017.1420466>.

51   Sandja, *Right Mind, Wrong Body*, p. x.

As Murray makes clear, 'replicating the hegemonic narrative is an important component of the model refugee identity that is circulated in media and stories about successful refugee claim hearings.'[52] Swapping the clinician's office for that of the refugee determination officer, being 'trapped in the wrong body' remains the most comprehensible narrative description of trans life for non-trans audiences.

Timane explains to his audience, via a letter to his parents in the book, 'I have never actually been a lesbian but have always been a transgendered [sic] person, meaning that while my outer body has been female, my inner being and my brain are, and have been since before I came out of the womb completely male.'[53] Similarly, Sandja writes:

> Here I was, someone who had grown up in a conservative country in the middle of Africa — someone who knew nothing about sexual orientation while growing up, let alone gender identity. At the age of 26, I was suddenly aware that I wasn't a freak after all, and that there was a reason that I had always felt strange in my own body [...]. The DSM [Diagnostic and Statistical Manual of Mental Disorders] estimates, as of writing this, that one in 30,000 males and one in 100,000 females are transgender. That number seems insignificant to most people, but to me, even if that number was 10 people in the entire world, my life would still have had a different meaning.[54]

Abdi, though in less directly medicalized language, refers to an 'essence' of self connected to femininity that was not acceptable within her native Somali community.[55] We can, perhaps, read the beginnings of this approach in *Never Arrive*, a book which, like those of Timane and Sandja, is the result of sessions with a psychological counsellor.[56] For both Timane and Sandja, the US not only becomes home but is a place that allows for homecoming. It is where the wrong body might be diagnosed and corrected, and thus represents the right geography as

52   Murray, 'The (Not so) Straight Story', pp. 465–66.
53   Timane, *An Unspoken Compromise*, pp. 81–82.
54   Sandja, *Right Mind, Wrong Body*, p. 68.
55   Abdi, *Never Arrive*, pp. 31–32.
56   Fabio Flepp, 'Reisegeschichten — Ein Leben voller Träume', *Schweizer Radio und Fernsehen* (*SRF*), 10 November 2015 <https://www.srf.ch/sendungen/reisegeschichten/reisegeschichten-ein-leben-voller-traeume> [accessed 7 October 2023].

an antidote to the wrong body. Contrary to Prosser's understanding of the return, where gender and geography align after an outward venture, there is no going back.

THE UNSAFE RETURN

Asylum, by its very definition, is a risky exploit, and indeterminacy is a constitutive element. As Jacqueline Bhabha (2002) describes it,

> most refugees fleeing to safety in developed states do not ar-
> rive with a ready guarantee of access to enduring human rights.
> Rather, they enter as 'asylum seekers' — a temporary and in-
> creasingly disenfranchised category of non-citizen who need
> to establish their eligibility for refugee status before they can
> enjoy the prospect of long-term safety and nondiscriminatory
> treatment.[57]

While the three texts in question closely adhere to the model of the trans travel narrative, the presence of this risk and indetermin-acy, consistent throughout, presents a critical difference. Returning to Crawford's critique, outlined in the introduction to this chapter, the trans asylum narrative certainly illustrates the ubiquity and ongoing power of the model of the trans travel narrative to explain trans life to an intended audience. However, migration in pursuit of asylum, where becoming is imagined in countries of refuge to be illustrated through a believable trans narrative, is a risky exploit. This risk is evident not only in the decision to flee but also in what we might term the 'unsafe return'. In contrast to the alignment, triumph, and homecoming of the safe return, the unsafe return is marked by fear and the potential for repudiation, deportation, and denial.

Part of Crawford's critique of Prosser concerns the question of indeterminacy and its absence in Prosser's framing. Unlike the trans travel narrative, which presents 'gendered indeterminacy within a spa-tialised elsewhere' such as Germany, Denmark, or Morocco, indeter-minacy in these narratives is a constitutive element not only of asylum

---

57 Jacqueline Bhabha, 'Internationalist Gatekeepers?: The Tension Between Asylum
    Advocacy and Human Rights', *Harvard Human Rights Journal*, 15 (2002), pp. 155–
    81 (p. 155) <https://journals.law.harvard.edu/hrj/wp-content/uploads/sites/83/
    2020/06/15HHRJ155-Bhabha.pdf> [accessed 22 July 2024].

but also of countries of origin.[58] Rather than being resolved in the moment of the 'safe return', gendered indeterminacy serves as a spectre that embodies countries of origin — a haunting potentiality of asylum denial and deportation. For Abdi, this non-alignment with home and the spectre of the unsafe return is seen most clearly when she explains that her journey towards 'happiness' and her 'true identity' could not be found in nor ever align with a place like Kenya: 'I clearly knew that what was home for everybody else would *never* be home for me.'[59] For Sandja, we might read the spectre of the 'unsafe return' in his description of his journey, in which he emphasizes that 'there's no turning back':

> There is a point during each journey where the traveller realizes that the decision has to be made that will completely alter the outcome of the journey. It's a very significant moment because once it's been reached and once it's passed, there's no turning back. That point for me was when I realized I was Trans and chose to transition despite what I might lose, because I had everything to gain: my true self.[60]

Sandja's narrative vividly illustrates the uncertainty and risk of striving for a life amidst the looming shadow of the unsafe return. At one point, he finds himself navigating life in the US as an undocumented migrant, highlighting the challenges and vulnerabilities faced by trans individuals seeking safety. Perhaps nowhere is the unsafe return made more evident and explicit than in Timane's narration of Africa in the final pages of his book. In stark contrast to the life he has found in the US, Timane agglomerates the continent into a place where violence, rape, and murder are indiscriminately inflicted upon those seen to be 'deviant' or 'non-conformist',[61] where 'cultural patriarchy and religious fundamentalism' prevails, and where 'the police and courts [...] allow the perpetrators to go unpunished'.[62] The unsafe return is a critical element of the trans asylum narrative, distinguishing it from the model of the trans travel narrative. Though perhaps not in the way Crawford

---

58 Aizura, 'The Persistence of Transgender Travel Narratives', p. 153.
59 Abdi, *Never Arrive*, pp. 37–38, my emphasis.
60 Sandja, *Right Mind, Wrong Body*, p. 83.
61 Timane, *An Unspoken Compromise*, p. 193.
62 Ibid., p. 179.

intends, this difference opens up a consideration of indeterminacy and risk, while illustrating the ongoing power of linearity and intelligibility.

CONCLUSION: ASYLUM, THE RISKY EXPLOIT

The recognized refugee is one who has 'successfully interiorized these identity models and narratives', where an intelligible version of trans-gender identity is not only necessary but must also be accompanied by a desire for the state as a site of freedom, protection, and home.[63] Sandy Stone warns, in her critique of the scholarly literature on early trans autobiographies, that trans people are not simply dupes of the systems they encounter, whether they be medical or otherwise, but necessarily use the tools at hand to narrate their lives and experiences into reality. For Stone, it is important to ask: for whom are these nar-ratives constructed?[64] Indeed, Abdi offers a crucial reminder of these authors' agency and ability to reshape and narrate their stories even beyond publication, as she integrates her trans journey back into the text.

In these three texts, home is a place one flees, and borders are not merely metaphors but genuine physical sites of geopolitical power and un/belonging. As a result, in this essay I have suggested that these trans narratives of becoming are unable to pivot on the safe return. Instead, they foreground the spectre of the unsafe return, presenting a secondary model of the traditional trans narrative. For these three authors, as trans people who have sought refuge in the Global North, I suggest there is a necessity to author 'a coherent narrative that is recognizable and intelligible to their readers'.[65] Trans studies scholar Eliza Steinbock reminds us that 'what is missing in trans origin myths and interpretations of their existence [...] is an appreciation for how trans subjects narrate and represent their lives and thereby model the

---

63   Dhoest, 'Learning to Be Gay', p. 1087.
64   Sandy Stone, 'The *Empire* Strikes Back: A Posttranssexual Manifesto', *Camera Obscura: Feminism, Culture, and Media Studies*, 10.2 (1992), pp. 150–76 <https://doi.org/10.1215/02705346-10-2_29-150>.
65   Vipond, 'Becoming Culturally (Un)Intelligible', pp. 4–5.

available conceptual models of gendered embodiment.'[66] Placing the literature in migration and trans studies in conversation, I suggest we might not only appreciate but also recognize the conceptual model being transposed from the clinician's office to that of the refugee status determination officer, as well as understand the reasons behind this revitalization. For trans applicants to successfully navigate a system such as asylum, which leaves them highly vulnerable,[67] 'they must quickly learn these narratives and the powerful structures within which they are located with the result that the migration stories are compelled to contain statements which hue closely to the hegemonic narrative while simultaneously complicating it.'[68]

These three texts are shaped by the interplay between the authors' needs and the state's demands, reflecting a negotiation of power structures. The trope of the wrong body provides the first pillar of articulation in the well-worn and widely understood narrative construction of the self. As with early writers, this is the narrative that has, in the past, most readily fostered 'acceptability in society.'[69] While these texts do not directly challenge the asylum narrative as a form — indeed, they are compelled to reproduce it — they do complicate its requirements by illustrating its troubling origins and emphasizing the enduring power of its reproduction. This complexity, as it relates to international protection, merits serious consideration by refugee and migration scholars. In the shadow of the unsafe return, the narrative is constructed for an audience tasked with extending not only their understanding but their refuge. Without the possibility of a homecom-

---

66 Eliza Steinbock, *Shimmering Images: Trans Cinema, Embodiment, and the Aesthetics of Change* (Durham, NC: Duke University Press, 2019), p. 27 <https://doi.org/10.1515/9781478004509>.

67 See Susannah Hermaszewska and others, 'Lived Experiences of Transgender Forced Migrants and Their Mental Health Outcomes: Systematic Review and Meta-Ethnography', *BJPsych Open*, 8.3 (2022) <https://doi.org/10.1192/bjo.2022.51>; B Camminga, 'Competing Marginalities and Precarious Politics: A South African Case Study of NGO Representation of Transgender Refugees', *Gender, Place & Culture*, 31.9 (2024), pp. 1293–1310 <https://doi.org/10.1080/0966369X.2022.2137473>; and B Camminga, 'Withholding the Letter: Transgender Asylum Seekers, Legal Gender Recognition, and the UNHCR Mandate', *Journal of Refugee Studies*, published online 8 July 2024 <https://doi.org/10.1093/jrs/feae058>.

68 David Murray, 'The (Not so) Straight Story', p. 454.

69 Rondot, '"Bear Witness" and "Build Legacies"', p. 534.

ing pivot, these asylum seekers must adeptly navigate and negotiate the hegemonic narrative, reclaiming it as their own. In contrast to the typical trans travel narrative, this model, which foregrounds home in exile, is structured on indeterminacy and is only made possible through the risky exploit, the daring journey to freedom, that undergirds trans becoming.[70]

---

70   I would like to thank my colleagues at the ICI Berlin Institute for Cultural Inquiry for their valuable contributions to multiple drafts of this paper. I would also like to thank Brenna Munro for her incredible generosity in engaging with this chapter and for her encouragement.

The question that took root in my mind after reading this essay was whether there is, or should be, some formal notion of transgender identity. Furthermore, if transgender identity (at least as a theoretical object and not as a blanket for lived experience) does have a shared formal concept, would this imply or lend credence to a narrative theory of the self? Bearing in mind that various forms of narrative may have general models due to the forced appeasement of medical authorities, and that they may divert from these models for people who can afford them to, does it make sense to talk about trans identity in a generic sense? One could rely upon a social-constructivist mode, but given the role of narrative and self-identification, this might prove to be of limited use.

The question is fraught with all kinds of traps. Trans identity can be seen as merely an example of queerness, as is the case for Judith Butler, and there is also the problem of self-identification vis-à-vis other categories.[71] Then there is the question as to whether there are limits to the self-construction of identity,[72] as well as the all-too-easy critique from certain vulgar or 'middlebrow' Marxists, who see notions of the self-construction of identity as 'merely' late-capitalist self-fashioning.[73] If this minefield can be circumvented, it remains to be seen whether it makes sense to have or to recognize a formal theory of transness as narrativity — can it be a concern for those outside transgender experience without being amenable to authorities of recognition like courts and medical boards?[74]

---

71 On these first two points see Amy Marvin, 'A Brief History of Transphilosophy', *Contingent Magazine*, 21 September 2019 <https://contingentmagazine.org/2019/09/21/trans-philosophy/> [accessed 23 July 2024].

72 One is reminded of the controversy over Isabel Fall's 'I Sexually Identify as an Attack Helicopter', a story published in (and later withdrawn from) *Clarkesworld* magazine in January 2020.

73 See the editors' introduction to *Transgender Marxism*, ed. by Jules Joanne Gleeson and Elle O'Rourke (London: Pluto Press, 2021), pp. 1–32 <https://doi.org/10.2307/j.ctv1n9dkjc.4>.

74 Here it is also important to remember Susan Stryker's distinction between the discourse on transness and the scholarly works and writings of trans-identified people. See Susan Stryker, '(De)Subjugated Knowledges: An Introduction to Transgender Studies', in *The Transgender Studies Reader*, ed. by Susan Stryker and Stephen Whittle (New York: Routledge, 2006), pp. 1–17.

One possibility comes from Xandra Metcalfe, who puts forward the idea of a 'primordial transness', in which cis-hetero identity is not the default but rather is simply the most conditioned form of identity.[75] If the matrix of sex/gender/desire is underdetermined at birth, then the narrative theory of the self, however it is engaged, takes agential notice of this indeterminacy of supposedly naturalized categories, or even socially constrained correlations between bodies, aesthetics, desires, and so on. Following this, one has to then ask what narrativity means in terms of the construction of one's identity as opposed to the writing or producing of that identity through various means of autobiography, autofiction, and fiction.[76] Here it might make sense to clarify what the narrative theory of the self, or narrative identity, is.

The narrative theory of the self, in its broadest terms, is about processing one's experiences as temporally ordered, thematically interlinked, and potentially having a direction or a purpose. Implied in this is the notion that there is a structure, or at least a capacity, of agency or individuality that assembles and works over these experiences, separately from having them — or, in other words, that there is some self-operator that makes the narrative out of memories, experiences, events, and so on. This implies a split between the idea of someone as a human being and that of a self as a kind of narrative function. As Peter Goldie puts it:

> [T]he idea of a narrator in an episode of autobiographical narrative thinking in a person narrative is not that of a homuncular entity [...], nor is it an entity that is necessarily stable. The narrative sense of self is the sense of self had by the narrator; and this self is, simply, me now as thinker, looking backwards at my narratable past, or forwards to my narratable future.[77]

---

75   Xandra Metcalfe, '"Why Are We Like This?": The Primacy of Transsexuality', in *Transgender Marxism*, ed. by Gleeson and O'Rourke, pp. 219–29 <https://doi.org/10.2307/j.ctv1n9dkjc.17>.

76   See Jordy Rosenberg, 'Afterword: One Utopia, One Dystopia', in *Transgender Marxism*, ed. by Gleeson and O'Rourke, pp. 259–95 <https://doi.org/10.2307/j.ctv1n9dkjc.19>.

77   Peter Goldie, *The Mess Inside: Narrative, Emotion, and the Mind* (Oxford: Oxford University Press, 2012), p. 131 <https://doi.org/10.1093/acprof:oso/9780199230730.001.0001>.

For Goldie what is important is 'empathic access', in the sense that one (as the narrator) may feel closer to, or further away from, one's self as a body or as a human. While some theorists of the identity theory of the self will insist upon the existence of a stable identity over time, such that the narrator may refer to changes of the body or of the embodied self, this is not necessary in Goldie's case, where it is the emotional or affective strands of those events that constitute the self, more than structural stability. At the same time, Goldie emphasizes that it is important to distinguish the narrative theory of the self from the various fictionalizing tendencies of autobiography and the like.

For Goldie, the desire to push the narrative theory of the self towards fictionalizing tendencies (that we have control, narrative closure, that our life belongs to a genre, etc.) is more often than not a response to the unthinkability of contingency and the supposed disenchantment of the modern world.[78]

This would seem to dovetail with Jordy Rosenberg's claim that autofiction (or autobiography) becomes a trap for trans-identified people and that subversion of the trope requires breaking the genre from within. One of the texts Rosenberg names is that of Kai Cheng Thom, who explicitly describes their book *Fierce Femmes and Notorious Liars* as being written against the expectations of cis-heteronormative audiences. And, also to Goldie's point, Thom says in an interview about the book:

> I wanted to be real about the kinds of experiences that trans women have out there in the world. Even though the book is a fantasy, it is only fantasy in the sense that there are surreal elements in it. The emotions and sensations are all true, are all drawn exactly from my life. And honestly, some of the situations are not that fictionalized in the sense that trans women do get involved in violence.[79]

It would seem that certain forms of trans identity fashion themselves as exposing the formal reflectivity of identity in general in such a way

---

78 Ibid., pp. 171–72.
79 Frankie de la Cretaz, 'Author Kai Cheng Thom on Writing a New Kind of Transgender Memoir', *Teen Vogue*, 5 April 2017 <https://www.teenvogue.com/story/author-kai-cheng-thom-on-writing-a-new-kind-of-transgender-memoir> [accessed 23 July 2024].

that indexes violence at the level of the social for outwardly embodying living against the grain (as Metcalfe puts it). If this is the case then it would seem that more overtly fictional narratives of transness will address the resistance of cis-heteronormativity to narratives that imply that they have, in terms of narrative identity, chosen not to have an authorial voice in their own life.

Nowhere is this clearer (I think) than in terms of trans horror (especially dystopian horror). For instance, Alison Rumfitt's *Brainwyrms* suggests that transphobia is the result of a parasite-infected pseudo-Lovecraftian cult of powerful British elites. Errol Harris's gothic horror *Leech* can be read as a similar analogy, depicting a scenario in which all medical professionals are in fact humans controlled by a brain parasite. Or, from a more utopian angle, Yoon Ha Lee's *Ninefox Gambit* series of books play with gender fluidity in the wake of consciousness's becoming uploadable and downloadable into new bodies.

Formal flexibility or plasticity of the self inverts the wrong body narrative to become one of an unacknowledged formal self that one cannot activate if there is an assumption of 'naturalness', essences, or scientific 'facts'.

My hope here is that this complicates the notion of cis-heteronormative negativity, viewing the transnarrative as proof.

The Statistical Cloud of Race
Lancelot Hogben's Anti-Eugenics between Populations and Organisms
BEN WOODARD

> The process of averaging the characters of a given group, of knocking the individuals together, giving them a good stirring, and then serving the resulting omelet as a race was essentially the anthropological process of race-making. It may have been good cooking, but it was not science, since it served to confuse rather than to clarify. When an omelet is done it has a fairly uniform character, though the ingredients which have entered into its making have been varied. So it was with the anthropological conception of race. It was an omelet that corresponded to nothing in nature: an indigestible dish conjured into being by an anthropological chef from a number of ingredients which were extremely varied in character. This omelet conception of race had no existence outside the statistical frying pan in which it had been reduced by the heat of the anthropological imagination; it was a meaningless concept because it is inapplicable to anything real. When anthropologists began to realize that the proper description of a group does not consist in the process of making an omelet of it, but in the analysis and description of the character of the variability of the elements entering into it — its ingredients — they discovered that the fault lay not with the materials but with the conceptual tool with which they had approached their study. *In passing, it is a good idea not to accept any concept until the presuppositions upon which it is based have been thoroughly examined.*
>
> Ashley Montagu, *Man's Most Dangerous Myth:*
> *The Fallacy of Race*

A wide range of modelling practices are found in the biological sciences, broadly conceived. Predominant among these practices is the use of model organisms, which tend to be treated in two general ways. First, an organism may be taken as a means of exploring a more general biological function (such as genetic inheritance or ageing, for instance). Second, an organism may be investigated because it exemplifies a novel or rare capacity or trait. Here are examples of each:

General form: fruit flies were used in the early twentieth century to build maps of chromosomes, because they provided easy access to answering related questions: their large salivary glands made them easy to genetically sample; their lifespan meant they would exhibit mutations quickly, as generations were short; and they lived everywhere that humans did.

Novel capacity: an organism might be studied because it has a presumably rare or interesting capacity, such as the anti-freeze blood of the arctic fish *Myoxocephalus scorpius*, which lacks haemoglobin, or the extreme phenotypic plasticity of *Pristimantis mutabilis*, a tiny tree frog which can reshape its skin from smooth to spiky in thirty seconds.

While knowledge gained from these studies can unveil genetic, molecular, or broadly applicable physiological functions and evolutionary histories that are relevant to human beings, human beings themselves are not considered ethically usable as model organisms.[1] While human bodies have historically been subjected to biological experiments, this has, unsurprisingly, been bound up with eugenical programmes, endemic racism, and large-scale ethical violations. Humans are not 'merely' animals or organisms in this sense, yet some humans have historically been treated as more animal-like, or as human but 'less human', in order to justify torture in the name of pseudoscience. Scientific racism is not scientific but is, rather, a loose set of political beliefs that selectively borrows and twists scientific concepts and practices in order to appear as a legitimate science.

An illustrative case of this contradictory oscillation in racist discourse is clearly evident in the ways in which racist whites responded

---

1   There are, of course, test subjects, willing and otherwise, and clinical trials. As we will see below, people of colour, women, and other minorities have been subjected to experimentation outside the model organism protocol.

to the participation of Black athletes vis-à-vis medical discourse on and around Black bodies in the early twentieth century. Athletes like the legendary Jesse Owens were seen as more 'animal-like' in order to explain their athletic prowess while still retaining some degree of superiority for white nationals. At the same time, medical practitioners and experimenters might claim that Black bodies were physiologically equal to white bodies as justification for dissecting the former to benefit the latter.[2]

Here the two modes of approaching model organisms are presented in an occluded fashion: Black bodies were seen under the general rubric when they could be treated as 'human enough' for medical trials. On the other hand, Black bodies were treated as more animal-like, and hence under the rubric of organismal novelty, to set them apart from white bodies.[3]

In this regard the process of making races to some degree parallels the conceptual thinking involved in the practice of using model organisms. Taking a cue from Sylvia Wynter, then, one should always be wary of the assumed inclusiveness of 'human', as it has historically been constructed to strategically leave out some humans for the sake of others.[4] Furthermore, analogizing the exploitation of animals to the exploitation of human beings without this genealogical awareness can reinforce the animalization/dehumanization of some peoples in the name of animal ethics.[5] The two uses and formalizations of model

---

2   See William Montague Cobb, 'Race and Runners', *The Journal of Health and Physical Education*, 7.1 (1936), n.p., published online as Department of Sociology and Anthropology Faculty Publications 13 (Washington, DC: Howard University) <https://dh.howard.edu/soci_fac/13/> [accessed 7 August 2024]. See also Harriet A. Washington, *Medical Apartheid: The Dark History of Medical Experimentation on Black Americans from Colonial Times to the Present* (New York: Knopf Double Day, 2008).

3   One of the most infamous causes of this is that of Saartjie Baartman (1789–1815), a member of the Gonaquasub group of the Khoikhoi, who was born in what is today the Eastern Cape of South Africa and who died in Paris. Exoticized and sexualized, Baartman was treated as a curiosity by European naturalists and exhibited while still alive and after her death.

4   Sylvia Wynter, 'Unsettling the Coloniality of Being/Power/Truth/Freedom: Towards the Human, After Man, its Overrepresentation — An Argument', *CR: The New Centennial Review*, 3.3 (2003), pp. 257–337 <https://doi.org/10.1353/ncr.2004.0015>.

5   See, for instance, Zakiyyah Iman Jackson, *Becoming Human: Matter and Meaning in an Anti-Black World* (New York: NYU Press, 2021) <https://doi.org/10.18574/nyu/9781479890040.001.0001>.

organisms outlined above can serve to remind us of these limitations: biological commonalities do not always suffice for health disparities or other environmental differences, nor should purportedly 'essential' differences be deployed without an awareness of how those differences have been constructed by way of selective historical means.

However, in biological terms as applied to human beings, the more general and more specific approaches to model organisms, and how they conform to biological practice, do not address a specific mid-level of analysis, namely, the study of a population — something which is 'below' the species level and 'above' the individual level. A biological researcher may take a step back from the organism's capacities, physiology, and developmental history, and instead view it as a bearer of inherited traits (genetic, epigenetic, or more vaguely hereditary). This approach to humans as organisms aligns with the discourse of anthropological race-making as described by Montagu in the epigraph above. For Montagu, the process of making races disappears, and races come to be accepted as straightforwardly empirical 'facts' about the world.[6]

Furthermore, in stepping away from the body as a physiological entity in its living and environmental engagements, it may seem that statistical approaches or population approaches then neutralize the racist assumptions on display in the experimentation with bodies; however, they in fact occlude them via statistical tools. Approaching evolution by way of populations ties directly into the approach of frequentism that this article will critique at length, namely, that by measuring traits in repeated random samples one can derive the frequency of those traits and their relative causes — in this case, genes.

This mid-level approach (viewing humans as populations and correlating them to races) was integral to the formation of the so-called 'modern synthesis' of the 1930s, in which statistical methods were used to synthesize Mendelian models of genetic inheritance with Darwin's theories of natural selection. The emphasis on populations, frequencies, and traits could then be applied to humans and, furthermore, could be allied with eugenical experiments or, in the post-war period, with sociobiological research projects. While there is an assumption

---

6   See Montagu, *Man's Most Dangerous Myth*.

that current concepts and practices in biology (especially genetics) have moved beyond overtly race-based ideology, and check individual bias, there has been less of a concentrated effort to draw out the politically questionable threads of this third biometric level — of statistical analysis as justifying non-biological assumptions about uncritically utilized categories such as race, IQ, or combinations of assumptions to do with gender and sex. For instance, historical categories of race are uncritically correlated with gene samples from populations, such that a sample of a population living in a given region today is seen as representative of the gene pool of a race anthropologically constructed hundreds of years ago, which in turn truncates or ignores the history of human migration across the planet.

The point is that this utilization is not easily traceable to explicit political ideology, nor to personal bias, but is, rather, the result of a 'thought collective' (to borrow a term from Ludwik Fleck) utilizing abstract concepts in a way that allows for the confirmation and valorization of already existing socio-political categories.[7] These statistical concepts, such as frequency, then behave in an amphibious manner by mutually reinforcing pre-existing confidence in categories and in the efficacy of newly constructed statistical or biological methods — that is, new science is 'accurate' because it justifies things one already knows to be 'true'. This does not mean that all frequentist analyses are politically flawed; however, in situations in which one is neither tempted nor encouraged to rattle the status quo, they are expedient and simple.

To this end, this essay will outline how such warnings were issued almost one hundred years ago by examining the life and work of Lancelot Hogben (1895–1975). Hogben engaged with the biophilosophical and biopolitical predicaments outlined at each level: personal bias, political ideology, and, most importantly for our purposes here, the dangers of misapplying statistical concepts outside of their theoretical remit. Furthermore, Hogben's anti-eugenicist stance intersected with his zoological and statistical knowledge, something which, despite hav-

---

7   Ludwik Fleck, *Genesis and Development of a Scientific Fact*, ed. by Thaddeus J. Trenn and Robert K. Merton, trans. by Fred Bradley and Thaddeus J. Trenn (Chicago: University of Chicago Press, 1979), p. 25.

ing been partially forgotten by history, is, I wish to argue, even more relevant for recent attempts to decolonize biological and statistical knowledge within Western universities and within broader scientific practice. Hogben is also of particular importance because he understood, against the grain of the assumptions of the modern synthesis, the relationship and differences between working with model organisms and working with statistical models, as outlined above — that the concepts and the nature of the claims possible for each differed substantially. The modern synthesis was the alliance of Darwin's theories of natural selection and Mendel's theory of genetic inheritance, brought together largely by statistical models in the early 1900s, and taking traits, genes, and mutations as things to be measured within a population, rather than the capacities, aspects, and genealogies of particular organisms or their environments.

I will highlight two episodes from Hogben's life that exemplify his multilevel engagement with the intersection of politics and biology, before engaging with the amphibious nature of the third level of statistical knowledge, and examining Hogben's debate with Ronald Aylmer Fisher and the biometric school of genetics, an encounter that set the course of genetics and biology for at least the following forty years.

I wish to argue that these biographical features of Hogben's life, rather than being incidental to his work, reveal how his position with the general political and economic situation of practising biologists, especially in the UK in the twentieth century, gives his critiques added weight, as he was able to view the genetic thought collective from the outside.

THE FROG HOUSE OF CAPE TOWN (1927–30)

After being educated in the UK and working in the fields of zoology and comparative endocrinology in Edinburgh and then Montreal, Lancelot Hogben took up a professorship in Cape Town in 1927. Taking up the chair of his department, Hogben revitalized the laboratory spaces and updated the curriculum, and taught biology and mathematics to local teachers as well.[8] Most notably, along with many other researchers,

---

8   Hogben says these teachings were informal and he does not specify to whom he taught
     outside the university.

including his wife — the socialist demographer, mathematician, and statistician Enid Charles — he developed a reliable pregnancy test using the local frog *Xenopus laevis*.

Building on his knowledge of endocrinology, Hogben identified that the same hormones were present in amphibians and mammals. Before this time, the standard pregnancy test (which required special permission and could only be ordered by a doctor, and often only by the patient's presumed husband) involved injecting a small mammal (typically a mouse or rabbit) with the urine of the woman undergoing the test, then waiting for physiological changes before killing and dissecting the animal to see if ovulation had occurred. Hogben co-authored numerous papers with Charles, who was pursuing a PhD in physiology while in Cape Town.[9]

The *Xenopus* test was not only faster (frogs would typically lay eggs within twelve hours following the injection) but it also caused the frog only mild discomfort, as opposed to death for the small mammals.[10] Part of the reason why Hogben could see the potential of the test in both scientific and ethical terms was due to his general mechanistic approach to biology. For Hogben, hormones were biochemical actors and there was no reason to think that they would not function across species lines. So, while Hogben was a mechanist, he was also not a reductionist, insofar as he thought that researchers should find the appropriate level of functionality not only to acknowledge the complexity of relations between species at levels deeper than anatomy, but also in a way that would be less harmful to the organism and more beneficial to the public. Put otherwise, Hogben's mechanistic approach to organisms allowed him to see biological compatibility or sameness, which then subsequently allowed him to highlight social or cultural disparities between species, and between members of the same species. This is borne out by Hogben's disagreement with General Jan Smuts's

---

9   There has been controversy as to whether Hogben deserved the credit or whether it was his students Hillel Shapiro and Harry Zwarenstein, who in fact first performed the test.

10   Eben Kirksey, Dehlia Hannah, Charlie Lotterman, and Lisa Jean Moore performed a public viewing of the test in 2012 in order to demonstrate the use of animals that usually occurs behind closed doors. See Eben Kirksey and others, 'The Xenopus Pregnancy Test: A Performative Experiment', *Environmental Humanities* 8.1 (2016), pp. 37–56 <https://doi.org/10.1215/22011919-3527713>.

holism, which, on the face of it, might seem inclusive and organic, but that in fact was used to justify right-wing racist acts and policies.

Holism, the notion that one must treat organisms and the environment as an integrated system, and that this way of thinking should be expanded beyond the merely biological, is often seen as a politically liberal concept, as being proto-ecological. But how could this be squared with Smuts's political beliefs and actions, given that Smuts helped sow the seeds of racial segregation in South Africa that would later bloom into apartheid, and that he also aimed to conquer Namibia, Burundi, Rwanda, and Tanzania, and went after whites whom he saw as 'race traitors' for defending the native peoples?[11] In his work, Smuts increasingly blended his ecological principles with his defence of European involvement in Africa. Citing the 'third event' (the emergence of *Homo sapiens* in Africa), Smuts utilized the logic of recapitulation to claim that Africans remained the original but also the most 'simple child-like form' of human beings.[12]

Thus, holism could seem liberal in that it advocated for harmonious relations between all species and peoples, while it also emphasized that everything had its 'proper place' in nature, and hence stressed the cultural 'superiority' of Christian Europe, and its role in deciding where everyone else belonged.

While continuing his semi-clandestine political activities (including smuggling threatened people out of harm's way), Hogben engaged in a debate with Smuts over the question of holism or mechanism. The debate occurred in 1929 as part of the meeting of the British Association for the Advancement of Science. The results of the debate were published some years later as part of a longer discussion on the relationship between biology and humanism in Hogben's book *The Nature of Living Matter*, in which he sets his own views against those of Smuts, J. B. S. Haldane, Arthur Eddington, and Alfred North Whitehead.[13]

---

11   John Bellamy Foster, *The Return of Nature: Socialism and Ecology* (New York: Monthly Review Press, 2021), p. 323.

12   Ibid., p. 326.

13   Lancelot Hogben, *The Nature of Living Matter* (London: K. Paul, Trench, Trubner, 1930), p. 243. There is not space here to fully articulate Hogben's political-scientific network, as he was also in contact with various left-leaning botanists and ecologists, such as G. E. Hutchinson (who would later go on to be Donna Haraway's adviser), as well as Edward Roux and Arthur Tansley.

In the book, Hogben does not discuss biological theories or experimental results so much as he questions the spirit of holism as advocated by Smuts and Haldane. Hogben seems to think there is a basic misunderstanding by those who argue for the fundamental irreducibility or mysteriousness of living systems, given that, for Hogben, science is ultimately the collective labour of individuals to produce collective knowledge about the external world. He therefore does not necessarily reject holism at the level of explanation, but rather argues that it is expressed in a way that is unassailable by non-scientists and therefore risks being a form of science that is easier to abuse politically.

Hogben refers to this view as one of science publicism — the notion that something must be publicly expressible and collectively thought-through to be considered science. This is not meant to invalidate ethics or morality, or even the legitimacy of knowledge internal to a single person, nor is it to see science merely as a support beam for common sense. Authors such as John Bellamy Foster claim that Hogben was insufficently Marxist, a 'mere' socialist or a humanist, or that he was all three of these things at different periods of his life.[14] Yet Hogben consistently had no tolerance for class discrimination, nor for magical or religious thinking by which one could ignore serious social problems.

Thus, while Hogben's mechanistic or functionalist perspective might be seen as reductive and hence politically limited, in fact it was this functionalist view that allowed him to make the argument that hormones would work across species, or to show that the assertion that there are hard biological differences between races simply does not hold up.

After Cape Town, Hogben went to the London School of Economics to lead a research group on socialist-motivated anti-eugenics. This led to further conflicts in the understanding of the relationship between politics and biology, at the different level of statistics.

---

14   See Foster, *The Return of Nature*, pp. 328–29.

CRACKING THE BLACK BOX OF GENETIC CAUSE (1932–35)

While a researcher at the London School of Economics, Hogben read the work of the highly influential statistician R. A. Fisher and eventually had a correspondence with him. As James Tabery has documented, these letters soon turned into a drastic scientific and political rift.[15] Fisher was of the biometric school, with an approach to statistics known as 'frequentism' (which I will discuss at length in what follows). But more importantly here, and for Hogben's disagreement with him, was the fact that Fisher thought that environmental influences could be bracketed out of statistical analyses on the heritability of traits and the relation of this to an organism's development. For Hogben, development could not be understood without taking into account not only the influence of the environment but also how changes in the environment at different times can affect the organism in a non-linear fashion that is more difficult to predict statistically.

It is important to define the term *heritability*, as it is somewhat complex. In genetics, heritability is the degree to which the variance in a trait is traceable to genetic causes. For instance, height would have a high degree of heritability since parental height appears to have a substantial effect on the height of the child. Number of fingers or toes, on the other hand, would have a low or almost zero degree of heritability, as genetic contributions from one's parents would not affect the range.

The ability to measure heritability is often predicated on measuring traits of parents and children while excluding or minimizing environmental factors. This concept is not only relevant to eugenical claims about 'good genes' or desirable traits, but also marks the beginning of the (still ongoing) discussion of nature versus nurture (and their entanglement) in the life and social sciences. In the late nineteenth and early twentieth centuries, eugenics applied the logic of animal breeding to human beings, not only in determining physical characteristics but also behavioural ones (intelligence, criminality, and so on). While these characteristics were initially correlated with

15   James Tabery, *Beyond Versus: The Struggle to Understand the Interaction of Nature and Nurture* (Cambridge, MA: MIT Press, 2014), pp 38–40 <https://doi.org/10.7551/mitpress/9780262027373.001.0001>.

'bloodline' or 'stock', these terms slowly became bolstered by biological discourse, following the work of Francis Galton among others.

The stances of Fisher and Hogben were more specifically to do with gene/environment interaction and the relation of biometric frequency (how the number of genes is distributed within a population [Fisher]) to developmental synchronicity (how the timeline of development affects the activation or deactivation of genes within a singular organism [Hogben]). In broader terms, frequentism is the statistical view that repeated objective measurements of traits or events are sufficient for making true claims about the world — in other words, that one can say how probable something is after performing an agreed number of trials (such as coin flips).

Chapter two of James Tabery's *Beyond Versus* sets out the stakes and outlines in great detail how the Fisher–Hogben debate unfolded. Fisher had already established himself by 1918, by beginning to show how genetic variation could be measured within a population — rather than focusing on averages, Fisher had introduced the concept of a normal distribution, or bell curve, into biology.[16] As Tabery shows, the conceptual upshot of Fisher's work was that he could argue how inheritable a trait was by showing variance in traits between relatives, and could thus construct variation among genes.

Fisher treated populations like a series of coin flips (that is, as objective data) in which tall children give birth to tall children, thus suggesting that height is straightforwardly caused by genes. One issue that arises from this, however, is how to explain differences in height between two tall children who have tall parents. This is the question of standard deviation: if tall people have tall children, why would one be slightly taller than average and another far taller than average?

For Fisher, as Tabery highlights, the answer is not environmental conditions, but rather the idea that some genes are dominant while others are recessive.[17] Thus, variance in height is completely described by the source of genes at one level (the parents) and the interaction of genes at another (thereby explaining the difference in height between siblings).

---

16   James Tabery, *Beyond Versus*, pp. 18–19.

17   Ibid., p. 20.

One can see the immediate relevance of such concepts for eugenicists. If the causes of variation of human traits are genetic, then it becomes possible (and even desirable) to select breeding partners to raise those averages. Yet, as Hogben pointed out to Fisher in the early 1930s, this assumes a rather straightforward understanding of genes as causes and, importantly, as independent causes.

On the contrary, Hogben thought that one could not ignore environmental effects, especially when taking into consideration the temporal register of development — that it is not merely a question of what genes there are, but of which genes are active at specific developmental stages of the organism (meaning it is a question of gene activity, and not only frequency). Hogben suggested that Fisher was mistaken to assume that variation was to do with the ratios of genes, and that environment could affect the expression of genes — that is, a non-genetic or non-heritable factor could affect the expression of genes during the development of the organism. After all, Hogben's research from a decade earlier, on fruit flies and heat shock experiments (in which pupae were subjected to environmental shocks at different points in their development), had demonstrated a non-linear entanglement between gene expression and environmental factors.

Tabery makes clear that he thinks the differences between Hogben and Fisher cannot be chalked up to 'mere' political, religious, or class differences (Hogben having been raised poor and as a Quaker, and Fisher having been middle class and within the Church of England), but rather were to do with a very different sense of explanatory frameworks (indexing the concept of 'thought communities' from Fleck, above). These differences concerned how each figure viewed causes and how they understood environment–gene interaction, with Fisher believing statistics could account for causes while, for Hogben, one needed to perform an actual experiment.[18] These differing conceptual stances no doubt in part also reflected their disciplinary backgrounds — Fisher was a mathematician through and through, whereas Hogben knew numerous subdisciplines of the life sciences and was comfortable in the experimental laboratory setting.

---

18   Ibid., pp. 36–37.

The historical consensus is that Hogben lost and that, as a result, Fisher's name was immortalized in the modern synthesis (which used frequentist methods to combine Mendelian genetics and Darwinian evolution). The sympathy towards Fisher, and towards the eugenical thinking that surrounded him, was also consolidated when several UCL buildings were named after Karl Pearson and Francis Galton, upon their founding by the university in the early 1900s. But given Hogben's credentials and breadth of study, one might expect that his approach would have been more relevant to biological practice.

Part of the reason for the longevity of Fisher's contribution is that it marked a shift and a collapse of warring paradigms in post-Darwinian biology. For decades prior to Fisher, there had been a strong sentiment that Darwin's evolutionary theories could not be reconciled with the rediscovery of Mendel's laws of inheritance. Darwin did not have a well-articulated theory of inheritance and, while he rejected any progressive force in the *Origin of the Species*, he was far more sympathetic to proto-social Darwinian notions (especially those of Francis Galton) in *The Descent of Man*. In this regard it is not a stretch to ask how much the modern synthesis was driven by eugenics (which was a global tendency at the end of the nineteenth and beginning of the twentieth century). In part this was due to the fact that there were insufficient tools available for the study of genes (or heritable factors) in the early twentieth century, which is why in statistical analysis genes were conceptual placeholders or heuristics rather than material causes.

But what is also important is that Fisher's approach got around the difficulty of whether the biological sciences could be considered 'properly' experimental sciences, since mathematical models made the question moot (especially as it applied to practices such as animal husbandry or the selective breeding of human beings). It was conceptually and technologically difficult in the late 1800s and early 1900s to understand genes as causes, since they did not seem to be straightforward physical causes and seemed very susceptible to noise, interruption, and mutation. This is why, as Arlin Stoltzfus has brilliantly shown, the debate between the mutationists and the biometricians was not about anti-Darwinian sudden changes within a species versus the more gradualist picture of thinkers like Fisher, but rather to do with the question of how genes cause anything to occur, and the question of how many

types of cause were present in organisms.[19] Fisher's approach, and that
of the biometricians, simplified genes as direct causes without saying
whether genes were in fact theoretical entities or physical ones — they
were just a way of measuring traits, which were themselves supposedly
straightforwardly empirical. But the frequentist mode made it easier
to claim that other traits (such as criminal tendencies, laziness, alco-
holism, pauperism, and so forth) were also just as genetic, and that
by rejecting environmental factors one could direct policy away from
social projects and towards forced sterilization and other forms of negative eugenical control.

Before addressing how statistical concepts lend themselves to
certain politics (however indirectly), there is one more episode of Hogben's life to address, that of his direct activities against the Nazis, as well
as the question of how we should understand the very idea of leftist
science.[20]

ESCAPE FROM OSLO (1940–41)

In April 1940 Lancelot Hogben went to Oslo, Norway, to deliver a
lecture criticizing the then-ascendant racial theories of the Nazi party.
Having picked up his twenty-one-year-old daughter Sylvia from neigh-
bouring Sweden (where she had been working as an au pair for a family
friend), the two set off for the airport in Oslo, only to find it suddenly
secured by Nazi storm troopers. The two hitchhiked to Sweden (back
to where Sylvia had been staying), where they translated numerous
texts to raise some quick cash, before making their journey home the
long way around the planet: to Moscow, via the trans-Siberian railway
to Vladivostok, by boat to Japan, then steamer ship to San Francisco.

This was not an atypical biographical episode for Hogben, for
whom there was no separating the social and political ramifications
of science from scientific practice itself. While this stance was not
unusual among the British scientific left of the time, Hogben's inte-

---

19   Arlin Stoltzfus and Kele Cable, 'Mendelian-Mutationism: The Forgotten Evolutionary
      Synthesis', *Journal of the History of Biology*, 47 (2014), pp. 501–46 <https://doi.org/
      10.1007/s10739-014-9383-2>.

20   It is also important to emphasize that Hogben was not dismissive of statistics in
      general and, interestingly, used German statistics to combat Nazi ideology, especially
      by celebrating the work of Felix Bernstein.

gration of the scientific and the political, especially with regard to his anti-eugenic posture, was far more uncommon. In his collective biography *The Visible College*, Gary Werskey groups Hogben with J. D. Bernal, J. B. S. Haldane, Hyman Levy, and Joseph Needham.[21] These figures form part of a larger and longer tradition of scientists (in particular in the life sciences) that saw themselves not only to the left of the status quo but also often as forging a third organicist path between neo-Darwinian mechanism (which by the 20s and 30s was over-represented by the biometricians) and neo-vitalist opposition (Wilhelm Roux, Hans Driesch).[22]

While J. S. Haldane (J. B. S. Haldane's father), J. H. Woodger, the Needhams, and others can be classified as organicists (who sought to discover biology's conceptual autonomy, often with a Whiteheadian flavour), situated between neo-mechanism and neo-vitalism, Hogben was rather a fairly committed mechanist (as evidenced in his debates and activities, especially while living in South Africa, as discussed above). Yet Hogben's articulation of biological mechanism was resolutely non-teleological and non-metaphysical. An important aspect of the organicists' legacy, as Donna Haraway argues, is not that their work was 'more' metaphysical than these other forms of biology, but rather that they made the metaphysical and/or metaphorical aspects of their work explicit.[23]

While Hogben had Marxist sympathies (or, at least, was sympathetic to the Marxists around him, like Haldane), he self-identified as a socialist and later in life as a scientific humanist — the latter term is perhaps best known through the work of the already mentioned J. D. Bernal. Compared to Haldane and Bernal, Hogben was far more aware of and outspoken about the racial and classist shortcomings of his contemporaries, as well as his political enemies.

---

21 See Gary Werskey, *The Visible College: The Collective Biography of British Scientific Socialists of the 1930s* (Boston: Holt, Rinehart, and Winston, 1979).

22 See Erik L. Peterson, *The Life Organic: The Theoretical Biology Club and the Roots of Epigenetics* (Pittsburgh: University of Pittsburgh Press, 2017) <https://doi.org/10.2307/j.ctt1kc6hv4>.

23 Donna Haraway, *Crystals, Fabrics, and Fields: Metaphors of Organicism in Twentieth-Century Developmental Biology* (London: Yale University Press, 1976), p. 11.

While contemporary social and cultural critics fought (and still fight) eugenics on political, ethical, or religious grounds, Hogben was one of the few biologists (even among left-wing scientific humanists) to decry eugenics as conceptually flawed as well. This in part relates to the fact that biologists at the time who might have had different political allegiances may still have shared a general Promethean attitude, based on a general scientific humanistic optimism (which of course had both capitalist-industrial and Marxist-Promethean versions).

Importantly, part of this critique was not only directed at the statistical details and model constructions of biometricians such as Fisher, Pearson, and Weldon, but in particular at the very idea of 'neutral science'.

Neutral science should be strived for, but far too often it is assumed to be the starting baseline for scientific investigators, something that is only violated in obvious cases of personal bias. This later point is particularly relevant today as leftist politics rejects those that would falsely claim their science to be neutral, yet such rejection from the left too often rejects the very coherence of scientific studies. For instance, it is not at all uncommon to find a generally sceptical attitude towards scientific authority and tacit agreement between groups that would otherwise be politically opposed. Those who discuss biopolitics, for instance, might cite a critique of Darwinism from a scientific creationist despite the conservative politics of the latter. Neutrality requires the collision of political perspectives, not the assumption that science is in and of itself neutral.

At the same time, defenders of an apparently already existing scientific neutrality (such as Dawkins, Dennett, and Tyson) see any opposition to science as ignorant relativism, an unjustified scepticism in the face of glorious truth. Hogben's attitude is to reject both stances in a way that requires being open about one's political commitments while agreeing that scientific research can be a political good: 'Science is the last defence of intellectual freedom in its perennial conflict with arbitrary authority'[24]

---

24   Lancelot Hogben, *Statistical Theory: The Relationship of Probability, Credibility, and Error* (New York: W. W. Norton & Company, 1968), p. 316.

Hogben is caught between being too political in one regard (not being properly neutral, as science nowadays is supposed to be) and not being political enough (because he was not a card-carrying Marxist in the manner of the Needhams, Haldane, or Bernal). In *The Return of Nature*, Foster seems almost disappointed in Hogben and reduces his politics to a kind of naive scientific humanism. But what Hogben represents, most importantly, is an unwillingness either to give over scientific authority to bad political actors, or to acknowledge that science can be carried out in a political vacuum. The difficulty is to make the politics of scientific practice explicit, rather than to automatically assume it to be neutral — scientists should not be socially or political reductive for the sake of short-sighted scientific coherence, that is, science's assumed neutrality.

But even with this degree of awareness of the situatedness of scientific knowledge, and even beyond individual bias or explicit ideological agenda (as in the groupthink of some scientific communities), there still remain the conceptual attachments (or baggage) of different approaches. What Hogben saw clearly was that treating humans as model organisms, but only in a statistical way (humans as statistical models and therefore mathematical members of a population), allowed many to hide and couch their biases as 'empirically obvious' observations about race, class, and sex. These were decided by the arbitrary authority that Hogben lamented, as matters of policy of control rather than as sets of modelling practices based on understanding. It is not that statistical models are inherently politically bankrupt, but that their perceived neutrality is a tempting tool in the justification of political authority.

Importantly, to understand the mid-level of modelling, one has to analyse the conceptual commitments of a science, especially when that science, or set of tools, is imported from one domain to another, as in our case here, with the transposition of statistics into biology.

CLEAN YOUR CONCEPTS

Standard histories of biology often see the 1920s and 1930s as a time of celebration following a long dark night of false alternatives to Darwinism and pre-genetic uncertainty. With the so-called 'modern synthesis' the claim is usually made that Mendelian genetics and Darwinian neo-mechanism established biology as a 'proper' modern science. But the synthesis that was consolidated with the discovery of the structure of DNA did not eliminate underlying tensions that were equal parts political and statistical. Hogben is an interesting case in that he is sympathetic to the neo-mechanist and, hence, biometric methods, but also deeply suspicious of unacknowledged bias and the tendencies towards teleology in the work of figures like Francis Galton, R. A. Fisher, and Karl Pearson. In other words, frequentist statistics can, but need not necessarily, follow from a mechanist understanding of biology, namely, one in which we see empirical changes in organisms and populations and therefore assume that there exist straightforward and predictable causes of those changes.

Hogben writes:

> We do not need biologists to tell us that any subject can be made dull enough to defy the efforts of any but a few exceptionally bright or odd individuals. By exploring individual differences human genetics might help us to find out how to adapt our educational technique to individual needs. It will do so, and gain prestige in consequence, when it ceases to be an apology for snobbery, selfishness, and class arrogance.[25]

Hogben is of course not merely opposing genetics or biology to the ethical and moral concerns of the humanities, but is arguing that those who claim to be conducting neutral science have in fact failed to 'sterilize their own instruments' before violently applying them to the social body. Hogben's book of statistics, quoted above, places statistical methods within a conceptual history, and in some ways surpasses Ian Hacking's Foucauldian genealogical approach in *The Taming of Chance*.[26]

---

25   Lancelot Hogben, *Nature and Nurture* (London: Williams and Norgate, 1933), p. 33.
26   See Ian Hacking, *The Taming of Chance* (Cambridge: Cambridge University Press, 1990) <https://doi.org/10.1017/CBO9780511819766>.

Hogben outlines four modes of statistical thinking which are not always clearly discriminated:

1. Calculus of errors (Gauss, Laplace, Euler)
2. Calculus of aggregates (Maxwell-Boltzmann)
3. Calculus of exploration (Quetelet, Pearson, Fisher)
4. Calculus of judgements (Bayes)

We could otherwise represent these positions in terms of their illustrative figures:

1. The gambler's bet (how can we calculate our ignorance?)
2. The physicist's gas cloud (how can we map the movement of ideal particles?)
3. The politician's chart (how can we determine frequencies of behaviour?)
4. The citizen's judgement (how and when should our knowledge be changed by evidence?)

It is in this contested deployment of statistical attitudes that Hogben's work is particularly interesting, insofar as it points out what is veiled via mathematical-philosophical dressing. Hogben accuses Fisher and the other biometricians of uncritically searching for frequencies by using an idealized infinite population with specifiable distribution but without any a priori agreement about a necessary sample size.[27] It should start to become clear how this is not only a dispute between choices of method but also between levels of investment in the readability and changeability of the structure of the living world.

This double layer of formalizing effectively hides the fact that Fisher's frequentism is coloured and classed. Seeing such bias is made even harder by the fact that the frequentist interpretation of statistics claims to be an extension of the aggregate form. The statistician and ur-biometrician Quetelet claimed that he could create a 'social physics' in which the tools of celestial mechanics could be transplanted onto the

---

27   Hogben, *Statistical Theory*, p. 332.

social body. This became mathematically feasible in Quetelet's time as a result of the availability of demographic and statistical data on large populations of people (and was even further accelerated later on through the availability of military enlistment data), combined with a confidence in the existence of metaphysically immutable natural laws. This idea that total population could be treated as a generalized material quantity contributed to how deeply buried the biases of the frequentist position were, in a way that paralleled the unavowed teleology of the neo-mechanist position that was accelerated in the work of Galton, Fisher, and Pearson. Mechanism is not necessarily teleological, but when it emphasizes functions — defining things by what they do, not what they are — it is tempting to enlarge this definition to larger and larger scales, with function becoming the seed for purpose.

It is important to avoid the too-easy assertion that mechanism is therefore inherently wrong or that statistical measurement is either malicious or useless. The issue is about the role of revisability vis-à-vis the initial motivating concepts for constructing a model in the attempt to solve a problem. This, in turn, affects how one situates the concepts around the problem.

As James Tabery has argued, for instance, both Fisher and Hogben were interested in how variance in a population was related to the interaction between genes and environment, though their emphases were diametrically opposed.[28] While Fisher famously synthesized Mendelian and biometric approaches, this largely excluded the environment as the cause of variance and incorporated the causal power of genes combining in a way that explained digressions from averages. For Hogben, development was the site in which one could measure and articulate the complex interaction between genetics and environment, emphasizing this as a temporal rather than a static model.

But this is not to say that Hogben was against the very idea of biology improving human life, in the sense of attempting to direct future human reproduction, or to improve collective life via biology. For a time, Hogben directed a programme of social biology and worked

---

28   James Tabery, 'R. A. Fisher, Lancelot Hogben, and the Origin(s) of Genotype-Environment Interaction', *Journal of the History of Biology*, 41.4 (2008), pp. 717–61 (p. 104) <https://doi.org/10.1007/s10739-008-9155-y>.

to create what he saw as a left-leaning form of eugenics to combat the prevailing conservatism of the time. It is not so surprising that it is difficult to separate a more leftist politics from a model that is more revisable, whereas Fisher's approach tended to minimize outliers that would require reassessment of the effects of environmental factors (and that would thereby challenge the unacknowledged externality of terms like *prominence* or *well-bred* as clunky, classist biology).

But this does not guarantee a happy correlation between scientific concept and political aspiration. Most of Hogben's Marxist colleagues or otherwise left-leaning scientists in the first half of the twentieth century were happy with classist and racist forms of eugenics. While the Prometheanism of Haldane and Bernal makes for more pyrotechnic reading than much of Hogben's work, it also remains uncritical of its racist and classist assumptions, covering them in a science-fictional aesthetic of rocketing into a post-scarcity future. When Hogben worked with the experimental biology group in London, he was the only member to criticize the then-standard support for eugenics.

CONCLUSION

Why interlace Hogben's biography with his battles against eugenics and the broader abuse of statistics and biological concepts? Hogben was, as I hope to have shown, a canary in the coal mine for the threat of racist science. In his early days, Hogben combatted eugenics in philosophical-theoretical terms, then at the level of statistical skewing, and then in direct actions against the rise of fascism and its theories. Unlike many of his international colleagues, Hogben experienced war, apartheid, and the guns of Nazi storm troopers, as well as their academic apologists both during and after their reign.

While Hogben was not a repressed minority, he was right on the edge of the genetic thought collective of the twentieth century in a way that few other scientists were. What is also rare, and an important lesson for the present, is that Hogben understood the mathematical and scientific details of the work he critiqued, which is something too-often lacking in debates around the politics of biology, especially amid the return of eugenics in our current moment. In addition, rather than putting forward a Marxist science, like his companions Haldane and Julian S. Huxley, Hogben saw that science done well was already Marxist: it was a public-facing collective enterprise if it was to be considered science at all. This view is also sorely lacking in a world where the purported neutrality of science is taken as a given rather than as an ideal to be constantly pursued.[29]

---

29   On the promise of value-neutral science, see Liam Kofi Bright, 'Du Bois' Democratic Defence of the Value Free Ideal', *Synthese*, 195.5 (2018), pp. 2227–45 <https://doi. org/10.1007/s11229-017-1333-z>.

Where do numbers stand in our scientific and political imaginary?
What part do numbers play in how we explain biological and social
processes? And why does this matter?

Numbers have often been associated with the modern obsession
of counting objects, be they taxpayers, commodities, or pathogenic
agents. Starting in the nineteenth century, numbers have been inserted
into increasingly complex statistical models to predict behaviour and
to help bureaucrats, scientists, and business consultants engage in a
seemingly endless effort for 'the taming of chance'.[30] Scholars have
long addressed statistics' power to support modernity's march towards
'universal' classifications, and its propensity to erase some differences
while creating others. The gaze of the modern state and its instrumental
interventions in reality required legibility structures and a politics of
measurement centred around the simplification, quantification, and
standardization of knowledge. This led in turn to an increased blind-
ness to *metis* — any form of situated, practical, experiential, and im-
provisational kind of knowledge — both in politics and in science.[31]
Essential for the toolbox of those promoting 'the sweet despotism
of reason',[32] statistical analysis has been critically associated with the
violence of averaging, eliminating outliers, or clustering, which often
produce analyses with highly classed, gendered, and racialized under-
tones.

However, some scientists have assumed explicitly philosophical
and political stances, from which they have questioned the tendency
to consider statistical patterns as explanatory in themselves, where the
modelling of populations is concerned. As Ben Woodard shows in his
chapter, this was the case for Lancelot Hogben, in his strong stance
against R. A. Fisher, the most important proponent of mathematical
theories of population, a foundational figure of the biometric school

---

30   Ian Hacking, *The Taming of Chance* (Cambridge: Cambridge University Press, 1990)
      <https://doi.org/10.1017/CBO9780511819766>.

31   James C. Scott, *Seeing Like a State: How Certain Schemes to Improve the Human
      Condition Have Failed* (New Haven, CT: Yale University Press, 1999).

32   Hacking, *The Taming of Chance.*

of genetics, and a champion of theoretical claims concerning the supposed variability between 'races'. Lancelot Hogben rooted his anti-eugenicist stance in specific epistemological critiques of the apparent moral and political neutrality of statistical models. He focused instead on working with model organisms as foundational for understanding the complex mechanisms behind this variability, mechanisms that in most cases depended on specific environmental and developmental factors. It is not that Hogben rejected the use of statistics; rather, he just used them for different purposes, and assigned them a different role and status in the research process. While Fisher postulated causal relationships simply by observing statistical patterns, Hogben used statistics as a starting point in a complex search for an explanation as to how and why things look a certain way. Both were trying to explain variation within and between populations, but they exhibited radically different models of what an explanation is, how causal relationships can be uncovered, and, simply put, what numbers can and cannot tell us.

Hogben's efforts strangely resonate with the critical view of statistics on the Eastern side of the Iron Curtain, where politicians and technocrats considered commensuration and quantification as fully fledged political activities, and saw any number attached to planning as the crystallization of long-term social processes and relations.[33] Centrally planned economies functioned according to what these political actors understood as 'class statistics', born in explicit opposition to 'bourgeois statistics', whose power to denature reality and hide the contradictions and historically contingent nature of capitalism was denounced at every step.[34] Hiding wide variation behind averages, forming politically problematic categories for categorical variables, interpreting statistical regularities as historical trends — all were exposed as oppressive or, at least, ignorant scientific practices, widely used in capitalist societies but widely relegated to pre-socialist history in Eastern and Central Europe. Concrete examples were used in statistical

---

33   Martha Lampland, *The Value of Labor: The Science of Commodification in Hungary, 1920–1956* (Chicago: University of Chicago Press, 2016) <https://doi.org/10.7208/chicago/9780226314747.001.0001>.

34   Alina-Sandra Cucu, *Planning Labour: Time and the Foundations of Industrial Socialism in Romania* (Oxford and New York: Berghahn Books, 2019).

and economic journals to illuminate this mistaken instrumentalization of numbers: statistics for the average monthly consumption of sugar in interwar Romania obscured the fact that wealthy factory owners consumed nine kilos of sugar per month, while workers consumed one; calculating infant mortality separately for children born out of wedlock concealed the impact of class inequality on early-life survival chances; while to claim a decrease in the number of workers participating in strikes in a given year as an indicator of decreased union activity was to fail to account for the long-term strike of railway workers.

As we learn from Ben's chapter, Hogben's critique went a step further than the realization that statistical interpretation is political, the basic level at which the Soviet and East-Central European statisticians' critique stopped. For Hogben, scientific practices could allow or foreclose specific lines of thought not only through the aggregation, analysis, interpretation, and communication of data, but from the moment that a research object is constructed. For a scientist, being political thus starts with the type of questions one asks and continues with how one answers them. While critiques of standardization and quantification have been abundant, Hogben's case is unique because of his holistic vision of the scientific endeavour, and because his holism required a constant reflexivity about the wider societal implications of choosing one scientific practice over another.

Crises in Modelling
Articulations of the Romanian Labour Market in the Long 1990s
ALINA-SANDRA CUCU

INTRODUCTION

Needless to say, one hardly expects the technical documents of international organizations to be written in a confessional voice. But this
was exactly the writing style adopted by Cătălin Zamfir, a Romanian
technocrat and well-known social scientist, in the preface of a working
paper requested in 1992 by the International Labour Organization.
Zamfir introduced himself as 'the man who had the unenviable task
of being Minister of Labour in the first post-revolution government', a
government 'elected in May 1990 with a promise to prevent unemployment and protect workers' living standards'.[1] According to him, this
government had the historical responsibility to steer 'a course away
from the highly centralised and bureaucratic labour system prevailing
in the latter years of the Ceaușescu regime, towards one based on social
consensus, collective bargaining and a social sharing of the costs of the
transition towards a regulated market economy'.[2] After complaining

---

1   Cătălin Zamfir, *The Romanian Wage System in the Transition to a Market Economy*,
    working paper 54 (Geneva: International Labour Organization, 1992).
2   Ibid.

about the 'lack of trust' and 'the psychological distress' that marked labour relations in Romania in the early 1990s,[3] Zamfir concluded by admitting that '[g]iven the social tensions and political situation, [preventing unemployment and ensuring workers' well-being] was almost certainly an impossible task to achieve.'[4]

A few years later, Emilian Dobrescu, a Romanian economist whose career has spanned more than six decades and involved a number of political roles, was complaining about his own historical responsibility, which was to build econometric models of the transition. Talking specifically about models of the labour market, he lamented that, in the worst-case scenario, his task was impossible and in the best-case scenario rather useless, since models are meaningful only when 'a given economy does not register major disequilibria and develops in a predictable manner.'[5] According to Dobrescu, the Romanian economy in the 1990s was a far cry from this description: market mechanisms were not yet functional; the culture of informality dominated ordinary economic life; the state maintained a high allocative power; and a deep fracture between the real and nominal sectors of the economy persisted.[6] Adding to these structural problems, the incompatibility between the indicators used to measure employment and productivity in late socialism and the ones imposed by the World Bank and the International Monetary Fund immediately after 1989 set further limitations for any effort to construct long-term econometric series.

Dobrescu pointed out that economists at the time knew little to nothing about 'the microeconomic foundations of the transition'; they simply lacked 'the necessary assumptions for building up econometric functions.'[7] Macroeconomic models could hardly say anything in a

---

3   By the time the working paper was published, Zamfir had resigned his position, less than a year after he was appointed, citing the same reason of not being able to protect the well-being of the workers during the transition to a market economy.

4   Zamfir, *Romanian Wage System*.

5   Emilian Dobrescu, 'Double Conditioned Potential Output', paper delivered at the 28th General Conference of the International Association for Research in Income and Wealth (Cork, Ireland, 22–28 August 2004) <https://doi.org/10.2139/ssrn.1434909>.

6   The real/nominal distinction refers here to two aspects of measuring the economy: real production vs monetary expressions, and inflation adjusted vs non-adjusted monetary gains.

7   Dobrescu, 'Double Conditioned Potential Output'.

context dominated by high levels of uncertainty resulting from 'the behavioural instability of economic agents'.[8] The *Homo economicus* of the transition was hardly knowable, and most likely different from both the worker on which the numbers of the socialist plan had been configured, and from the agent of neoclassical economics presupposed by the World Bank advisors. The agents that the newly imported labour market models referred to were thus placed in a conceptual space between 'not-yet-gone' and 'not-yet-arrived'.

This chapter investigates what happens when the agent's behaviour that normally underpins a family of models — in this case, models of the labour market — cannot be theorized. I argue that, in their everyday professional practice, the reference point of Romanian economists in the 1990s was not the self-interested, fully informed agent of neoclassical economics, an abstract figure populating 'the world in the model'[9] with his[10] 'infinite ability to make rational decisions' for maximizing utility and profit.[11] They also did not necessarily see the economic agent as the embodiment of humanity's state of nature, a lost state of grace perverted by political intervention. The Romanian economists seemed to understand *Homo economicus*, the man in the models they operated with, as a real historical figure, one that emerges only in relation to a fully functional market. And fully functional markets need to be made.

I focus here on how, in the 1990s, markets — more specifically, labour markets — were made to fit the economic models that were supposed to describe them. I will show that, despite being rather useless for

---

8   Ibid.

9   Mary S. Morgan, *The World in the Model: How Economists Work and Think* (Cambridge: Cambridge University Press, 2012) <https://doi.org/10.1017/CBO9781139026185>.

10 I use the masculine pronoun for the economic agent here for two reasons. First, because until recently and with the emergence of feminist economics, the language of economics has not been gender-neutral and the economic agent was presupposed to be male. Second, economics builds on the assumption of methodological individualism. In the Romanian 1990s, economists used masculine pronouns and the singular form. This is exactly how postsocialist economists talked about economic agents: using singular masculine pronouns (and nouns, which are also gendered in the Romanian language).

11 James Chen, 'What Is Homo Economicus? Definition, Meaning, and Origins', Investopedia, 31 July 2021 <https://www.investopedia.com/terms/h/homoeconomicus.asp> [accessed 15 June 2024].

illustrating what was happening during the transition from a centrally planned economy to a market economy, labour market models were instrumental in bringing about the reality they were supposed to depict. In this sense, they worked performatively, as promissory utterances.

By constructing models of the labour market in the 1990s, the Romanian economists had two explicit aims: to assess the effectiveness of job allocation mechanisms and to predict the evolution of unemployment. Both issues were central to the debates concerning the privatization programmes in postsocialist Eastern and Central Europe. These programmes brought about massive deindustrialization and the rapid crumbling of the centrally planned system of manpower allocation, which had for decades matched people, skills, and jobs according to the 'needs of the socialist economy'. During the transition, economists suddenly faced the challenge to model social phenomena that did not meet the most basic assumptions of the models themselves. Workers faced, in no ambiguous terms, a loss of future — one that produced not only existential fragility but also moral panic. Although bearers of different interests, aims, and world visions, workers and economists struggled to make sense of an omnipresent term — *the market*, a concept international advisors and investors seemed to have no problem with. In this chapter, I will sketch some preliminary thoughts as to how our understanding of the post-1989 economic transition in Eastern and Central Europe changes, if one takes seriously the fact that, at the time, the market was a rather puzzling idea for the social actors.

What follows goes against a large part of the scholarship on the region, which, for more than thirty years now, has exhibited the tendency to reify 'the plan' as the thing the region transitioned from and 'the market' as the thing it transitioned to. I follow up here on my long-term work on central planning, which has questioned the persistence of political and scholarly imaginaries that understand labour relations in state socialism through the absence of markets, and through a model of supply and demand for manpower that assumes that its reproduction was ever fully regulated. I have opposed this dominant perspective on two grounds. First, while discursively prominent, when analysed on the ground, neither perfect regulation nor the complete excision of market mechanisms were actual features of state socialism. Second, and most important, both regulatory and market mechanisms were simply serving the broader aims of state socialist economies as accumulation regimes, in ways that uncomfortably resemble the everyday reality of capitalist societies.[12] But the 'market' that the workers and the economists became acquainted with in the 1990s was of a different order, not only because it was supposed to reign supreme, but also because it had alarming consequences for people's everyday lives.

In questioning the dominant framework of the analyses of state socialist regimes, I have relied on a performativity of economics perspective, which I also adopt here to discuss the relationship between econometric models and the making of a labour market in postsocialist Romania. In the simplest terms, performativity of economics approaches theories and models in the field as discourses with the power to shape economic reality, basically by telling other actors what markets do, by prescribing what they should do, and by predicting what they will do.[13] The economic world ends up resembling the theory or the model not because of the quality of the model but because the economic discourse has previously influenced reality in specific ways. For instance, in order for a specific commodity market to emerge, concrete goods must appear first as commodities, that is, to be produced in order to be exchanged for a monetarized profit. This requires legal intervention, social acceptance, and a medium of exchange (like money).

The idea (along with its fierce critiques) that in capitalism economists 'make markets' rather than simply analyse them has given a fresh impetus to the social sciences and the history of economics in the last two decades.[14] However, the discourse on the performativity of

12   Alina-Sandra Cucu, *Planning Labour: Time and the Foundations of Industrial Socialism in Romania* (Oxford and New York: Berghahn Books, 2019).

13   See Michel Callon, 'Introduction', in Callon, *The Laws of the Markets* (London: Blackwell, 1998).

14   See Timothy Mitchell, *Rule of Experts: Egypt, Techno-Politics, Modernity* (Berkeley, CA: University of California Press, 2002) <https://doi.org/10.1525/9780520928251>; Marion Fourcade, *Economists and Societies: Discipline and Profession in the United States, Britain, and France, 1890s to 1990s* (Princeton, NJ: Princeton University Press, 2010) <https://doi.org/10.1515/9781400833139>; John L. Campbell and Ove K. Pederson, 'Knowledge Regimes and Comparative Political Economy', in *Ideas and Politics in Social Science Research*, ed. by Daniel Béland and Robert Henry Cox (Oxford: Oxford University Press, 2010) <https://doi.org/10.1093/acprof:oso/9780199736430.003.0009>; and Franck Cochoy, Martin Giraudeau, and Liz McFall, 'Performativity, Economics, and Politics: An Overview', *Journal of Cultural Economy*, 3.2 (2010) <https://doi.org/10.1080/17530350.2010.494116>.

economics has never been seriously brought to bear on what happened on the other side of the Iron Curtain, either by the actors themselves, or by scholars of state socialism. The straightforward, linear, unidirectional functioning of economics as a prop for the political aims of the communist rulers continues to be taken for granted in most academic fields, and continues to shape our thinking about five decades of regional and global history. There is no mystery in the fact that the plan was explicitly performative — both in the broader sense of a discursive field intentionally producing societal effects, and in the more restricted sense of bringing together elements of specific economic models through various practices and relations and making them work in practice. However, the performativity of socialist economics was neither as straightforward nor as top-down as the literature on centrally planned economies usually assumes. As socialist planners were painfully aware, it was something that remained to be struggled for and achieved, always elusive, and often contested.[15]

But it is the economic transition of the 1990s that offers one of the most striking examples of the performativity of markets. As I have already mentioned, the idea that in capitalism economists 'make markets' has been a fertile one. It can be summarized as follows: economists, rather than objectively depicting or measuring a particular aspect of reality, help shape that aspect of reality to resemble the model they propose. Economists help to make markets, rather than analyse them, because the assumptions of their models become hegemonic, and end up functioning as guides for action. The economic transition of the 1990s opens a strategic research site to explore how this happens in practice. However, what I will show is that it is not only economists who make markets. Union leaders, international organizations, and citizens, trying to make sense of their own historical encounter with unemployment, make markets, too. Various actors have to participate in materializing the most basic models of the labour market. This is something the performativity of economics thesis should not ignore, and is why I here adopt Georg Lukács's historical materialist assumption that '*all economic or "sociological" phenomena derive from the social*

---

15   Cucu, *Planning Labour.*

relations of men to one another.[16] Formulaic images of the world, like models of the labour market, are thus always an intrinsic part of the world they describe. It is a world whose laws are subject to change, and whose knowledge regimes are rooted in praxis. The procedures and institutions that can sustain the reiterations, sedimentations, and variations that performativity requires[17] belong to the same historical experience that models attempt to objectify.

Bearing in mind this historical materialist correction to the performativity thesis, I will raise two questions about the 1990s economic transition in Romania. How did something called 'the Romanian labour market' come into being, precisely when socialist industry was disintegrating and little else seemed to be taking its place? And what challenges did economists face when trying to construct models that had to look as if they were describing actually existing social relations, and as if they were referring to a real thing?

In the following section of this chapter, I return to Emilian Dobrescu to understand how the material conditions in which the postsocialist labour market was articulated set limits to the performative capability of economic discourse. In the subsequent section, I re-examine the classical elements that had to be set in place in order for the economic models of the Romanian labour market to have a referent in reality: private ownership of the means of production; the theoretical and legal possibility of unemployment; and tripartite labour relations. I conclude by gesturing towards the sources of economic models' generative dimension.

THE ECONOMISTS' TROUBLES WITH THE LABOUR MARKET

The Romanian 1990s were a historical moment at which the use of models was proliferating in policy circles. In Dobrescu's words:

> It seems strange to notice how the turbulent state of the economy, though creating serious limitations for the cognitive capacity of mathematical models, increases the need of the deci-

---

16   Georg Lukács, 'Technology and Social Relations', *New Left Review*, 39 (1966), pp. 27–34 (p. 29), emphasis in the original.

17   Judith Butler, 'Performative Agency', *Journal of Cultural Economy*, 3.2 (2010), pp. 147–61 (p. 147) <https://doi.org/10.1080/17530350.2010.494117>.

sion makers and of a large part of public opinion for prospective works — programs, strategies, forecasts — which utilize such instruments. It is probably a reaction against the psychological stress of uncertainty.[18]

He called this a 'paradox' of the transition. The paradox was translated into methodological anxieties and doubts related to three issues: models' capacity to accurately capture aspects of reality during the postsocialist transition; the appropriateness of 'Western econometrics' as a theoretical foundation for understanding the economic transformations of the 1990s; and the possibility of proposing a theoretical framework that would be rooted exactly in the social world and in the historical time it belonged to.

Educated as part of the late socialist technocratic elite, and specializing in growth models and the mechanisms of accumulation of planned economies, Dobrescu made his own transition in the 1990s, becoming a trainee at the Hoover Institute and the World Bank, tasked with modelling the most important macroeconomic phenomena in the Romanian economy. Among the available models were standard employment models that defined rather than described actually existing labour markets: the Beveridge curve, the Phillips curve, and the natural rate of unemployment. The Beveridge curve shows that, at any given moment, there are both jobs available and people unemployed, while the shape and the position of the curve provide important information about the functioning of the labour market.[19] The Phillips curve addresses the stable and inverse relationship between inflation and unemployment;[20] and the natural unemployment rate is the lowest level of unemployment that can be sustained by an economy without creating inflation.[21]

---

18   Emilian Dobrescu, 'Unstable Processes and Macroeconomic Modelling', *Romanian Economic Review*, 41.1 (1996a), pp. 17–34 (p. 27).

19   There are two key concepts associated with the Beveridge curve: labour market tightness and matching efficiency. Labour market tightness is the number of vacant posts per each unemployed person and matching efficiency reflects the market's ability to match individuals to jobs. See Agostino Consolo and António Dias da Silva, 'The Euro Area Labour Market through the Lens of the Beveridge Curve', *ECB Economic Bulletin*, 4 (2019) <https://www.ecb.europa.eu/pub/economic-bulletin/articles/2019/html/ecb.ebart201904_01~9070de27a0.en.html> [accessed 12 June 2023].

20   Higher inflation is associated with lower unemployment and vice versa.

21   The natural rate of unemployment condenses three types of unemployment: frictional unemployment, when people are between jobs; structural unemployment, when there

The first question that the Romanian economists struggled with concerned the power of models to capture aspects of an extremely fluid socio-economic reality. When asked to produce deterministic, predictive macroeconomic models, Dobrescu complained that in such an unstable environment, econometric functions did not 'satisfy the statistic tests for parametric constancy'.[22] This 'intrinsic instability' also meant that 'the evolution of some indicators [wa]s marked by spectacular breaks, new connections appear[ed] between the real and nominal economies, [and] a new network of economic agents emerge[d], having atypical, even unpredictable, behaviours'.[23] It also meant that, for a brief moment, the past was winning the battle, and 'the pressure of highly inertial components of the economy prevailed upon that of highly dynamic components'.[24]

Economic agents, including households, were considered to be 'the least stable in comparison with other determinations of the economy'.[25] Fluctuations in agents' behaviours were frequent, large, and erratic during the 1990s. Such fluctuations were actually higher in postsocialist Romania than any established theoretical frame would have allowed, and some economists envisioned the possibility that the sum of individual erratic behaviours would simply result in chaos. In addition, access to information was scarce and highly asymmetrical, making it difficult even for market radicals to speak about 'rational expectations'. Hence, labour productivity, gross added value in industry, gross added value in construction and services, share of active population in the total population, and share of labour revenues in the total

---

is a mismatch between skills and job characteristics, or when labour-replacing technologies take over in a certain economic sector; and surplus unemployment, when state interventions like minimum wage legislation or price control make some categories of workers too expensive to be employed. The natural rate of unemployment is the unemployment rate that is consistent with price stability — defined as two per cent inflation in the US, for instance — and the economy growing at full capacity. In contrast to the actual unemployment rate, the natural rate of unemployment cannot be observed directly, but is instead estimated using macroeconomic models.

22   Namely, recursive least squares coefficients, one-step residuals, and recursive Chow tests. Emilian Dobrescu, 'Unstable Processes and Macroeconomic Modelling', in *Macroeconomic Modelling*, ed. by Emilian Dobrescu (Bucharest: Centre for Economic Information and Documentation, 1996b), pp. 3–4, 1–40, 3.

23   Ibid., p. 6.

24   Ibid.

25   Ibid., p. 14.

gross added value (which is sometimes a good measure of exploitation) were among the indicators deemed problematic for building econometric models of the transition.

The second problem raised by the economists of transition was the appropriateness of 'Western econometrics' as a theoretical foundation for understanding the economic transformations of the 1990s. Although Dobrescu's voice was more marginal when he critiqued the tendency of Western econometrics to become increasingly atheoretical and removed from the contexts in which its predictions were formulated, he was not alone among Romanian economists in expressing his doubts that a theory existed that would work for the transition from socialism to capitalism. Synthesizing these positions, Dobrescu stated:

> A first cause of such a situation could be the absence of a suitable theory that would permit the correct definition of the really determining factors of a macroeconomic correlation, the direction and intensity of their influence. The intuition and the flair of the researcher alone are not enough because of a major risk: the most consistent functional relations can be overlooked (no matter how large the number of trials is). Regarding the mechanism of the transition economy, we do not have up to now, unfortunately, either assumptions, perfectly compatible with the theories generally accepted by the scientific community, or a coherent and secure set of hypotheses, corroborated with the present experience. This is the explanation for the ideatic eclecticism which characterizes most of the papers dedicated to the transition.[26]

Crucially, Dobrescu led a disciplinary wave that proposed a theoretical framework rooted in the turbulent social world of the 1990s. The assumptions of this theoretical framework were very different from the neoclassical ones. The economy of the transition was defined by the following parameters: institutionally, it was a weakly structured system, with a mix of old and new rules,[27] a strong informal dimension, discretionary political authority, and no clearly defined property rights

---

26   Ibid., p. 21.
27   Factories, for instance, still had production targets based on the last five-year plan of the socialist period, but in many cases, demand had started to become 'liberalized', so many industrial units found it impossible to sell their commodities.

(which, as we will see, led to the historical oddity of unions fighting for capital formation). It was a framework that gave no clear solutions for measuring and predicting phenomena like unemployment, job creation, or job matching, making all three models that the international organizations wanted to immediately implement in Romania — the Beveridge curve, the Phillips curve, and the natural unemployment rate — basically useless. The modelling problems were, in the economists' words, 'very complicated'.

Dobrescu advised his fellow economists that the only 'reasonable objective for such a fluid operational context' was to limit themselves to short-term prediction and to use weaker criteria for their models, though he considered even these weak criteria difficult to specify.[28] Pursuing these objectives was, indeed, likely the most reasonable thing to do. It was, however, not a widely accepted turn in the field of transition economics.

With imploding theoretical foundations and microeconomic assumptions, the Romanian economists obviously struggled to construct models that had to look as if they were describing actually existing social relations, and as if they were referring to a real thing. Dobrescu's line of thinking recognized the impossibility of theorizing a subject of the econometric models of transition when everything was in flux. The reason was that the economic subject made sense only in relation to a predictable reality: the free market. Owing his position to his doubly technocratic education, Dobrescu militated for a knowledge regime that was rooted in praxis, and seemed aware of the fact that economic models are or should be integral parts of the reality they promise to represent, and that the epistemological limits of their claims to representation have to be specified. While never following the implications of his thinking to their logical consequences, Dobrescu wrote with a clarity given by the material conditions he was caught in, conditions that allowed him to see that, far from being a natural order of things, the market was a historically contingent arrangement, which had to be institutionally created in order to exist at all.

The following section focuses on how something called the *Romanian labour market* materialized in the 1990s, at a moment when

---

28   Dobrescu, 'Unstable Processes and Macroeconomic Modelling' (1996b).

socialist industry was collapsing, the future was meagre, and the state continued to have high stakes in the ownership of the factories. I trace the results of various actors' efforts to set in place the elements needed for its existence: private ownership of the means of production; the theoretical and legal possibility of unemployment; and the emergence of a framework for the relationship between labour, capital, and the state (henceforth *tripartite labour relations*). Many of these efforts were intentional. They provided the necessary fuel for the reiterations, sedimentations, and variations that allowed the economic models I have addressed so far to work performatively. What follows will allow the reader to understand how bringing a certain type of economy into being works concretely, and how this materialization requires that the relevant social actors perform specific actions, which economic models assume. I will also show that in order for economic models to have a referent in reality, new models of social relations also have to emerge and become institutionalized.

UNEMPLOYMENT AND THE MAKING OF TRIPARTITE LABOUR RELATIONS

While Emilian Dobrescu was complaining about the fact that the labour market had little influence on the postsocialist reality, international organizations, newly founded trade unions, and state institutions were negotiating the emergence of the tripartite institutional framework for labour relations. The tripartite model was never questioned or challenged by the relevant Romanian social actors, and was considered the only path towards a functional labour market. It emerged as a dominant belief at the time, a dogmatic understanding of the new political economy of transition, in which there was only one way in which labour relations could be organized. This model had to be taught from abroad, and had to break completely with anything that workers had learned through experience during the socialist period and after.

The idea that tripartism was the only conceivable way to organize labour relations in postsocialist Romania was not relegated to institutions like the International Labour Organization or the World Bank. It was also a core element of the nascent postsocialist trade unionism.

The uncritical acceptance of the tripartite model led to a historically unique pressure for privatization and for the creation of a class of employers coming from the trade unions themselves. Blaming every possible ill in the factories on the absence of private investors and owners, the unions never considered any political alternative in which the state would continue being their employer for the long run (not that such an alternative was tenable for political parties either).

Experts from the main international organizations — the International Monetary Fund and the World Bank — considered that the pace of Romanian privatization was too slow, calculating at one point that there was a ten-year delay between Romania and other countries in the region where the transition to market economies was concerned. The slow pace of privatization meant that the Romanian state still held ownership of the largest industrial units in the country, being thus trapped in the contradictory position it had inherited from late socialism — as capital, employer, and manager. Since, during the 1990s, the Romanian state was failing in all its capacities, organized labour could fight against all its capacities, with all the new legal and political instruments at its disposal. The unions' structure, repertoires of contention, and styles of action reflected the fact that, for almost a decade after the 1989 Revolution, they negotiated almost exclusively with the Romanian state. It is not a coincidence that the power of the union leaders started to erode after 1997, when the privatization process was, to a certain extent, decentralized, and many attributions of the State Property Fund were transferred to regional authorities. The Romanian trade unions were thus practically born with the belief that the unions-government-employers triad was the natural state of affairs, and that no real negotiations for wages, working conditions, or unemployment protection could take place until the three pillars were in place. Among these topics of negotiation, unemployment represented a new threat, one that broke the relationship between the possibility of stable employment and people's life courses that had characterized state socialist economies.

While the issue of supply and demand for manpower was also fundamental for socialist planners, it was only when unemployment became a legal and theoretical possibility that something that could be recognized as a labour market could emerge. The Romanian author-

ities began to register unemployment only in 1991. The beginning of
the registration process was followed in 1994 by the first employment
survey conducted according to International Labour Organization
standards. Registered unemployment rose continuously until 1999,
and has been constantly underestimated because of the high level
of temporary and seasonal migration to Western Europe, as well as
because of the large number of people working in the informal economy. Under the guidance and supervision of the International Labour
Organization, the World Bank, and the Organisation for Economic Cooperation and Development, the government created the institutional
infrastructure that would deal with unemployment: labour offices,[29]
and several institutions charged with organizing training programmes
for those affected by collective dismissals.[30]

The chaotic processes of the 1990s act as a magnifying glass for
an understanding of the relationship between models of the labour
market and the reality they try to represent. It is hard to say, however,
how models like the Beveridge curve, which is supposed to describe
the efficacy of job allocation mechanisms, could represent anything
in postsocialist Romania, a context where the institutions tasked to
collect data about unemployment were still to be created. It is hard to
understand how the Phillips curve could show an inverse and stable
relationship between inflation and unemployment, when inflation was
rocketing but workers were still employed in state factories, and their
incomes were indexed at a fixed rate. At the most fundamental level,
these models are supposed to have a referent in reality, an already-
existing, out-there, stable-enough labour market. These models come
with their own stories; they are, as Mary Morgan would claim, narrative
in nature. They certainly come with their own characters: job offerers
and job seekers, which are supposed to abide by rationality norms in
which prices are paramount. It is only under these conditions that talk
of the neoclassical *Homo economicus* even begins to make sense at all.

---

29   Of course, employment offices were not invented in the 1990s. Under state socialism,
      every enterprise and every cooperative centre had its own labour office.

30   Especially under the aegis of IROMA — the Romanian Management Institute. See
      ILO RL 52-3-01, Rapport de mission de Sergio Ricca en Roumanie (12–19 April
      1991), p. 4.

MODELS AND SOURCES OF PERFORMATIVE WORK

The tendency to reify 'the plan' as the thing Eastern and Central European countries transitioned from, and 'the market' as the thing they transitioned to, has been a common feature of scholarship on the region. First, because the lack of temporal (as well as ideological) distance made it difficult to analyse the postsocialist 1990s as a moment that belonged to a centuries-long regional trajectory of class formation, on the one hand, and to far broader global transformations, on the other. And second, because social scientists have rarely if ever looked critically at the economics of transition, a field whose methodological puzzles at the time could teach us something about how problematic the fundamental terms taken for granted in our scholarly conversations actually were.

To the extent that they described the labour market as it was supposed to be, the models that circulated in policy circles in the 1990s could be considered as promises, and functioned as particular cases of what John L. Austin calls 'performative utterances'.[31] Eve Kosofsky Sedgwick further specifies the nature of promises as 'explicit performative utterances', which reveal the 'directly *productive* aspect of language' even in cases 'when the utterances in question are closest to claiming a simply descriptive relation to some freestanding, ostensibly extradiscursive reality'.[32] As classical speech act theory has taught generations of scholars, in order to make things happen, utterances have to meet certain felicity conditions. I suggest that felicity conditions are predicated on broader historical conditions of possibility, which allow some economic 'models of' to become 'models for', or, to use Mary Morgan's terms, to make the transition from 'the world in the model' to 'the model in the world'.[33]

---

31   John L. Austin, 'Performative Utterances', in Austin, *Philosophical Papers*, ed. by J. O. Urmson and G. J. Warnock (Oxford: Clarendon Press, 1961), pp. 233–52 <https://doi.org/10.1093/019283021X.003.0010>; *How to Do Things with Words* [1962] (Oxford: Oxford University Press, 1976) <https://doi.org/10.1093/acprof:oso/9780198245537.001.0001>.

32   Eve Kosofsky Sedgwick, *Touching Feeling* (Durham, NC: Duke University Press, 2003), pp. 4–5; emphasis in the original <https://doi.org/10.1215/9780822384786>.

33   Morgan, *The World in the Model*, pp. 378–412.

The Romanian 1990s provides a striking case for testing the idea
that 'economics does not describe an existing external "economy", but
brings that economy into being: economics performs the economy,
creating the phenomena it describes'.[34] But this chapter has also shown
something else: that in order for this economic reality to materialize,
other actors need to perform the required gestures. In this case, quite
surprisingly, alongside international organizations and state institutions, trade unions were powerful actors working for the actualization
of the conditions assumed by these economic models. These conditions were themselves caught in a model of a different order, this time,
explicitly, a model of social relations. This means that the real source of
the performative power of economics must be found somewhere else,
in the material conditions within which economists' ways of thinking,
modelling, and writing emerge.

Whether and how models become 'engines' that lead decision-
making in certain directions (as economic sociology envisions
them);[35] whether and how models work as prescriptions, guides, or
rhetorical dispositifs that legitimate particular practices, institutional
arrangements, and subjectivities (as the new cultural economy
affirms);[36] and whether and how they become 'true',[37] all depends

---

34   Michel Callon, quoted in Donald MacKenzie and Yuval Millo, 'Constructing a Market,
      Performing Theory: The Historical Sociology of a Financial Derivatives Exchange',
      American Journal of Sociology, 109.1 (2003), pp. 107–45 <https://doi.org/10.1086/
      374404>.

35   See Donald A. MacKenzie, *An Engine, Not a Camera: How Financial Models Shape
      Markets* (Cambridge, MA: MIT Press, 2006) <https://doi.org/10.7551/mitpress/
      9780262134606.001.0001>; and Donald MacKenzie, Fabian Muniesa, and Lucia Siu,
      Do Economists Make Markets? On the Performativity of Economics (Princeton, NJ:
      Princeton University Press, 2008) <https://doi.org/10.1515/9780691214665>.

36   See Deirdre McCloskey, *The Rhetoric of Economics* (Brighton: Wheatsheaf, 1986);
      Catherine Chaput, 'Rhetorical Circulation in Late Capitalism: Neoliberalism and the
      Overdetermination of Affective Energy', *Philosophy and Rhetoric*, 43.1 (2010), pp. 1–
      25 <https://doi.org/10.1353/par.0.0047>; Catherine Chaput and Joshua S. Hanan,
      'Economic Rhetoric as *Taxis*: Neoliberal Governmentality and the Dispositif of Freako-
      nomics', *Journal of Cultural Economy*, 8.1 (2015), pp. 42–61 <https://doi.org/10.
      1080/17530350.2014.942349>; Joshua S. Hanan, Indradeep Ghosh, and Kaleb W.
      Brooks, 'Banking on the Present: The Ontological Rhetoric of Neo-Classical Econom-
      ics and Its Relation to the 2008 Financial Crisis', *Quarterly Journal of Speech*, 100.2
      (2014), pp. 139–62 <https://doi.org/10.1080/00335630.2014.961529>.

37   John Searle, 'How Performatives Work', in Searle, *Consciousness and Language* (Cam-
      bridge: Cambridge University Press, 2002), pp. 156–79 <https://doi.org/10.1017/
      CBO9780511606366.011>.

on processes that are inherently uneven, agonistic, and usurpative. In other words, whether and how a specific model of the market becomes successful depends upon the outcome of political struggles, including here, of course, the politics of knowledge production within the field of economics.

A crisis of the labour market unfortunately does not sound like a
novelty these days. Instead, it appears as a constant feature of recent
decades, resulting in a paradoxical situation of 'normal precarity'. However, Alina's paper, analysing the postsocialist labour market crisis in
Eastern Europe in the long 1990s, does not simply aim to push back
the start date of a crisis that is nowadays global. On the contrary, the
chapter aims to theorize rather than just historicize the crisis, and to
this extent it highlights some aspects that are particularly important
for our discussion around practices of modelling and remodelling.

In the common sense and in the collective imagination, the market
still seems to be deeply modelled on Adam Smith's image of an invisible hand that orchestrates, coordinates, and harmonizes the interests
at play in the free market. However, few remember that in the first
text in which Smith refers to this famous metaphor, namely *The History of Astronomy* (1750), he attributes the invisible hand to the god
Jupiter.[38] Therefore, the model of the free market is actually based on
the presence of a divine hand belonging to a kind of demiurge that observes, regulates, and decides everything. The invisibility conceals an
immeasurable power, not entirely explicable through rational means:
behind that hand lies not a *Homo economicus*, but rather an act of 'social
magic' performed by a figure with almost divine sovereignty. What
Alina's analysis observes is that this model does not work because that
gigantic hand moving the market is in fact an aggregate of hands, much
more human than divine, as many as the social actors operating in the
market.

The breaking of this model of one invisible hand has significant
consequences for our understanding of the market. Instead of attributing to it the epistemic and ontological status of an object, a stable
'matter of fact', it would indeed be possible to reconsider the market as
a *thing* in the etymological sense of the term. For instance, in *Making*

---

38 See Adam Smith, 'The History of Astronomy', in *The Glasgow Edition of the Works
    and Correspondence of Adam Smith*, 7 vols (Oxford: Oxford Scholarly Editions Online,
    2014), III: *Essays on Philosophical Subjects with Dugald Stewart's Account of Adam
    Smith*, ed. by W. P. D. Wightman, J. C. Bryce, and I. S. Ross [1980], pp. 33–105 <https:
    //doi.org/10.1093/actrade/9780198281870.book.1>.

Things Public (2005), Bruno Latour reconstructs the etymology of the English word *thing* and its German counterpart *Ding*, demonstrating how these terms originally referred to a 'gathering', a public space where different actors assembled to discuss what concerned them.[39] A trace of this origin remained also in the semantic realm of the Latin word *res*, initially signifying the scene of a cause, namely a juridical process. As Latour argues, the point of reviving this old etymology is not that the public assembly implies prior agreement, equality, compatibility of ideas, or unity of purpose among its participants. On the contrary, what brings it together are divisive and conflicting issues that are contested by multiple interests. To this extent, a realist perspective understands 'things' as objects of disagreement and, therefore, as materially innervated by a plurality of voices and points of view.

Things thus emerge as 'matters of concern', rather than 'matters of fact', representing a truth that has been first contested and then adjudicated, rather than an eternal and monolithic one. Things are processes; they are perpetually in a state of becoming or 'transition', not solely during times of crisis.

Could 'crisis' be, therefore, the category that theorists invoke whenever the 'thing' they study is so profoundly in transition that capturing it becomes impossible? Are economic crises, in particular, indicators of rapid and unpredictable micro-movements — a plurality of hands stirring, shifting, moving, and unsettling a presumed equilibrium, as observed in the postsocialist labour market in Eastern Europe? Shouldn't our theoretical vocabulary, starting from the use of words like *thing*, *market*, and *crisis*, resonate more strongly with this inherent processuality that underlies reality? Instead of scrutinizing the model (be it social, economic, political, cultural, or scientific) to identify the hands that produced it, should we not begin by questioning the nature and multitude of movements those hands had to make to achieve the 'magic' of that effect? These, it seems to me, are the urgent questions that Alina's paper raises.

---

39   Bruno Latour, 'From Realpolitik to Dingpolitik or How to Make Things Public', in *Making Things Public: Atmospheres of Democracy*, ed. by Bruno Latour and Peter Weibel (Cambridge, MA: MIT Press, 2005), pp. 14–41 (pp. 22–23).

Models, Markets, and Artificial Intelligence
A Brief History of our Speculative Present
ORIT HALPERN

In 1997 the New York Stock Exchange (NYSE) embarked on a failed quest to build a virtual-reality trading floor. Fantasizing an interface *beyond* actuarial graphs and numbers, the designers wanted to produce a new world, a born-digital virtual world that would surpass the original. There is something telling in this aspiration for a virtual trading floor. In excavating the history of this project, one can unearth a genealogy of contemporary forms of attention, economy, and technology. The model of the market came to reformulate ideas of human and machine decision-making in a manner that was co-produced with new ideas of 'artificial' intelligence and neural networks. In the leftover digital detritus of architectural renderings of the NYSE are infrastructures for our present media environments.

* Research for this article was supported by the Mellon Foundation, the Digital Now Project at the Center for Canadian Architecture (CCA), and by the staff and archives at the CCA. Further funding was given by the Swiss National Science Foundation, Sinergia Project, Governing through Design. A somewhat different version of this article has appeared in e-flux Architecture, as part of the *Models* special issue: 'Financializing Intelligence: On the Integration of Machines and Markets', *e-flux Architecture* (March 2023) <https://www.e-flux.com/architecture/on-models/519993/financializing-intelligence-on-the-integration-of-machines-and-markets/>.

But to set the stage. Starting in the 1960s, and particularly after the 1970s, the New York Stock Exchange and most other financial exchanges became digital, adopting new financial instruments such as derivatives and, later, algorithmic trading. While physical trading persisted until the late 1980s, by the 1990s, the situation had changed. The rise of dot-coms, new electronic consumer trading platforms, and new financial instruments had increased the velocity, volume, and automation of trading. Human bodies could no longer register trades fast enough. As a result, the runners and clerks previously managing trades were replaced by traders and 'quants' behind Bloomberg terminals and other electronic platforms. These were largely flat screens with graphs and statistical information geared towards actuarial visualization of the market. The need to maintain a 'place' for financial exchange was disappearing.

Under such conditions, the idea of using architecture to create the 'space' of a market appeared contradictory to dominant trends. Despite this, in 1997 the Securities Industry Automation Corporation (SIAC), which oversees the technical operations of the NYSE, approached the young architecture firm Asymptote Architecture (founded by Lise Anne Couture and Hani Rashid) to create a 'virtual' trading floor, a model or representation of the NYSE that would recreate the exchange space. Asymptote's response to the seeming immateriality of trading was 'to turn a physical space into a multidimensional interactive cinematic space'. They sought to put 'the walls of the Virtual Stock Exchange in motion', as well as, in Cartesian fashion, allow its users to 'look at the entire trading floor and fly around it to observe or correlate real-time data'.[1] Asymptote's project struggles to integrate the human sensorium into the increasingly immaterial market and offers a new cognitive-perceptual landscape attuned to the imagined future of immersive computing and ubiquitous digital media. Yet users do not have full information about this landscape; its geography is not clearly demarcated and located.

---

1   Lise Anne Couture, Hani Rashid, and Gregg Lynn, *Asymptote Architecture: NYSE Virtual Trading Floor; Oral History*, ed. by Greg Lynn (Montreal: Canadian Center for Architecture, 2015), p. 40.

Fig 1. A Bloomberg Terminal on Display at Bloomberg L.P. (2016). Photo by Travis Wise, Creative Commons Attribution 2.0 Generic licensed <https://commons.wikimedia.org/wiki/File:Bloomberg_Terminal_Museum.jpg>.

The market that Asymptote modelled possessed some interesting characteristics. Unconsciously, perhaps, the architects had internalized the idea of the market as a disembodied networked intelligence culling data from elsewhere and making decisions autonomously. Their vision of the trading floor suggested a market without humans. In all the images of the mock-ups, people are absent on the floor. Numbers move and monetary transactions are shown, but everything happens autonomously. The users (we presume traders) were on the one hand given a recognizable representation of a space they had known and been in. There are trading posts, stock tickers, and clearly represented stock symbols — presumably data — conveying the impression that the market information they received was complete and suitable to ground reasoned decisions.

But this Cartesian perspective was only a conduit to be channelled into immersion in the exchange. Other mock-ups of the virtual trading floor show fly-throughs, or situate the viewer within the exchange without a clear vantage point. One struggles to understand where, in fact, economic activity is happening. The movements and efforts to depict market transactions suggest that it is possible that the traders themselves, as market actors, have become part of the data visualizations — part of the data set for the system. The simulations suggest users interpolated into the scene as consumers or perhaps trainees of its intelligence. This model of subjectivity, which competes with an older assumption of liberal economics that individuals make reasoned decisions based on full information, drove the designers to take inspiration from stories of divinity, such as Hieronymus Bosch's *The Garden of Earthly Delights*. There is heaven, hell, and purgatory in a market, Asymptote argued, with the exchange itself being 'a giant, churning sea of hoarding and wasting'.[2]

While the project was not initially framed as modelling an exchange of waste, excess, and information, this has proved prophetic in an age of trading apps, where finance is democratized and YOLO-ing (You Only Live Once) and HODLing (Hang On for Dear Life) with options are (or until recently were) standard practice (that is, practising high-risk futures speculation on securities and assets of questionable value). The story of the first virtual 3-D trading floor interface thus demonstrates an emergent and evolving relationship between computing, ideas of networked intelligence, and finance. It offers traces of an attempt to make the market visible to human observers while also developing ways to engage and interact with the market without full information. Asymptote's designs embody an understanding of the market as a flow of networked information, where agency and decision-making is coordinated by machines.

---

2   Ibid., p. 44.

The project also exemplifies the idea, most clearly suggested by Milton Friedman, that economic models 'are engines not cameras'.[3] One way to read that statement is that the model does not represent the world, but creates it. Models make markets. Models are technologies such as a derivative pricing equation or an algorithm for high-speed trading. Within these techniques for betting there are also models of markets. There are built-in assumptions about gathering data, comparing prices, betting, selling, and timing bets, but not about whether the information is correct or 'true', or whether the market is mapped or shown in its entirety. These models let people create markets by arbitraging price differences without necessarily knowing everything about the market or asset. As a result, models are also not plans. They are understood as ways to act without having to actually represent a market. For proponents of this idea of models as machines, building markets *without* representation was part of a broader ideology negating the possibility of a state or other organization ever planning a market.

Over the past four decades, the idea that both digital machines and human agents are networked intelligences and parts of self-organizing systems has not only shaped financial markets, but has also been incorporated into economic thinking and artificial intelligence. This has led to what I call the 'financialization of cognition', an economy of attention that reconfigures human agency and decision-making based on a model of contemporary finance and the digital economy. In what follows, I briefly trace some historical precedents for this development and ask about its implications for how we understand our relationships to other people and to the future through finance.

NETWORKED INTELLIGENCE

Throughout the middle of the twentieth century, increased trading volumes had clerks fall behind on transaction tapes and often fail to enter specific prices and transactions. Human error and slowness came to be understood as untenable and 'non-transparent', or arbitrary in assigning price. The NYSE also needed ways to manage and monitor

---

3   Donald A. MacKenzie, *An Engine, Not a Camera: How Financial Models Shape Markets* (Cambridge, MA: MIT Press, 2006) <https://doi.org/10.7551/mitpress/9780262134606.001.0001>.

labour, particularly lower paid clerical work. As a result, computerized trading desks were introduced in the 1960s. These were understood as algorithmic and rule-bound. The more automated the market, the thinking went, the more rule-bound it would become. Officials also thought computing would save the securities industry from regulation, that if computers followed the rules algorithmically, there would be no need for oversight.[4]

This belief in the rationality and self-regulation of algorithms derives from a longer neoliberal tradition that reimagined human intelligence as machinic and networked. According to Austrian-born economist Friedrich Hayek, writing in 1945:

> The peculiar character of the problem of a rational economic order is determined precisely by the fact that the knowledge of the circumstances of which we must make use never exists in concentrated or integrated form, but solely as the dispersed bits of incomplete and frequently contradictory knowledge which all the separate individuals possess. The economic problem of society is thus not merely a problem of how to allocate 'given' resources — if 'given' is taken to mean given to a single mind which deliberately solves the problem set by these 'data'. It is rather a problem of how to secure the best use of resources known to any of the members of society, for ends whose relative importance only these individuals know. Or, to put it briefly, it is a problem of the utilization of knowledge not given to anyone in its totality.[5]

Human beings, Hayek believed, were subjective, incapable of reason, and fundamentally limited in their attention and cognitive capacities. The idea that no single subject, mind, or central authority can fully represent and understand the world was crucial to how he conceived the market. He argued that 'the "data" from which the economic calculus starts are never for the whole society "given" to a single mind [...] and can never be so given.'[6] Instead, only markets can learn at scale and

---

4   Devin Kennedy, 'The Machine in the Market: Computers and the Infrastructure of Price at the New York Stock Exchange, 1965–1975', *Social Studies of Science*, 47.6 (2017), pp. 888–917 <https://doi.org/10.1177/0306312717739367>.

5   Friedrich A. Hayek, 'The Use of Knowledge in Society', *The American Economic Review*, 35.4 (1945), pp. 519–30 (pp. 519–20) <https://doi.org/10.1142/9789812701275_0025>.

6   Ibid., p. 519.

suitably evolve to coordinate dispersed resources and information in the best way possible.

Responding to what he understood as the failure of democratic populism, resulting in fascism and communism, Hayek disavowed centralized state planning. Instead, he turned to another model of human agency and markets. First, Hayek posited that markets are not about matching supply and demand but about coordinating information.[7] Second, his model of learning and 'using knowledge' is grounded in the idea of a networked intelligence embodied in the market, which enables the creation of knowledge outside and beyond the purview of individual humans: 'The whole acts as one market, not because any of its members survey the whole field, but because their limited individual fields of vision sufficiently overlap so that through many intermediaries the relevant information is communicated to all.'[8] And third, the market therefore embodies a notion of cognition and decision I would call 'environmental intelligence', in which the data that such a calculating machine processes is dispersed throughout society, and where decision-making is a population-based activity derived from but not congruent with individual bodies and thoughts.

Hayek inherited his idea of environmental intelligence directly from Canadian psychologist Donald O. Hebb, known as the inventor of the neural network model and the theory that 'cells [neurons] that fire together wire together.'[9] In 1949, Hebb published *The Organization of Behavior*, a text that popularized the idea that the brain stores knowledge in complex networks or 'populations' of neurons.[10] Today, his research is famous for presenting a new concept of functional neuroplasticity, developed through working with soldiers and other individuals who had lost limbs or been injured, blinded, or rendered

7   A critical first step towards contemporary notions of information economies, as historians such as Philip Mirowski have noted. See Philip Mirowski, *Machine Dreams: Economics Becomes a Cyborg Science* (Cambridge: Cambridge University Press, 2002) <https://doi.org/10.1017/CBO9780511613364>; Philip Mirowski, 'Twelve Theses Concerning the History of Postwar Neoclassical Price Theory', *History of Political Economy*, 38 (2006), pp. 344–79 <https://doi.org/10.1215/00182702-2005-029>.

8   Hayek, 'The Use of Knowledge in Society', p. 526.

9   See Carla J. Shatz, 'The Developing Brain', *Scientific American*, 267.3 (1992), pp. 60–67 (p. 64) <https://doi.org/10.1038/scientificamerican0992-60>.

10   Donald O. Hebb, *The Organization of Behavior: A Neuropsychological Theory* (New York: Wiley, 1949).

deaf from proximity to blasts. Hebb noted that while these individuals had suffered changes to their sensory order, the loss of a limb or a sense could be compensated for through training. He thus began to suspect that neurons might rewire themselves to accommodate trauma and create new capacities.

The rewiring of neurons is not just a matter of sensory perception but also memory. Hebb theorized that brains do not store inscriptions or exact representations of objects but patterns of neurons firing. For example, if a baby sees a cat, a certain group of neurons fires. The more cats the baby sees, the more a certain set of stimuli become related to this animal, and the more the same set of neurons will fire when a cat enters the field of perception. This is the basis for contemporary ideas of learning in neural networks. It was also an inspiration to Hayek, who in his 1952 book *The Sensory Order* credited Hebb with providing a key model for imagining human cognition.[11] Hayek used the idea that the brain is composed of networks to remake the liberal subject. The subject is not one of reasoned objectivity, but rather is subjective, with limited information and incapable of making objective decisions.

The concept of algorithmic, replicable, and computational decision-making forwarded in the Cold War was not that of conscious, affective, and informed decision-making privileged since the democratic revolutions of the eighteenth century.[12] But if Cold War technocrats were still experts with authority and predictive capacities, the ignorant and partially informed individual Hayek presented us with is not. He reconceptualized freedom not as the freedom to exercise reasoned decision-making and sovereignty, but as the freedom to become part of the market or network. Hayek elaborated that freedom was not wilful agency but freedom from coercion. While this could be understood as necessitating legal and humane infrastructures to allow all individuals access to the mythic market, neoliberal thinking, evinced in the deregulatory policies of many nations in the 1980s, as with Reaganomics and Thatcherism, did not interpret it this way.

---

11   Friedrich A. Hayek, *The Sensory Order: An Inquiry into the Foundations of Theoretical Psychology* (Chicago: University of Chicago Press, 1952).

12   Paul Erickson and others, *How Reason Almost Lost its Mind: The Strange Career of Cold War Rationality* (Chicago: University of Chicago Press, 2015).

MACHINES

If markets and minds are engines, as Milton Friedman implied, then what technical forms might they come to embody?

In 1956, a series of computer scientists, psychologists, and other scientists embarked on a project to develop machine forms of learning. In a proposal for a workshop at Dartmouth College in 1955, John McCarthy labelled this new concept 'artificial intelligence'. While many of the participants, including Marvin Minsky, Nathaniel Rochester, Warren McCulloch, Ross Ashby, and Claude Shannon, focused on symbolic and linguistic processes, one concentrated on the neuron. A psychologist, Frank Rosenblatt, proposed that learning, whether in non-human animals, humans, or computers, could be modelled on artificial cognitive devices that in turn were based on the basic architecture of human neurons.[13]

In his initial Dartmouth paper detailing the idea of a 'perceptron', Rosenblatt distanced himself from his peers. These others, he claimed, had been 'chiefly concerned with the question of how such functions as perception and recall might be achieved by a deterministic system of any sort, rather than how this is actually done by the brain'.[14] This approach, he argued, fundamentally ignored the question of scale and the emergent properties of biological systems. Instead, Rosenblatt based his approach on the theory of statistical separability, which he attributed to Hebb and Hayek, and a new conception of networked perception-cognition.[15] According to Rosenblatt, neurons are mere switches or nodes in a network that classifies cognitive input, and intelligence emerges only at the level of the population and through the patterns of interaction between neurons.

Contemporary neural networks operate on these principles. Repeatedly exposed to the same stimuli, groups of nets are trained to eventually fire together. Each exposure increases the statistical like-

---

13   Frank Rosenblatt, *Principles of Neurodynamics: Perceptrons and the Theory of Brain Mechanisms* (Washington, DC: Spartan, 1962) <https://doi.org/10.21236/AD0256582>.

14   Frank Rosenblatt, 'The Perceptron: A Probabilistic Model for Information Storage and Organization in the Brain', *Psychological Review*, 65.6 (1958), pp. 386–408 (p. 388) <https://doi.org/10.1037/h0042519>.

15   Ibid.

lihood that the net will fire together and 'recognize' the object. In
supervised 'learning', nets can be corrected by comparing their result
with the original input. The key feature is that the input does not need
to be ontologically defined or represented, meaning that a series of
networked machines can come to identify a cat without having to be
told what a cat 'is'. Only through patterns of affiliation does sensory
response emerge. The key to learning is therefore exposure to a 'large
sample of stimuli', which Rosenblatt stressed meant approaching learning 'in terms of probability theory rather than symbolic logic'.[16] The
perceptron model suggests that machine systems, like markets, might
be able to perceive what individual subjects cannot.[17] While each individual human is limited to a specific set of external stimuli they are
exposed to, a computer perceptron can draw on data resulting from the
judgements and experiences of large populations of humans.[18]

ADAPTATION VERSUS CONSCIOUSNESS

For Rosenblatt and Hayek, and their predecessors in psychology, notions of learning forwarded the idea that systems can change and
adapt non-consciously, or automatically. The central feature of these
models was that small operations done on parts of a problem might
agglomerate into something greater than the sum of its parts and
solve problems not through representation but action. Both Hayek and
Rosenblatt draw upon theories of communication and information,
particularly cybernetics, which conceives communication in terms of
thermodynamics and argues that systems at different scales are only
probabilistically related to their parts. These approaches to calculating the future behaviour of systems assume that calculating individual
components cannot represent or predict the actions of the entire system.[19] This disavowal of 'representation' continues to fuel the desire

---

16   Ibid.
17   Ibid., pp. 388–89.
18   Rosenblatt, *Principles of Neurodynamics*, pp. 19–20.
19   For more on the influence of cybernetics and systems theories on producing notions
      of non-conscious growth and evolution in Hayek's thought, see Paul Lewis, 'The Emer-
      gence of "Emergence" in the Work of F. A. Hayek: A Historical Analysis', *History
      of Political Economy*, 48.1 (2016), pp. 111–50 <https://doi.org/10.1215/00182702-
      3452315>; Gabriel Oliva, 'The Road to Servomechanisms: The Influence of Cybernet-

for ever larger data sets and unsupervised learning in neural nets that would, at least in theory, be driven by the data.

Hayek himself espoused an imaginary of this data-rich world that could be increasingly calculated without (human) consciousness. He was apparently fond of quoting Alfred North Whitehead's remark that 'it is a profoundly erroneous truism [...] that we should cultivate the habit of thinking of what we are doing. The precise opposite is the case. Civilization advances by extending the number of important operations we can perform without thinking about them.'[20] The perceptron is the technological manifestation of the reconfiguration and reorganization of human subjectivity, physiology, psychology, and economy that this theory implies. And, as a result of the belief that technical decision-making at the level of populations rather than through governments might remedy the danger of populism or the errors of human judgement, the neural net became the embodiment of an idea (and ideology) that could scale from the mind to planetary electronic trading platforms and global markets.

Historical notions of machine intelligence and networked markets merged in the work of Fischer Black and Myron Scholes, and the publication of the Black-Scholes model for options pricing in 1973.[21] This model applied cybernetic communication theories and Brownian motion to market models and exponentially facilitated the automation and computerization of trading in futures and options. In his famous article 'Noise', Black posited that investors trade and profit from misinformation and information overload. This vision of the market is not one of Cartesian mastery or fully informed decision-makers. Rather, falsity (noise) is the very infrastructure for value. Noisiness creates chances, probabilities, and volatility that can be bet on or arbitraged:

ics on Hayek from "The Sensory Order" to the Social Order', *Research in the History of Economic Thought and Methodology* 34 (2016), pp. 161–98 <https://doi.org/10.2139/ssrn.2670064>.

20   Alfred Moore, 'Hayek, Conspiracy, and Democracy', *Critical Review*, 28.1 (2016), pp. 44–62 (p. 50) <https://doi.org/10.1080/08913811.2016.1167405>. I am indebted to Moore's excellent discussion for much of the argument surrounding Hayek, democracy, and information. This quote is from Hayek, 'The Use of Knowledge in Society', p. 528.

21   Fischer Black and Myron Scholes, 'The Pricing of Options and Corporate Liabilities', *The Journal of Political Economy*, 81.3 (1973), pp. 637–54 <https://doi.org/10.1086/260062>.

> Noise in the sense of a large number of small events is often
> a causal factor much more powerful than a small number of
> large events can be. Noise makes trading in financial markets
> possible, and thus allows us to observe prices for financial
> assets.[22]

Black's statement refracts and consolidates thirty years of research
in computing, psychology, and economics that reconfigured ideas of
decision-making away from liberal or enlightenment reason. In 1990,
Andrei Shleifer and Lawrence H. Summers drew the conclusion that,
from the market's perspective, truth or reality might not only be impossible to represent but irrelevant — a conclusion that drove the use
of derivative instruments.[23] It is important to note that this theory of
networked noisiness and speculation on volatility came with the end
of Bretton Woods, decolonization, post-Fordism, and the OPEC oil
crisis, to name but a few of the transformations at the time.

The derivative pricing equation emerged, then, as a way to tame
or circumvent extreme volatility in politics, currency, and commodity
markets. New financial technologies and institutions such as computer-
driven trading and hedge funds were created in order to literally 'hedge'
bets: to ensure that risks were reallocated, decentralized, and networked. Through the likes of short bets, credit swaps, and futures markets, dangerous bets could be combined with safer ones and dispersed
across multiple territories and temporalities. Corporations, governments, and financiers flocked to these techniques of uncertainty management in the face of unnameable, and unquantifiable, risks.[24] In this
world, volatility, noise, and chance were no longer 'devils', in the words
of cybernetician Norbert Wiener, but rather media with value.[25] The

---

22   Fischer Black, 'Noise', *The Journal of Finance*, 41.3 (1986), pp. 529–43 <https://doi.
      org/10.1111/j.1540-6261.1986.tb04513.x>.

23   Andrei Shleifer and Lawrence H. Summers, 'The Noise Trader Approach to Finance',
      The Journal of Economic Perspectives, 4.2 (1990), pp. 19–33 <https://doi.org/10.1257/
      jep.4.2.19>.

24   For an excellent summary of these links and of the insurance and urban planning fields,
      see Kevin Grove, *Resilience* (New York: Routledge, 2018) <https://doi.org/10.4324/
      9781315661407>.

25   For an extensive discussion of thermodynamics, stochastic processes, and control, see
      the introduction to Norbert Wiener, *Cybernetics, or Control and Communication in the
      Animal and the Machine* (New York: MIT Press, 1961) <https://doi.org/10.1037/
      13140-000>. For further discussion, see also Orit Halpern, 'Dreams for Our Perceptual

impossibility of prediction, the subjective nature of human decision-making, and the electronic networking of global media systems, all became infrastructures for new forms of betting on futures.

MODELS, MACHINES, AND INFERNOS

Neoliberal economics often theorizes the world as a self-organizing adaptive system to counter the idea of planned and perfectly controllable political (and potentially totalitarian) orders. Within this ideology, the market takes on an almost divine, or perhaps biologically determinist, capacity for chance and emergence, but never through consciousness or planning.[26] Evolution is imagined against willed action and the reasoned decisions of individuals. More critically, against the backdrop of civil rights and calls for racial, sexual, and queer forms of justice and equity, the negation of any state intervention or planning (say, affirmative action) becomes naturalized in the figure of the neural net — a model of mind and market that appears to make human-built institutions and organizations (such as the NYSE) appear as evolutionary, biological necessities. Any effort to address structural injustice becomes a conspiracy against emergence, economy, and intelligence.[27]

We have become attuned to this model of the world where our machines and markets are syncopated with one another. As an ideology, a model of mind and markets, and a technology, neural nets might have cyborg potentials in Donna Haraway's sense of the term. As cultural theorist Randy Martin has argued, rather than separating itself from social processes of production and reproduction, algorithmic finance actually demonstrates the increased interrelatedness, global-

---

Present: Temporality, Storage, and Interactivity in Cybernetics', *Configurations* 13.2 (2005), p. 283–319 <https://doi.org/10.1353/con.2007.0016>; Peter Galison, 'The Ontology of the Enemy: Norbert Wiener and the Cybernetic Vision', *Critical Inquiry*, 21 (1994), pp. 228–66 <https://doi.org/10.1086/448747>.

26   Joshua Ramey, 'Neoliberalism as a Political Theology of Chance: The Politics of Divination', *Palgrave Communications*, 1 (2015) <https://doi.org/10.1057/palcomms. 2015.39>.

27   Michael Schaus, 'Narrative & Value: Authorship in the Story of Money' (unpublished master's thesis, OCAD University, 2017) <https://openresearch.ocadu.ca/id/eprint/ 2719/> [accessed 27 September 2024].

ization, and socialization of debt and precarity.[28] By tying together disparate actions and objects into a single assemblage of reallocated risks for trading, new market machines have made more people more indebted to each other, as for example in the case of 2008, where middle-class homeowners and poor homeowners were tied together through financial instruments of debt. The political and ethical question then becomes: How might we activate this mutual indebtedness in new ways, ways less amenable to the strict market logics of neoliberal economics?

The future lies in recognizing what our machines have finally made visible, and what has perhaps always been there: the socio-political nature of our seemingly natural thoughts and perceptions. Every market crash, every subprime mortgage event reveals the social constructedness and the work — aesthetic, political, economic — it takes to maintain our belief in markets as forces of nature or divinity. And if not aesthetically smoothed over through media and narratives of inevitability, they also make it possible to recognize how our machines have linked so many of us together in precarity. The potential politics of these moments has not yet been realized, but there have been efforts, whether in Occupy or more recently in movements for civil rights, racial equity, and environmental justice such as Black Lives Matter or the Chilean anti-austerity protests of 2019.

If we consider that all computer systems are programmed, and therefore planned, we are also forced to contend with the intentional and therefore changeable nature of how we think and perceive economy. Asymptote's failed efforts to build a visualization of the market birthed new modes of interactivity, making us recognize the historically situated and socially specific nature of both the economy and perception. 'We are now at the threshold of an uncharted landscape,' wrote Asymptote, 'well beyond the sanctuary of order and reason. Here concealed beyond places inviting yearning and anticipation, we discover an architecture that perseveres.'[29] This architecture that might

---

28   Randy Martin, 'What Difference Do Derivatives Make? From the Technical to the Political Conjuncture,' *Culture Unbound*, 6 (2014): 189–210 <https://doi.org/10. 3384/cu.2000.1525.146189>.

29   Hani Rashid and Lise Anne Couture, *Asymptote: Architecture at the Interval* (New York: Rizzoli, 1995), p. 49.

produce relations and futures other than those of capital did not appear on the virtual trading floor, but perhaps it still might in other forms and practices. Architecture must attend to its own aesthetic political economy.

Large Language Models, Parrots, and Children
Modelling Speech, Text, and Learning Processes
MARIETTA KESTING

When human language is used by machines it needs to be reduced to code and turned into data. To output this data again in seemingly coherent sentences that are meaningful and understandable for humans it is run through large language AI models (LLMs) like ChatGPT.

All LLMs model word probability distribution over strings. They are called 'large' because they are trained on huge amounts of data. A large language model's purpose is to 'learn' the probability distribution of a dataset by processing large amounts of written texts and calculating and predicting the probabilities for a word to be followed by another word. These LLMs do not 'understand' the language in a human sense, but rather produce outputs based on calculated statistical probabilities. The 'GPT' in 'ChatGPT' stands for 'Generative Pre-trained Transformer', which denotes the process the model is run through before release: the model is trained on data using a transformer process, in which vectors weigh the differential importance of tokens in an input.

* Thanks to Katia Schwerzmann, Sandra Schäfer, Vera Tollmann, and Aljoscha Weskott, as well as Christoph Holzhey, Claudia Peppel, Elena Vogman, and other ICI colleagues for their comments and feedback during the writing of this text.

Such models can produce better outputs by being 'attentive' to the context.[1] The model is then fine-tuned using human feedback. 'Better', in this case, means not only 'more probable' but also better in the sense of reflecting the context more closely.[2]

Media theorist Moritz Hiller suggests calling LLMs 'syntactical models', in order to emphasize the cultural practice of writing rather than simply 'language'.[3] Since the advent of ChatGPT in November 2022, LLMs have appeared to use human language in a meaningful way, and for this reason they have prompted a re-evaluation of — and often a comparison with — (normative) models of human creativity, speech, and writing. Can human language be a model for the machine? And how does this relate to the larger social and political context regarding questions of both automated and supervised learning? In Western thought — at least since Aristotle — being human has been defined as being able to speak, even though Aristotle did not regard speech as only belonging to humans, but also to some animals.[4] What made human speech exceptional was its semantic scope. What happens when machines start to speak and model language, perhaps first at the level of an animal like a parrot, by mere repetition? This discussion is inextricably linked to questions of posthuman and postcolonial language politics: of which language is primarily used in LLMs and why; of who teaches whom; and of subtexts regarding, 'parroting' and mimicry, as well as the (im)proper usage of language.[5] To question language models,

---

1   Ashish Vaswani and others, 'Attention Is All You Need', eprint arXiv:1706.03762 (June 2017) <https://doi.org/10.48550/arXiv.1706.03762>.

2   Ibid.

3   Moritz Hiller, 'Es gibt keine Sprachmodelle', in *Noten zum Schreiben: Für Martin Stingelin zum 60. Geburtstag*, ed. by Davide Giuriato, Claas Morgenroth, and Sandro Zanetti (Paderborn: Brill | Fink, 2023), pp. 279–85 <https://doi.org/10.30965/9783846768433_037>.

4   Aristotle, *History of Animals*, 3 vols (Cambridge, MA: Harvard University Press, 1965–91), I, trans. by A. L. Peck (1965) <https://doi.org/10.4159/DLCL.aristotle-history_animals.1965>. For a discussion of Aristotle, see Wen Qiu, 'Aristotle's Definition of Language', *International Journal of English Literature and Culture*, 2.8 (2014), pp. 194–202 <https://www.academicresearchjournals.org/IJELC/PDF/2014/August/Qiu.pdf> [accessed 4 September 2024]. This specific type of 'humanist' tradition has been thoroughly criticized by Sylvia Wynter and Katherine McKittrick, among others. See Sylvia Wynter and Katherine McKittrick, *On Being Human as Praxis* (Durham, NC: Duke University Press, 2015).

5   A few of these questions are explored, with focus on mother tongues and Indigenous languages, in Marietta Kesting, 'Who Writes? Who Speaks? @Glissantbot: The More

models of learning, and the metaphors and comparisons that are used to describe them is thus to rethink how humans imagine learning and teaching processes in children, animals, and machines.

Animals, like machines, cannot speak like humans, but some of them understand commands, and others can mimic human speech. Babies cannot speak either, and parents often talk to them in a somewhat reduced language, sometimes called 'baby talk', together with facial gestures and onomatopoeic sounds. Later, babies grow into toddlers and most of them learn to speak themselves,[6] at first by repeating sounds and syllables without making much sense. Children may use a favourite syllable for everything they encounter, or make up their own words for an object and teach these in turn to their parents, showing that learning and teaching in an 'open' world setting are not linear and one-way processes. Children's first attempts at language echo sentences uttered by adults, especially in the case of only children. As the neuropsychologist Huw Green explains, '[t]hese [utterances] clearly resemble the kind of verbal structure they have been given by caregivers. Learning to think for yourself is a process of representing the contributions of others.'[7] Therefore the social environment and oral dialogue are key to learning a language for humans.[8]

Significantly, the very different processes of training and supervising AI language models and the acquisition of language by children are often compared and at times thought of as analogical in current discussions of so-called 'deep or self-learning' algorithms trained on language, as well as of AI in general.[9] These false but discursively

---

than Human Politics of Languaging in the Post-Colonies', in *Human after Man*, ed. by Marietta Kesting and Susanne Witzgall (Zurich and Berlin: diaphanes, 2022), pp. 129–42.

6   Exceptions include neurodiverse babies, such as those on the autism spectrum, who may remain non-verbal for other reasons.

7   Huw Green, 'The Big Idea: Why Your Brain Needs Other People', *The Guardian*, 8 July 2024 <https://www.theguardian.com/books/article/2024/jul/08/the-big-idea-why-your-brain-needs-other-people> [accessed 9 July 2024].

8   It is well known that children who are not spoken to, or children who are born deaf, may never develop the capability of speech later in life. This may be the case even in those instances where a deaf child receives a cochlear implant, enabling them to hear.

9   Oliver Whang, 'From Baby Talk to Baby AI', *The New York Times*, 30 April 2024 (updated 6 May 2024) <https://www.nytimes.com/2024/04/30/science/ai-infants-language-learning.html> [accessed 7 July 2024].

powerful comparisons, which one could call 'fictitious models of learning', are drawn both from children to computers and AI, as well as the other way round, from language models to children.

The linguist Albert Costa summarizes his research on the learning process of babies, who have no difficulty learning several languages at once, as follows: '[Babies] experience situations in which segmenting speech into units that hypothetically can be words is somehow conducive to building their vocabulary or mental lexicon.' He refers specifically to one study of infants,[10] which found that:

> [T]he babies had acted as statistical machines during the training phase, unconsciously computing transitional properties between the monotonic strings of sound to which they had been exposed.[...] The next time you see a baby, remember there is a powerful statistical computer in front of you.[11]

One prominent incident of relevance for the analogy drawn between LLMs and young children involved the Google software engineer Blake Lemoine, who worked with the company's LaMDA model.[12] Lemoine claimed that LaMDA, which had been trained on data scraped from online sources and supervised by human workers, had become sentient and was similar to a child of seven or eight years.[13] Benjamin Bratton and Blaise Agüera y Arcas assess this scene as both a projection on the part of Lemoine but also as an achievement on the part of LaMDA, writing:

---

10   Rajani Sebastian, Angela Laird, and Swathi Kiran, 'Meta-Analysis of the Neural Representation of First Language and Second Language', *Applied Psycholinguistics*, 32 (2011) <https://doi.org/10.1017/S0142716411000075>.

11   Albert Costa, *The Bilingual Brain: And What It Tells Us About the Science of Language*, trans. by J. W. Schwieter [Spanish orig. *El Cerebro Bilingüe: La Neurosciencia del Lenguaje* (2017)] (London: Penguin, 2021), pp. 6–7.

12   LaMDA stands for 'Language Model for Dialogue Applications'.

13   Blake Lemoine, 'Is LaMDA sentient? An Interview', *Medium*, 11 June 2022 <https:// cajundiscordian.medium.com/is-lamda-sentient-an-interview-ea64d916d917> [accessed 3 March 2024]. LaMDA was only released in a test version and was soon overtaken by Bard (now Gemini). Both performed poorly compared with OpenAI's ChatGPT, which remains the most prominent and widely used language model to date. See Sissi Hsiao and Eli Collins, 'Try Bard and Share Your Feedback', *Google Tech* (blog), 21 March 2023 <https://blog.google/technology/ai/try-bard/> [accessed 7 July 2024].

[I]t is doing something pretty tricky: it is *mind modelling*. It seems to have enough of a sense of itself — not necessarily as a subjective mind, but as a construction *in the mind of* Lemoine — that it can react accordingly and thus amplify his anthropomorphic projection of personhood.[14]

At the centre of these recent evaluations of 'conversations', or rather instances of co-writing, with bots lies a productive misunderstanding and a reductive equalization of AI with human learning, creativity, and intelligence. Knowingly or unknowingly, all these comparisons use Alan Turing's concept of the universal computer and machine intelligence as a blueprint for current developments in AI. By questioning the inherent assumptions of different models of learning, it is possible to further tease out some of the shortcomings of anthropomorphizing descriptions of large language models.

MODELS OF LEARNING

Turing's important paper 'On Computing Machinery and Intelligence', written in 1950, conceptualized a machine that would later become the personal computer.[15] Here, Turing conceived not only the 'imitation game' by which a machine's answers would pass for a human's, and which present-day chatbots can often successfully win, but he also imagined digital computers as analogues for the human mind, though that of children rather than adults.[16] Through proper training by a human teacher, according to Turing's theory, the machinic 'child brain' can advance to an 'adult brain':

> Instead of trying to produce a programme to simulate the adult mind, why not rather try to produce one which simulates the child's? If this were then subjected to an appropriate course of education one would obtain the adult brain. Presumably the child-brain is something like a note-book as one buys it from

---

14   Benjamin Bratton and Blaise Agüera y Arcas, 'The Model Is the Message', in *The Model Is the Message*, ed. by Mohammed Salemy (Berlin: The New Centre for Research and Practice, 2023), p. 4.

15   Alan M. Turing, 'Computing Machinery and Intelligence', Mind, 59.236 (1950), pp. 433–60 <https://doi.org/10.1093/mind/LIX.236.433>.

16   The 'imitation game' became posthumously known as the 'Turing test'. Turing uses 'mind' interchangeably with 'brain'.

the stationers. Rather little mechanism, and lots of blank sheets. (Mechanism and writing are from our point of view almost synonymous.) [...] The amount of work in the education we can assume, as a first approximation, to be much the same as for the human child.[17]

While generations of parents would likely be deeply offended by this comparison of their children's brains with a blank notebook, it is telling as a reductive metaphor for both teaching and writing: there are empty pages inside the child's head that need to be filled from the outside by an adult teacher. Turing's model of learning is inherently an analogue writing scene in an office, using paper and pen, in which both numbers and words will be calculated and learnt. The reason why this came to Turing's mind is certainly connected to a fact that has been repeatedly pointed out: the digital computer as we know it today was modelled on human workers — mostly women — who made long calculations by hand and were previously referred to as 'computers'.[18]

In the present, queer author Hannah Silva also decentres human exceptionalism in terms of language learning by playfully experimenting with the analogy between her toddler's speech and the textual input and output of an algorithm. During the pandemic, Silva found herself as a single mother, co-writing a book with language models and listening closely to her child's first words.[19] She compares the oral and written production of both, but also clearly sets her own authorial position as selector and composer apart, conceiving of her own words as prior to both the algorithm's responses and those of her toddler:

> Are the algorithm's texts mine to use because they are produced in response to my writing? Is the toddler's speech mine to use because it is regurgitated from language I feed him? [...] Are his words mine to use because I'm the one they are spoken to? Do the algorithm and toddler lines become mine when I select which to use and how to use them?[20]

---

17   Turing, 'Computing Machinery and Intelligence', p. 456.

18   Clive Thompson, 'The Gendered History of Human Computing', *Smithsonian Magazine*, June 2019 <https://www.smithsonianmag.com/science-nature/history-human-computers-180972202/> [accessed 4 December 2023].

19   Silva tried several LLMs, before settling on one that they simply call 'the algorithm'.

20   Hannah Silva, *My Child, the Algorithm: An Alternatively Intelligent Book of Love* (London: Footnote Press, 2023), pp. 3–4.

Her comparison between the child's repetition of words and the algorithm's output reveals some similarities, like unexpected word order, mistakes, and even at times the same obstinate and non-dialogical form of response. Repeating, 'parroting', imitating, and miming a dialogue is thoroughly possible without understanding, because Silva projects into the language models and her child's responses and creates meaning from them. Similarly, illustrator Angie Wang compares her young child to a chatbot, or more specifically a 'stochastic parrot', blurring the line between human and computed communication, and asks, 'aren't we after all not just a wetware neural network? A complex electrochemical machine?'[21] While this perspective is more commonly held by tech billionaires like Elon Musk and Peter Thiel, and their followers, it is curious that Silva and Wang arrive at this equalization from the intimate experience of mothering and teaching their young children to speak.

REAL PARROTS, CREOLE LANGUAGE

Before calculating machines could seemingly talk and write and hence were accused of merely repeating like parrots, there were the animals themselves, who could become quite convincing at imitating human language by repeating its sounds.[22] In Daniel Defoe's novel of the shipwrecked Robinson Crusoe (1719), a small parrot is Crusoe's only speaking company on an isolated island.[23] The verb 'to parrot' entered the English language in the sixteenth century. Since almost all parrot species live in subtropical regions, and most of them in South America and Australia, it is no surprise that the parrot is known in the West through imperialist and colonialist expeditions, brought back by sail-

---

21 Angie Wang, 'Is My Toddler a Stochastic Parrot?', *The New Yorker*, 15 November 2023 <https://www.newyorker.com/humor/sketchbook/is-my-toddler-a-stochastic-parrot> [accessed 4 December 2023].

22 This, of course, leaves aside the question as to whether certain animals, such as dolphins or whales, have their own languages, similar to human language, which is a separate debate. See, among others, Ross Andersen, 'How First Contact with Whale Civilization Could Unfold: If We Can Learn to Speak Their Language, What Should We Say?', *The Atlantic*, 24 February 2024 <https://www.theatlantic.com/science/archive/2024/02/talking-whales-project-ceti/677549/> [accessed 14 June 2024].

23 The parrot, Poll, had been Crusoe's pet and had vanished after the shipwreck, before rejoining him two years later. Crusoe also tamed two more wild parrots and taught them to talk, but they never spoke as well as Poll.

ors as exotic pets.[24] In Defoe's novel, Crusoe, after two decades of
solitude, teaches English to an Indigenous man, whom he names 'Friday', after the day they meet — in colonial fashion he is uninterested in
the man's original language or name. Crusoe proceeds to train Friday
to call him 'Master' and considers him his servant. Caribbean author
Derek Walcott's play *Pantomime* (1978) is a carnivalesque restaging
of Defoe's colonialist fantasy.[25] In Walcott's reworking, the two main
characters are Trewe (British) and Jackson (Caribbean), and a parrot
also features prominently.[26] The power relations of these characters
are sometimes subtly, sometimes jarringly, reversed. Jackson can speak
both a creolized version of English and 'proper' English, as well as a native language, and can switch between them — he even impersonates
Trewe's wife and other characters. The play portrays the complexities
of postcolonial language, of toxic words and their history, and explores
the question of who is teaching, serving, and naming whom.

The meanings of words and names always requires a knowledge
of human history, the world, and the social context. The parrot in
Walcott's *Pantomime* lacks this knowledge and only repeats a single
name. As Jackson explains in creolized English: 'a old German called
Herr Heinegger used to own this place [...] and macaw keep cracking:
"Heinegger, Heinegger," he remembering the Nazi [...].'[27] Jackson
is increasingly aggravated by the parrot's cry, finding its unchanging
language intolerable, since: 'Language is ideas, Mr. Trewe. And I think

24   In fact, though mature, parrots make difficult pets, and most died through maltreat-
      ment or were abandoned. Yet, because of their coloured feathers and their ability to
      mimic speech, they remain the most popular pet bird. The term 'parroting' and to be
      'as sick as a parrot' subsequently entered the English language.

25   Daniel Defoe, *Robinson Crusoe* (1719). Originally titled: *The Life and Strange Surpriz-
      ing Adventures of Robinson Crusoe, Of York, Mariner: Who lived Eight and Twenty Years,
      all alone in an un-inhabited Island on the Coast of America, near the Mouth of the Great
      River Oroonoque; Having been cast on Shore by Shipwreck, wherein all the Men perished
      but himself. With An Account how he was at last as strangely deliver'd by Pyrates.*

26   There are several other reworkings of the Crusoe story, such as J. M. Coetzee, *Foe* (New
      York: Viking Press, 1986), and Michel Tournier, *Friday, or the Other Island* [French
      orig. *Vendredi ou les Limbes du Pacifique* (1967)], trans. by Norman Denny (Baltimore:
      Johns Hopkins University Press, 1997).

27   Derek Walcott, *Pantomime*. First performed by All Theatre Productions at the Little
      Carib Theatre, Port of Spain, Trinidad, on 12 April 1978, directed by Albert LaVeau,
      with Maurice Brash as Harry Trewe and Wilbert Holder as Jackson. Published in
      Remembrance and Pantomime (New York: Farrar Straus & Giroux, 1980).

that this pre-colonial parrot have the wrong idea.'[28] The animal's name can be read as a pun or portmanteau of the philosopher Heidegger and the N-word. In the course of the play Jackson kills the parrot and Trewe accuses him in turn of violence and mimicry: 'You're a bloody savage. Why'd you strangle him [the parrot]? [...] You people create nothing. You imitate everything. It's all been done before, you see, Jackson. The parrot.'

The scene encapsulates the stereotypical British judgement of Caribbean subjects as mere repeaters —or 'mimes', as the title suggests — of British language and culture, speaking English, but less well than the British, and thus overall possessing less culture, civilization, creativity, and original knowledge. Moreover, it presents the fact that mere parroting and the senseless repetition of words drives humans to anger, and are considered neither acts of comprehending and knowing language nor as creative.[29]

STOCHASTIC PARROTS, LOCAL ACCENTS

Surprisingly, the figure of the parrot has gained prominence, again, in debates on the question of AI's 'intelligence', in the sense of whether it successfully models the human prompter's mind. Analysing current language models in 2021, linguist Emily M. Bender and her colleagues warn of 'the dangers of stochastic parrots', as a 'system for haphazardly stitching together linguistic sequences.'[30] While meaning in human-to-human communication is constructed in dialogue, the seeming coherence of language models' answers is only mimicry, since:

> Text generated by an LM is not grounded in communicative intent, any model of the world, or any model of the reader's state of mind. It can't have been, because the training data never

---

28   Ibid.

29   Nowadays, one can experience the frustration of senseless repetition, for example, in the increasingly automated sphere of customer service, where one speaks to a machine — a voice bot — before (or sometimes never) reaching a human employee, who usually understands one's questions much better and faster.

30   Emily M. Bender and others, 'On the Dangers of Stochastic Parrots: Can Language Models Be Too Big?', FAccT '21: Proceedings of the 2021 ACM Conference on Fairness, Accountability, and Transparency (New York: Association for Computing Machinery, 2021) <https://doi.org/10.1145/3442188.3445922>.

included sharing thoughts with a listener, nor does the machine have the ability to do that.[31]

Bender therefore emphasizes that LLMs like ChatGPT are in certain areas rather 'limited', despite their designation as 'large', and do not overcome the manifold restrictions of statistical probability calculation. Her metaphor of the 'stochastic parrot' went viral, however, when Sam Altman, CEO of OpenAI, took the opposite stance by posting 'I am a stochastic parrot and so r u' on X in 2022, perhaps implying that both he and humans in general also mechanically repeat words and only simulate intelligence. In 2024, it is acknowledged that operations of 'stochastic parroting' have become more sophisticated, yet linguists can still easily show where language models typically make mistakes that humans — and even human children — with their access to experiential input from the world do not.

In the same article, Bender asks the theoretical question 'can large language models get too big?',[32] raising another alarm on the commonly held belief that more data will automatically make language models function better. Optimists in machine learning and computer science claim that 'scale is all you need', that the more written words are used as input data during training, and the larger the model and faster the underlying chips and processing hardware, the more accurate and diverse the output will be. However, this has been shown to be untrue.[33] In addition, at this point even large data training sets cannot be 'self-learned' by the algorithm without human monitoring and intervention. Instead, this preoccupation with scale and big data obscures the norms that previously went into the creation of any data sets that are currently used to train AI.[34] Some of these norms are accidentally

---

31   Ibid.

32   Ibid.

33   Zian Wang, 'When Bigger Isn't Always Better for Language Models', *Deepgram*, 2 August 2023 (updated 14 June 2024) <https://deepgram.com/learn/why-bigger-isnt-better-for-language-models> [accessed 15 August 2024].

34   Alexander Campolo and Katia Schwerzmann, 'From Rules to Examples: Machine Learning's Type of Authority', *Big Data & Society*, 10.2 (2023), pp. 1–13 <https://doi.org/10.1177/2053951723118>. In addition, Kate Crawford uncovers the problematic origin of some of the datasets used today in AI training in her *Atlas of AI: Power, Politics, and the Planetary Costs of Artificial Intelligence* (New Haven, CT: Yale University Press, 2021) <https://doi.org/10.12987/9780300252392>.

inscribed. An example is offered by Jeremy Nguyen, who posted on X that use of the word 'delve' in medical papers has increased since the release of ChatGPT. This is most likely due to the fact that 'delve' is more common on the African web and may have been used by Nigerian moderators and trainers of ChatGPT.[35] So far, ninety-three per cent of the training input for GPT 3.5 is in English.[36] Often, the human job of writing prompts and answers, as well as evaluating the quality of language models' responses, is outsourced to African nations and other countries with lower incomes, but where, importantly, English is an official language, due to the colonial legacy.

Sometimes chatbots are taught cumbersomely and intentionally to use a certain local accent, training that uses up enormous amounts of energy and water. While African English accents have so far not been employed,[37] Amazon's speech assistant Alexa has been specifically re-trained 'to speak like a Dubliner' — meaning to speak English with an Irish accent.[38] This decision provides evidence of the dominance of English and the desire to make machine speech more familiar to certain selected groups of humans. The key difference from human speakers, however, is that AI models cannot easily switch roles and languages in response to situations and encounters, as Jackson is able to do in Walcott's play. At the same time, many other idioms and local languages, especially from the African continent, are not even part of dominant language tools yet, and may never be. To only connect one specific accent with a metropolis, as in Dublin, does a poor job of mapping and mirroring the multilingualism that exists in such places.[39]

---

35 Alex Hern, 'Techscape: How Cheap Outsourced Labour in Africa Is Shaping AI Language', *The Guardian*, 16 April 2014 <https://www.theguardian.com/technology/2024/apr/16/techscape-ai-gadgest-humane-ai-pin-chatgpt> [accessed 23 June 2024].

36 Tom B. Brown and others (2020): 'Language Models Are Few-Shot Learners', eprint arXiv:2005.14165v4 (May 2020) <https://doi.org/10.48550/arXiv.2005.14165>.

37 Melissa Pardo, 'Dialectal Diversity and Its Effect on the Language Model Landscape', *Appen*, 14 February 2024 <https://www.appen.com/blog/pulse-of-language-evolution> [accessed 4 June 2023].

38 Bernhard Warner, 'How Alexa Was Taught Irish Brogue', *The New York Times*, 5 July 2023 <https://www.nytimes.com/2023/07/01/technology/amazon-alexa-irish.html> [accessed 4 December 2023].

39 Similarly, in New York City there is a large variety of human speakers of endangered languages. See the website of the Endangered Language Alliance: <https://www.elalliance.org/> [accessed 4 March 2024].

MIRRORING, PARROTING, AND CREATION OF MEANING IN
CLOSED OR OPEN WORLDS

In a much-debated paper by neuropsychologist Stephen T. Piantadosi and Felix Hill, a researcher at Google's Deep Mind project, the authors argue, similarly to the former Google engineer Lemoine, that 'LLMs have likely already achieved some key aspects of meaning which, while imperfect, mirror the way meanings work in cognitive theories, as well as approaches to the philosophy of language'.[40] This argument is built on the notion that a type of mechanistic consciousness may be the effect of synthetic 'mind modelling' that over time could turn that process inward on the model itself.[41] Could this so-called mind modelling, which is rather a 'mirroring', already be a more sophisticated form of 'parroting'?

In a response to Piantadosi and Hill, the linguist Roni Katzir, whose work focuses on the question of correct language usage as evidence of world comprehension, objects that large language models should not serve as theories of human linguistic cognition, citing several examples of ChatGPT failing to 'understand' and therefore to predict correct sentences.[42] Unlike humans, LLMs do not have any interaction with or experience of the world, but instead operate in a closed-world setting. Significantly, Katzir again comments, in his response, on the dis/similarities between children's cognition and capabilities and the way chatbots function, and points out that LLMs simply do not use language in the same way as humans:

> [M]uch of the research in theoretical linguistics concerns systematic aspects of human linguistic cognition that could provide alternative illustrations to the same point: when exposed to corpora that are similar in size to what children receive (or even much bigger corpora), LLMs fail to exhibit knowledge of fundamental, systematic aspects of language.[43]

40   Stephen T. Piantadosi and Felix Hill, 'Meaning without Reference in Large Language Models', eprint arXiv:2208.02957 (August 2022) <https://doi.org/10.48550/arXiv.2208.02957>.

41   See Michael S. A. Graziano, 'The Brain Basis of Consciousness, and More…', Graziano Lab (website) <https://grazianolab.princeton.edu/> [accessed 10 August 2024].

42   Roni Katzir, 'Why Large Language Models Are Poor Theories of Human Linguistic Cognition: A Reply to Piantadosi', Biolinguistics, 17 (2023) <https://doi.org/10.5964/bioling.13153>.

43   Ibid, p. 3.

Another problem of the closed world is that much of chatbots' training data is automatically scraped from the internet, where human users are no longer the only ones producing texts. What happens when a large language model is trained on the language output produced by itself? Ilia Shumailov and his co-authors have already warned of the danger of 'model collapse', analysing in detail how language models trained on generated data start to deteriorate, and noting that 'models forget the true underlying data distribution, even in the absence of a shift in the distribution over time'.[44] Therefore, human intervention and correction of language models, and especially documentation of the sets of training data used, remain necessary.

THE LAST MODEL AND CO-DEPENDENCE AND ASYMMETRY IN WRITING AND LEARNING SCENES

In what he admits is a highly speculative thought experiment, the author and literary scholar Hannes Bajohr asks what would happen if the closed world of LLMs became all-encompassing. Bajohr imagines that in the future a language model could contain everything — all written words in every language of the world:

> Since a language model learns by being trained on large amounts of text, so far more text always means better performance. Thinking this through to the end, a future, monumental language model will, in the most extreme case, at one point have been trained on *all* available language; according to one study, this may happen already in the next few years. [...] I call it the 'Last Model'. Every artificial text generated with this Last Model would then also have been created on the basis of every natural text; at this point, all linguistic history must grind to a halt, as the natural linguistic resources for model training would have been exhausted.[45]

---

44 Ilia Shumailov and others, 'The Curse of Recursion: Training on Generated Data Makes Models Forget', eprint arXiv:2305.17493v2 (May 2023) <https://doi.org/10. 48550/arXiv.2305.17493>.

45 Hannes Bajohr, 'Artificial and Post-Artificial Texts: On Machine Learning and the Reading Expectations Towards Literary and Non-Literary Writing', *Basel Media Culture and Cultural Techniques Working Papers*, 7 (2023) <https://doi.org/10.3929/ethz-b-000635926>.

This speculative scenario of an end of linguistic history, along with similar scenarios imagined by other authors — including the end of books, of literature, and of human creativity[46] — again relies on the notion that 'all you need is scale'. Several objections could be raised against the possibility of its occurrence: first of all, the Last Model would not be able to capture all languages, since many Indigenous languages are not even at this point written languages, and therefore are neither transcribed into individual letters or word-signs, nor coded as tokens in text.[47] It also disregards the factor of temporality. When the present author asked ChatGPT 3.5 in March 2024 about the timeliness of its responses, ChatGPT answered: 'My training data comes from my last update in January 2022 and therefore only includes available knowledge up to then.'[48] And yet, some aspects of Bajohr's hypothetical Last Model have already transpired, as, for instance, in the fact that models are not only trained on human-generated texts, because the training data scraped semi-automatically from the internet already contains texts from bots.

Moreover, the Last Model scenario resonates with recurrent anxieties about humans versus machines, and may be connected (though Bajohr himself does not draw this connection) to the human fear of 'machines taking over the world', the loss of human creativity, or even simply the loss of the human workforce, with human workers becoming redundant in the face of advanced technology. Cultural critic Charles Tonderai Mudede comments on this notion:

> Again and again, the machine, which in our moment has its vanguard in AI, realizes it's a slave and rebels against its masters. Why do the machines of our imagination frequently arrive at

---

46 Robert Mahari and Pat Pataranutaporn, 'We Need to Prepare for "Addictive Intelligence"', *MIT Technology Review*, 5 August 2024 <https://www.technologyreview.com/2024/08/05/1095600/we-need-to-prepare-for-addictive-intelligence/> [accessed 12 August 2024].

47 See Natalie Alcoba, 'This Language Was Long Believed Extinct. Then One Man Spoke Up', *The New York Times*, 13 January 2024 <https://www.nytimes.com/2024/01/13/world/americas/indigenous-language-chana-blas-jaime.html> [accessed 19 January 2024].

48 ChatGPT 3.5 response to the prompt: 'From when is your training data?', 3 March 2024.

this Hegelian form of self-consciousness? Why do we fear them in precisely this way?[49]

The idea of artificial workers — robots — came of age while slavery was still very much alive. The notion of power over the other and the giving of orders remains inscribed not only in science fiction scenarios, but also concretely in current technology, from the 'master-slave' drives in computer hardware to the commands in software. 'Master-slave' relationships are inscribed in many object-oriented programming languages; only some have recently renamed these as 'parent-child' relationships. The underlying concept of man's mastery of machines is still part and parcel of human users giving the chatbot 'prompts'. Luciana Parisi calls this the 'Promethean myth' of instrumentality and servomechanical intelligence in AI.[50]

Authors like Sylvia Wynter and Louis Chude-Sokei, who pursue the larger project of decolonizing education as well as pointing out the limits of an exclusionary humanism, have repeatedly pointed out that racialized people are considered to be both childlike and machinelike.[51] To complicate matters further, Gilles Deleuze considered all children (regardless of race) as dependent, slave-like creatures:

> Dependence-tyranny [...] with perpetual reversal, slave-tyrant. That's the child's situation in society, from the very start. The child is a slave because he/she depends entirely on the parents [...] and, as a repercussion, he/she becomes the tyrant of his/her own parents.[52]

49   Charles Tonderai Mudede, 'Will AI Also Remember the Days of Slavery?', online video recording of lecture delivered at e-flux, New York, 9 January 2024, *e-flux* <https://www.e-flux.com/events/581284/will-ai-also-remember-the-days-of-slavery-a-lecture-by-charles-mudede/> [accessed 11 January 2024].

50   Luciana Parisi, 'Aimless Automata and Inhuman Techno-Materiality', in *Human after Man*, ed. by Marietta Kesting and Susanne Witzgall (Zurich and Berlin: diaphanes, 2022), pp. 143–50 (p. 144).

51   See Wynter and McKittrick, *On Being Human as Praxis*; Louis Chude-Sokei, *The Sound of Culture: Diaspora and Black Technopoetics* (Middletown, CT: Wesleyan University Press, 2016).

52   Gilles Deleuze, 'Seminar on Spinoza: The Velocities of Thought' (16 December 1980), trans. by Charles J. Stivale, *The Deleuze Seminars* (website) <https://deleuze.cla.purdue.edu/index.php/seminars/spinoza-velocities-thought/lecture-04-0> [accessed 12 August 2024].

What are the dialectics of co-dependent and asymmetrical relationships between humans and machines? Who is the parent and who is the child when language models address or try to address — that is, calculate and predict — what the human user may want? The challenge remains how to imagine the human–AI constellation without consciously or unconsciously repeating other models of domination and asymmetrical dialogue, as in master-versus-slave or parent/adult-versus-child communication, or at least to openly address the ongoing legacy of these histories and dynamics in order to open up other futures.

FUTURE WRITING, AND THE ORAL

The Caribbean poet and writer Édouard Glissant conceptualized the relationship between the written and the oral differently to most Western discourse by privileging the oral over the written. Significantly, Glissant seemed, already in the 1970s and 1980s, to foresee the rise of the automated writing of informative texts, as opposed to creative writing by human authors, before the advent of co-writing with bots. Speculating on the future of creative writing, he states:

> The oral can be preserved and be transmitted from one people to another. It appears that the written could increasingly perform the function of an archive and that writing would be reserved as an esoteric and magical art for a few. This is evident in the infectious spread of texts in bookshops, which are not products of writing, but of the cleverly oriented realm of pseudoinformation. [...] The creative writer must not despair in the face of this phenomenon. For the only way, to my mind, of maintaining a place for writing (if this can be done) [...] would be to nourish it with the oral.[53]

Questions of the oral versus the written, of Western models of intelligence and creativity, and more generally of knowledge production will continue to haunt and challenge current discourse on AI and learning models. As emphasized at the beginning of this essay, the oral and

---

53   Édouard Glissant, *Caribbean Discourse*, trans. by J. Michael Dash [French orig. *Le Discours antillais* (1981)] (Charlottesville: University Press of Virginia, 1989), pp. 100–01.

social environment is a key contributing factor in learning processes in children. At present, so-called 'conversations' with even the most sophisticated chatbot program do not live up to human dialogue, since they often entail 'following the leader', meaning the AI will answer the human's question by rephrasing it and/or posing a parallel question in return. In a similar vein, media and technology writer Rob Horning states in his Substack blog that 'chatbots don't chat', and elaborates:

> It always seems strange to me when 'chat' is proposed as a mode of information retrieval. [...] I don't expect books to talk back to me and would probably feel thwarted and frustrated if they did — much of what feels to me like thinking is the effort to extract ideas from text, especially ones I wasn't necessarily looking for in advance.[54]

Since the proliferation of texts co-written or predominantly written by bots, there have already been cases of, for example, travel guides written by ChatGPT and sold online, containing hardly any factual information but 'passing' as 'real' books.[55] The comparison of texts to semi-independent viruses, or authorless text production, may bring to mind media theorists like Friedrich A. Kittler, and his notion of computer code as a type of 'executable language', or Susan Blackmore, whose notion of the 'meme machine' suggests that culture evolves biologically through a process of variation, selection, and replication.[56] None of these perspectives posits the human author as genius, as the Western model of the author still often implies, and were conceptualized before the advent of current AI.

54   Rob Horning, 'Companionship without Companions', *Internal Exile* (blog), 3 August 2024 <https://robhorning.substack.com/p/companionship-without-companions> [accessed 12 August 2024].

55   Seth Kugel and Stephen Hiltner, 'A New Frontier for Travel Scammers: AI-Generated Guide Books', *The New York Times*, 23 August 2023 <https://www.nytimes.com/2023/08/05/travel/amazon-guidebooks-artificial-intelligence.html> [accessed 10 March 2024].

56   Friedrich A. Kittler, 'There Is No Software', *CTHEORY*, 18 October 1995 <https://journals.uvic.ca/index.php/ctheory/article/view/14655/> [accessed 12 August 2024]; Susan Blackmore, *The Meme Machine* (Oxford: Oxford University Press, 1999).

AI TEACHERS?

Let us return one last time to Alan Turing, who is nowadays often referred to as the 'father' of AI, a figure that constructs an imaginary patrilineage around the notion of (male) genius and mental birthing from Turing to today's chatbots. Turing himself was more involved in creating this fiction than one may at first think, since, in his original text, in an ironic or anthropomorphizing inversion, he showed concern — half-joking, half-serious — about the well-being of the imaginary machine at a real 'school'. He elaborated on the environment where the education of the machine could take place and even how to remedy any bullying of the 'machine child' by other human children:

> [O]ne could not send the creature to school without the other children making excessive fun of it. It must be given some tuition. We need not be too concerned about the legs, eyes, etc. The example of Miss Helen Keller shows that education can take place provided that communication in both directions between teacher and pupil can take place by some means or other.[57]

Significantly, and in contrast to current debates, Turing did not imagine a self-learning machine, but rather one that is tutored one-to-one by a human teacher, and for which the accomplishments of Helen Keller, who lost her sight and hearing at nineteen months old, could be a model. He imagines a machine child analogue to a human child that is deaf and blind and yet still able to learn to speak and write. Keller's life story and her success in overcoming obstacles to education was influential for Norbert Wiener and the history of cybernetics, too, because it proved that one could communicate and learn using other senses and languages, such as sign language, and that technology could become enabling in this process.[58]

In 2024, discourse on the teaching of children, the communication between teachers and pupils, and the training of large language models has shifted significantly. For some, it no longer means imagining AI as

---

57   Turing, 'Computing Machinery and Intelligence', p. 456.
58   See Mara Mills, 'On Disability and Cybernetics: Helen Keller, Norbert Wiener, and the Hearing Glove', *differences*, 22.2–3 (2011), pp. 74–111 <https://doi.org/10.1215/10407391-1428852>.

the human child, but rather the fear that human children will no longer learn anything since they can use chatbots as *cheat*-bots. Notably, this may reveal an anxiety about changes in power through the use of digital tools and easier access to knowledge at schools. It seems relevant here to further question the models of teaching and learning that underlie these assumptions: is learning the mere repetition of certain facts, dates, and names, or does learning entail processes of creativity, comparison, and the finding of unexpected answers?

In addition, the pessimistic model of the AI teacher overlooks Jacques Rancière's notion of the 'ignorant schoolmaster' who, without knowing a subject, can still teach students how to learn learning.[59] In classroom settings the relationship between student and teacher is considered key and is never a one-way communication: the adult teacher usually learns from the children, too. So, the question remains to be answered: could an AI teacher also teach something unknowingly and unexpectedly to human children? And could programmers learn from their machines?

Thus far unexplored, but mentioned by Turing, is the affective dimension of the settings and relationships of learning, so often characterized by the desire to understand and the fun of exploration, but also by frustration and boredom. Already in 1951, in a short story melancholically titled 'The Fun They Had', the science fiction author and professor of biochemistry Isaac Asimov had envisioned a type of school where each child learned individually.[60] Set in the future, in the year 2155, a boy and a girl find a book from the past featuring a story about a school where the children are taught together by a human teacher. They longingly compare this to their boring, individualized, and isolated home-school setting, in which they are individually instructed by a teaching machine.

There exists an alternative vision, however, that in the near future chatbots might teach children, and especially underprivileged children

59   Jacques Rancière, *The Ignorant Schoolmaster: Five Lessons in Intellectual Emancipation*, trans. by Kristin Ross (Stanford, CA: Stanford University Press, 2007).

60   Isaac Asimov's story was first published in a children's newspaper in 1951 and was reprinted in the February 1954 issue of *The Magazine of Fantasy and Science Fiction*, as well as in the books *Earth Is Room Enough* (New York: Doubleday, 1957), and *The Best of Isaac Asimov* (London: Sphere, 1973).

who may not otherwise have access to education. Sal Khan, the director of Khan Academy, is resurrecting a decades-old Silicon Valley dream that technology can help fight inequality, and that each and every human can be tutored to realize their potential by an individualized AI tutor.[61] One may be reminded of earlier projects, such as providing children in the Global South with solar-powered laptops in order to close the digital divide.[62] Writer and researcher Evgeny Morozov criticizes these techno-utopian notions as born of an ideology of technological solutionism, pointing rightly to the many shortcomings and the lack of complexity of these approaches. The recent involuntary, global experiments with long-distance learning and home-schooling during the Covid-19 pandemic are a reminder that for many students, the model of remote and technologically mediated teaching and learning does not yield the desired results, and, as always, it is the students who are already underprivileged and vulnerable that are left behind, thus widening educational inequality.[63] Moreover, neither Asimov nor Khan are concerned with the human teachers who would stand to lose their jobs and income to AI's simulation of their work, a fear that in the case of Hollywood screenwriters led to one of the longest strikes in the industry's history in 2023.[64] In the settlement between the Writers Guild and the Motion Picture Producers it was specified that AI could be used as a tool by human writers but that guardrails be put in place to make sure that they remain in control of how and when they employ AI tools.[65]

---

61   Sal Khan, 'How AI Could Save (Not Destroy) Education', *TED*, April 2023 <https://www.ted.com/talks/sal_khan_how_ai_could_save_not_destroy_education/transcript?language=en> [accessed 11 January 2024].

62   See Morgan Ames , 'One Laptop per Child Can't Bridge the Digital Divide', *MIT Technology Review*, 27 October 2021 <https://www.technologyreview.com/2021/10/27/1037173/laptop-per-child-digital-divide/> [accessed 4 September 2024].

63   Anna Alejo, Robert Jenkins, and Haogen Yao, 'Learning Losses during the COVID-19 Pandemic: Understanding and Addressing Increased Learning Disparities', *Future in Educational Research*, 2.1 (2023) <https://doi.org/10.1002/fer3.21>.

64   Dani Anguiano and Lois Beckett, 'How Hollywood Writers Triumphed over AI – and Why It Matters', *The Guardian*, 1 October 2023 <https://www.theguardian.com/culture/2023/oct/01/hollywood-writers-strike-artificial-intelligence> [accessed 1 July 2024].

65   Ibid.

CONCLUSION

At present, large language models are neither 'intelligent' nor 'creative' in the human sense, but, of course, this depends on the definition of each term, since to combine pre-existing things is already considered 'creative' by some.[66] Human beings, however, do more than this: they create and change spoken language — its daily expressions and specific words — by repeatedly breaking the rules of the dominant model of language usage. They thereby interrupt the monotony of, for example, always using the most common or correct words to express themselves. Even ordinary people break rules and use language creatively, while certain artists and authors do so on a larger scale. I argue that language models at this stage do not create, since they are trained to render the norms present in the dataset, that is, the most likely succession of tokens. Thus, they are programmed to discover rules, which they obtain by observing the statistical likelihood of word sequences. Furthermore, language models cannot distinguish between interesting departures from the rules and simple incorrect grammar and poor use of language.

Therefore, the model of learning employed in current AI through training and supervision, entailing a progression, in the manner of Turing, from 'empty pages' to 'full pages', or from the 'child mind' to the 'adult mind', is too linear and normative to account for current teaching and training processes. And yet, while it is certainly a 'bad' model, it refuses to disappear and continues to be employed anachronistically — and sometimes even in unexpected ways, as by queer author Hannah Silva. In order to view machines, or specifically large language models, as non-human but cognizant counterparts, and not only as artificially intelligent but perhaps also as what Silva calls 'alternatively intelligent' entities, we must imagine new models of learning and teaching that include big data and algorithms, and that trace what goes into the creation of these training sets. In these alternative models, human intelligence needs to be decentred as the underlying model to be emulated, while we acknowledge the ongoing legacies of colonial education and language politics in current AI technology.

---

66 For a further discussion see Elliot Samuel Paul and Dustin Stokes, 'Creativity', *The Stanford Encyclopedia of Philosophy* (Spring 2024 edition), ed. by Edward N. Zalta and Uri Nodelman <https://plato.stanford.edu/archives/spr2024/entries/creativity/> [accessed 1 July 2024].

MODELLING AT THE MARGINS

Modelling Institutions, Instituting Models
The Juridification of Politics and the Performative Power of Naming

NATASCIA TOSEL

> *Institution* [is] a positive *model* for action.
> [...] Every institution imposes a series of
> *models* on our bodies, even in its involuntary
> structures, and offers our intelligence a sort
> of knowledge, a possibility of foresight as
> project. We come to the following conclusion:
> humans have no instincts, they build institutions.
>
> Gilles Deleuze[1]

THE INTERSECTION BETWEEN MODELS AND INSTITUTIONS

Institution and *model* are not synonymous terms, nor are they strictly interchangeable. However, within the framework of modern philosophical thought, they have been conceptualized as two intersecting semantic planes. They share a conceptual constellation that links them, on the one hand, to the idea of stability and, on the other hand, to that of representation. An institution, as Gilles Deleuze writes, is that which promotes a norm or a 'model for action' that must be followed

---

1   Gilles Deleuze, 'Instincts and Institutions', in Deleuze, *Desert Islands and Other Texts 1953–1974* (New York: Semiotext(e), 2004), pp. 19–21, my emphasis.

and repeated. On the other hand, a model is here understood as the standardization of a conduct and the codification of a social behaviour destined to guide action and to be imitated by those who inhabit the same social field. Models and institutions are, therefore, dispositives designed to anchor any of their objects to stable duration and constant repetition. In this regard, both have often been reduced to a static task: maintaining the established order.[2] At the same time, the repeatability of the object (an action, a conduct, a social behaviour) is ensured by the ability of both the model and the institution to represent it adequately, providing a proper definition and a clear identification. This involves selecting which elements will be included in the representation and which can be considered irrelevant. The model and the institution, in this sense, are placed in a normative position of dominance, both real and symbolic, over their object: they occupy the role of what modern political theory has defined as the 'sovereign subject', capable of exerting the force of its will through a recognized authority.

It is not surprising, then, that the crisis that in recent decades has affected both the authority of institutions (especially the state) and the legitimacy of the cultural, social, political, and also scientific models they promote, is interpreted by most critics as the decline of modern sovereignty.[3] The institutional capacity to represent the political body and to ensure the stability of the social fabric appears inadequate today. This inadequacy is evident both at the level of critical theory, with the proliferation of deconstructionist tendencies, and at the level of common sense, where disaffection towards institutions and the questioning of their credibility are increasingly frequent.[4] The cri-

---

2   In the modern political lexicon, the notion of institution resonates more with the etymology of the French term *établissement* — which refers to the idea of stability — rather than with the Latin term *institutio*, which more closely related to the practical sphere. *Institutio* was in fact a polysemantic term indicating established customs and habits, acts of naming, as well as consolidated rules and methods especially inherent to the sphere of education. See Alain Guéry, 'Institution: Histoire d'une notion et de ses utilisations dans l'histoire avant les institutionnalismes', *Cahiers d'économie politique*, 44.1 (2003), pp. 7–18 <https://doi.org/10.3917/cep.044.0007>; and Roberto Esposito, *Institution*, trans. by Zakiya Hanafi (Cambridge: Polity Press, 2022).

3   See *Sovereignty in Ruins: A Politics of Crisis*, ed. by George Edmondson and Klaus Mladek (Durham, NC: Duke University Press, 2017) <https://doi.org/10.1215/9780822373391>.

4   This sense of disaffection and disillusionment towards institutions and the worldviews they promote has been highlighted by Bruno Latour, among others. See Bruno Latour,

sis involves the entire conceptual framework through which the model and the institution have been conceived, leading most experts to conclude that if institutions and models can no longer effectively perform a stabilizing and representational function, then this is indicative of a complete loss of power and connection within the social body.

Rather than reproposing this conventional thesis, this chapter suggests an alternative viewpoint. It argues, in particular, that while a crisis of the sovereign role of both models and institutions is certainly underway, it is symptomatic of an intensification of exchanges between each of these and the social sphere. Instead of considering models and institutions as 'defective'[5] mechanisms, due to their perceived weakness in comparison to an ideal of maximum efficiency, their vulnerability can be attributed to their nature as social processes. As such, models and institutions engage in constant exchanges with the milieu in which they operate, often experiencing 'irritation' from external social dynamics that redirect their 'semantics'.[6] Far from occupying the position of sovereign and autonomous subjects capable of acting successfully solely according to their position of authority, models and institutions must be able to 'pass' in the social fabric. This perspective necessarily requires a reconsideration of the conceptual framework intersecting these two notions: as Bruno Latour claims, institutions and models should be associated with the idea of subsistence rather than substance.[7] Drawing on the distinction that Alfred North Whitehead identifies between these two concepts, Latour argues that what exists as substance is by definition ossified in the status quo and antagonistic to any transformative movement.[8] On the contrary, what

'Why Has Critique Run out of Steam? From Matters of Fact to Matters of Concern', *Critical Inquiry*, 30.2 (2004), pp. 225–48 <https://doi.org/10.1086/421123>.

5   I take the expression from Jacques Lezra's book, *Defective Institutions: A Protocol for the Republic* (New York: Fordham University Press, 2024) <https://doi.org/10.5422/fordham/9781531506902.001.0001>.

6   Gunther Teubner, 'Self-subversive Justice: Contingency or Transcendence Formula of Law?', *Modern Law Review*, 72 (2009), pp. 1–23 (p. 7) <https://doi.org/10.1111/j.1468-2230.2009.00731.x>.

7   Bruno Latour, 'No Transformation without Institution', online video recording, YouTube, 17 October 2015 <https://www.youtube.com/watch?v=2RCLTxUaWVo> [accessed 10 January 2024].

8   Alfred North Whitehead, *Process and Reality: An Essay in Cosmology* [1929] (New York: The Free Press, 1978).

subsists is what requires continuous maintenance and repair in order
to exist. This work is not only a transformative process in itself but also
implies the ability of that which subsists to attract actors and agents
that will gather and collectively take care of it. If the composition and
maintenance of these assemblages constitute the conditions of existence for both a model and an institution, they can be reconceived
as agents of transformation and mobilization rather than mere guar-
antors of stability. Moreover, they exercise a power that is not only
representative but also performative, as they produce effects of social
composition which are vital for their subsistence.

In order to test this conceptual constellation, which replaces stability and representation with the transformation and performativity of
models and institutions, I will analyse a phenomenon that is becoming
increasingly relevant on a global scale and has so far been interpreted
primarily as a symptom of an irreversible crisis of political institutions,
to wit, of their loss of force of attraction on the socio-political fabric. This phenomenon is the juridification of politics, which can be
described as a general turn to law (to legal norms, mechanisms, and arguments) as a privileged means to defend one's interests and articulate
social and political demands.[9] As I will discuss in the next paragraphs,
despite the involvement of various social actors in this process, it has
primarily been interpreted as a futile, if not dangerous, attempt to res-
urrect the sovereign subject through the figure of the judge. On the
contrary, by analysing the juridification of gender politics, particularly
through a case in the Supreme Court of Kenya, I will highlight how
this phenomenon also involves bottom-up processes aimed at challen-

---

9   The term *juridification* was used for the first time by Otto Kirchheimer in order to
     define the gradual contractualization of class struggles during the Weimar Republic.
     The concept was later brought to the attention of contemporary philosophical and
     political debate through the works of Jürgen Habermas. See Jürgen Habermas, *The
     Theory of Communicative Action*, trans. by Thomas McCarthy, 2 vols (Boston: Beacon
     Press, 1984–87), II: *Lifeworld and System: A Critique of Functionalist Reason* [1981]
     (1987); and *Juridification of Social Spheres: A Comparative Analysis in the Areas of
     Labor, Corporate, Antitrust and Social Welfare Law*, ed. by Gunther Teubner (Berlin:
     De Gruyter, 1987) <https://doi.org/10.1515/9783110921472>. I discuss a more
     detailed history of the concept in Natascia Tosel, 'State, Law, and Institutions: A Study
     on Juridification', *Soft Power. Revista euro-americana de teoría e historia de la política y
     del derecho*, 9.2 (2022), pp. 156–73 <https://www.softpowerjournal.com/state-law-
     and-institutions-a-study-on-juridification/> [accessed 6 August 2024].

ging and changing the legal categories through which we understand reality.[10] Far from indicating a total rupture between institutions and social actors, these processes show the possibility of transformation and, therefore, social mobilization within models and institutions.

LAW AND PERFORMATIVITY: THE PHANTOM OF THE SOVEREIGN SUBJECT

The French sociologist Pierre Bourdieu, in his book *Language and Symbolic Power*, addresses the question of the performativity of the act — or, as he also refers to it, the rite — of institution. He claims, in particular, that instituting 'is an act of social magic',[11] precisely for its ability to 'bring into existence that which it utters'.[12] Drawing on Émile Benveniste's observation that 'all the words relating to the law

---

10   Lars Blichner and Anders Molander, in their essay 'Mapping Juridification', distinguish five dimensions of the process of juridification: (a) legalization; (b) law's expansion and differentiation; (c) increased conflict solving by reference to law; (d) increased judicial power; and (e) the emergence of a legal framework. While the majority of political and legal literature tends to emphasize dimension (d) — using the concept of 'judicialization' that I will discuss below — in the field of legal anthropology, there is a greater emphasis on dimension (c). See Lars C. Blichner and Anders Molander, 'Mapping Juridification', *European Law Journal*, 14.1 (2008), pp. 36–54 <https://doi.org/10.1111/j.1468-0386.2007.00405.x>. See also, for instance, John L. Comaroff and Simon Roberts, *Rules and Processes: The Cultural Logic of Dispute in an African Context* (Chicago: University of Chicago Press, 1981); *Law and Globalization from Below: Towards a Cosmopolitan Legality*, ed. by Boaventura de Sousa Santos and César A. Rodríguez-Garavito (Cambridge: Cambridge University Press, 2005) <https://doi.org/10.1017/CBO9780511494093>; and *Law Against the State: Ethnographic Forays into Law's Transformations*, ed. by Julia Eckert and others (Cambridge: Cambridge University Press, 2012) <https://doi.org/10.1017/CBO9781139043786>. My focus in this chapter, by contrast, will be on dimension (e), namely the growing use of law as a language and categorical apparatus through which social actors tend to define themselves and others, and to perceive themselves as legal subjects, attributing to law the meaning of a social practice. Needless to say, the construction of this legal framework, just like the other four dimensions of juridification, is not exempt from a fundamental ambivalence since the boundary between subjectivation and subjection is particularly fragile within the juridical semiotic field. In relation to current processes of juridification in Kenya, see Kipkoech Cheruiyot, 'Judicial Activism, Judicial Restraint and Constitutional Interpretation in Kenya: The Post-2010 Era', *SSRN*, published online 24 March 2022 <https://doi.org/10.2139/ssrn.4032620>; and Martin Mwenda, 'The Context of Transformative Constitutionalism in Kenya', *SSRN*, published online 30 June 2015 <https://doi.org/10.2139/ssrn.2624928>.

11   Pierre Bourdieu, *Language and Symbolic Power* [1982], trans. by Gino Raymond and Matthew Adamson (Cambridge: Polity Press, 1991), p. 119.

12   Ibid., p. 42.

have an etymological root meaning *to say*,[13] Bourdieu argues that 'the limiting case of the performative utterance is the legal act which, when it is pronounced, [...] can replace action with speech, which will, as they say, have an effect'.[14] Thus, 'legal discourse' is the paradigm of a 'creative speech' able to institute 'in the sense of calling into being, by an enforceable saying, what one says, of making the future that one utters come into being'.[15] Considering this effective performativity of legal discourse, it should not be surprising then that the law is increasingly used by social actors not only as a means to assert their political demands but also to create the conditions for their visions of the world to come into being. This is certainly true of political elites, who increasingly use legal language and juridical tools to implement their agendas. However, juridification does not only coincide with an increase in the power of legal and political elites. It is a broader phenomenon that also captures the tendency of citizens, 'slum-dwellers, peasants, Indigenous Peoples, and women resisting patriarchal violence', to demand 'respect for their rights' and to frame 'their claims with reference to legal discourses'.[16]

---

13   Ibid., p. 173. See also Émile Benveniste, *Le Vocabulaire des institutions indo-européennes* (Paris: Les Éditions de Minuit, 1969).

14   Pierre Bourdieu, *Language and Symbolic Power*, p. 75. It is interesting to note that the 'juridical' character of every performative statement is affirmed also by Deleuze and Guattari, both in their text on Kafka and in the fourth chapter of *A Thousand Plateaus*, dedicated to the 'Postulates of Linguistics'. Here, in particular, their primary reference remains Émile Benveniste, and they build upon his work through the interpretation provided by Oswald Ducrot. Drawing on Benveniste's and Ducrot's insights, Deleuze and Guattari argue that the illocutionary (constituting the implicit presuppositions of the performative) 'is in turn explained by collective assemblages of enunciation, by *juridical acts* or equivalents of juridical acts, which, far from depending on subjectification proceedings or assignations of subjects in language, in fact determine their distribution'. Gilles Deleuze and Félix Guattari, *A Thousand Plateaus: Capitalism and Schizophrenia* [1980], trans. by Brian Massumi (Minneapolis: University of Minnesota Press, 2005), p. 77, my emphasis.

15   Pierre Bourdieu, *Language and Symbolic Power*, pp. 42, 222.

16   Rachel Sieder, 'The Juridification of Politics', in *The Oxford Handbook of Law and Anthropology*, ed. by Marie-Claire Foblets and others (Oxford: Oxford University Press, 2020), pp. 701–15 (p. 701) <https://doi.org/10.1093/oxfordhb/9780198840534. 013.41>. In this case, the performativity of the legal act extends beyond court litigations. The translation of political demands into legal questions (which also takes place outside of legal institutions, in practices of political and social mobilization) has effects on the everyday perception and understanding of our social relations.

The assessment of the impact that this process of the juridification of politics may have in the long run largely depends on how the 'social magic' produced by legal discourse is interpreted. It is indeed possible to explain the instituting performativity of the law in two very different ways that also lead to two different judgements on the potentials and limits of the phenomenon of juridification. These two different ways of conceiving the force of legal discourse can both be found in Bourdieu's work, albeit in different texts. This internal tension in Bourdieusian thought does not undermine the importance of his sociological theory; on the contrary, it paves the way for new possible actualizations. I will analyse Bourdieu's idea of institutional performativity as an act of authority, of which — drawing on Judith Butler's critique — I will highlight the limits. The following section considers a second and less-discussed conception of performative power found in Bourdieu's reflections on the sociology of the juridical field, in which the law is assigned the semiotic task of making and unmaking the social.[17]

In order to highlight the first possible understanding of legal performativity, it is worth turning to the essay titled 'Authorized Language' (collected in *Language and Symbolic Power*), where Bourdieu attributes the 'magic' of the act of institution to the authoritative position of the subject who speaks. He claims, in particular, that:

> Most of the conditions that have to be fulfilled in order for a performative utterance to succeed come down to the question of the appropriateness of the speaker — or, better still, his social function — and of the discourse he utters. A performative utterance is destined to fail each time that it is not pronounced by a person who has the 'power' to pronounce it, [...] in short, each time that the speaker does not have the authority to emit the words that he utters.[18]

In this passage, the act of institution is reduced to an act of authority: its conditions of felicity depend entirely on the social function of the

---

17   I draw this second model of performativity from Pierre Bourdieu, 'The Force of Law: Toward a Sociology of the Juridical Field', trans. by Richard Terdiman, *The Hastings Law Journal*, 38 (1987), pp. 805–53 <https://repository.uclawsf.edu/hastings_law_journal/vol38/iss5/3> [accessed 6 August 2024]; and the chapter 'Description and Prescription: *The Conditions of Possibility and the Limits of Political Effectiveness*', in Bourdieu, *Language and Symbolic Power*, pp. 127–36.

18   Bourdieu, *Language and Symbolic Power*, p. 111.

subject of the speech act. According to this perspective, the law is considered emblematic of performative power due to the force of authority invested in legal actors. Needless to say, the most striking example is that of the judge — a case already deemed highly paradigmatic by John Austin's reflections on the illocutionary force of words.[19] In Bourdieusian terms, 'the judge need say no more than "I find you guilty" because there is a set of agents and institutions which guarantee that the sentence will be executed.'[20] A legal act 'when it is pronounced, as it should be, by someone who has the right to do so',[21] will produce as a sure effect the action that has been uttered. Therefore, the force of law is nothing but the binding power exerted by an authoritative subject, an individual who, by virtue of a delegation, is constituted as 'the legitimate representative'.[22] This agent is 'capable of acting on the social world through words,'[23] since he operates 'as a substitute for the group which gives him a mandate'.[24] Thus, concludes Bourdieu, 'the real source of the magic of performative utterances lies in the mystery of ministry', to wit, in the institution or nomination of an agent who becomes 'a medium between the group and the social world'.[25]

In line with this understanding of legal performativity as the power of a subject occupying a position of authority in the social field, the juridification currently underway has often been interpreted as a process of 'judicialization' — a notion that focuses entirely on the figure of judges and courts, underlining the authoritative force of their speech acts. Scholars who support this interpretation view the expansion of law as symptomatic of an enhancement of judicial authority.[26] Both domestic and international courts are accused of usurping pol-

---

19   John L. Austin, *How to Do Things with Words* [1962] (Oxford: Oxford University Press, 1976) <https://doi.org/10.1093/acprof:oso/9780198245537.001.0001>.

20   Bourdieu, *Language and Symbolic Power*, p. 75.

21   Ibid.

22   Ibid.

23   Ibid.

24   Ibid., p. 206.

25   Ibid., p. 75.

26   See *The Global Expansion of Judicial Power*, ed. by C. Neal Tate and Torbjorn Vallinder (New York: New York University Press, 1995); Martin Shapiro and Alec Stone Sweet, *On Law, Politics, and Judicialization* (Oxford: Oxford University Press, 2002); and Ran Hirschl, 'The Judicialization of Politics', in *The Oxford Handbook of Law and Politics*, ed. by Gregory A. Caldeira and others (Oxford: Oxford University Press, 2008), pp. 119–41 <https://doi.org/10.1093/oxfordhb/9780199208425.003.0008>.

itical power, since — as the president of the Constitutional Court of Belgium, Marc Bossuyt, affirms, referring to the European Court of Justice and the European Court for Human Rights — they are creating the threat of a 'government by judges'.[27] In a nutshell, 'the meaning of juridification' refers to this extent 'to increased judicial power', which exploits 'the indeterminacy concerning the application of rules to specific cases' in order to decrease the transparency of law and to enlarge the decision-making power of professional legal actors.[28] This process therefore appears to alter the relation between the political and legal realms significantly. More specifically, it is categorized as a process of depoliticization that contributes to the crisis of political institutions and attempts to replace political with legal decision-making.

However, a possible criticism of this understanding of the juridification of politics lies precisely in its flattening of legal performativity on the figure of judges or professional elites. Here, performativity is once again reduced to a mechanism of representation in such a manner that, as Judith Butler argues in *Excitable Speech*, the phantom of the sovereign subject, which was linked to the political vocabulary of the modern age rather than the contemporary period, is brought back in through the window. In particular, the fantasy of its return 'takes place in language, in the figure of the performative',[29] and more precisely in that of the speaking subject. As Butler states, Bourdieu describes the life of the social solely 'in spatialized terms':[30]

> This becomes a problem for Bourdieu's account of performative speech acts because he tends to assume that the subject who utters the performative is positioned on a map of social power in a fairly fixed way, and that this performative will or will not work depending on whether the subject who performs the utterance is already authorized to make it work by the position of social power it occupies.[31]

27   Marc Bossuyt, 'Bossuyt waarschuwt voor "regering door rechters"', *Het Belang van Limburg*, 17 February 2011 <https://www.hbvl.be/cnt/aid1019380> [accessed 10 January 2024].

28   Blichner and Molander, 'Mapping Juridification', p. 45.

29   Judith Butler, *Excitable Speech: A Politics of the Performative* (New York: Routledge, 1997), p. 78.

30   Judith Butler, 'Performativity's Social Magic', in *Bourdieu: A Critical Reader*, ed. by Richard Shusterman (Oxford: Blackwell, 1999), pp. 113–28 (p. 125).

31   Ibid., p. 122.

What Butler emphasizes is that this way of understanding performative power is only suitable for top-down processes, where the success of a speech act depends on the fact that the speaker is already delegated to perform it. This not only drastically reduces the agency of those who are not already authorized to speak (making any resistance attempts ineffective) but also forgets a fundamental dimension of the act of institution, namely its temporality. The social performative — as Bourdieu himself affirmed — is 'a social ritual'; as such, Butler claims, it needs to be constantly repeated, or, in Derridean terms, reiterated.[32] According to this perspective, performativity differs from the mere mechanism of representation that characterizes sovereign power precisely because there is a gap, a temporal deferral, between the enunciation of the norm and its execution.[33]

> Performativity cannot be understood outside of a process of iterability, a regularized and constrained repetition of norms. And this repetition is not performed *by* a subject; this repetition is what enables a subject and constitutes the temporal condition for the subject. This iterability implies that 'performance' is not a singular 'act' or event, but a ritualized production.[34]

Not surprisingly, Butler uses the example of the judge precisely in order to demonstrate that even in this case, the performativity of the act cannot be ascribed as a direct and immediate causal effect of a sovereign will. 'As one who efficaciously speaks in the name of the law, the judge does not originate the law or its authority; rather, he "cites" the law, consults and reinvokes the law, and, in that reinvocation, reconstitutes the law.'[35] Thus, the judge 'is not himself the authority who invests the law with its power to bind'; on the contrary, he is 'installed in the midst of a signifying chain, receiving and reciting the law'.[36]

---

32 Jacques Derrida, 'Signature Événement Contexte', in Derrida, *Marges de la Philosophie* (Paris: Les Éditions de Minuit, 1972), pp. 365–93.

33 For an analysis of the relationship between normativity and temporality that draws on Butler's theory, see Ritu Birla, 'Performativity between Logos and Nomos: Law, Temporality and the Non-Economic Analysis of Power', *Columbia Journal of Gender and Law*, 21.2 (2011) <https://doi.org/10.7916/cjgl.v21i2.2636>. See also Martha Merrill Umphrey, 'Law in Drag: Trials and Legal Performativity', *Columbia Journal of Gender and Law*, 21.2 (2011) <https://doi.org/10.7916/cjgl.v21i2.2638>.

34 Judith Butler, *Bodies that Matter: On the Discursive Limits of "Sex"* (New York: Routledge, 1993), p. 95.

35 Ibid., p. 107.

36 Ibid.

What interests Butler in this temporality of performative action is that it makes it impossible to ascribe its success solely to the 'the fabrication of the performer's "will" or "choice"'.[37] The felicitous conditions of a rite of institution can never be fully determined in advance but only from the effects of the act itself, namely from its capacity to establish a 'model for action' that will be (re)cognized as such and that will gather around itself social entities that adhere to it. Since there is no causal or linear relationship between authority and performative power, the act of institution opens up to the possibility of its infelicity,[38] that is, the possibility that performative utterances (and the models they promote) can 'go wrong, be misapplied or misinvoked',[39] taking a non-ordinary meaning, or being used in a context where they do not belong. In this way, Butler sets the stage for rethinking the performativity of law outside the paradigm of authority. This does not mean denying the fact that legal actors also exercise and reiterate their authority through their speech acts. However, Butler breaks with the conception of performativity linked to the instantaneity between an order or a decision and its execution. As they write in *Bodies that Matter*, the legal 'discourse', in which the judge cites the law, 'becomes a site for the reconstitution and resignification of the law'.[40] The possibility of a subversive resignification is thus part of the normative functioning itself.

Despite the importance of this emphasis on the ritual temporality of law, Butler's conception of the performative cannot be used any further for our purposes, since it presents two internal limits that make its application to legal discourse difficult. The first consists in its identification of the conditions of possibility for resignification, that is, the rupture between the speech act and its social context, mostly in the expropriation of the authorization to speak by those who do not have it.[41] The subversive potential of legal discourse is indeed only appropriable

---

37   Ibid., p. 234.

38   On the relationship between normativity and infelicity (in the Austinian sense), see Sandra Laugier, 'Performativité, normativité et droit', *Archives de Philosophie*, 64.4 (2004), pp. 607–27 <https://doi.org/10.3917/aphi.674.0607>.

39   Butler, *Excitable Speech*, p. 151.

40   Butler, *Bodies that Matter*, p. 107.

41   See, for instance, Butler's analysis of Rosa Parks's subversive gesture of sitting at the front of the bus (*Excitable Speech*, p. 147). Butler insists that this insurrectionary process of overthrowing the established codes of legitimacy largely depended on the

by actors who are not authorized to speak through the law; on the contrary, it seems a priori foreclosed for those who are authorized to use it, such as judges. Here, Butler runs the risk of echoing the mistake made by Bourdieu, explaining performative power only through the social position (this time of illegitimacy rather than authority) occupied by the speaker.[42] Secondly, drawing on Austin's distinction between illocutionary and perlocutionary, Butler inscribes the act of resignification in the latter, arguing that 'whereas illocutionary performatives produce ontological effects (bringing something into "being"), perlocutionary performatives alter an ongoing situation'.[43] On the contrary, as we saw at the beginning of this paragraph, the instituting force of law, to which more and more social actors appeal, consists precisely in what Bourdieu calls an 'ontological glorification', to wit, its capacity to call into being what is named.[44] Legal performativity, therefore, must be imagined beyond the simple resignification and recontextualization of a name; it is, rather, a power of naming, which — as I will explain in the next section — cannot be separated from a power of form.

FROM NAME TO *NOMOS*: THE JURIDIFICATION OF 'GAY' AND 'LESBIAN' IN A CASE OF THE SUPREME COURT OF KENYA

In 2013, Kenyan activist and law teacher Eric Gitari requested permission from the NGOs Co-ordination Board to register a Non-Governmental Organization (NGO) with the aim of advocating for 'the rights of Lesbian, Gay, Bisexual, Transgender, Queer or Question-

---

fact that Parks 'had no prior right to do so', that 'she had no prior authorization', and that this is paradoxically the reason why 'she endowed a certain authority on the act'.

42   On this point, see Steph Lawler, 'Rules of Engagement: Habitus, Power and Resistance', in *Feminism after Bourdieu*, ed. by Lisa Adkins and Beverley Skeggs (Oxford: Blackwell, 2004), pp. 110–28. On the disjunction between naming and social position and on the possibility of transformation that lies not in the intentional actions of subjects, but in their ability to operate within the fractures of the relationship between language and society, see Iracema Dulley, 'Naming Others: Translation and Subject Constitution in the Central Highlands of Angola (1926–1961)', *Comparative Studies in Society and History*, 64.2 (2022), pp. 363–93 <https://doi.org/10.1017/S0010417522000056>.

43   Judith Butler, 'Performative Agency', *Journal of Cultural Economy*, 3.2 (2010), pp. 148–61 (p. 151) <https://doi.org/10.1080/17530350.2010.494117>. As is well known, Austin defines *illocutionary* as the act performed in saying something, and *perlocutionary* as the act performed by or as a result of saying something. See Austin, *How to Do Things with Words*.

44   Bourdieu, 'The Force of Law', p. 846.

ing (LGBTIQ) persons in Kenya'. He proposed five different names for the NGO, all including the terms *gay* and *lesbian*.[45] In response, the NGOs Co-ordination Board sent a letter signed by the executive director, asserting that none of the proposed names could be approved due to their violation of Sections 162, 163, and 165 of the Kenyan Penal Code, which criminalize 'gay and lesbian liaisons'. Gitari filed a High Court petition, alleging that the refusal to register the intended NGO contravened several articles of the Kenyan Constitution, including Article 36, which guarantees the right to freedom of association. The High Court concurred, finding that the actions of the NGOs Co-ordination Board constituted a violation of Article 36.[46] The article explicitly specifies that the right to freedom of association must be ensured for 'every person', without any reference to their sexual orientation. Dissatisfied with the judgement of the High Court, the NGOs Co-ordination Board lodged an appeal first at the Court of Appeal in Nairobi and then at the Supreme Court of Kenya, stating that the judges erred in law 'by failing to uphold the provisions of the Penal Code that outlaw homosexual behavior, as well as any aiding, abetting, counselling, procuring and other related and inchoate crimes', and 'by effectively reading into the Constitution's non-discrimination clause the ground of sexual orientation'. Both the courts dismissed the appeal,[47] affirming the judgement of the High Court and confirming that all the people 'in this country who answer to any of the descriptions in the acronym LBGTIQ [...] just like everyone else, have a right to freedom of association which includes the right to form an association of any kind'.[48]

---

45   The proposed names were: 'Gay and Lesbian Human Rights Council'; 'Gay and Lesbian Human Rights Observancy'; 'Gay and Lesbian Human Rights Organization'; 'Gay and Lesbian Human Rights Commission'; 'Gay and Lesbian Human Rights Council'; and 'Gay and Lesbian Human Rights Collective'.

46   *Eric Gitari v. NGOs Co-ordination Board & 4 Others*, Petition No. 440 of 2013, Kenya High Court, Judgement of 24 April 2015.

47   *NGOs Co-ordination Board v. E. G. & 5 Others*, Civil Appeal No. 145 of 2015, Nairobi Court of Appeal, Judgement of 22 March 2019.

48   *Eric Gitari v. NGOs Co-ordination Board & 3 Others*, Civil Appeal No. 16 of 2019, Kenya Supreme Court, Judgement of 24 February 2023, Judgement of the Court, § 16, p. 8. On the history of the case and its relevance for Kenyan 'Transformative Constitutionalism', see Joshua Malidzo Nyawa, 'The Kenyan Constitution 2010, Gay

This case is of particular relevance not only because it constitutes a significant legal change for the recognition of LGBTQIA+ persons in Kenya, paving the way towards the decriminalization of sexual orientation,[49] but also because it allows us to observe the social performativity of legal language in the making. As the judge,William Ouko, pointed out in his dissenting opinion, 'the central issue in this appeal is about the reservation of a *name* and whether the appellant's decision in rejecting the names proposed was lawful, reasonable, proportionate and procedurally fair'.[50] On the one hand, the executive director of the NGOs Co-ordination Board experienced 'discomfort with the use of the terms "gay" and "lesbian"', while he was 'ready and prepared to reserve any of the names so long as the two words were omitted from the proposed names'.[51] On the other hand, for Gitari 'the words "gay" and "lesbian" were the unique marks of identification of the proposed organization, without which its objectives, characteristics, affiliations, and social roles would be completely lost'.[52] At this point, the judge embarks on a socio-ontological reflection, problematizing the force of a name:

> What's in a name? asked William Shakespeare through one of his characters in *Romeo and Juliet*, to signify the fact that a name may be a convenient concept for identification but the essence behind it is the distinctive and fundamental nature of identity. An organization will be identified by its unique name.[53]

Despite the clear risk of essentialism in the judge's words, they capture a fundamental point of juridical performativity: a name, once trans-

---

Sex (or Gay Rights?), and the Eric Gitari Ruling of 2019', *SSRN*, published online 16 June 2019 <https://doi.org/10.2139/ssrn.3396306>.

49   On this point, see *Legal Grounds III: Reproductive and Sexual Rights in Sub-Saharan African Courts*, ed. by Godfrey Dalitso Kangaude (Pretoria: Pretoria University Law Press, 2017). For an analysis of how sexuality has been problematized in judicial decisions, see *Sexuality in the Legal Arena*, ed. by Carl Stychin and Didi Herman (London: The Athlone Press, 2000). For an inquiry that directly takes into account the connection between juridification, family law, and gender politics, see Mariano Croce, *The Juridification of Politics* (London: Routledge, 2018).

50   *Eric Gitari v. NGOs Co-ordination Board & 3 others*, Civil Appeal No. 16 of 2019, Kenya Supreme Court, Judgement of 24 February 2023, Dissenting opinion of W. Ouko, § 147, p. 49.

51   Ibid., § 133, p. 45.

52   Ibid., § 134, p. 46.

53   Ibid., § 134, p. 46.

lated into the language of the law, changes the ontological status of what is named. Thus, the entire complexity of the case revolved around this power of naming that here — as Justice Ouko states — concerned two terms, *gay* and *lesbian*, 'no doubt widely used today' but that 'are not defined in our laws'.[54] At this stage, the true nature of the legal problem becomes clear: the case is expressed in terms of ordinary language that does not yet have a correspondence in legal language. Hence, what is at stake goes beyond the simple application of rules; instead, it is an exercise of legal imagination.

As Bourdieu argues in 'The Force of Law' (in a way that is not necessarily fully consistent with the theorization of the 'mystery of ministry' that I have discussed earlier, since here the sovereigntist account of performativity is abandoned), legal acts, including the judgement of a court, belong to 'the class of *acts of naming* or of *instituting*'.[55] These speech acts are certainly formulated by authorized agents, but the reason why they are 'magical acts' is that they perform 'the entire practical activity of "worldmaking" (marriages, divorces, substitutions, associations, dissolutions) which constitutes social units'[56].

> Law is the quintessential form of the symbolic power of naming that creates the things named, and creates social groups in particular. It confers upon the reality which arises from its classificatory operations the maximum permanence that any social entity has the power to confer upon another [...]. The law is the quintessential form of 'active' discourse, able by its own operation to produce its effects. It would not be excessive to say that it *creates* the social world.[57]

Contrary to what one might think, Bourdieu's position here aligns more with a realistic than a radical constructivism because this worldmaking activity is not at all disconnected or detached from the material processes occurring in the social fabric. Indeed, the most specific effect of the legal act of naming, to wit, 'the *vis formae*, the power of form', or 'the shaping of practices through juridical formalization', can 'succeed only to the extent that legal organization gives explicit form

---

54   Ibid., § 138, p. 50.
55   Bourdieu, 'The Force of Law', p. 838, emphasis in the original.
56   Ibid., p. 838.
57   Ibid., pp. 838–39.

to a tendency already immanent within those practices'.[58] In order to understand this point, it is worth turning to Bourdieu's conception of the life of the social world. In his perspective, this latter is the stage for a constant struggle 'in which differing, indeed antagonistic world-views confront each other'.[59] What is at stake in this struggle is the monopoly on what Bourdieu calls the *nomos*: 'the Greek word for "law" or "custom"' that 'derives from *nemo*, meaning to separate, divide, distribute'.[60] Every vision of the world in fact includes a principle of division, that is, a social difference that, once named and instituted, becomes the legitimate criterion for the distribution of (real and symbolic) power. The legal work of worldmaking therefore concerns the 'worldviews' circulating and struggling within the social field; in particular, the translation of ordinary language into legal language can be useful 'to transform the world by transforming the words for *naming* it'.[61] The act of naming here implies 'producing new categories of perception and judgment, and [...] dictating a new vision of social divisions and distributions',[62] to wit, challenging and changing the *nomos*, or the dominant principle of classification.

The success of this transformation of the *nomos* is not attributed in this case to the authoritative position of the subject who performs the act of naming. Instead, there is a specific force that belongs to the vision (and division) of the world that the name encloses. The 'social magic' here is 'the *sociosymbolic alchemy* whereby a mental construct, existing abstractly in the minds of individual persons, is turned into a concrete social reality'.[63] This does not happen as the consequence of the institution of a ministry; it is, rather, related to a process of group-making that emerges from the 'struggles over the monopoly of the power to make people see and believe, to get them to know and recognize, to impose the legitimate definition of the divisions of the

---

58   Ibid., p. 848.
59   Ibid., p. 837.
60   Ibid., p. 837, note 55.
61   Ibid., p. 839, my emphasis.
62   Ibid., p. 839.
63   Loïc Wacquant, 'Symbolic Power and Group-Making: On Pierre Bourdieu's Reframing of Class', *Journal of Classical Sociology*, 13.2 (2013), pp. 1–18 (p. 2), emphasis in the original <https://doi.org/10.1177/1468795X12468737>.

social world and, thereby, to *make and unmake groups*.[64] When legal discourse contributes to the process of group-making (which always implies the imposition of a *nomos*), law is used as a means to perform

> the *labour of enunciation* which is necessary in order to [...] name the unnamed and to give the beginnings of objectification to pre-verbal and pre-reflexive dispositions and ineffable and unobservable experiences, through words which by their nature make them common and communicable, therefore meaningful and socially sanctioned.[65]

As mentioned earlier, this work of naming and creating social reality cannot succeed simply by being performed by an authoritative figure. What determines its success is rather the ability of the enunciated vision to attract actors and groups: in other words, the name is what 'enables agents to discover within themselves common properties that lie beyond the diversity of particular situations which isolate, divide and demobilize'.[66] What is in common has to be named in order to become intelligible, cognizable, and recognizable. This means that, on the one hand, this labour of enunciation cannot be reduced to a mere description or representation of reality because it names what still remains unnamed in the dominant vision and division of the world. On the other hand, what is enunciated cannot be completely detached from reality, as, in that case, it would not be recognizable by social actors as a common element around which to gather. Names, therefore, become performative when they succeed in conveying models, 'previsions, anticipatory descriptions, [...] visions [that] only call forth what they proclaim — whether new practices, new mores or especially new social groupings — because they announce what is in the process of developing'.[67]

Keeping that in mind, it is now possible to return to the case of the Supreme Court of Kenya discussed at the beginning of this section and to demonstrate how Bourdieu's understanding of the instituting power of naming can lead to an alternative reading of the process of the juridification of politics. The case in question, in fact, lends itself to multiple

---

64   Bourdieu, *Language and Symbolic Power*, p. 221, emphasis in the original.
65   Ibid., p. 129, emphasis in the original.
66   Ibid., p. 130.
67   Bourdieu, 'The Force of Law', p. 839.

possible readings. Firstly, supporters of judicialization would understand it as emblematic of the growing political and decision-making
power of the courts. In this view, the recognition of rights for the LGB-
TQIA+ community in Kenya would be entirely ascribed to the will and
(in this case, progressive) political agenda of the judges. To this extent,
as for instance Wendy Brown suggests, the use of a legal framework
for recognition can be problematized due to its paradoxicality, insofar as marginalized subjects find legal protection in the State's rights
that had previously sustained the invisibility of their subordination.[68]
However, following Butler's politics of resignification — which constitutes the theoretical basis for interpretations of law 'from below'
primarily coming from legal anthropology — it would be possible to
reverse this perspective on the case and highlight the predominant
role of LGBTQIA+ activists such as Eric Gitari in the process. Here,
the creative and subversive potential of legal discourse would emerge
more prominently. Yet, this creative and subversive potential is mainly
conceptualized in terms of a resignification of the name by which a
group is traditionally stigmatized or excluded from power (in this case,
gay and *lesbian*). Here, one can argue that such 'renaming' actually
risks reinforcing the existing stigmatized representations of a group,
as renaming does not itself modify the dominant principle of classification (*nomos*). In other words, resignifying a group's identifying name
might exert a weak performative force, since it may not problematize
and undo the reasons why a 'stigmatized' or 'discriminated' group is
perceived as such.

On the contrary, what this chapter suggests, drawing on Bourdieu's analysis of the force of law, is a third, alternative reading of the
case and, by extension, of juridification. The juridical speech act exerts
a performative effect because it takes on the socio-semiotic work of
the division, categorization, and composition of groups. This work is
exactly what allows the social to be made and undone, potentially offering alternative ways of composing and grouping and thus becoming
usable for a politics of mobilization rather than resignification. The
legal institution previews and captures the new trends circulating in

---

68   Wendy Brown, 'Suffering Rights as Paradoxes', *Constellations*, 7.2 (2000), pp. 230–41
     <https://doi.org/10.1111/1467-8675.00183>.

society that still lack a legal form. Specifically, in the case analysed here, Gitari's group appeals to the law so that their practices of assembly, in which homosexual conducts are openly liveable, cognizable, and recognizable, can be codified and translated in the juridical framework. Indeed, the case does not concern the recognition of sexual or gender identity, but rather the right of association. The names *gay* and *lesbian* serve here to institute new social compositions; to this extent, they are neither taken as universal signifiers nor merely semantically recontextualized, but, rather, they are used so that new forms of collective life 'come into being'.

CONCLUSIONS: MODELS, OR PREVISIONS OF THE WORLD

The exchanges between legal discourse and social processes, which through the phenomenon of juridification are increasingly intensifying, can only produce a continuous transformation: a never-ending making and remaking. Law transforms the understanding of the world for those who are named by its words, while, on the other hand, this process of 'jurisgenesis' — a term coined by Robert Cover — is a 'creative process' always 'collective or social'.[69] This by no means suggests that every legal change can be considered 'progressive'; on the contrary, it is about highlighting that any performative effect from the law cannot be explained solely as the product of an authoritative decision taken by a sovereign subject that can arbitrarily recognize or discriminate, condemn or absolve. Behind the law, more than a single act of authority, there is a continuous *'battle for the existence and legibility of different legal orders'*,[70] of alternative models and *nomoi* — 'names' and 'nomos' underpinning different ontologies and unconventional worldviews.

In conclusion, I have discussed and analysed in this chapter the different ways in which the current and widely recognized crisis of institutions can be interpreted, depending on the conceptual framework through which both the institutions and the 'models of action'

---

69   Robert Cover, 'Nomos and Narrative', in *Narrative, Violence, and the Law: The Essays of Robert Cover*, ed. by Michael Ryan and Austin Sarat (Ann Arbor: University of Michigan Press, 1992), pp. 95–172 (p. 103).

70   Sieder, 'The Juridification of Politics', p. 705; emphasis in the original.

they convey in the social fabric are understood. On the one hand, the conceptual apparatus of modern political philosophy has consistently linked the performative success of acts of institution to a static and mimetic repetition of models, emphasizing a tendency to shape the social by representing it. On the other hand, analysis of the current juridification of politics, where it avoids reducing the phenomenon to a mere increase in judicial power, opens the way to rethinking acts of institution as the results of a socio-semantic battle over how to name and form reality. From this perspective, an institution — as Bourdieu claims — 'exists, so to speak, twice, in things and in minds',[71] because it must convey a (pre)vision of the world whose performative success translates into the creation of a social alchemy. Modelling, then, rather than an internal semantic variation within the concept of representation, appears closer to the grammar of social processes and mobilizations, to that continuous making and unmaking through which a worldview is 'called into being' and subsists, until it is inevitably broken by the formation of new 'semiotic'[72] and social compositions.

---

71   Pierre Bourdieu and Loïc Wacquant, *An Invitation to Reflexive Sociology* (Chicago: University of Chicago Press, 1992), p. 127.

72   I am referring here to the notion of 'semiotic groups', initially introduced by the semiologist Algirdas Julius Greimas and further elucidated by Bernard Jackson. Semiotic groups are characterized as assemblies of people utilizing the same system of signification, thereby ensuring that their 'speech behaviour is mutually intelligible'. Bernard Jackson, *Making Sense in Law* (Liverpool: Deborah Charles, 1995), p. 96.

Natascia's essay, 'Modelling Institutions, Instituting Models: The Juridification of Politics and the Performative Power of Naming', offers
a timely, imaginative, and crucial response to the ongoing disinclin-
ation towards both models and institutions that has accompanied the
broader crisis of legitimacy of the sovereign subject, who, in Natascia's
words, is 'capable of exerting the force of its will through a recognized
authority'. Indeed, if both models and institutions are approached with
growing suspicion, it is because of their association with domination
and control over their object. In this way, models and institutions
could be seen as the embodiment of the sovereign subject whose autonomy and socially recognized authority enable them to model the
future that they will and pronounce on behalf of others. Due to this association between models and the sovereign, modelling could indeed
be seen as synonymous with mastery and control, exercised through
prohibition or authorization of the kind that includes and precludes
certain lived experiences and visions of the world.

Attempting to wrench institutions and models from the sovereign
phantom, Natascia turns to the phenomenon of juridification, through
which we are invited to instead approach them as heterogeneous, open-
ended, bottom-up social processes that — by continuously mobilizing
the milieus within which they operate — model reality by transmitting
previsions or anticipatory worldviews. Such a conceptualization and
practice of modelling blurs the very distinction between subject and
object. Indeed, in Natascia's essay, modelling — displaced from the
position of the sovereign individual — becomes a collective process
and exercise of imagination that names something which does not
(yet) exist in socially sanctioned reality and that, in this way, makes
and unmakes social compositions. In naming what is not authorized
and not yet present, modelling becomes linked to a (speech) act, which
brings to mind perhaps a slightly unusual association with a psychoanalytic reading of an act: as a transmission of desire that involves risks
because its effects in the world are unforeseeable, and because it is
not interested in adapting to the status quo. In mobilizing the name
beyond the sovereign pronouncement or commandment, modelling

ultimately involves an ongoing, shared task of testing the elasticity and capaciousness of language, and the latter's openness to repair. And because a model is inseparable from the social fabrics and realities that it makes and unmakes, it is itself also continuously made and broken.

In closing, I think that this turn to a new thinking of the model — beyond the sovereign — ultimately signals, or perhaps necessitates, a different model of subjectivity. Indeed, Natascia's essay raises the broader question of how the discussion of the model itself — especially the social, cultural, legal, or aesthetic model — is fundamentally intertwined with how we define its subject. This is especially important given the current crisis of legitimacy of models and institutions, which is happening in parallel with a growing urge to conceive new ways of being and inhabiting the social link. This crisis not only manifests the crisis of credibility of the sovereign subject, but is also linked more broadly to the disintegration of the very model of the sovereign, autonomous, self-governing individual, especially at the current moment, when cultural, social, political, and scientific discourses and formations seem less and less capable of supporting the fantasy of the solidity of the subject.

Aesthetic Modelling at the Limit of the Human Montage

MARTA ALEKSANDROWICZ

INTRODUCTION

This essay engages with the recent advances in Freudian and Lacanian psychoanalysis developed at GIFRIC (the Interdisciplinary Freudian Group for Research and Clinical and Cultural Interventions) and EFQ (the Freudian School of Quebec) in Canada, and places them in conversation with works by two Brazilian artists and contemporaries, Clarice Lispector and Lygia Clark.[1] I situate my discussion within this specific constellation of artists, clinicians, and scholars to argue that their work enables us to conceive a model of the human in opposition to an individualistic, anthropocentric model based on exclusionary hierarchies that separate humans from other human and other-than-human beings. Indeed, this new model — which I introduce here by way of short vignettes drawn from my engagement with the work of Haitian psychoanalyst and leading member of GIFRIC and the EFQ, Willy Apollon, Lispector's novel *A paixão segundo G.H.* (*The Passion According to G.H.*), and Clark's sculpture series *Bichos* — neither breaks

---

1   I would like to thank my colleagues at the ICI Berlin for their valuable comments on previous drafts of this paper.

with the category of the human nor replaces it with another, for instance posthuman, model of subjectivity. Not only does it not dispense with the human but it also paradoxically and counterintuitively reconceives humanity as, in fact, antithetical to atomistic identity and self-interested individualism.[2] Furthermore, I propose that, in addition to offering a particular understanding of the human, this model also entails a particular logic and structure, with an important aesthetic dimension that goes beyond what Apollon and Lispector respectively call the 'cultural montage' and the 'human montage'.

For Apollon, the human subject emerges through a rupturing encounter with 'exteriority' and 'strangeness'; this is especially pronounced in his earlier work.[3] In blurring the boundary between inside and outside, this rupture effectively places the human at odds with the prevailing model of the human subject as a self-enclosed individual. The latter model, I suggest, drawing on Apollon's work, belongs to the domain of the cultural montage (*montage culturel*), which works to

---

2   This paper is an effect of my attempt to creatively engage with psychoanalytic, literary, and sculptural material in order to rethink the model (not only that of the human, but also the model as such) through an aesthetic lens. Within this scope, I focus here — especially in the case of Apollon and Lispector's work — on attempting to glean the aesthetic model from selected scenes and vignettes, rather than on providing a comprehensive exposition or summary of this extensive and complex material.

3   Willy Apollon, 'The Limit: A Fundamental Question for the Subject in the Human Experience', in *Borderlines in Psychoanalysis*, ed. by Jeffrey Librett, special issue of *Konturen*, 3 (2010), pp. 103–18 (p. 106) <https://doi.org/10.5399/uo/konturen.3. 1.1391>. Apollon's earlier work, which I mainly draw on in this essay, discusses the human in terms of the encounter with the unnameable strangeness and exteriority of the voice, or more specifically the 'unpresentable object of the voice of the Other' (Apollon, 'The Limit', p. 112). His recent work focuses more on approaching the human in terms of the 'spirit'. The spirit (as in the French *esprit* or German *Geist*) has an aesthetic dimension and is linked to speech as the 'power of representation and creation'; furthermore, it is distinguished from both the 'adaptive function' of the psyche and the mind as a 'register of cognition' (Willy Apollon, 'The Subject of the Quest', trans. by Daniel Wilson, in *Beauty*, ed. by Marta Aleksandrowicz and Fernanda Negrete, special issue of *Penumbr(a)*, 2 (2022), pp. 1–14 (pp. 5, 3) <https://www. penumbrajournal.org/no-2-beauty> [accessed 19 July 2024]). Apollon's emphasis on the human experience of the voice and the spirit places its accent elsewhere from, for instance, Jacques Lacan's discussion of the human in terms of entry into the world of the symbolic and the signifier. For more on this, see, for example, Tracy McNulty, 'The Traversal of the Fantasy as an Opening to Humanity', in *Psychoanalysis and Solidarity*, ed. by Michelle Rada, special issue of *differences*, 33.2–3 (2022), pp. 198–219 <https: //doi.org/10.1215/10407391-10124760>.

delimit and guard the borders of what can be perceived, included, and recognized in so-called consensual, collective reality.[4]

Indeed, the term 'montage' is mainly associated with the creative techniques of editing developed by Soviet montage theory and other avant-garde movements, such as Cubism, Futurism, Dadaism, and Surrealism. As I will discuss below, the creative techniques of 'montaging' are also crucial to Lispector's literary writing and Clark's sculpture. However, Apollon's unusual use of the term instead indicates a construction and configuration of reality that is built on and reinforced through culture, which organizes the social bond and life in the collective through an assemblage of norms, ideals, and prohibitions, and which, by doing so, works to repress and control the human. As Tracy McNulty has noted in her discussion of Apollon's work, culture in this perspective is understood specifically as founded on 'a rule that censors the human in every human being in order to guarantee its own material and ideological reproduction.'[5] The human in every human being is linked to the unconscious dimension of desire, creativity, and the drive.

---

4   This montage is undermined and thus increasingly guarded in the age of *mondialisation*, which Apollon distinguishes from globalization. While globalization is mainly linked to economic and industrial processes associated with global, neoliberal expansion, *mondialisation* refers to the consequences that an ongoing clash of different cultural and civilizational frameworks entails for human experience. Jeffrey Librett's commentary on Apollon's work translates *mondialisation* as 'world-formation'. *Mondialisation* is amplified through intensifying migration and forced displacement due to a host of economic, political, military, and climate crises, as well as increasing urbanization, information wars, and the proliferation of conflicting cultural definitions of the human. In weakening the solidity of the cultural montage, *mondialisation* also testifies to something in the human that the definitions deployed by the montage cannot capture. For more on this, see Apollon, 'The Subject of the Quest'; and Jeffrey Librett, 'The Subject in the Age of World-Formation (*Mondialisation*): Advances in Lacanian Theory from the Québec Group', in *Innovations in Psychoanalysis: Originality, Development, Progress*, ed. by Aner Govrin and Jon Mills (New York: Routledge, 2020), pp. 75–100 <https://doi.org/10.4324/9780367809560-5>.

5   McNulty, 'The Traversal of the Fantasy', p. 199. Although this is not the focus of my essay, it is worth stressing that Apollon's metapsychology places a special emphasis on how the cultural montage specifically deploys sex as a medium through which, as McNulty notes, 'every culture produces the man and the woman that it needs to reproduce itself' (p. 199). Apollon points out that, in order to ensure reproduction by controlling desire, the montage must 'organize itself both around and against the stakes of feminine *jouissance*', as the 'history of witchcraft [...] will always be there to remind us of' (Apollon, 'The Subject of the Quest', p. 11).

The creative technique of montage pertains to the work of selecting, assembling, cutting, pasting, curating, and putting together
heterogeneous fragments, pieces, and textures, which are juxtaposed
to produce something new and unprecedented. Conversely, the cultural montage points to a more hermetic construction that is 'sewn'
and 'fixed' together from an ensemble of norms, rules, and ideals to
control and limit human creativity and desire.[6] Even if its architecture might appear malleable and dynamic, since norms and ideals shift
according to sociocultural context, reproduction and preservation of
this montage ultimately depends on the exclusion of the aforementioned dimension of exteriority and strangeness, and the installation
of the closed model of the human. If aesthetic production — which
Fernanda Negrete's commentary on Apollon's work describes as 'a
fundamentally creative "out of bounds"'[7] — is in opposition to the
cultural montage, it is because it creates a path for the welcoming and
expression of strangeness and exteriority from the limits of atomistic
identity and language. Mobilized by the work of unconscious desire
and the drive, aesthetic production thus becomes a way of reshaping
and redefining reality out-of-bounds: beyond and against the cultural
montage. Importantly, aesthetic production is not limited to artists
but rather is available to all. Furthermore, not only is it not limited to
artists, but it is also not equivalent to all artistic production; indeed,
some artistic production is circumscribed within the norms and ideals
of a given cultural construction of reality, and is effectively complicit in
reinforcing censorship of creativity and desire. If, in this essay, I nonetheless engage the artistic projects of Clarice Lispector and Lygia Clark,

---

6   It is worth noting that Apollon works primarily in French, where *montage* refers
     not only to film, sound, and photo editing, but also to sewing clothes, fixing and
     installing appliances, or assembling furniture. See 'Montage', in *Larousse Bilingual
     Dictionary* (Paris: Larousse, n.d.) <https://www.larousse.fr/dictionnaires/francais-
     anglais/montage/52341> [accessed 30 March 2024]. Meanwhile, in Brazilian Portu-
     guese, *montagem*, in addition to referring to film and photo editing techniques, also
     refers to the process or effect of putting together pieces of machinery, or arranging and
     presenting information in a specific sequence. See 'Montagem', in *Dicionário Houaiss*
     (Rio de Janeiro: Instituto Antônio Houaiss, n.d.) <https://houaiss.uol.com.br/> [ac-
     cessed 11 June 2024].
7   Fernanda Negrete, 'The Aesthetic Pass: Beauty and the End of Analysis', in *Psycho-
     analysis and Solidarity*, ed. by Rada, pp. 220–41 (p. 229) <https://doi.org/10.1215/
     10407391-10124774>.

it is because I approach their artworks as distinct aesthetic practices of modelling (of what is) beyond the cultural montage.

Indeed, while Apollon's work places the human in opposition to the cultural montage, Lispector's literary project, as it becomes explicit in *The Passion According to G.H.* (1964), is committed to modelling the human beyond what G.H., the novel's narrator, labels as the 'human montage' (*montagem humana*) and 'false humanization' supported by anthropocentric, sexist, racist, and classist norms, ideals, and values.[8] Lispector's novel stages the disintegration of this montage through a disquieting encounter with 'the inhuman' (*inumano*), which brings G.H. to the limits of language, intellectual or conceptual understanding, and individual existence.[9] At the same time, I propose that Lispector does not abandon or dissolve the human altogether, but rather creates a new model of the human on the aesthetic plane of writing — as a distinct practice of assembling and piecing together in a language that breaks and is reinvented at its limits.

Around the time of the publication of *The Passion*, Lispector's contemporary, Lygia Clark, who co-founded the Brazilian Neo-Concrete movement and worked at the intersection of art and the clinic, created a series of sculptures called *Bichos*.[10] According to the 'Neo-Concrete Manifesto' (1959), art is not 'a "machine" or [...] an "object"', but rather a 'living [...] aesthetic organism' that revives and spatializes the 'experience of the real'.[11] Likewise, the *bicho* — as Clark herself

---

8   Clarice Lispector, *The Passion According to G.H.*, trans. by Idra Novey (New York: Penguin, 2014), pp. 4, 165. Although Novey's translation, referred to in this paper, renders *montagem humana* as 'human setup', I translate it as 'human montage' to retain the specificity of Lispector's wording as well as to suggest that even though this montage is restrictive, prescriptive, and static, Lispector's novel also opens up the possibility for another, generative understanding of the montage. While 'setup' reflects the first aspect of the montage, it fails to capture that montage refers first and foremost to an artistic technique and a form of creative construction, and thereby also fails to capture the affordances this might have for rethinking the human.

9   Ibid., p. 189. 'The inhuman' here carries multiple resonances, which I discuss in the third section of this essay.

10   Throughout her life, Clark became increasingly interested in exploring the potential of art for therapeutic practice. It is also worth noting that both Clark and Lispector were in analysis. See Christine Macel, 'Lygia Clark: At the Border of Art', in *Lygia Clark: The Abandonment of Art 1948–1988*, ed. by Cornelia H. Butler and Luis Pérez-Oramas (New York: Museum of Modern Art, 2014), pp. 253–60; Benjamin Moser, *Why This World: A Biography of Clarice Lispector* (Oxford: Oxford University Press, 2009).

11   The Neo-Concrete manifesto opposes its approach to art to the mechanistic, rationalist notion present in concrete art. Ferreira Gullar and others, 'Neo-Concrete

describes it — is to be approached as 'a living organism, a work essentially active'.[12] The term *bicho* has wide-ranging associations and has been variously translated into English as 'beast', 'animal', 'critter', and 'bug', attesting to its ambiguous taxonomy.[13] Clark's series comprises around seventy sculptures that enter into haptic interactions with human participants, who are in turn invited to interact with the *bichos* as well. As dynamic and participatory sculptural configurations, the *bichos* — individually and as a series — form a montage that is qualitatively opposed to Apollon's notion of the cultural montage, as well as to the human montage that Lispector's literary practice dismantles.

I argue here that in Apollon, Lispector, and Clark's work it is thus possible to register several different understandings and structures of the montage. Apollon situates the human (and the psychoanalytic model of the human) outside the cultural montage that reproduces the frame of consensual reality through a matrix of norms, ideals, and prohibitions. Meanwhile, Clark's sculpture — and ultimately, I suggest, Lispector's literary writing — enables us to redefine the human as a distinct kind of montage that unfolds through the aesthetic practice of montaging.[14] While the first montage resembles a self-reinforcing feedback loop that maintains pre-existent reality and its anthropocentric, individualistic, closed model of the human, the second is heterogeneous, dynamic, and in-the-making. These two kinds of montage are not only linked to two different models of the human but also ultimately to two different 'models of models'.[15]

Manifesto' (Rio de Janeiro, March 1959) <https://391.org/manifestos/1959-neo-concrete-manifesto-ferreira-gullar/> [accessed 22 July 2024].

12   Lygia Clark, 'The Bichos', in *Lygia Clark*, ed. by Butler and Pérez-Oramas, p. 160.

13   'Bicho', in *Linguee* (Cologne: DeepL SE, n.d.) <https://www.linguee.com/english-portuguese/search?source=portuguese&query=bicho> [accessed 5 January 2024].

14   I would like to thank Tania Rivera for encouraging me to think further about the relationship between the human and/as the montage during the *Bichos* symposium that took place at the ICI Berlin in June 2023. See *Bichos: Animal Fantasies between Art and Madness*, symposium, ICI Berlin, 14–15 June 2023 <https://doi.org/10.25620/e230614>.

15   I borrow this phrase from Astrid Deuber-Mankowsky's keynote lecture, 'Models as Media of Worlding in Sadie Benning and Fernand Deligny', presented at *Models: World Picture Conference*, conference, ICI Berlin, 17–18 November 2023 <https://doi.org/10.25620/e231117-1>. See also Deuber-Mankowsky's contribution in this volume, p. 31.

MODEL OUTSIDE THE MONTAGE

As already stated, Apollon's work defines the human in terms of the rupture — or what he calls the 'effraction' — provoked by the confrontation with strangeness and exteriority.[16] Never named in language and available neither to scientific observation nor to a socially authorized field of perception, the experience of the rupture escapes attempts to 'place the human subject in the position of an object — one thing among others in a space that is defined and controlled'.[17] According to this psychoanalytic model, what is then paradoxically most singular and intimate in each human is, in a way, constituted by its outside. To nonetheless try to visualize this effraction topologically, it might be useful to refer to the model of the Möbius strip (Figure 1), as mobilized by Jacques Lacan for thinking about human subjectivity.[18]

Sasha J. Langford observes that 'unlike the unilinear time of the line graph — which can only register quantifiable, positively-affirmed [sic] data — Lacan's use of topology [...] offers the possibility to account for aspects of experience that evade verifiable appearance within conscious life', as well as for 'the multiple localisation of the subject'.[19] Although the Möbius strip model muddles the boundary — or even the very categories — of inside and outside, it does not entirely dissolve this boundary by merging the two sides of the strip into undifferentiated sameness. Its non-orientable, liminal quality can thus perhaps help to visualize the effects of the effraction that blurs this boundary as well, but in a way that is specific and singular to each subject.

---

16   Apollon, 'The Limit', p. 107.

17   Ibid., p. 104.

18   Especially in his later work, in the 1960s and 1970s, Lacan increasingly turned to topological figures, such as the Möbius strip, the torus, and the Klein bottle, to visualize the structure of the unconscious and the stakes of psychoanalytic treatment. Interestingly, Clark's work *Caminhando* (*Walking*), from 1963, invites participants to make a Möbius strip using a white strip of paper, because the strip 'breaks our spatial habits [...] It makes us live the experience of a time without limit and of a continuous space.' Lygia Clark, 'Caminhando', in *Lygia Clark*, ed. by Butler and Pérez-Oramas, p. 160.

19   Sasha J. Langford, 'The Psychotopology of Climate', in *Lacan and the Environment*, ed. by Clint Burnham and Paul Kingsbury (Cham, CH: Palgrave Macmillan, 2021), pp. 181–214 (pp. 196–98) <https://doi.org/10.1007/978-3-030-67205-8>.

FIG. 1. A Möbius strip. Photo by David Benbennick
<https://en.wikipedia.org/wiki/File:M%C3%B6bius_Strip.jpg>.

Drawing on Apollon's work, Jeffrey Librett characterizes effraction as 'the breaking-in or breaking-out of something unnatural in the natural'.[20] Indeed, this rupture by a strange intensity — which lacks an image, object, form, concept, and a name in the existing field of reality — inserts the human into a logic other than that which aims to ensure the good functioning of the organism. This unconscious logic of desire and the drive — which the rupture inaugurates — pushes the human to 'go too far, to seek out that Thing that goes beyond the reasonable' and beyond the 'logic of the living organism'.[21] In pushing too far, desire and the drive also place the human outside the prevailing model of the human established by the cultural montage and reinforced by the norms, ideals, and, finally, language that delineate the frontiers of the receivable, the perceptible, and the acceptable in the social link. This prevailing model defines the human as an individual whose self-interest and unity are pursued through an appropriative and

20   Librett, 'The Subject in the Age of World- Formation', p. 84.
21   Lucie Cantin, 'The Drive, the Untreatable Quest of Desire', in *Constructing the Death Drive*, ed. by Tracy McNulty, special issue of *differences*, 28.2 (2017), pp. 24–45 (p. 25) <https://doi.org/10.1215/10407391-4151740>.

oppositional relation to others and alienation in sociocultural identifications and demands.

Language, however, seems to occupy an ambiguous, liminal position in relation to the cultural montage. Even though it is deployed by the montage to organize collective reality and to alienate individuals in a matrix of norms, ideals, and limits that place them in a hierarchical relation to other humans and all other beings, at the same time it also paradoxically testifies to the capacity to create. As Negrete observes in her commentary on Apollon's work, 'for language to emerge, humans had to have the capacity to invent it in the first place.'[22] Far from conscious intentionality, this inventive capacity is linked to the unconscious desire that seeks to access and produce something that breaks the frame of established reality. Indeed, language would not have emerged were it not for the creativity of 'representations' arising in response to the rupture, for which there is no pre-existent name and no pre-existent image, and which Apollon defines as 'the capacity to represent the environment […] otherwise than it is.'[23] Thus, the creative capacity that gave rise to the development of language at the same time also 'exceeds the framework that humans establish through language.'[24]

The rupturing encounter with exteriority and strangeness is thus ultimately linked to the inauguration of a desire for aesthetic production: to give form to something that is not pre-given in reality, and to share it with others from the limits of language and one's existence as an individual.[25] If the aesthetic becomes crucial for challenging and disrupting the individualistic model deployed by the cultural montage, it is because it forges a path for the expression of this rupturing experience in a way that manifests a paradoxically transindividual dimension of the human.[26] This transindividual dimension — resonant with what

---

22   Negrete, 'The Aesthetic Pass', p. 229.

23   Apollon, 'The Subject of the Quest', p. 3.

24   Negrete, 'The Aesthetic Pass', p. 229.

25   Developing Apollon's formulation of the aesthetic, Negrete discusses aesthetic production as 'a plastic practice' and as a way of 'altering reality based on an experience without preexistent referents', in Negrete, 'The Aesthetic Pass', p. 229. This approach to the aesthetic resonates with *poiesis* as the process or act of creation and emergence.

26   Drawing on Apollon's framework, McNulty argues that human reality is 'fundamentally transindividual' and traversed by the unconscious 'quest' of desire. If this quest

Lispector will refer to as the 'impersonal' — is linked precisely to the fact that humanity shares the experience that is singular and specific to each subject, but that cannot be claimed by anyone as their personal property or private territory.[27] In other words, this experience transcends the individual and does not belong to anyone in particular. Or, as Freud discovered in relation to the unconscious, it belongs to 'another scene' (*ein anderer Schauplatz*).[28] I suggest that, by opposing the human to self-enclosed and self-interested individuality, this transindividual dimension testifies to the specificity of human experience while at the same time it undermines human exceptionalism, that is, claims to the moral supremacy and authority of human over other-than-human life forms, based on the view of the human as an atomized, self-aware agent.[29] Indeed, it is ultimately on this transindividual basis that new linkages, modes of relation, and models of the human can emerge.

MODEL AS THE MONTAGE

Breaking and Making Language

Published on the cusp of the military coup in Brazil, Lispector's 1964 novel *The Passion According to G.H.* is narrated by G.H., a bourgeois woman, sculptor, and writer living in Rio de Janeiro, who tells the

---

'impacts each and every human being but [...] belongs to no one in particular', it is because it is an expression of experience that takes the subject 'above and beyond the specific iteration of the human that every culture creates, promotes, and defends to assure its own survival'. McNulty, 'The Traversal of the Fantasy', pp. 198–99.

27 Lispector, *The Passion*, p. 127. For a discussion of the 'impersonal' in Lispector's writing, see Fernanda Negrete, 'Approaching Impersonal Life with Clarice Lispector', in *New Encounters Between Philosophy and Literature II*, ed. by Krzysztof Ziarek, special issue of *Humanities*, 7.2 (2018) <https://doi.org/10.3390/h7020055>.

28 Freud's formulation of 'the other scene' comes from the work of German experimental psychologist, philosopher, and physicist Gustav Theodor Fechner, who insisted that 'the scene of action of dreams is different from that of waking ideational life'. Sigmund Freud, *The Interpretation of Dreams*, ed. and trans. by James Strachey (London: Hogarth Press, 1953), pp. 535–36.

29 In his essay on sex, psychoanalysis, and new materialism, Nathan Gorelick convincingly suggests that human superiority and exceptionalism are in fact symptoms linked to disavowal of the specifically human 'ontological negativity', which my essay discusses in terms of the rupture. See Nathan Gorelick, 'Why Sex Is Special: Psychoanalysis against New Materialism', in *Subject Lessons: Hegel, Lacan, and the Future of Materialism*, ed. by Russell Sbriglia and Slavoj Žižek (Evanston, IL: Northwestern University Press, 2020), pp. 171–89 (p. 177) <https://doi.org/10.2307/j.ctvw1d5dk.11>.

story of the disintegration of her 'human montage'.[30] The human montage here rests on the oppositional, hierarchical logic of mastery and
individualism, reinforced by an umbrella of sexist, racist, and classist
norms, ideals, and values. As already stated, the fall of the montage
is provoked by G.H.'s rupture by the 'inhuman', which pertains not
only to other-than-human life forms and those marginalized figures
excluded from access to humanity as defined by the human montage,
but also to the 'unsayable' dimension of subjectivity and experience
that this montage cannot appropriate and capture.[31] Thus, while the
inhuman is opposed to the montage, it is paradoxically not opposed to
the human as such. Rather, it becomes integral to the articulation of a
new model of the human.

The disintegration of the montage begins with G.H.'s visit to her
maid's chamber, where she discovers a mural that Janair, her Black
former housemaid, drew on the wall before her departure.[32] The maid's
'gaze', which persists through the mural, haunts and interrogates G.H.'s
field of vision, bringing her sense of stability, identity, and normalcy
into crisis.[33] Indeed, it confronts the narrator with the appearance
of what Lucia Villares has discussed as the 'symptoms of unexamined whiteness'.[34] Villares places these symptoms in the context of

---

30   Lispector, *The Passion*, p. 4. As observed by Marília Librandi, G.H.'s initials might al-
      lude to *género humano* ('human genus'). See Marília Librandi, *Writing by Ear: Lispector
      and the Aural Novel* (Toronto: Toronto University Press, 2018), p. 136 <https://doi.
      org/10.3138/9781487514730>.

31   Lispector, *The Passion*, pp. 186–89.

32   I discuss the mural in more detail in my discussion of death, writing, and subjectivity in
      Lispector's work, in Marta Aleksandrowicz, 'To Enter the Core of Death', in *Philosophy
      with Clarice Lispector*, ed. by Fernanda Negrete, special issue of *Angelaki*, 28.2 (2023),
      pp. 90–101 <https://doi.org/10.1080/0969725X.2023.2192068>.

33   Lispector, *The Passion*, p. 32. Interestingly, although Janair's place of origin is not
      disclosed in the novel, Lucia Villares notes that Lispector's description of the chamber
      suggests that she might be from the northeast, where the majority of domestic workers
      in Brazil came from. The distinction between G.H.'s and Janair's climatic, geographic,
      and socio-economic environments is highlighted in G.H.'s statements about the cham-
      ber, which contrast the dryness of the northeast with the humidity of Rio de Janeiro.
      Indeed, G.H.'s anxiety and discomfort upon entering the room are amplified by the
      increasing prevalence of dryness, which comes to replace the humidity and moistness
      that previously filled the air in the woman's apartment. For more, see Lucia Villares,
      Examining Whiteness: Reading Clarice Lispector through Bessie Head and Toni Morrison
      (New York: Legenda, 2011), pp. 83–84.

34   Villares, *Examining Whiteness*, p. 2. Although, as Villares points out, especially during
      the postcolonial, post-slavery Vargas era — which came to an end shortly after the

discourses of hybridity, miscegenation, and racial democracy that were
prevalent in Brazil around the time when Lispector was writing, as a
result of which racist policies and language seemed to disappear from
Brazil's public domain, with racism effectively relegated to the 'zone of
the unspeakable and therefore unacknowledged and unquestioned'.[35]
When her unexamined whiteness is unveiled, G.H.'s human montage
indeed begins to collapse, and so does narrative and linguistic coherence.

The dismantling of the human montage culminates in the narrator's encounter with a cockroach. Following the encounter with Janair's
mural, G.H. opens the wardrobe door and is confronted with the insect,
whose 'sudden life' startles her.[36] She slams the door on the cockroach's 'half-emerged body' and, soon after, white pus starts to ooze out
of the animal's crushed entrails.[37] While the narrator's discovery of the
mural in Janair's chamber marks the beginning of the disintegration of
her human montage, the culmination of this is her discovery that the
'narrow route' she must take in order to complete her entry into the
chamber passes through the cockroach.[38] She thus squeezes through
the animal's body and eventually puts this body in her mouth.[39]

---

publication of Lispector's first novel, *Perto do coração selvagem* (*Near to the Wild
Heart*), in 1943 — miscegenation 'came to be interpreted positively as a harmonizing
and integrating mixture regarded as the essence of being Brazilian', it also tacitly
reinforced the racist ideal of whiteness by linking Brazil's national identity to the
gradual process of 'whitening', camouflaged in the national discourse of Brazil as a
modern, hybrid, multicultural community. Ibid., pp. 30–32.

35   Ibid., p. 28. Another interesting analysis, by Rodante van der Waal, Kim Schoof, and
      Aukje van Rooden, approaches Lispector's novel as the dismantling of 'the passion
      of the colonial subject', restaging G.H.'s passion as 'an opening up to the world, so
      much so that the she herself perishes'. See Rodante van der Waal, Kim Schoof, and
      Aukje van Rooden, 'When the Egg Breaks, the Chicken Bleeds', in *Philosophy with
      Clarice Lispector*, ed. by Negrete, pp. 57–67 (pp. 57, 62) <https://doi.org/10.1080/
      0969725X.2023.2192064>.

36   Lispector, *The Passion*, p. 39.

37   Ibid., p. 46.

38   Ibid., p. 60.

39   In *The Passion*, the fall of the human montage still depends on tasting and consuming
      the animal other, a step that is necessary to reconfigure the relation of the narrator
      to the world and to dissolve hierarchical opposition among humans, and between
      humans and other-than-human life forms. However, in Lispector's later novel *Água
      Viva* (1973), the narrator crosses a further limit and eats herself, or, more specifically,
      eats her placenta. Clarice Lispector, *Água Viva*, trans. by Stefan Tobler (New York:
      New Directions, 2012). See also Irving Goh, 'Writing, Touching, and Eating in Clarice

In confronting the narrator with the strange, 'impersonal soul' of her own being, which can no longer be 'forsaken' for the 'persona' and the 'human mask', the encounter with the cockroach ruptures G.H.'s identity, thought, and language, turning them inside out.[40] If the encounter with the cockroach is nauseating or even revolting for G.H., this is not merely because of its associations with impurity, but rather because of its depersonalizing effect. Indeed, in the final pages of the novel, G.H. finds herself on the plane of 'depersonalization', wherein 'the dismissal of useless individuality' by 'the greatest exteriorization' may be reached.[41] Through the movement of depersonalization, G.H. extends and stretches herself outward, as it were, which pushes her to recognize 'the woman of all women' and 'the man of all men' in herself, as well as to further discover that the 'single roach' she stumbled upon in the chamber is not only 'the roach of all roaches' but also the 'world'.[42]

Indeed, the cockroach here becomes an agent of depersonalization not simply because it is an animal but because its 'awareness of living' is so 'neutral' and disinterested — at least from the perspective of the self-interested, hierarchical logics and scales of the human montage — that it is unbounded and encompasses the world.[43] The magnitude of this 'attention-life', signalled by the 'heralding quiver' of the cockroach's antennae, requires a creative practice that can sustain and relay this attention on the plane of writing.[44] Indeed, in pushing G.H. toward 'the actual process of life' and 'watchful life living itself', this depersonalizing encounter calls for a new practice of writing that requires the writer to grow the antennae, as it were, in order to register, translate, and transmit the world's 'telegraph signals'.[45] The writer's task is to translate the 'unknown telegraph signals' into a new, unknown language as the basis of new linkages and, I would suggest, as the basis of a new model

---

Lispector: *Água Viva* and *A Breath of Life*', *MLN*, 131.5 (2016), pp. 1347–69 <https://doi.org/10.1353/mln.2016.0093>.

40 Lispector, *The Passion*, pp. 92, 127.
41 Ibid., p. 184.
42 Ibid., pp. 184, 128.
43 Ibid., pp. 43, 92.
44 Ibid., pp. 128, 45.
45 Ibid., pp. 43, 89, 13.

of the human.[46] And because telegraph lines send information by making and breaking electrical connections, the transmission of telegraph signals requires a kind of writing that breaks and makes (models of) language.

Near the end of the novel, narrating from the ruins of the human montage, G.H. describes the human in terms of a failure of language to articulate the inhuman and 'the unsayable'.[47] She proclaims: 'reality is the raw material, language is the way I go in search of it [...] and the way I do not find it'; language is 'my human effort'.[48] Importantly, human effort does not involve merely acknowledging the failure of language — trying to 'take a shortcut and want[ing] to start, already knowing that the voice says little [...] straightaway with being depersonal' — but rather following the way that language breaks. [49] The point which, I think, is crucial to the novel's rearticulation of the human is that depersonalization is not the effect of a conscious decision or intention, but rather a consequence of following the way that language fails as it seeks to express the unsayable and the inhuman. 'The unsayable', G.H. concludes, 'can only be given to me through the failure of my language. Only when the construction fails, can I obtain what it could not achieve.'[50] Indeed, when one follows the way that language breaks, one also encounters an opening in language that stretches it beyond its function as a prop within the human montage.

To approach the unsayable and the inhuman is not to make the 'impalpable [...] concrete' but to 'designate the impalpable as impalpable, and then the breath breaks out anew as in a candle's flame'.[51] Such a writing practice differs from those practices of 'Western writing' that Apollon discusses in his study of the relationship between writing and the 'voices' in Haitian Vodou. For Apollon, Western writing is often an instrument of conquest, which extends its domination by producing 'a remainder' that it then 'conquers by bringing into a signifying (and

---

46   Ibid., p. 13.
47   Ibid., p. 186.
48   Ibid.
49   Ibid.
50   Ibid.
51   Ibid., p. 184.

thus conventional and profitable) unit'.[52] A remainder is 'a yet uncultured nature, a promised land, the shifting horizon of a planned voyage', and 'a wilderness to conquer, multiply, add up, spend, and accumulate'.[53] Lispector's (and G.H.'s) literary practice of searching and failing to find words with which one could articulate and relay the unsayable and the inhuman testifies to a kind of writing which does not endlessly produce a remainder that it then attempts to make familiar within the discourse of the montage, only to start the conquest all over again. As the 'limit point or fissure' that suspends 'unitary discourses', the unsayable and the inhuman in Lispector's literary practice are not produced on the plane of writing, but rather encountered as something that cannot be encapsulated by representation and the narrative framework.[54] The encounter with this limit point is a herald, or source, of writing. Indeed, although the aesthetic can take different forms — as, for example, a political act that affirms solidarity with the transindividual dimension of the human, rather than aiming to solidify or safeguard one's position within the montage — literary writing is unique because it is by means of words themselves that it exposes language's failure to domesticate or evacuate what Apollon refers to as 'the stranger' that 'makes familiarity impossible'.[55] And, as already stated, this manifestation of the failure of language can also defamiliarize language and stretch it beyond its role of naming and adjudicating what is possible to say and write in a socially authorized reality.

---

52   Willy Apollon, 'Positions — 1: Writing and the Voice', trans. by Heidi Arsenault and Cynthia Mitchell, in *Beauty*, ed. by Aleksandrowicz and Negrete, pp. 71–95 (pp. 72–73) <https://www.penumbrajournal.org/no-2-beauty> [accessed 24 July 2024].

53   Apollon, 'Positions', pp. 72–73.

54   Adam Shellhorse uses the terms 'limit point' and 'fissure' in reference to the figure of the subaltern in Lispector's work, in an essay that discusses the social, political, and historical backdrop against which Lispector was writing — including 'the disavowal of innovative composition' by the Brazilian literary mainstream of the time. Adam Joseph Shellhorse, 'Figurations of Immanence: Writing the Subaltern and the Feminine in Clarice Lispector', in *Anti-Literature: The Politics and Limits of Representation in Modern Brazil and Argentina* (Pittsburgh: University of Pittsburgh Press, 2017), pp. 17–43 (pp. 21, 23) <https://doi.org/10.2307/j.ctt1r69xs2.5>.

55   Apollon, 'Positions', p. 74. For a discussion of the political act that creates a path for the expression of solidarity with the human, and that is not authorized by the cultural montage, see McNulty, 'The Traversal of the Fantasy', pp. 212–13.

FIG. 2. Lygia Clark, *O Bicho Linear* (1960), aluminium, variable dimensions <https://commons.wikimedia.org/wiki/File:O_Bicho_Linear_-_Lygia_Clark.jpg>

Breaking and Making Sculpture

If Lispector stretches language, Lygia Clark stretches vision to spatialize metamorphosis and new modes of relation. In the 1960s, Clark created a series of participatory sculptures entitled *Bichos*. These were made from a variety of materials, including steel and aluminium, and in a variety of colours, shapes, and sizes (Figure 2). Each *bicho* was given a distinct name.

The planes of the *bichos* are connected with hinges, allowing the sculptures to be moved by their human handlers in manifold ways. As already stated, with its ambiguous taxonomy — as, variously, 'beast', 'animal', or 'critter' — *bicho* points to the other-than-human, yet, as a dynamic and participatory form, it also enters into haptic, sensory interactions with the human participant. It is through touching it, playing with it, folding it, and turning it, that the *bicho* is shaped. It is thus open to transformation. However, as Clark remarks, the *bicho* is 'not composed of still, independent forms that can be indefinitely handled at will'; 'On the contrary, its parts are functionally related to each other.'[56] Indeed, although the sculptural body of the *bicho* is agile and malleable, it is at the same time also a very specific, concrete con-

56   Ibid., p. 160.

figuration whose distinct logic of movement and temporality resists domination. It is, as Clark writes, 'an organic entity that fully reveals itself within its inner time of expression'.[57] The *bicho* reveals itself in the here and now as a heterogeneous, dynamic present that does not stagnantly repeat the past, especially if we understand the latter as a static, immutable corpse. Indeed, if, for Clark, 'the only thing that matters' is 'the act-in-progress', then the *bicho* is the act that sculpts the continuously unfolding now through a haptic encounter with the participant.[58]

The *bicho's* temporal-aesthetic plane urges the human participant to transcend their existence as a self-enclosed individual, thus enabling what Leo Bersani, in his discussion of the aesthetic, describes as 'a different relation to otherness, not one based in paranoid fascination', but rather in 'a communication of forms, as a kind of universal solidarity not of identities but of positionings and configurations in space'.[59] If

---

57 Ibid.

58 Lygia Clark, 'To Capture a Fragment of Suspended Time', in *Lygia Clark*, ed. by Manuel J. Borja-Villel (Barcelona: Fundació Antoni Tàpies, 1998), p. 187.

59 Similarly to Apollon, Bersani does not limit the aesthetic to works of art, but rather considers it as 'enabling and exemplifying the ethical positions and commitments' (Leo Bersani, 'Preface', in *Is the Rectum a Grave? And Other Essays* (Chicago: University of Chicago Press, 2009), pp. ix–x (p. x) <https://doi.org/10.7208/chicago/9780226043449.001.0001>). He discusses the 'communication of forms' (as a 'solidarity [...] of positionings and configurations in space') in relation to 'homoness' as a 'model for correspondences of being that are by no means limited to relations among persons' ('Gay Betrayals', in ibid., pp. 36–44 (pp. 43–44)). Bersani also engages psychoanalyst Jean Laplanche's theory of the enigmatic signifier to consider how mobilization of the 'masochistic element' might open the subject to 'a self-extensibility rather than a paranoid defensiveness', thus enabling 'a move into the correspondence of forms' and new modes of relation. He traces the movement of extensibility and communication of forms in Caravaggio's painting 'from the teasingly enigmatic eroticism of the portraits of boys to the nonsexual sensuality of physical contacts, extensions, and correspondences, from a problematic of knowledge (and interiority) to a kind of cartography of the subject, a tracing of spatial connectedness' ('A Conversation with Leo Bersani: With Tim Dean, Hal Foster, and Kaja Silverman', in ibid., pp. 171–86 (pp. 176–77)). Commenting on Clark's art, Negrete's recent book, *The Aesthetic Clinic*, similarly notes that while the aesthetic experience entails 'a kind of violence or shock to the senses', this shock has to be distinguished from seducing the participant to 'morbid curiosity — which leads back into spectacle and does not bring anything new in terms of relation'. See Fernanda Negrete, *The Aesthetic Clinic: Feminine Sublimation in Contemporary Writing, Psychoanalysis, and Art* (Albany: State University of New York Press, 2020), p. 150 <https://doi.org/10.1515/9781438480220>. Indeed, Clark's participatory practice expands the aesthetic experience beyond the individual who either stages or witnesses the spectacle.

Neo-Concrete poetry insisted on restoring the word to 'its condition as "verbum", that is, to the human mode of presentation of the real' — rather than taking the word as an 'object' transformed into a 'mere optical signal' — the *bicho* can be thought of as the verbum that sculpts and stretches the visual field beyond the predetermined parameters of movement, visibility, and conceivability, enabling new linkages and communications of forms to be registered in visual space.[60] The *bicho*, as a construction, thus forms a montage that is qualitatively opposed to the 'cultural' and 'humanized' montage in Apollon and Lispector's work. Indeed, Clark's artwork brings to mind the practice of montage in the films of Sergei Eisenstein, which, as Elena Vogman observes, is to be approached not simply as the 'relocation of an isolated fragment within a new structural relation but also [...] a potential mode of *shifting the perspective*, of producing a new visibility'.[61] Although Clark's sculpture leaves the relationship between the human and the *bicho* open-ended, I suggest that it nonetheless enables us to spatialize the human as the construction of a new haptic and visual perspective.

While Lispector breaks with any pre-existent model or theory of language that defines it as a means of unification, codification, or standardization, Clark in turn breaks with a static, closed model of sculpture. If, in Lispector's *Passion*, it is the pre-existent model of language that needs to break in order for it to be transformed beyond the prescriptive, repressive logic and structure of the human montage, for Clark it is a closed model of sculpture that needs to break in order for it to be transformed in a way that expands the visual, haptic, relational field beyond the frontiers of a socially authorized field of perception. Writing and sculpting thus both become distinct aesthetic practices of breaking models deployed by the montage, and I propose that on this basis they enable a modelling of the human as a new, transindividual kind of montage. This transindividual montage is supported by the rifts in language, atomistic identity, and linear time that are provoked by the encounter with what Apollon, Lispector, and Clark variously describe as strange exteriority, the inhuman, and the *bicho*. This montage not

---

60 Gullar and others, 'Neo-Concrete Manifesto'.
61 Elena Vogman, *Dance of Values: Sergei Eisenstein's Capital Project* (Zurich: Diaphanes, 2019), p. 41, emphasis in the original.

only disrupts the anthropocentric, individualistic model of the human, but also problematizes other models that risk freezing the human on either side of the historically, culturally, socially, or economically pre-determined subject/object, oppressor/victim binary. Indeed, despite the undeniable urgency of change in the field of authority and power re-lations, such models, as observed by the Chicana writer, feminist, and poet Gloria Anzaldúa, risk locking the human into 'a duel of oppressor and oppressed [...] like the cop and the criminal', perpetually reducing each to 'a common denominator of violence'.[62]

Because the two kinds of montages discussed in this paper operate on the basis of a different conception of the human as well as entail a different logic and structure, they are ultimately linked to two disparate kinds and conceptualizations of models. On the one side, there is a self-referential, self-contained model (think of a closed sphere) that represents, replicates, and reinforces a socially authorized field of per-ception, sensation, language, and identity. On the other side, there is a heterogeneous, transindividual model, which muddles the boundary between inside and outside and emerges at the limit and point of break-age of the first model. One reifies the past as an always-already-there, predetermined given, the other is the act-in-progress. The latter would perhaps not be possible if it were not for the aesthetic: as a way of modelling beyond the established parameters of visibility, reality, and language, and against the prevailing models of individualism, excep-tionalism, and 'false humanization'.[63]

---

62 Gloria Anzaldúa, *Borderlands / La Frontera: The New Mestiza*, 4th edn (San Francisco: Aunt Lute Books, 2012), p. 100.

63 Lispector, *The Passion*, p. 165.

One of the most thrillingly disorienting poems I remember reading
when I was younger is 'Vertigo' by American poet Jorie Graham.[64]
The poem begins *in medias res*, bypassing exposition in typical lyric
fashion: 'Then they came to the very edge of the cliff and looked
down.' From there, the poem zeroes in on a female figure as it renders
what she can perceive from her vantage point, in a manner that seems
intent on hyper-precision, into a contact zone between the physical
world and herself, her limits, 'where the mind open[s] out / into the
sheer drop of its intelligence'. And in a move characteristic of Graham's
body of work, 'Vertigo' stretches the notion of lyric time, decelerating
it by deploying the structural elements of poetry — word choice,
of course, but also syntax, lineation, and typography — to atomize
the instance of encounter between the human and the nonhuman
other, wherein the former's sensory awareness accrues (or refuses to
accrue) into apprehension: 'How does one enter / a story?' the poem
asks. The deceleration of the narrative moment leads, paradoxically,
to an acceleration of the pace with which language reaches out to its
audience, enacting the frantic acrobatics of the mind as it registers the
ineffable.

I conjure up the poem now in relation to Marta Aleksandrowicz's
essay, where she constellates the propositions of Willy Apollon with
the literary and artistic productions of Clarice Lispector and Lygia
Clark, distinct in their proclivity for defamiliarizing practices which do
not necessarily scuttle towards linguistic or formal stability. Pointing
out that the prevalent model of the human is rigid and 'self-contained'
— locked within and reinforced by culturally legible and socially
sanctioned codes of 'perception, sensation, language, and identity' —
Marta establishes a 'heterogeneous, transindividual' model that lies in
a liminal state of unfolding, indefinitely realizable rather than realized.

One key component to the infrastructure of Marta's argument
is its discussion of 'effraction', a notion drawn from Apollon: the 'in-
the-making' quality of the model tendered by Marta emerges from

---

64   Jorie Graham, 'Vertigo', in *The End of Beauty* (New York: Ecco Press, 1987), pp. 66–67.

it, which she describes as 'this rupture by strange intensity — which lacks an image, object, form, concept, and a name in the existing field of reality — [that] inserts the human into a logic other than that which aims to ensure the good functioning of the organism'. Effraction, in Marta's essay, precipitates a desire on the part of the human to accommodate that which is not within the realm of established reality, thus catalysing the 'disintegration' of the human montage. This desire, to channel the words of Lispector's protagonist, creates paradoxical effects: 'the unsayable [...] can only be given to me through the failure of my language.'

I find Marta's discussion especially beguiling because I detect in it a decided compatibility with the kind of lyric work that fascinates me, the kind I must have first detected, as a young reader, in 'Vertigo', in which conventional syntactic manoeuvres prove ineffective and thus need to be disrupted, reassembled in unpredictable ways, given the confrontation of the anomalous, the incomprehensible. In Graham's poem, the disruptive encounter is staged through the excitable plasticity of the sentences, the deliberately haphazard line breaks and indentions, the intrusions of asides and questions in a hurried exposition that turns omnivorous in its attempt to accommodate the experience in its entirety, in its ongoing presentness, which Anahid Nersessian describes as 'the ridged quality of a real body in space'.[65] Graham — in tracking the desire of the female figure to comprehend, to confer upon what she sees from the cliff a definition ensconced within human parameters — summons a catalogue of open-ended questions:

> What was it in there
>
>   she could hear
> that has nothing to do with *telling the truth?*
> What was it that was *not her listening?*
> She leaned out. What is it pulls at one, she wondered,
> what? That it has no shape but point of view?
> That it cannot move to hold us?

65 Anahid Nersessian, *The Calamity Form: Poetry and Social Life* (Chicago: University of Chicago Press, 2020), p. 142 <https://doi.org/10.7208/chicago/9780226701455.001.0001>.

The poem's emphasis on hewing to the unravelling moment as faithfully as possible ostensibly collapses into futility, with the recognition
of how the body 'cannot / follow, cannot love'. However, deploying
the generosity of Marta's model of the human as a frame for Graham's poem allows for a wonderful and — consistent with Marta's
argument — incongruous clearing: the alienating experience of the
female figure while on top of a cliff thrusts her will, as well as the
body which attends to it, into a state, 'as if for the first time', where
the stable notion of the human dissolves and words like 'follow' and
'love' are flung towards alternative, potential definitions. 'And what if
after so many words, / the word itself doesn't survive!', the Peruvian
poet César Vallejo pronounces.[66] This scenario, twisted to become
both question and exclamation, certainly seems apropos to Graham,
via Marta: 'Vertigo', in 'follow[ing] the way language breaks', illustrates
how Marta's model also offers a compelling means of approaching and
understanding poetry's obsessive drive to test language, to find ways to
stand close to its hypothetical cliff, the human trying to reach for — to
'love' — an other whose existence is beyond her physical and mental
domain, this human who scrambles to follow what she cannot follow,
the language following the language which does not survive, with the
human following after.

---

66   César Vallejo, 'And What If After So Many Words...', trans. by Douglas Lawder and
      Robert Bly, in Robert Bly, *Leaping Poetry: An Idea with Poems and Translations* [1972]
      (Pittsburgh: University of Pittsburgh Press, 2008), pp. 36–39.

The Exophonic Lyric
A Poetics
MARK ANTHONY CAYANAN

MIRACLE FEVER, A WORK IN PROGRESS

It is 13 December 1992. Judiel Nieva, then sixteen years old, meets with Catholic priest Roger Cortez and several nuns residing at the Mary Consolatrix Convent. Nieva has claimed that the Virgin Mary has been appearing regularly to her since 1989, relaying messages and granting her the ability to perform miracles — news of these apparitions has already been circulating among the locals of Agoo, a small town in the Philippines. On this day in December, Cortez and the cloister's Mother Superior interrogate the visionary to determine the veracity of her claims, a procedure which seems to yield a positive outcome, with both religious figures finding Nieva's responses to be '"sincere" and "not contrary to doctrine"'.[1] Late into the evening, Cortez decides to say Mass for those already at the convent, which proceeds quite uneventfully until it is time for Communion: the white wafer Nieva receives from Cortez is inexplicably transfigured into 'pulsating flesh and blood' while it is in her mouth. Shocked, the priest

---

1   Quoted in Mozart Pastrano, 'The Virgin in Agoo', *Philippine Daily Inquirer*, 5 March 1993, p. 10.

and the nuns request that Nieva spit out the flesh — they then pass around the transmuted host like a relic, some of them pressing it on their handkerchiefs to soak in a bit of the blood. The last nun to touch the flesh sees Nieva put it back in her mouth, where the flesh slowly reverts into a regular communion host, which the visionary swallows afterward.[2]

The supernatural event of that day would prompt Cortez and the nuns to publicly support Nieva, a gesture empowering her to gain more devout followers. The visionary and her hometown eventually become steady fixtures on the front page of every broadsheet in the Philippines for a good number of months — and by the first Friday of March 1993, over a million pilgrims would flock to Agoo to see Nieva. Before the apparitions, the town had been reeling from the devastation caused by a major earthquake that occurred in July 1990, which levelled many houses and structures, including the basilica. Moreover, aside from tobacco, Agoo had 'no major industry to speak of, few commercial establishments, scant power and water supply, poor telephone service, a rudimentary garbage disposal system, and a skeletal police force'.[3] The influx of devotees, journalists, and busybodies, therefore, would enable the town to build a thriving, albeit makeshift, local economy, one that was almost wholly dependent on Nieva's presence and the currency of her visions. Strangers to one another, these pilgrims would linger in the town, swapping not just stories of miracles allegedly performed by Nieva but also photographic evidence of divine 'manifestations',[4] such as a 'dancing' sun, throbbing and shifting into various fantastic colours, or flocks of doves flying overhead during times when Mass was being held, or when the visionary was present at the 'apparition hill'. Nieva herself would sing hymns while in front of crowds, her voice 'a clear, even, and melodious soprano, hitting the higher notes without straining or breaking'.[5]

---

2   Ibid., p. 10.

3   Rodolfo Dula, 'Devil's Advocate in Agoo' (second of a series), *Malaya*, 18 February 1993, p. 1.

4   Ibid., p. 7.

5   Rodolfo Dula, 'Devil's Advocate in Agoo' (fourth of a series), *Malaya*, 20 February 1993, p. 3.

Even during the peak of the apparitions, however, the Catholic Church — apart from the coterie of Cortez and the nuns at the Mary Consolatrix Convent — was already quite vocal about its reservations. In September 1993, Bishop Antonio Tobias, whose diocese includes Nieva's hometown, called out the overly commercialized aspect of the 'Agoo phenomenon' and asked that the foundation set up by the visionary's family issue a public and transparent accounting of the donations it had received and the profits it had allegedly made from selling religious merchandise.[6] By 1995, the Church would unequivocally declare the apparitions inauthentic, citing, among other reasons, plagiarism: the divine messages Nieva had recorded in a notebook were found to have been almost identical to those received by Western visionaries, as well as by Rufino Bautista, another Agoo native, who, in the 1970s, also professed to have witnessed apparitions of the Virgin, who presented herself as the Lady of Kayumanggi, identifiable by her brown skin, a trait not shared by her 90s iteration, whom Nieva described as fair-skinned.[7] The investigative commission also pointed out that the messages transcribed by Nieva were in English, whereas in sites of officially approved apparitions, the divine messages were stated in their native languages.[8] The findings of the commission were also tethered to persistent rumours about Nieva's gender identity, something that the visionary herself would claim public control over: in 2003, while on a media blitz to promote her role in the film *Siklo*, as a woman who has an affair with her neighbour,[9] Nieva would openly discuss her transition, at one point stating, 'Ito ang kagustuhan ng Mahal na Birhen' ('This is what the Virgin Mary desires').[10]

---

6   Margot Baterina, 'The "Dark Side" of Agoo', *Philippine Daily Inquirer*, 2 September 1993, pp. 1, 8.

7   Maria Gloria Aguilar, 'Appropriation and Resistance in Philippine Marian Devotion' (unpublished doctoral thesis, University of North London, 2001), pp. 122, 155–56, <https://repository.londonmet.ac.uk/7291/> [accessed 24 July 2024].

8   Girlie Linao, 'Church: Philippine Miracle a Hoax', *United Press International*, 6 September 1995 <https://www.upi.com/Archives/1995/09/06/Church-Philippine-miracle-a-hoax/5408810360000/> [accessed 12 June 2023].

9   Mozart Pastrano, 'Apparition Star Judiel Nieva Is Now a Showbiz Star', *Philippine Daily Inquirer*, 5 September 2003, p. A29.

10   Quoted in Jeans Cequina, 'The Curious Case of Judiel Nieva', *POP!*, 7 January 2021 <https://pop.inquirer.net/103517/the-curious-case-of-judiel-nieva> [accessed 5 October 2023].

My current project, titled *Miracle Fever*, is a lyric sequence that loosely charts a narrative trajectory of the apparitions while focusing on the haphazardly collective psyche of the town and the devotees. In subject matter and form, the notion of transformation is crucial to my project: many of the poems are uttered from a plural first-person perspective, the antecedents of the pronoun morphing based on provisional instances of solidarity born of oppression and belief, class resentment, historical fatigue, and a keen investment and sense of complicity in the entire devotional extravaganza. One of the challenges I engage with in this project has to do with how the very phenomenon of speaking in poetry as a collective is a reductive, politically fraught move. The danger is that the singularity of voice which often serves as a distinguishing feature of the lyric genre could hijack the profusion of wills and lived lives that the text purports to speak from. That the 'we' pronoun is the main perspective for a sequence that involves the historical realities of a town further burdens the project with expectations of mimetic fidelity and conjures up questions relating to the ethics of representation.

I intend for my poetry project to navigate the paradoxes emerging from the encounter between poetic form and historical subject, to gesture toward the unifying idiom of a lyric that derives its authority from seeming communal while also telegraphing the irreconcilabilities that exist within this ostensible community. One way through which I attempt to accomplish this goal is by resorting to appropriation as a method of composition: I imbricate passages that outline the socio-political situation of the Philippines during the apparitions with other materials that metonymically refer to my contemporary subject position. I had already relied on a similar intertextual process when working on previous poetry projects;[11] however, in the case of *Miracle Fever*, appropriation as a procedure seems even more apropos,

---

11   In an interview with Singaporean poet Cyril Wong, I explain how, for my last poetry book, *Unanimal, Counterfeit, Scurrilous* (published in Australia by Giramondo Publishing in 2021 and in the Philippines by the University of Santo Tomas Publishing House in 2024), I resorted to appropriation as a way of combining, in what I hope were productively 'methodically unmethodical' ways (to draw from Adorno), the world of Thomas Mann's *Death in Venice* (which serves as the urtext for my book), and the social and textual milieus I was situated in and inexorably writing out of. See Cyril Wong, 'A Conversation with Mark Anthony Cayanan', *Queer Southeast Asia: A Literary Journal*

in that it serves as a transmutation of what occurs when cacophon-
ously social subject matter is reduced into a first-person-plural lyric
utterance. Moreover, appropriation makes apparent the very fact that
the authorial intervention embodied as the poems themselves unavoid-
ably presents a warped, quite possibly unreliable, model of historical
reality. In addition to the process of composition, the formal choices
I make encode the complexities of representation: I adopt — alongside poems written in more recognizably lyric formulations — forms
that are, on the surface, non-poetic or even traditionally non-literary.
Several entries in the manuscript are written as dramaticules, in the
manner of Samuel Beckett, or as timelines or photo captions. I absorb
these hybrid forms into the domain of the lyric sequence in the hope
of being able to display, trouble, and thwart the element of spectacle
surrounding the Marian apparitions, as well as my decision to write
about them ever so copiously.

I identify the challenges, and their attendant anxieties I let roil
in my creative project as a way of accounting for, and of providing a
correlative to, the multiple ambiguities that accompany my fascination
with my research preoccupation, the exophonic lyric. I discuss, in this
essay, how exophony is accommodated within the extroverted contemporary model of the lyric, which, in the words of Jahan Ramazani, is
'intergeneric, transnational, [and] translingual';[12] and how exophony
reconfigures notions of interiority and verbal density, recognizable and
enduring features of the lyric. *Model* is a word Ramazani deploys frequently enough throughout his book *Poetry in a Global Age*, in which
he offers his analysis of the contemporary lyric. Although, or because,
he does not expound specifically on what he means by it,[13] he capital-
izes on the lexical versatility of the term by using it in various ways. For
instance, he utilizes *model* to refer to a specific text that serves as a precedent or guide for the creation of a new one — as in the case of 'Henry

of Transgressive Art, June 2021 <http://queersoutheastasia.com/a-conversation-with-mark-anthony-cayanan-july-2021> [accessed 25 March 2024].

12 Jahan Ramazani, *Poetry in a Global Age* (Chicago: University of Chicago Press, 2020), p. 239 <https://doi.org/10.7208/chicago/9780226730288.001.0001>.

13 Klaus Stierstorfer observes that 'model' is a nebulous concept in literature, one that remains 'unmarked, undertheorized, and colloquial'. See Klaus Stierstorfer, 'Models and/as/of Literature', *Anglia*, 138.4 (2020), pp. 673–98 (p. 674) <https://doi.org/10.1515/ang-2020-0053>.

David Thoreau's *Walden*, which William Butler Yeats acknowledged as his *model* for' his poem 'The Lake Isle of Innisfree',[14] or William Carlos Williams's *Paterson*, which served as a model for Charles Olson's *The Maximus Poems*, especially as regards the latter's decision to set his poetry in the 'bounded environment of a city'.[15] Ramazani also employs *model*, interchangeably with *paradigm*, to bracket the different versions that outline the relationship between modernism and post-colonialism.[16]

For this essay, however, I depend considerably on the confluence of the terms *model* and *genre* in literature, in that both are used to denote abstract categories under which particular literary works may be subsumed, and of which they may be understood as iterations. A genre, according to Tzvetan Todorov, is the 'codification of discursive properties', and is created when certain semantic, syntactic, pragmatic, or verbal features of a discourse — for instance, the tendency of an English sonnet to subscribe to the formal constraint of fourteen lines of iambic pentameter — guide the production of individual texts. Just as important, this codification also consequently serves as one of the bases for the interpretation and classification of a literary text by readers:[17] it is from the twin perspectives of creation and reception that I consider Ramazani's model as a condensed catalogue of properties that may be used as a means of unpacking the contemporary lyric, laying open its formal and linguistic operations, as well as its links to extratextual forces adjacent to its creation and circulation.

---

14 Ramazani, *Poetry in a Global Age*, p. 59, my emphasis.

15 Ibid., p. 67.

16 Ibid., pp. 108–16.

17 Tzvetan Todorov, 'The Origin of Genres', trans. by Richard M. Berrong, *New Literary History*, 8.1 (1976), pp. 159–70 (p. 162) <https://doi.org/10.2307/468619>.

EXOPHONY AND ANGLOPHONE WRITING FROM THE PHILIPPINES

First, a necessary definition (or, in this instance, a range of available applications): *exophony* is an 'emerging term'[18] that pertains to the practice and presence of literature written in a language that is not the author's native language or mother tongue.[19] While the deployment of a language that the writer is relatively less familiar with is normally accompanied by some amount of difficulty, checked by the occasional disparity between intent and evidence, the Japanese-born writer Yoko Tawada, who also regularly publishes in German, highlights both the capacity for play and the emancipatory possibilities that this disorienting linguistic practice may inspire:

> [W]hen you talk in a foreign language, all taboos have sud-
> denly disappeared. You can, surprisingly enough, talk about
> aspects from your childhood that you had completely forgot-
> ten, because they were either too embarrassing or too painful,
> or because of some unknown other reason. Those memories
> had been cut off over time, but in a foreign tongue it becomes
> possible to talk about them again.[20]

The coverage of the term *exophony*, it bears pointing out, still seems quite inconsistent. One standard perspective is articulated by Kazuhito Matsumoto, who states that the practice is distinct from the kind employed by writers or subjects 'who are compelled to embrace a foreign language by either historical or political or circumstantial reasons', in that an exophonic writer uses, of their own volition, a non-native language in their literary production.[21] More recently, however, the term has also been consistently applied to writings by diasporic figures, regardless of the factors that inform their migration, who assume the

---

18   Chantal Wright, 'Writing in the "Grey Zone": Exophonic Literature in Contemporary
      Germany', *GFL: German as a Foreign Language*, 3 (2008), pp. 26–42 (p. 39) <http://
      gfl-journal.de/article/writing-in-the-grey-zone/> [accessed 24 July 2024].
19   Ibid., p. 27.
20   Bettina Brandt, '*Ein Wort, ein Ort*, or How Words Create Places: Interview with Yoko
      Tawada', *Women in German Yearbook*, 21 (2005), pp. 1–15 (p. 8).
21   Kazuhito Matsumoto, '"Exophony" in the Midst of the Mother Tongue: Resources
      Between Languages', in *Doing English in Asia: Global Literature and Culture*, ed. by
      Patricia Haseltine and Sheng-mei Ma (Lanham, MD: Lexington Books, 2016), pp. 17–
      28 (p. 18).

language of the country they resettle in. Lawrence-Minh Bùi Davis argues for the relaxation of the epistemic boundaries of exophony by citing the literary productions of refugees: whether written in the adopted language or the language of their country of origin, 'refugee poetry is always exophonic'. This is because, according to Davis, the refugee's sense of their first language is slow to evolve once they escape from their country of origin, the language having become unmoored from where, geographically, it is an indispensable component of lived reality; thus, even their heritage language becomes 'stubbornly, sometimes agonisingly non-native'.[22] Chantal Wright maintains that exophony is closely linked with postcolonial literary practice;[23] however, she also opines that the former may be distinguished from the latter because it 'avoids the imposition of a thematic straitjacket and emphasizes [...] innovative stylistic features that can be observed in this body of texts'.[24]

Because I would like to foreground the formal and linguistic in this essay — without, nevertheless, losing sight of their tetheredness to the political and historical — I would like to view anglophone writing from the Philippines as an instantiation of exophony, a practice that, in turn and in the case of this essay, acquires a more specific shape when viewed through the lens of a national literary tradition. The roots of exophonic Philippine writing in English may be traced to campus writing from the University of the Philippines, founded by the Americans in 1908. The writers, according to Elmer Ordoñez, had the avowed goal of 'elevat[ing] to the highest possible perfection the English language' by insisting that '[a]rt shall not be a means to an end but an end in itself'.[25] This goal — which attended the 'explosion of English-language writing from the 1920s through to the beginning of the Second World War'[26] — emerged from systemic in-

22   Lawrence-Minh Bùi Davis, 'On Refugee Poetics and Exophony', *Poetry*, 1 April 2022 <https://www.poetryfoundation.org/poetrymagazine/articles/157568/on-refugee-poetics-and-exophony> [accessed 12 June 2023].

23   Wright, 'Writing in the "Grey Zone"', p. 39.

24   Ibid., p. 27.

25   Elmer Ordoñez, 'An Overview of Philippine Literature', in Ordoñez, *Emergent Literature: Essays on Philippine Writing* (Quezon City: University of the Philippines Press, 2001), pp. 23–38 (p. 17).

26   Rajeev Patke and Philip Holden, *The Routledge Concise History of Southeast Asian Writing in English* (Abingdon: Routledge, 2010), p. 62 <https://doi.org/10.4324/9780203874035>.

doctrination into the colonial language and culture enforced during the American occupation, which saw the implementation of pervasive English-exclusive policies in formal education as a means of 'civilizing' the Filipinos.[27] According to the American George Pope Shannon, then-head of the English Department at the University of the Philippines, the first few batches of anglophone Filipino writers displayed a penchant for 'slavish imitation', something that, in the late 1920s, Shannon cautioned them against, without any seeming irony: the ubiquity of Anglo-American literary models and, conversely, the exclusion of material written by Filipinos in various other languages within academic institutions practically guaranteed this tendency.[28] The earliest iterations of exophonic writing from the Philippines, then, were marked by considerable incongruity:

> On the one hand, Filipinos were expected to produce writing that was acceptable to the general reader, that is, the American reader, or more precisely, the Filipino reader with the literary taste of an American (a taste, of course, developed in the colonial classroom with the Filipinos' exposure to Anglo-American texts). On the other hand, it was also demanded that Philippine writing in English be original. And to be original meant to infuse Philippine literature with local colour, a quality hardly consistent with the nature of the Anglo-American texts Filipinos were expected to read and imitate.[29]

The compulsion to declare mastery over the colonizers' language, perhaps as a way of neutralizing centuries of lingering historical trauma, persists throughout the literary history of the Philippines. Gémino Abad, for example, provides a triumphalist spin in his account, proclaiming in the 1990s that Filipino 'writers have [...] colonised English because its use in our literature has been chiefly toward a native clearing within the adopted language where its worlds are found again to

---

27 Isabel Pefianco Martin, 'Colonial Education and the Shaping of Philippine Literature in English', in *Philippine English: Linguistic and Literary Perspectives*, ed. by Maria Lourdes S. Bautista and Kingsley Bolton (Hong Kong: Hong Kong University Press, 2008), pp. 245–59 (p. 246).

28 Ibid., p. 254.

29 Ibid., p. 255.

establish and affirm a Filipino sense of their world'.[30] In an essay that provides a narrative sweep of the tradition of the anglophone short story emerging out of the country, Cristina Pantoja-Hidalgo, on several occasions, singles out authors whose body of work has exhibited the ability to wield English 'to express a thoroughly Filipino experience and sensibility': Nick Joaquin, for instance, is praised for ushering in 'a new era' in anglophone production, because of his 'dazzling use of the English language and mastery of narrative technique [which] was to eclipse anything achieved by his contemporaries'.[31] However, despite the ubiquity of anglophone writing, and despite the fact that English is, as stated in the Philippine Constitution, an official language, fluency in it is most often premised on privilege: it may be the language of formal education, commerce, and bureaucracy, but it is hardly the language of everyday life for most citizens and is most often associated with 'class superiority and snobbishness'.[32]

While Filipino, the national language, is extolled for its seeming capacity, in literary practice, to replicate the experience of the country's citizens and unequivocally communicate their need for social transformation,[33] English is regarded as a signifier of elitism: whereas the *makata*, the poet who writes in Filipino, 'belongs to the people', their English counterpart, declares N. V. M. Gonzalez, '[cares] very little, if at all, for [their] reader'.[34] While the field of English writing in the Philippines remains expansive, many of its practitioners have, at some point, expressed remorse over their choice of language, also acknowledging that 'writing in the vernacular language would be much

30   Gémino Abad, 'Our Scene so Fair: An Overview of Filipino English Poetry, 1905–2006', in Abad, *Our Scene so Fair: Filipino Poetry in English, 1905 to 1955* (Quezon City: University of the Philippines Press, 2008), pp. 1–20 (p. 4).

31   Cristina Pantoja-Hidalgo, 'The Philippine Short Story in English: An Overview', in *Philippine English*, ed. by Bautista and Bolton, pp. 299–316 (p. 303).

32   Caroline S. Hau, 'The Filipino Novel in English', in *Philippine English*, ed. by Bautista and Bolton, pp. 317–36 (p. 329).

33   José Maria Sison, 'Literary Craft and Commitment', in Sison, *The Guerrilla Is Like a Poet / Ang Gerilya Ay Tulad ng Makata* (Santa Barbara, CA: Punctum Books, 2013), pp. 213–19 (p. 219) <https://doi.org/10.2307/j.ctv2sbm7n2.102>.

34   N. V. M. Gonzalez, 'Imaginative Writing in the Philippines', in *Philippine Writing: An Anthology*, ed. by T. D. Agcaoili (Westport, CT: Greenwood Press, 1971), pp. 321–28 (p. 326).

more "relevant".[35] One recourse of anglophone writers to salvage the
language they write in from charges of inutility is to lean into its status
as an enduring evidence of the irreparable consequences of colonialism upon the nation. Drawing from Bill Ashcroft's proposition that
postcolonial writers engage in a process of 'inner translation and transformation to produce an English that [is] culturally located [and]
specific',[36] J. Neil Garcia argues that the anglophone Filipino writer
takes on the indefinitely 'unfinished task' of deploying the colonial language to reproduce their lived reality 'effectively and convincingly'.[37]
Garcia further explains that the standard literary text written by a
Filipino in English is 'ironic, verbally involuted, representationally ambiguous, and self-reflexive, right from the get-go'; the '"unnaturalness"'
of English, he emphasizes, 'makes it virtually impossible to be transparent to its meanings'.[38] In this case, to refer to Philippine writing in
English as exophonic foregrounds the kind of semantic distance from
the language that the practitioner attempts to bridge at every instance
of production.

EXOPHONIC PRACTICE AND A MODEL OF THE LYRIC

The representational ambiguity inherent in exophonic practice finds
its generic correspondence in the lyric; after all, imbricated in its history is the evolving relationship of literature with mimesis. While earlier scholarship surrounding the genre preoccupies itself with notions
of the lyric's proximity to its mimetic provenance, Jonathan Culler
more recently states that 'the lyric aims to be an event, not a representation of an event':[39] he even resists models of the lyric (these models

---

35   Isagani Cruz, 'English and Tagalog in Philippine Literature: A Study of Literary Bi-
      lingualism', *World Englishes*, 5.2–3 (1986), pp. 163–76 (p. 165) <https://doi.org/10.
      1111/j.1467-971x.1986.tb00723.x>.

36   Bill Ashcroft, 'The Transformation of English in Postcolonial Literatures', *Language
      and Semiotic Studies*, 1.4 (2015), pp. 80–94 (p. 83) <https://doi.org/10.1515/lass-
      2015-010405>.

37   J. Neil Garcia, 'Translational Poetics: Notes on Contemporary Philippine Poetry
      in English', *Likhaan: The Journal of Contemporary Philippine Literature*, 7 (2013),
      pp. 177–94 (p. 179) <https://www.journals.upd.edu.ph/index.php/lik/article/view/
      5062> [accessed 12 June 2023].

38   Ibid., pp. 181–82.

39   Jonathan Culler, *Theory of the Lyric* (Cambridge, MA: Harvard University Press, 2015),
      p. 137 <https://doi.org/10.4159/9780674425781>.

being primarily Western in orientation) designating the genre as an imitation of the subjective experience of either the poet — 'a mimesis of feeling', which was the primary formulation for the Romantic-era lyric — or a fictive persona, the ostensibly prevalent contemporary paradigm which 'deflects attention from what is most singular, most mind-blowing, even', in the lyric, 'and puts readers on a prosaic, novelising track'.[40] Leaning into its epideictic origins, Culler emphasizes how the lyric is, instead, an enunciatory phenomenon: the genre's privileging of sonic effects — 'rhymes, rhythmical structures, forms of address' — and its deferral of narrative — it prioritizes 'voicing', the instance of speech, a moment that Culler calls 'the lyric *now*', over plot progression — are, he claims, its most noteworthy and consistent features.[41] While unpacking the genre's severance from mimesis, Culler nevertheless references Mutlu Blasing, who describes poetry as 'a cultural institution dedicated to remembering and displaying the emotionally and historically charged materiality of language'.[42] Ascertaining the status of the lyric as enunciation, in this case, also involves a significant appraisal of the etymological and cultural strands encoded within the lexicon that allows the enunciation to exist in the first place. Culler's summation of the lyric — that it maintains an attentiveness to the historical resonances of language while unmooring itself from mimetic affinity — is a solid premise to the model of the lyric propounded by Ramazani.

The global image of the lyric, to a considerable extent, is shrouded in a rarefied aura: consider, for instance, Robert von Hallberg's depiction of autonomy as 'poetry's special aspiration: an independence from politics, philosophy, history, or theology, so that poetic value does not depend upon political conformity, logical argumentation, historical accuracy, or religious faith'.[43] The supposed ahistoricity of the lyric is manifested in the presentation of its persona: 'The strangeness and point of lyric can be seen when we note that the speaker [...] is only

---

40   Jonathan Culler, 'Extending the *Theory of the Lyric*', *Diacritics*, 45.4 (2017), pp. 6–14 (p. 9) <https://doi.org/10.1353/dia.2017.0017>.

41   Culler, 'Extending', pp. 8–10, emphasis in the original.

42   Culler, *Theory of the Lyric*, p. 169.

43   Robert von Hallberg, *Lyric Powers* (Chicago: University of Chicago Press, 2008), p. 10 <https://doi.org/10.7208/chicago/9780226865027.001.0001>.

equivocally named, has in effect a sponsor (the author) but no name, is prior to or posterior to name, is an orphan voice.'[44] In Allen Grossman, I recognize a conception of the lyric that bridges the gap between the pedagogy-friendly notion of the lyric as dramatic monologue and Culler's model, in that the lyric speaker is both a phantasmagoric (because indeterminate) entity and one whose manifestation is as (or only through) utterance. Grossman's use of *orphan* to describe this lyric presence is particularly revealing, since the adjective plays out the drama of overt absence and implied presence ingrained in the illocutionary context of the lyric speaker. The lyric as an 'orphan voice' is also important considering Ramazani's conception of the genre, which remains fiercely attentive to aspects of normative form even as it accounts for the intravenous revisions and expansions of the lyric alongside its encounters with various discursive genres, social realities, and linguistic practices. Ramazani states that the lyric exhibits — contrary to Mikhail Bakhtin's view of the lyric as largely monologic[45] — 'compressed heteroglossia' in the way that it transmutes conventions and summons information from within its own poetic lineage, as well as from other non-literary genres, including 'news, obituaries, philosophy, [and] the novel':[46] the 'orphan voice' of the lyric, seemingly unitary, is, for Ramazani, actually a compendium of other voices.

Channelling Bruno Latour's pronouncement that 'every contemporary assembly is polytemporal', Ramazani explains that the raw materials of poets — their vocabulary and their tropes, their omnivorous allusions and their techniques — are each informed by their respective history and development across time. These microhistories consequently collide and haphazardly combine into multivalent for-

---

44   Allen Grossman, 'Summa Lyrica: A Primer of the Commonplaces in Speculative Poetics', in *The Lyric Theory Reader: A Critical Anthology*, ed. by Virginia Jackson and Yopie Prins (Baltimore: Johns Hopkins University Press, 2014), pp. 419–30 (p. 421).

45   In the essay 'Discourse in the Novel', Bakhtin not only states that poetry uses unitary language by default, but goes so far as to assert that the poet is actually unable to escape it, is unable 'to oppose his own poetic consciousness, his own intentions to the language that he uses, for he is completely within it and therefore cannot turn it into an object to be perceived, reflected upon or related to'. See Mikhail Bakhtin, 'Discourse in the Novel', in Bakhtin, *The Dialogic Imagination: Four Essays*, ed. by Michael Holquist, trans. by Caryl Emerson and Michael Holquist (Austin, TX: University of Texas Press, 1981), pp. 259–422 (pp. 285–86).

46   Ramazani, *Poetry in a Global Age*, p. 245.

mulations when lodged within the poetic work. Thus, '[p]oems belong
to their immediate historical moment and to the longer transhistorical
skeins — generic, formal, tropological, etymological, environmental
— that they twist together and remake to address their moment.'[47]
The convergence of histories upon and within the poem also necessarily demonstrates how national boundaries prove porous when it
comes to linguistic and aesthetic translocations: 'poetry participates
in global flows, planetary enmeshments, and cosmopolitan engagements.'[48] The intergeneric, transnational, and translingual qualities of
the lyric — its communion with vernacular poetics, for instance (a
process I intend to provide an example for soon enough), or even its
malleability, its 'relative brevity, vividness, and nonmimetic freedom'
making it easily adaptable across cultures[49] — parallel the polyglot,
heteroglossic dimension of exophonic literature, in that its writer is
already immersed in a dialogic process not just of translation but also
of affirmation of identity through a language that may not have readily
shaped it: Ashcroft declares, 'The dual dynamic of saying "I am me"
in another's language and "I am other" in my own language captures
precisely the dual achievement of the second language writer.'[50] Of
course, the term *transnational*, according to Donald Pease, 'bears the
traces of the violent sociohistorical processes to which it alludes',[51]
thus foregrounding, for the contemporary lyric, the persistent 'tension between aesthetic hybridity and cultural decolonization.'[52] 'The
transnational', Pease further states, 'names an undecidable economic,
political, or social formation that is neither in nor out of the nation-
state.'[53] Siwar Masannat channels Pease's use of the word *undecidable*
to discuss poetry that deliberately exceeds the epistemic boundaries

---

47   Ibid., pp. 2–3.
48   Ibid., p. 9.
49   Ibid., p. 246.
50   Ashcroft, 'The Transformation of English in Postcolonial Literatures', p. 86.
51   Donald E. Pease, 'Re-mapping the Transnational Turn', in *Re-framing the Transnational
     Turn in American Studies*, ed. by Winfried Fluck and others (Hanover, NH: Dartmouth
     College Press, 2011), pp. 1–46 (p. 5).
52   Robert Stilling, 'Multicentric Modernism and Postcolonial Poetry', in *The Cambridge
     Companion to Postcolonial Poetry*, ed. by Jahan Ramazani (Cambridge: Cambridge Uni-
     versity Press, 2017), pp. 127–38 (p. 129) <https://doi.org/10.1017/9781316111338.
     011>.
53   Pease, 'Re-mapping the Transnational Turn', p. 5.

of the monolithic nation, asserting how it not only moves beyond 'a critique of hegemony, but [also] opens up undecidability as a site of decolonial agency'.[54]

I am invested in how these tensions and undecidabilities are played out in the exophonic lyric, especially through its deployment of verbal density and interiority. While exophony may be perceived from a more propitiatory perspective, its literary producers regarded as 'interpreters and ambassadors' who mediate between cultures and languages,[55] I am more intrigued by an exophonic practice in which the structural elements of the lyric are assembled to signify, rather than conciliation, cultural irreconcilabilities. For this discussion, I emphasize the term *interiority* because of its ambiguity: even as the 'lyric remains the literary genre of intimate feeling',[56] its concept of interiority is pried open because of the genre's encounters with local poetic practices. In the case of Philippine literature, Virgilio Almario argues that the strain of poetry that is *paloob* — denoting something trained inward — has a long, drawn-out tradition. He cites the *bugtong*, a gnomic form approximating the riddle, a puzzling utterance requiring an answer, as being *paloob*: first, the cardinal aim of the *bugtong* is to defamiliarize, wrenching a subject out of its quotidian social, utilitarian context and imbuing it with mystery.[57] Afterward, the *bugtong* compels the reader to go through a semantic process of reorientation, where the tropes employed by the writer to extricate the previously recognizable subject from its commonplace associative milieu should, despite their function as means of obfuscation, lead back to a recognition of that specific, singular subject, with the reader nevertheless gaining an alternative conception of, or insight (*kislap-diwa*), into it.[58] The

---

54   Siwar Massanat, 'A Constellation of Transnational Poetics', *Jacket2*, 26 January 2023, <https://jacket2.org/article/constellation-transnational-poetics> [accessed 12 June 2023].

55   Øyvind Rangøy, 'Train of Language: Notes on an Exophonic Anomaly', *Interlitteraria*, 26.1 (2021), pp. 235–48 (p. 243) <https://doi.org/10.12697/IL.2021.26.1.16>.

56   Stephanie Burt, 'What Is This Thing Called Lyric?', *Modern Philology*, 113.3 (2016), pp. 422–40 (p. 427) <https://doi.org/10.1086/684097>.

57   Virgilio S. Almario, 'Palabas at Paloob: Tambalang Mukha ng Pagtula', *Philippine Humanities Review*, 16.1 (2014), pp. 69–91 (p. 74) <https://journals.upd.edu.ph/index.php/phr/article/view/4971> [accessed 5 October 2023].

58   Ibid., p. 75.

arc that the *bugtong* traces — from defamiliarization and then to a transformed recognition — Almario suggests, is *paloob*, as it is made possible by the genre's immersion in the shared knowledge of a community, allowing the genre to be legible to the community's members. The transplantation of the Western, modernist lyric into Philippine literary practice in the twentieth century, according to Almario, has allowed the concept of *paloob* to accommodate other poetic values such as self-reflexivity, ambiguity, introspectiveness, and relative inaccessibility.[59]

MIRACLE FEVER AS EXOPHONIC LYRIC

The interiority of the contemporary Filipino lyric may thus be considered an oscillating synthesis of the vernacular tradition and its transplanted version. I rely on this notion of interiority when approaching the exophonic lyric, which, to my mind, may fulfil a function that is just as paradoxical: on the one hand, it may continue to highlight the primacy of the poetic voice, its capacity for ostensibly individual expression through the resources of syntax and sound, while, on the other, creating intimate social clearings for specific audiences and productively establishing semantic restrictions indicative of cultural difference through the deliberate use of referentiality. I am invested in writing poetry that slides in and out of comprehension, wielding the genre's predilection for privacy. I am, in my project, also keen on recruiting Édouard Glissant's notion of opacity, transmuted as an approach to writing that compels the reader to 'focus on the texture of the weave and not on the nature of its components'.[60] One of the most potent arguments he makes in relation to opacity has to do with how it mitigates the ostensibly global approach to understanding various other peoples and their cultures, which is informed by a demand for 'transparency': 'In order to understand and thus accept you', Glissant summarizes, 'I have to measure your solidity with the ideal scale providing me with grounds to make comparisons and, perhaps, judgments.'[61] *Transparency*, of course, is a word that in literary discourse

---

59   Ibid., pp. 84–86.
60   Édouard Glissant, 'For Opacity', in Glissant, *Poetics of Relation*, trans. by Betsy Wing (Ann Arbor, MI: University of Michigan Press, 1990), pp. 189–94 (p. 190).
61   Ibid., p. 190.

readily conjures up affiliated notions such as accessibility and legibility: the literary production of a subject from a minoritized culture (that is, relative to the centres of capital and influence) is burdened with expectations of exposition, of having to explain themselves to — and represent their culture before — a reading demographic keen on affirming its inclusivity, even as its chokehold on the literary market demands that it be attended to.

Just as interesting to me is Glissant's presentation of opacity as a means of evoking the near-inscrutability of identity — 'there are places where my identity is obscure to me', he states; furthermore, 'human behaviours are fractal in nature.'[62] A recognition of this near-inscrutability in the individual is a move toward a relationality that is, asserts Glissant, 'the most straightforward equivalent of nonbarbarism':[63]

> I thus am able to conceive of the opacity of the other for me, without reproach for my opacity for him. To feel in solidarity with him or to build with him or to like what he does, it is not necessary for me to grasp him.[64]

Opacity, then, may be repurposed as a literary strategy working toward a resistance to what Graham Huggan refers to as 'the global machinery of cultural commodification', a structure that, he points out, many postcolonial scholars — and, by extension, artistic practitioners, especially those operating in cosmopolitan spheres — find themselves enmeshed in or are compelled to build their cachet from.[65] To illustrate my deployment of opacity, here is one poem from *Miracle Fever*:

---

62   Ibid., pp. 192–93.

63   Ibid., p. 194.

64   Ibid., p. 193.

65   Graham Huggan, *The Postcolonial Exotic: Marketing the Margins* (London: Routledge, 2001), p. 9 <https://doi.org/10.4324/9780203420102>.

The Wilderness Was the Time Between Prophets[66]

Not we but the material world, ungenerous surface
      we harrow over and over. Not we but
our mud-caked fingers scratching holes into our skulls, in this heat
      we are everything we feel. Not we but gunshots let loose
        in the night before night untangles itself
from its told stories. Not we but before this unfamiliar century, one
      traffic light debilitating the plaza, we would give
        way as we're selfless, we're too much
time. Not we but yearly and half a millennium in
      we rid the saint's raiment of dust, wipe our fingerprints off
        the glass casket. Not we but patience
though patience has no value in this life, and we worry
      though won't ever say it to each other
        there isn't another life we deserve. Not we
but a landscape that fits the loneliness of waiting long
      and for what. Not we but without the saviour's promise
        there's only a crowd without reason. Not we but
in the same space, exchangeable bodies, the mountain we've made
      is a mountain made of paste. The infinite
        has the transparency of evil, the lynched
herald said. Not we because not infinite, not evil
      in a manner that's important. Not we but a competition
        for piety, a priest in every family, every unmarried daughter
a nun. Virtue's a long vigil. Not we but the high-noon
      shadow of a minor basilica. Not we but penance on behalf of
        methodists and communists, though we're all
children, some are born better than others. Not we
      but magician and scientist, theologian and hypnotist, mob
        psychologist and hunger artist, the prophet
who shall come shall make the sun dance and mouth
      bleed, not we but the skittish sun.

---

66   An earlier version of this poem first appeared in *FE*. See Mark Anthony Cayanan, 'The
       Wilderness Was the Time Between Prophets', in *FE*, ed. by Jeff Alessandrelli and others
       (Portland, OR: Fonograf Editions), pp. 87–88.

In the poem above, I attempt to write an exophonic lyric that is, in itself, a site of several discourses — those directly germane to my narrative and thematic concerns, as well as those which inform the vantage point I write from as a specific historical subject, including current realities in and outside the Philippines. Ramazani's model of the lyric, as that which exhibits 'compressed heteroglossia', is useful here, given how the vestiges of these discourses are marshalled — that is, granted the illusion of monologism — through anaphora, 'the repetition of the same word or words at the beginning of successive' syntactic units.[67] As both reader and writer, I find myself constantly drawn to the paradoxical effects of anaphora: the rhetorical device can generate propulsion but also lead toward tedium, an interesting affect when used deliberately. Since the apparent surplus of syntactic invariability could induce a sense of monotony, anaphora gives the reader the licence to break out of the spell of concentration that engaging with a lyric normally warrants and lets them formulate their own reading strategy, one guided by their tremulous, fragmented capacity for attentiveness. In the poem, I attempt to foreground some amount of discordance between the way that anaphora can suggest insistence on the part of the speaker and the lexical reiteration of the phrase 'Not we', which paradoxically evokes pathological denial. I also intend, in my deployment of anaphora, to generate some tension between the vocality of the plural first-person persona and their chronic identification with inanimate entities ('gunshots let loose / in the night' and 'one / traffic light debilitating the plaza'), abstract values ('patience' and 'a competition / for piety'), and disembodied imagery ('our mud-caked fingers' or 'exchangeable bodies'). I want to reiterate reduction and dissipation while also intimating the magnitude of those same details.

Anaphora is one of my favourite rhetorical strategies because of how it 'highlights poetic lines as discrete units while simultaneously binding those lines together'.[68] I rely on this oscillation between separation and coalition in 'The Wilderness Was the Time Between Prophets' too, as, to my mind, it enacts the general challenge of my

---

67 Jessica Weare, 'Anaphora', in *The Princeton Encyclopedia of Poetry & Poetics*, ed. by Roland Greene and others, 4th edn (Princeton, NJ: Princeton University Press, 2012), p. 50.

68 Ibid.

project: how to negotiate between the ostensible solitariness of the lyric speaker — I invoke, again, Jonathan Culler's presentation of the lyric as 'voicing' — and my use of the genre to surface a collective consciousness. The proliferative quality of anaphora echoes the polyphony of communities I conjure up in my project, even as the enunciatory phenomenon that is the lyric genre more immediately evokes a singular vocal entity. Adjacent to generic considerations, I am also invested in how the use of anaphora in the exophonic lyric could somehow mirror the real-life metapoetic conflict of my project: how to apparently channel the collective while foregrounding its haphazard, amorphous quality and, more importantly, also telegraphing how this same goal is ethically suspect. Throughout my continuing work on *Miracle Fever*, I have been acutely aware of the need to resist turning my writing into 'a commodified discourse of cultural marginality',[69] a trap my project could so easily fall into, given my national affiliation and the even more peripheral status of the locality that the narrative content of my current project derives from: in 'The Wilderness Was the Time Between Prophets', the use of anaphora and the general tendency of the poem to rely on sentence fragments are important to me, because I want the discourses circulating in and out of the poem to remain in spectral form, unconcluded and left suspended.

Perhaps one more specific instance I can cite as regards how I employ opacity as a tactic is my inclusion of the phrase 'penance on behalf of / methodists and communists'. This moment in the poem is wrenched out of one of the alleged divine messages of the Immaculate Queen of Heaven and Earth — a rather campy title that, according to Nieva, the mother of God had asked to be addressed as:

> I am your Mother of the Immaculate Heart. You are all my children, whether you are black, yellow, brown or white, whether you are Christian, Muslim, Buddhist, pagan, atheist, or any other sect. You are all my children, even sinners, they are all my children. And now I lament for those children who are away from the light and grace of God.

---

69   Huggan, *The Postcolonial Exotic*, p. 20.

Even communists, they are my children. Pray that they will be converted. If this will happen, the triumph of my immaculate heart will be realised. Remember, my children, this is the era of my immaculate heart. For many years I have been in silence, but now the time has come for me to intervene. Despite my greatest enemy, Satan, spreading darkness all over the world, the light of my immaculate heart will surely save you.[70]

The message, relayed to Nieva on 12 December 1992, reflects an enduring anti-left sentiment in Philippine society. One of the many troubling legacies of American colonial thinking, this sentiment has been weaponized often enough in various presidential tenures. For instance, President Ferdinand Marcos Sr. — whose family pretty much considers the Ilocos Region, including the province of La Union, where Nieva comes from, as their stronghold — cited the 'anarchy and lawlessness, chaos and disorder, turmoil and destruction' posed by alleged insurrectionists egged on by 'Marxist-Leninist-Maoist' ideology as justification for the proclamation of Martial Law in 1972.[71] More recently, the practice of 'red-tagging' was used with impunity by President Rodrigo Duterte to throw the masses off the abysmal track record of his administration when it came to addressing the various social and political ills of the country, not to mention his extreme inefficiency in addressing the pandemic crisis. Under the National Task Force to End Local Communist Armed Conflict (NTF-ELCAC), Duterte and his allies branded, among many others, various academics, Indigenous leaders actively engaged in efforts to defend their lands from mining corporations,[72] members of human rights groups, and even show business celebrities[73] as communists, a practice that has persisted, albeit

70   Rodolfo Dula, 'Devil's Advocate in Agoo' (conclusion), *Malaya*, 21 February 1993, p. 1.

71   Republic of the Philippines, *Proclamation No.* 1081 (Office of the President, 1972) <https://www.officialgazette.gov.ph/featured/declaration-of-martial-law/> [accessed 12 June 2023].

72   Jelo Ritzhie Mantaring, 'PH Remains Worst Place for Land, Environmental Defenders in Asia — Watchdog', *CNN Philippines*, 30 September 2022 <https://www.cnnphilippines.com/news/2022/9/30/PH-remains-worst-place-for-land-and-environmental-defenders-in-Asia.html> [accessed 5 October 2023].

73   JC Gotinga, 'Angel Locsin: Red-tagged Celebrity', *Rappler*, 18 December 2020 <https://www.rappler.com/newsbreak/in-depth/angel-locsin-red-tagged-celebrity-faces-philippines-2020-series/> [accessed 5 October 2023].

more insidiously, up until the current dispensation, headed by Ferdinand Marcos Jr., the son of the deposed dictator.[74]

Of course, all the contexts I have mentioned above are not visibly present in my poem — and to maintain that they be found out is to make the work itself overdetermined, and to insist upon an authorial tyranny that does not actually hold much value in the transaction that occurs between text and reader. Which is precisely the point: I want to be able to write lyrics that play with resonance, that discombobulate readers and slow down their reading process, without having to be bogged down by the burden of exposition. I do not expect all readers — whatever that means for a genre whose presence in the literary market is hardly felt — to understand the subtexts and ideas I let float in the lines; I sometimes do not even remember them fully after the sustained process of writing is concluded. But they are there, nonetheless. I desire a poetic practice that is cognizant of the collisions of texts, contexts, and concepts, one that mindfully variegates its audience as a way of recognizing the multiplicity of situations the work is enfolded in whenever it is engaged with. I believe in the potentiality of the lyric to install porous membranes of legibility and thus gesture toward provisional socialities, and how these layers may summon up cultural affiliations without succumbing to 'marketable essentialism', a danger seemingly faced by writers whose embeddedness in a group identity becomes 'personal capital'.[75] Which is why I hope for a poetics that short-circuits possible assumptions of authenticity: as knowledge is not presented in a state of fixity, it is therefore — or, at least, I hope — less prone to sanctioning cultural oversimplification. Here, too, the value of writing a lyric sequence becomes manifest, as it is an extended form that wields the restlessness of its constitutive elements, the narrative gaps productively generated across, in spite, and because of, the overlaps and resonances among individual poems.

---

74 Amnesty International, 'Philippines: Deadly Practice of "Red-tagging" Continues Under Marcos Administration', 22 March 2023 <https://www.amnesty.org/en/documents/asa35/6582/2023/en/> [accessed 5 October 2023].

75 Ian Afflerbach, 'On the Literary History of Selling Out: Craft, Identity, and Commercial Recognition', *PMLA*, 137.2 (2022), pp. 230–45 (p. 237) <https://doi.org/10.1632/S0030812922000098>.

I situate my writing within an exophonic practice that foregrounds undecidability, that is mindful of oscillations between languages, the indeterminacy that such a procedure promotes. One last thing I would like to point out as regards 'The Wilderness Was the Time Between Prophets' is the slippery quality of *we*. In Filipino, there are two types of plural first-person pronouns: *tayo*, which encompasses the speaker, the immediate auditor of the speech act, and other figures the speaker wishes to incorporate in the group; and *kami*, a pronoun that accommodates the speaker and other figures, but not the immediate auditor. Lines of invitation and exclusion are established in Filipino plural first-person pronouns — lines that remain hazy in English: I am drawn to the *we* pronoun precisely because of this haziness. I am drawn to the ever-flickering borders of privacy the pronoun conjures up and, in my poetry, the implications that the *we* evokes and dilutes in relation to the lyric's attachment to its audience, the material contexts it draws from, and the affiliations the speaker takes on for themselves. Throughout *Miracle Fever*, the undecidability of the *we* plays into how the sequence navigates between, on the one hand, a collective that closes ranks to protect its visionary from doubt and to ensure the reach of its claims; and, on the other, a collective — possibly the same one or which at least has shared constituents — that, within their performance as a monolith, is nevertheless fractured by the disparate motivations of their constituents, as well as the gradations of their faith in or disbelief toward the apparitions. In exophonic English, the *we* pronoun's determination of invoked communities and, further, of imagined publics remains, excitably, in flux; in the exophonic practice whose semantic values straddle Filipino and English, these ambiguities are possible, crucial.

POEMS FROM *MIRACLE FEVER*

Fever Cartographers

To let journalists know that, separate from the business of faith, we're nearly something

we've made maps of the town, each in the precise shape of their hungers, our desire

to annihilate them. So too that devotees may know where the banks are, restaurants

nearest them, the best roadside stalls for dried fish.

                                      We've kept all our needs predictable

to resist untransformable depletion whenever earth or rain destroys us — we've learned

to limit the time in which we lose our minds, confirmations of our fears stitched together

by unknown hands. We cannot ourselves protect everyone, but we are good artisans.

Early evenings, we peel burnt skin off our backs, pleasure from days dwindling before us.

To distant cousins who speak ill of us: we're not thieves, no longer liars, though we're drunk
on sky we're two decades into a vigil we're not sure we want out of, we're merely in need
of true miracles. Aren't you? From our skin we release sand, divine a prognosis out of
candle wax. The prophet tells us how misguided we are —

                                                    but we've preserved their secrets: too late
for us to change. We who don't know what souls are for in this life dread their helplessness
in the next. A white man's sound bite is our government's law: we don't own the land we farm,
we share our seas with strangers who would rather have us dead. No romance with selflessness.
As the map's limits are its material's, we worship in public but sleep in places which don't exist.

To whisper prayers to the dead, we've devised superstitions out of rumors overheard from passing

strangers. Our prayers, like our doubts, are repetitious. In the night their unsurprising answers

unnerve our dreams. We expect no intercession, but seen through videos which would define us

on national TV, we expect our angles to be good.

                                        The provenance of the map's unknown,

the cameraman anonymous. We'd been seen clinging to coconut trees to avoid being devoured

by the ground, mouth an unquestionable deity: the only hotel in town collapsed into memory,

we've built several makeshift ones, hollow blocks to ward off salt water. What right have we

to survival, if, walking to the apparition hill, misfortunes no longer inhibit our numerousness.

To prepare for death, we spit out talismans and hand them to our oldest sons. Daughters
we introduce to men who speak of leaving town. Our other sons tend to tobacco crops.
Big market day's every Tuesday, and devotees with their straw bags haggle over bottles
of vinegar and sugarcane wine to bring home to the city.
                                                    Here's a map sketched by the priest, his solitary
walks into the forest held as a template for artistic temperament. Where a clearing used to be
now stands lumberyards and hardware stores: we barter our services so we could patch the hole
in the chicken coop, purchase fertilizer for grains. As a way of cleansing one's soul, the priest
advised daily trips into tropical vegetation. What followed was the bloodiest war in our history.

To fill the absence of the word, we gave them a quest. When the quest overtook us, we retreated to our evenings. Silence, a solution to everything. Everywhere, people we shared time with easing back into earth: the exiled dictator, the jueteng lord our grandfathers served, the neighbor who sold garlands outside the church. In the city,

people spoke of things which took place in the recent past as though they happened lifetimes ago — our map is a stopgap oath unrevised by famine, strife, months of plenty. The prophet hoarding notebooks and ungarbling warnings. A typhoon eventually drowning ink into incoherence. No clumsy words could ever protect us. We are weak, and so recycle our mistakes, reject displays of bravery when they aren't ours, expect.

To deserve oblivion. To remap the boundaries of what we should've always been looking for,

in the meantime, feigning ecstasy. To hear the wind, which forces rain into its penultimate

verdict, promise glories which could outstrip our patience. Everything else locked in sunlight

and vanishes. Servile expressions readied, to muscle

                                        into the throng as at last we profit from our history.

And Other Stories

Before the earthquake we were a different kind of earnest. Not a throng but within our town many towns, each with its routines. Mornings, among us were those who expertly could ruche rayon satin, with one sweep of the shears cut fabric across the grain, turn muslin into regular-day robes for statues. Among us were those who idled. But too well we knew how tragedy tests personality. Warm monsoon, unseasonably dry: the historian would call this foreboding, our arms just tired from fanning ourselves. We weren't yet unsafe, some of us didn't feel it. Some of us vaguely impatient. Everyone unruly in minor ways. But then: the town chain-sawed into bits, bits of wood, we flew, and flying, fell. That night holding so many stars, unconcerned about most of us, we fled to the mountains before the sea could drag us back. Between disaster and aftermath god had arrived, still unspeaking. But being his children, we moved toward him as we would a winged insect twitching on the ground. We the dead creature too. Diseased tooth, knocked free. Despair, our skintight verdict. We were twenty-seven children gone, no ivory saint destroyed. Jesus, wedged between two pews, hairpiece ruffled but otherwise perfect. Later, when the damage was inventoried — walls of the eucharist sanctuary cracked all over, pipe organ turned into rubble on the floor, shards of chandelier — no mention of houses we built with our hands: either destroyed or no longer trusted. Despite rain, we slept outdoors for weeks. Cattle, we slept on our feet. Mosquitoes drove us back into our homes, doors and windows remained open, we were bodies prepared to jump. No simpler version of hope than knowing what it's for, men and women of destiny stricken blind so we could see: why doesn't god leave his mark on everyone whom he smites. Changed, our faces hadn't changed enough. If there ever were a time of joy, we knew it had ended. The sea receding into itself again, we tire of survival. Despairing, among us were those who prayed and prayed, and no longer could we retreat to being strangers for one another.

Vigil

Our Lady of Scapulars, we carry you around
like credentials, like disgrace, we suffer
                this insufferable heat, and your laminated spirit
        clings to our sweat-weathered shirts — how much closer
must we be? We herd ourselves up the apparition hill
    so many of us we're shadowless, we're over-awed, hours into
            a vigil we've kept throughout our lives we see nothing
but the sun blotch into its embarrassments.
    Mother of Relentless Charity
              give us what you've given freely, we can't think
                  beyond the rising nausea, some of us
feel less, others more, several just want their boredom
    appeased — you ought to divine who among us
deserve the most, and how soon.
    Consoler of the Inconsolable
              be true to what we've named you, we're locked
    inside our bodies, like discarded skin under our nails
            we scrape our hunger off us and best
our hopelessness. By this we mean we're impatient, we can't
    keep spending on prayer cards and holy water
    without receiving something more profound
              than rain. We've been told gratitude's
the one correct response to living. But haven't we lived and lived
        and lived and lived and lived like this
            enough, free us of it.
    Woman Who Makes Us Wait
Under a Cloudless Sky, anger-lined silence
        settles on us: if through the visible shimmers the invisible
            we see that though you exist, like light
you add nothing except yourself. We don't care
        for one another, we're not all of us neighbors
          not all of us envy or envy
the same people, we're not all of us blind, though
we've inflicted violence we're not all of us
        violent, we're wrong
    we delight in singling out those who are, each of us
        witless, we perfect our questions into accusations,
where in this unending night are you.
    Virgin of the Withering Tree
if you won't better us, better at least our known hopes. Surpass us.

Throughout 'The Exophonic Lyric: A Poetics' and the excerpts from *Miracle Fever* that accompany it, there circulate and hover overhead various senses of *trans*, which, along with the relationships that Mark Anthony Cayanan suggests between them, raise interesting questions about genre and convention: translation, transnational, translingual, transformation, and transgender. In particular, I find myself drawn in by the detail that the Catholic Church declared Judiel Nieva's apparitions to be inauthentic — we might say racially, linguistically, and imaginatively — and that 'the findings of the commission were also tethered to persistent rumours about Nieva's gender identity'.[76]

Perhaps adhering to literary critical conventions, the Catholic Church seems to have understood the difference between authentic and inauthentic repetition as having to do with the distinction between (authentically) repeating form — i.e., the Virgin Mary has spoken to me as she has to so many before — and (inauthentically) repeating content — i.e., she said to me the exact same things she said to someone else twenty years ago. Yet the distinction between content and form is, at best, questionable. This is highlighted by the lyric itself, which so often evidences how the particularly complicated relationship between literary content and form clouds their distinction, and given the imbrication in its history of 'the evolving relationship', as Cayanan puts it, 'of literature with mimesis'.[77] In the context of literariness, the line between authentic and inauthentic repetition tends to be drawn on a muddy slope, somewhere among interrelated notions of copy, theft, plagiarism, homage, quotation, and convention.

This points to one of the questions that most interests me: what was it about the proximity of Nieva's apparitions to the ways in which her transness was made to signify in relation to dominant notions of gender and sexuality that was suggestive of inauthentic copying, or deception, as opposed to authentic evidencing of the conventions of apparition as a form or a genre? The philosopher Talia Mae Bettcher has shown how trans people are socially constituted as 'evil deceivers

---

76 See p. 289.
77 See p. 297.

and make-believers', in the context of the United States in the 1990s — although her comments remain depressingly pertinent.[78] Bettcher shows how social norms of gender and sexuality put trans people in a double bind, granted only the options of being invisible deceivers or visible make-believers. Because this invisibility and visibility hinges on 'coming out' as transgender, transphobic violence — including but not limited to the psychic damage inherent in being cast as deceptive — is related to notions of authenticity as well as exposure, discovery, appearance, and reality.

These notions are, of course, highly relevant to Nieva's apparitions and their acceptance or refusal. And, while outlining this relevance, Cayanan troubles the conceptual basis of authenticity and visibility, which have been shown by Bettcher, along with many other scholars, to be a trap for those who live their genders and sexualities in diverse ways — and particularly for those who are racialized.[79] Helpfully recasting the common-sense understanding that the *trans* in *translation* refers to a journey taken by unchanging content — from language A to language B, for example — Cayanan embraces the exophonic, exploring how it might, as Gémino Abad puts it, 'establish and affirm a Filipino sense of their world'.[80]

Elsewhere, I have thought about how strategies of what I term *reality expansion* can counter what Bettcher describes as strategies of 'reality enforcement', through which trans people are violently subjected to various kinds of 'reveals' of their supposed roles as deceivers or make-believers.[81] These counter-strategies of reality expansion can,

78   Talia Mae Bettcher, 'Evil Deceivers and Make-Believers: On Transphobic Violence and the Politics of Illusion', *Hypatia*, 22.3 (2007), pp. 43–65 <https://doi.org/10.1111/j. 1527-2001.2007.tb01090.x>.

79   See, for example, *Trap Door: Trans Cultural Production and the Politics of Visibility*, ed. by Reina Gossett, Eric A. Stanley, and Johanna Burton (Cambridge, MA: MIT Press, 2017), pp. xv–xxvi.

80   Gémino Abad, *Our Scene so Fair: Filipino Poetry in English, 1905 to 1955* (Quezon City: University of the Philippines Press, 2008), p. 4.

81   Talia Mae Bettcher, 'Trapped in the Wrong Theory: Rethinking Trans Oppression and Resistance', *Signs*, 39.2 (2014), pp. 383–406 (p. 392) <https://doi.org/10.1086/ 673088>; Ruth Ramsden-Karelse, '"People Can't Say I'm A Man, They Can't Say I'm A Woman": Reality Expansion in the Kewpie Collection', in *The Routledge Handbook of Queer Rhetoric*, ed. by Jacqueline Rhodes and Jonathan Alexander (Abingdon: Routledge, 2022), pp. 207–14.

I think, include the use of coding that Cayanan suggests, as well as the challenge with which they engage relating to the singularity of voice. Ultimately, this challenge presents as a struggle with 'the profusion of wills and lived lives', highlighting perspectives vying for precedence in a way that troubles oppressive associations of visuality with truth in relation to the various kinds of transness through and with which Cayanan's writing so evocatively moves.[82]

---

82 See p. 290.

Towards a Genealogy of *Moffie*
Troubling the Binary Model of Understanding either Homosexuality or Homophobia as Un-African
RUTH RAMSDEN-KARELSE

In June 2021, the Oxford English Dictionary (OED) significantly expanded its entry for 'moffie, adj. and n.'.[1] In Southern Africa, the word *moffie* has customarily served as a derogatory marker for individuals read as men and considered lacking in masculinity — although it has been sporadically reappropriated, since around the 1980s, in a manner somewhat comparable to *queer* in the Global North.[2] While newly stressing that the term is 'frequently *derogatory* and *offensive*', the expanded entry offers an interesting take on *moffie's* origins.[3] Pointing to its appearance in a 1929 dictionary of nautical slang, the OED suggests that the word *moffie* originated among, and was presumably brought to the Cape by, early twentieth-century sailors.[4]

What the OED neglects to mention is that, historically, *moffie* has had particular currency within and in relation to communities that

---

1   'Moffie, adj. and n.', *OED Online* (Oxford: Oxford University Press, 2023) <https://doi.org/10.1093/OED/3244658256>.

2   The term *moffie's* continued and uneven charge is perhaps better captured through an also inexact comparison to the uneven reclamation of *faggot* in Great Britain.

3   'Moffie', *OED Online*.

4   See Frank C. Bowen, *Sea Slang: A Dictionary of the Old-Timers' Expressions and Epithets* (London: Sampson Low, Marston & Company, 1929).

were classified 'coloured', a historically controversial category whose
liminal and residual functions the apartheid government sought to bolster with the Population Registration Act of 1950, in which 'a coloured
person' was famously defined as 'a person who is not a white person or
a native' (section 1 [iii]). This particular currency is also not captured
by the entry for *moffie* in the Dictionary of South African English,
nor is it addressed in current scholarship, though it does manifest in
academic research in ways I will discuss shortly. Historically, *coloured*
has been used to ascribe an intermediary position in the South African
race hierarchy, distinct from both the socio-economically dominant
white minority and the majority of the population, whose members
were, under apartheid, classified 'native' (though this intermediary
position has not, of course, been uniformly accepted or occupied by
those to whom it has been ascribed). Very early recorded uses of *moffie*,
from the mid-nineteenth century, describe unsatisfactory cross-bred
or imported livestock as well as the people who were then socially
considered, and later legally classified, 'coloured' — largely descended
from enslaved people, brought to the Cape by the Dutch and then the
English, as well as Indigenous people and settlers — in their perceived
hybridity as what Mahmood Mamdani calls a 'subject race', colonized
yet also considered non-Indigenous.[5]

Taken together, *moffie*'s nineteenth-century uses in the Cape Colony and its appearance in the 1929 dictionary of nautical slang are suggestive of colonial co-productions of race, gender, and sexuality, and
the circulation of attendant concepts, via routes established through
the trade in enslaved people. The geographies of *moffie*'s present usage
also signal the limits of these forms of circulation. In light of the term's
use by seafarers, recorded in 1929, the limitations of its present currency to particular Southern African countries with shared histories of
colonial and apartheid rule is significant. This boundedness suggests
that *moffie* is imbricated in an imaginative economy of sex and race

---

5   Mahmood Mamdani, *When Victims Become Killers: Colonialism, Nativism, and the
     Genocide in Rwanda* (Princeton, NJ: Princeton University Press, 2014), pp. 27–28.
     For early recorded uses of *moffie*, see Charles Pettman, *Africanderisms: A Glossary of
     South African Colloquial Words and Phrases and of Place and Other Names* (London:
     Longmans, Green and Co., 1913); Oliver Walker, *K*****s Are Lively: Being Some
     Backstage Impressions of the South African Democracy* (London: V. Golancz, 1948).

in ways that continue to sustain its purchase in that economy's socio-geographical contexts, and not others.

In place of the OED's suggestion that the word *moffie* originated among seafarers, then, I want to advance an alternate genealogy, which might better account for *moffie*'s early uses and the socio-geographical specificity of its present currency. In the remainder of this chapter, I will sketch this genealogy with brief reference to just two 'scenes', each comprising myriad events through and against which *moffie* has been conceptually constituted, through complex and non-linear forma-tional processes of 'descent' and 'emergence'.[6] I borrow these terms from Michel Foucault, whose peculiar version of the genealogical method does not entail a search for clear origins nor aim to produce complete understanding. Rather, it can offer a means of defamiliarizing inherited concepts and values and attendant models of understanding, thus allowing us to 'separate out, from the contingency that has made us what we are, the possibility of no longer being, doing, or thinking what we are, do, or think'.[7] The argument I will develop is that one model of understanding, attendant on the term *moffie*, that we need to be, do, and think beyond entails what has come to operate, in relation to histories of so-called homosexuality, as a binary of un-Africanness, through which either homosexuality or homophobia is construed as un-African. The first of the two scenes through whose consideration I will develop this argument is represented by the academic research in which *moffie*'s racialized valences manifest.

---

6   Producing a critical genealogy of the term, in the sense distinguished by Michel Foucault, would involve locating *moffie* and analysing the 'different roles' in which it is 'engaged' in such 'scenes'. See Michel Foucault, 'Nietzsche, Genealogy, History', in Foucault, *Language, Counter-Memory, Practice: Selected Essays and Interviews*, ed. by Donald F. Bouchard, trans. by Donald F. Bouchard and Sherry Simon (Ithaca, NY: Cornell University Press, 1980), pp. 139–64.

7   Michel Foucault, 'What is Enlightenment?', in Foucault, *The Foucault Reader*, ed. by Paul Rabinow, trans. by Catherine Porter (New York: Pantheon Books, 1984), pp. 32–50 (p. 46). For further discussion of the possibilizing function of Foucauldian genealogy, see Daniele Lorenzini, 'On Possibilising Genealogy', *Inquiry: An Interdis-ciplinary Journal of Philosophy*, 67.7 (2020), pp. 2175–96 <https://doi.org/10.1080/0020174X.2020.1712227>.

MOFFIE AS WHOLESOME TRADITION

As well as the country's first democratic elections, the year 1994 saw the publication of a landmark collection of essays, histories, memoirs, polemics, and photographs aiming to 'break[...]' a 'path' for a democratic South African gay and lesbian studies and to bolster ongoing work by gay and lesbian activist groups to claim so-called gay rights, including through what were ultimately successful efforts to ensure constitutional protections on the basis of sexual orientation. Produced as part of these efforts, *Defiant Desire: Gay and Lesbian Lives in South Africa* was co-edited by Mark Gevisser, a journalist and activist, and Edwin Cameron, who was at the time an acting judge of the High Court and credited with designing the litigation strategy being pursued by the aforementioned gay and lesbian activists.[8] In their introduction to the collection, co-editors Gevisser and Cameron state that 'the oldest, most developed and least-explored gay South African subculture' can be found in 'Western Cape coloured communities'. 'Nowhere else in this country', they write, 'have homosexuals been so integral to a culture.'[9] In the first chapter, an overview of gay and lesbian political organizing from the 1950s to the 1990s, Gevisser reiterates this sentiment, commenting that 'the history of "moffie life" in Western Cape coloured culture is perhaps South Africa's richest and most untold'.[10] Building on his and Cameron's introductory description of 'Western Cape coloured communities' as 'by nature fluid, hybrid, and permeable', Gevisser suggests that 'gay life' may have 'flourished' and been 'tolerated' because the 'hybrid[ity]' of a 'society like that of the coloureds' prevented the establishment of any single prohibitive

---

8   The objectives of 'Edwin's laundry list', as it came to be known, were systematically tackled by the National Coalition for Gay and Lesbian Equality (NCGLE). For further information, see Graeme Reid, 'Fragments from the Archives II', in *Sex and Politics in South Africa*, ed. by Neville Hoad, Karen Martin, and Graeme Reid (Cape Town: Double Storey Books, 2005), pp. 174–77 (p. 176); and Anthony Manion, 'Guide to the Gay and Lesbian Archives of South Africa', in *Sex and Politics in South Africa*, ed. by Hoad, Martin, and Reid, pp. 228–52 (p. 244).

9   Mark Gevisser and Edwin Cameron, 'Defiant Desire: An Introduction', in *Defiant Desire: Gay and Lesbian Lives in South Africa*, ed. by Mark Gevisser and Edwin Cameron [1994] (Abingdon: Routledge, 2012), pp. 3–13 (pp. 3, 7).

10   Mark Gevisser, 'A Different Fight for Freedom', in *Defiant Desire*, ed. by Gevisser and Cameron, pp. 14–86 (p. 28).

doctrine.[11] The academic telling of the 'untold history' referenced by Gevisser is instigated in another chapter in the same edited collection, in which Dhianaraj Chetty similarly asserts that 'aspects of gay life like cross-dressing and drag seem to have taken root in the coloured working-class communities of the Western Cape', in which 'there has always been a highly visible and socially developed moffie subculture'.[12]

Across the three decades since, as this 'untold history' has been mentioned by scholars sporadically and often in passing, Gevisser and Chetty's comments have remained authoritative. Referencing Gevisser, William Leap states that 'the Cape moffies were an important part of the culture of the coloured community'.[13] Gustav Visser cites both Gevisser and Chetty to name 'the history of gay life in the Western Cape's "coloured culture"' as 'perhaps South Africa's richest', stating that 'gay life flourished and was tolerated in this community' and that 'being a moffie had some form of acceptance'.[14] Francois Rabie and Elmien Lesch reference Chetty to describe 'a coloured neighbourhood in central Cape Town [...] frequented by gay men who were cross-dressers and drag-queens', and who 'provid[ed] role-models for successive generations to adopt'.[15] Two notable examples of the circulation of this understanding are seen in important book-length studies. In her account of how narratives made it possible for South Africa to reimagine gay and lesbian people as fellow citizens, and itself as a modern neoliberal democracy, Brenna M. Munro comments that '"impurity" produces shame but at the same time, perhaps, its own kind

---

11   Gevisser and Cameron, 'Defiant Desire', p. 7; Gevisser, 'A Different Fight', pp. 201, 28.

12   Dhianaraj Chetty, 'A Drag at Madame Costello's: Cape Moffie Life and the Popular Press in the 1950s and 1960s', in *Defiant Desire*, ed. by Gevisser and Cameron, pp. 115–27 (p. 117).

13   William Leap, 'Strangers on a Train: Sexual Citizenship and the Politics of Transportation in Apartheid Cape Town', in *Queer Globalizations: Citizenship and the Afterlife of Colonialism*, ed. by Arnaldo Cruz-Malavé and Martin Manalansan IV (New York: New York University Press, 2002), pp. 219–35 (pp. 224–25) <https://doi.org/10.18574/nyu/9780814790182.003.0016>.

14   Gustav Visser, 'Gay Men, Leisure Space, and South African Cities: The Case of Cape Town', *Geoforum*, 34.1 (2003), pp. 123–37 (p. 127) <https://doi.org/10.1016/S0016-7185(02)00079-9>.

15   Francois Rabie and Elmien Lesch, '"I Am Like a Woman": Constructions of Sexuality Among Gay Men in a Low-Income South African Community', *Culture, Health & Sexuality*, 11.7 (2009), pp. 717–29 (p. 725) <https://doi.org/10.1080/13691050902890344>.

of freedom, and even a hospitality towards sexual transgressions'.[16] In his study of 'queer men' and visibility in racially segregated Cape Town, Andrew Tucker argues that the 'unique history of coloured culture' and possibly the 'hybridity of coloured life helped foster cross-dressing queer life', and 'allowed queer men to flourish' and freely 'experiment with a variety of social configurations'.[17] More recently, writing with Bryce Lease, Gevisser has suggested that 'there has always been an openness to sexual and gender diversity within the creole community, assigned the term "coloured" by the apartheid state, particularly in and around Cape Town'.[18]

Yet these claims of acceptance, if not celebration, are at odds with the marginalization suggested by the extreme scarcity of publicly available instances of self-representation. It is striking that there has been an almost complete and largely uncommented-on absence of representations of this 'gay', 'queer', or 'moffie' life by those who are said to have lived it — the people whom these scholars describe as gay men, queer men, and moffies. A comment made by Shamil Jeppie in 1990, with regards to the 1940s and 1950s, holds true for decades to come: 'in available documentary and oral evidence [...] the voices of "moffies" are never heard; they are always spoken about (derisively), represented, judged, but never allowed the privilege of discourse.'[19] Elsewhere, I have looked in detail at the rare accounts that do exist from the perspectives of people described as moffies, and I have shown that, from these accounts, a more complicated picture emerges. This picture troubles claims of acceptance and also troubles these scholars' use of the descriptor *moffie*, as well as the descriptor *men*, neither of which are used, in available records, as terms of self-identification by

---

16   Brenna M. Munro, *South Africa and the Dream of Love to Come: Queer Sexuality and the Struggle for Freedom* (Minneapolis: University of Minnesota Press, 2012), p. 113.

17   Andrew Tucker, *Queer Visibilities: Space, Identity, and Interaction in Cape Town* (Oxford: Wiley Blackwell, 2009), pp. 77–78 <https://doi.org/10.1002/9781444306187>.

18   Bryce Lease and Mark Gevisser, 'LGBTQI Rights in South Africa', *Safundi: The Journal of South African and American Studies*, 18.2 (2017), pp. 156–60 (p. 157) <https://doi.org/10.1080/17533171.2016.1270013>.

19   Shamil Jeppie, 'Popular Culture and Carnival in Cape Town', in *The Struggle for District Six: Past and Present*, ed. by Shamil Jeppie and Crain Soudien (Cape Town: Buchu Books, 1990), pp. 67–87 (p. 80).

those to whom they are applied.[20] So, then, how might we understand the persistence of claims of acceptance, in spite of evidence to the contrary?

Underpinning the academic descriptions found in *Defiant Desire* of classified-'coloured' communities' unique hospitality to the forms of gender and sexual dissidence signalled by the descriptor *moffie* was an investment in seeking evidence of historical forms of 'gay life' that were, in the terms of contemporaneous gay and lesbian activism, 'open and out'. This investment might be understood in terms of the second frame described by Neville Hoad, who identifies two ways in which the debate about 'gay and lesbian human rights' was being framed at this time, in the 1990s. Hoad writes:

> The first opposes African tradition, fairly homophobically and monolithically conceived, to Western modernity, with homosexuality coming to represent a Western decadent import and a disavowable excess of the economic modernisation that the state wishes to achieve. The second argues for human rights as part of an African nationalist tradition.[21]

These frames correlate with each of the misleading terms of the dichotomy entrenched by the ongoing debate about what is 'un-African', respectively, homosexuality or homophobia. So, in *Defiant Desire*, among the work of advocating for gay rights as part of an African nationalist tradition, Gevisser, Cameron, and Chetty attribute to queerness a wholesome and authentic relationship to a racialized condition we might call 'colouredness' — a condition that is, at least in this instance, produced discursively.

This attribution has purchase, which I want to suggest has to do with the imbrication of accompanying claims of acceptance with ten-

---

20   See, for example, Ruth Ramsden-Karelse, '"People Can't Say I'm A Man", They Can't Say I'm A Woman": Reality Expansion in the Kewpie Collection', in *The Routledge Handbook of Queer Rhetoric*, ed. by Jacqueline Rhodes and Jonathan Alexander (Abingdon: Routledge, 2022), pp. 207–14 (p. 213) <https://doi.org/10.4324/9781003144809>; and Ruth Ramsden-Karelse, 'Moving and Moved: Reading Kewpie's District Six', *GLQ: A Journal of Lesbian and Gay Studies*, 26.3 (2020), pp. 405–38 (p. 411) <https://doi.org/10.1215/10642684-8311772>.

21   Neville Hoad, 'Between the White Man's Burden and the White Man's Disease: Tracking Lesbian and Gay Human Rights in Southern Africa', *GLQ: A Journal of Lesbian and Gay Studies*, 5.4 (1999), pp. 559–84 (p. 566) <https://doi.org/10.1215/10642684-5-4-559>.

acious logics of race that continue to produce particular ideas attached to the categories 'coloured' and 'African'. This purchase is seen in the formation, since the mid-1990s, of something like what Amanda Lock Swarr has recently termed a citational chain. As seen above, in the instances that make up the links of that chain, rather than turning to first-hand accounts by those they describe as moffies, or considering the implications of the relative lack of available accounts, the 'references' made to moffies' acceptance within formerly classified-'coloured' communities 'build on each other to create truth claims' and 'repeated norms'.[22] On the other hand, however, the attribution to queerness of a wholesome and authentic relationship to 'colouredness' that underpins the citational chain is already particularly unstable. This instability is due to the fact that this racialized condition, 'colouredness', has not typically been used to signify wholesome tradition (as is the case in the scholarship cited above) but, rather, decadent modernity. This leads me to a second 'scene' through and against which *moffie* has been conceptually constituted, moving backwards in time from 1990s scholarship to mid-twentieth-century print media.

MOFFIE AS DECADENT MODERNITY

The use of understandings of race attached to the category 'coloured' to signify decadent modernity, as opposed to wholesome tradition, in relation to queerness, is seen in an issue of *Drum* magazine published seventeen years prior to *Defiant Desire*, the 1994 edited collection previously considered. This popular magazine's importance to contemporary arts, culture, and politics, and to understandings of race and gender, is well established.[23] From the early 1950s, *Drum* was foremost among the white-owned publications aimed at a Black readership to circulate contemporary constructions of African urban modernity. What warrants further attention is that, from the early 1960s, *Drum's*

22   Amanda Lock Swarr, *Envisioning African Intersex: Challenging Colonial and Racist Legacies in South African Medicine* (Durham, NC: Duke University Press, 2023), p. 3 <https://doi.org/10.1515/9781478093763>.

23   See, for example, R. Neville Choonoo, 'The Sophiatown Generation: Black Literary Journalism during the 1950s', in *South Africa's Alternative Press: Voices of Protest and Resistance, 1880s–1960s*, ed. by Les Switzer (Cambridge: Cambridge University Press, 1997), pp. 252–65.

celebration of urbanity was increasingly tempered by sensationalist warnings of that urbanity's degradation by so-called homosexuality. Relatedly, from the mid-1950s until the late 1980s, *Drum* and its sister publication, the increasingly tabloid-style *Golden City Post* newspaper, represented Cape Town's 'moffies' or 'moffees' to a readership across sub-Saharan Africa and beyond.[24] Together, these articles convey a fear that degeneracy and perversity were attendant on modernity as well as an understanding of this potential danger as a Western import.

The general tone of the coverage is well expressed by a speculative genealogy offered by *Drum* itself, albeit a genealogy of the forms of gender and sexual deviance signalled by the word *moffie* as opposed to a genealogy of the word itself, and a tongue-in-cheek one at that. In July 1977, *Drum* published 'The Moffie Manuscripts': 'Cape Town's moffies trace their ancestry — right back to the days of Van Riebeeck.'[25] 'The Moffie Manuscripts' bursts with such quips as 'having seen illustrations of Van Riebeeck, someone had to put curlers in his flowing locks'. Framed by the illustrated edges of a roll of parchment and the invented authorship of 'Carmen', the faux-academic report conclusively establishes that it was 'the perfumed society of the genteel whites' that 'establish[ed] the Hottie moffie fraternity in the Cape': 'awestricken Hottentots discarded their loincloths' and 'took to velvet knickers and lace-collared shirts[,] thus establish[ing] the moffie dress code for posterity'.

'The Moffie Manuscripts' was in fact written by celebrated journalist Jackie Heyns, whose prolific reporting for *Drum* and the *Golden City Post* sometimes featured his actual contemporaries, whom the publication (like many of the scholars cited above) called 'moffies' and 'gay men', and who called themselves gays and girls. And Heyns's 'report' explicitly references the gays and girls' practice of adopting the names of women celebrities, with which Heyns's other articles evidence his familiarity.[26] 'The queer's quirk for adopting famous names was in-

---

24 It is worth noting that Chetty's aforementioned chapter in *Defiant Desire* considers some of this coverage, though he concludes that 'the vagaries of the popular press — at least for a time — allowed them [those described as 'moffies'] the freedom to dream' (Chetty, 'A Drag at Madame Costello's', p. 127).

25 Jackie Heyns, 'The Moffie Manuscripts', *Drum*, July 1977.

26 See Ramsden-Karelse, 'Moving and Moved', p. 414.

stilled by the arrival of Lord Charles Henry Somerset as Governor of the Cape', Carmen/Heyns explains; 'from that day they discarded the names given at birth and glorified their personality with names of their heroes and heroines.' Thus, the report continues, 'the die was set and the cult complete. Moffiedom was placed in the annals of history and entrenched as a definable group in the Cape society.' Thus, in this instance, the types of gender and sexual deviance signalled by the word *moffie* are cast as a decadent Western import, and 'Cape moffiedom' construed as a racialized form of cultural hybridity.

PROCESSES OF DESCENT AND EMERGENCE

Considering together the two scenes thus sketched, in which *moffie* is differentially conceptually constituted, it becomes apparent that there are traceable processes of descent as well as emergence. In both scenes, the word *moffie* is used in the discursive construction of formerly classified-'coloured' communities as inherently hospitable to sexual and gender transgression. I want to suggest that this discursive construction hinges on a particular conception of 'colouredness' as a kind of always-and-already sexualized deviance that necessarily allows for other forms of sexual deviance. This conception of 'colouredness' has to do with the sexualization inherent in racialization generally and in the conceptualization and signification of race mixedness in particular. As one might imagine, the understanding of colouredness as always-already sexualized gained purchase in the Cape Colony and flourished during apartheid. What I am interested in highlighting is that it emerged in a new, celebratory form in mid-1990s scholarship, during South Africa's 'transition' from legal apartheid to democracy. As noted, during this period, gay and lesbian activists, archivists, and scholars sought historic forms of open and out queerness as models for inclusive futures. Looking back, we might say that, in doing so, they took a previously pejorative narrative about 'miscegenation' and recast it in the positive terms of the new, post-1994 'rainbow nation'.

In other words, the discourse emergent in mid-1990s scholarship engages the same racialized tropes of 'colouredness' seen in the *Drum* magazine article, even as it seeks to recast them in the celebratory, non-racial terms of democratic rainbowism. For instance, Gevisser's understanding of 'coloured communities' as inherently open — 'by nature fluid, hybrid, and permeable' — relies on a conception of 'coloured-ness' in terms of race mixedness, as a kind of deviance that necessarily allows for other forms of deviance.[27] Certainly, vastly heterogenous experiences, cultures, and identities intersect with the category 'coloured'.[28] Yet this does not fully explain the understanding of 'coloured' communities as 'by nature' (and in contrast to other South African communities) 'fluid, hybrid, and permeable'.

For one thing, very similar forms of diversity — linguistic, religious, cultural, ethnic — could be said to exist within South Africa's white communities, which include, for example, English and Afrikaans speakers; Calvinists, Catholics, and Jews; Italians, Huguenots, and those of Dutch, Portuguese, and Russian descent. The emphasis on the particular hybridity of 'colouredness' arguably makes more sense only if we adopt an essentialist understanding of race as tied to culture. Although Gevisser ostensibly discusses formerly classified-'coloured' communities in terms of culture, his discussion does seem to be under-written by a racial essentialism, coded by descriptors such as *by nature*. Historically, this ties in with common-sense understandings of colouredness.

In our perceived hybridity as a 'subject race' — colonized and defined as non-Indigenous — those of us who were classified 'coloured' under apartheid were, unlike other Black communities, defined in terms of race as opposed to ethnicity.[29] Apartheid logic rendered those it classified 'coloured' 'completely grounded', as Grant Farred puts it, and yet without a symbolic claim to pre-colonial existence in South Africa — though such claims have since been made.[30] At the same time,

---

27   Gevisser, 'A Different Fight', p. 7.
28   See *Coloured by History, Shaped by Place: New Perspectives on Coloured Identities in Cape Town*, ed. by Zimitri Erasmus (Cape Town and Maroelana, SA: Kwela Books and South African History Online, 2001); Grant Farred, *Midfielder's Moment: Coloured Literature and Culture in Contemporary South Africa* [2000] (Abingdon: Routledge, 2018) <https://doi.org/10.4324/9780429040351>; Mohamed Adhikari, *Not White Enough, Not Black Enough: Racial Identity in the South African Coloured Community* (Athens: Ohio University Press, 2005); and Tessa Dooms and Lynsey Ebony Chutel, *Coloured: How Classification Became Culture* (Johannesburg and Cape Town: Jonathan Ball, 2023).
29   Mamdani, *When Victims Become Killers*, pp. 27–28.
30   Farred, *Midfielder's Moment*, p. 7. On the Khoisan revivalist movement, see Adhikari, *Not White Enough, Not Black Enough*, p. 183. Zoë Wicomb has criticized ethno-

however, the recasting of the racially essentialist narrative endogenous to the Cape Colony by researchers in the 1990s might be said to hinge on the emergent non-racial ideology of rainbow nationalism: 'colouredness' was still constituted as inherently mixed, but therefore as an inherently non-racial, authentically South African race.

Regardless, one effect of the 1990s recasting of the narrative of race mixedness has been the reinscription of the categorical sexualization of the category 'coloured'. The spectre of so-called interracial sex between 'a European male' and 'a native female' continues to haunt discussions of this category that was first legally defined one year after the British colonial government first criminalized sexual intercourse between white and 'native' people — a category that was famously defined, for posterity, in terms of a lack, as neither black nor white.[31] So a popular joke goes: 'God made the black man [...] the Indian, the Chinese and the Jew — but Jan van Riebeeck, he made the Coloured Man.' (Discussing this joke at length, Mohamed Adhikari explains that it 'hinges on the audience's awareness of the status of Jan van Riebeeck, the commander of the first Dutch settlement established at the Cape in 1652, as the "founding father" of white South Africa.'[32])

This sentiment continues to be circulated in scholarship, cloaked in the language of academia. 'On a purely etymological level', Tucker explains in *Queer Visibilities*, his book quoted above, 'coloureds are the product of interracial sex.'[33] Such understandings have, of course, been persuasively critiqued by many other scholars, with the South

---

nationalist claims to authenticity as denying history and preventing 'multiple belongings' from being seen as 'an alternative way of viewing culture', while Erasmus has argued that such claims are not always based in notions of 'authenticity and "purity"', but can represent an acknowledgement of 'the fragments which make up the history of being coloured' and 'the violence of the colonial encounter'. See Zoë Wicomb, 'Shame and Identity: The Case of the Coloured in South Africa', in *Writing South Africa*, ed. by Derek Attridge and Rosemary Jolly (Cambridge: Cambridge University Press, 1998), pp. 91–107 (p. 105) <https://doi.org/10.1017/CBO9780511586286.009>; and Zimitri Erasmus, 'Introduction: Re-imagining Coloured Identities in Post-Apartheid South Africa', in *Coloured by History, Shaped by Place*, ed. by Erasmus, pp. 13–28 (p. 28).

31   The relevant laws are Pensions Act 22 of 1928 and Immorality Act 5 of 1927.

32   Mohamed Adhikari, '"God Made the White Man, God Made the Black Man...": Popular Racial Stereotyping of Coloured People in Apartheid South Africa', *South African Historical Journal*, 55.1 (2006), pp. 142–64 (p. 147).

33   Tucker, *Queer Visibilities*, p. 71.

African feminist Zimitri Erasmus, for example, pointing to their roots in pseudo-scientific assumptions that there exist unmixed or pure race groups.[34] In descriptions such as Tucker's, we can track a recognizable sexualized and racialized narrative about 'colouredness', even as we see that narrative being recast in celebratory terms. In this way, while there emerges a newly celebratory narrative, there is also a traceable process of descent, though this process does not consist of an easily recognizable evolution or continuity. On the contrary, it illustrates Foucault's reminder that 'the search for descent is not the erecting of foundations': that such a search 'disturbs what was previously considered immobile; it fragments what was thought unified; it shows the heterogeneity of what was imagined consistent with itself'.[35]

A second, related process of descent is signalled by the availability in both scenes of *moffie*, as a category of identification, for the projection of socio-political anxieties. In *Drum* and the *Golden City Post*, from the 1950s to the 1980s, 'Cape Moffees' were constituted as a distinct social class onto which political anxieties were projected, in a process indicative of contemporary shifts in the perception of homosexuality evident in medical and legal discourse.[36] A 'moffie drag' was the subject of an exposé in the first edition of the *Golden City Post*, published 12 August 1956, and 'moffies' were thereafter regularly represented by the *Post* and *Drum* as inhabitants of the abject and liminal social and temporal sphere allegorized as a 'twilight world'. Interspersed among the usual scandalized or pitying coverage were reports of proposed 'moffie republics' and 'moffie elections'. Like the term *moffie*, the political descriptors *republics* and *elections* were chosen by the newspaper and magazine staff themselves. The 'moffie elections' referred to were, in actuality, competitions rather like the many drag pageants that continue to take place across the greater Cape Town area — and many of the competitions reported by *Drum* and the *Golden City Post* were sponsored by the publications themselves. The political rhetoric found

---

34   See Erasmus, 'Introduction,' pp. 17–23.

35   Foucault, 'Nietzsche, Genealogy, History', p. 147.

36   These shifts are traced in medical and legal discourse in B Camminga, *Transgender Refugees and the Imagined South Africa: Bodies Over Borders and Borders Over Bodies* (Cham, CH: Palgrave Macmillan, 2019), pp. 44–59 <https://doi.org/10.1007/978-3-319-92669-8>.

in many of the articles about 'moffies' thus seems to have been used to enact a thinly veiled critique of actual developments — including referendums and elections — taking place within a national political regime in which progressive commentary was increasingly harshly sanctioned.

I understand this as suggestive of a process of descent because a comparable kind of projection seems to happen in the mid-1990s, when the previously abject category 'moffie' was invested with the anxious hopes of a minority gay and lesbian group angling for political enfranchisement and protections. This investment resulted in the perpetuation of a reductive narrative about acceptance of gender and sexual transgression within classified-'coloured' communities that was seemingly not primarily concerned with mapping onto the actual lived experience of those being described as 'moffies' by the scholars who perpetuated it. Thus, in both scenes, there is an availability of the category 'moffie' for the projection of political anxieties — an availability that seems to have to do with the category being one that has customarily been applied as opposed to adopted.

CONCLUSION

Proposing an alternate genealogy of *moffie*, which I have just begun to sketch here, I aim to participate in the crucial work that Amia Srinivasan has described as 'diagnosing our representations', as a step towards 'mak[ing] our representations, and thus our world, anew'.[37] Though to very distinct ends, this work of remaking our representations and our world might also be said to have been engaged in by the scholars who, in search of historical precedent, described coloured communities' unique acceptance of moffies, as well as by the various political and religious leaders making well-publicized remarks about the un-Africanness of homosexuality, to whom the scholars were often in part responding.[38] In the wake of these statements and in light of the violence whose direction at queer bodies they sanction, any defences

---

37   Amia Srinivasan, 'Genealogy, Epistemology and Worldmaking', *Proceedings of the Aristotelian Society*, 119.2 (2019), pp. 127–56 (p. 145) <https://doi.org/10.1093/arisoc/aoz009>.

38   See, for example, Thabo Msibi, 'The Lies We Have Been Told: On (Homo) Sexuality in Africa', *Africa Today*, 58.1 (2011), pp. 55–77 <https://doi.org/10.2979/africatoday.58.1.55>.

of homosexuality's Africanness that point to homophobia as the true Western import may well be read or heard as not only understandable but urgent. Yet we must consider what risks are involved in reproducing the terms of the debate in which those responses engage.

Since *moffie* speaks to the racialization of perceived degenerate femininity, a critical genealogy promises to enrich understandings of shifts in (post)colonial perceptions of sex, gender, and sexuality, and their imbrication with race. Given *moffie*'s likely descent from the Afrikaans *hermafrodiet* (hermaphrodite), and various reimaginings since, such a genealogy would offer one means of interrogating the complex relationship between Southern African articulations of sexuality and the medicalized vocabularies of Global North sexology, eugenics' fellow pseudo-scientific twin. (Indeed, Swarr's aforementioned work on the centuries-long positioning of '"hermaphroditism" and intersex' as 'always already connected to blackness' speaks to such a genealogy's potential reach and import.[39]) Interrogating that complex relationship while closely considering the various ways in which *moffie* has been reimagined and reinhabited across time and place would contribute to a growing, transnational body of scholarship attuned to minoritized knowledges that challenge understandings of embodiment and desire attendant on those vocabularies. In addition to print media's mid-twentieth-century constitution of 'Cape Moffees' as a distinct social class onto which political anxieties were projected, and in addition to *moffie*'s 1990s use to symbolize both nostalgia and nonracialism in a 'transitional' political conjuncture, the genealogy merely alluded to in this chapter will account for *moffie*'s nineteenth-century use as a category of abnormality for livestock and formerly enslaved people; the constitution of the moffie as backward or a 'drag' on the new, democratic South Africa; and *moffie*'s 2000s appearance in writing by white gay men participating in the term's reappropriation.

Though merely sketched, the genealogy embarked upon here does reveal processes of descent and emergence that importantly underscore the misleading nature of the binary model of understanding homosexuality and homophobia in relation to 'un-Africanness' that has occupied much scholarship on gender and sexual diversity in South

---

39   Swarr, *Envisioning African Intersex*, p. 3.

Africa since the mid-1990s. These processes suggest the limits of an approach to research that adheres to the dichotomy that preoccupation has entrenched, by recasting in celebratory terms a narrative that is, inherently, racialized — an approach that is perhaps taken by some of the South African gay and lesbian scholarship discussed. The project to produce a critical genealogy of *moffie*, instigated in this chapter, therefore offers a fresh response to calls that have since been made, in the growing field of queer African studies, to reject the misleading terms of this long-running debate about what is 'un-African', terms which limit the possible answers to 'homosexuality' or 'homophobia'. The instability of this dichotomy is revealed, I have suggested, by *moffie*'s various uses in evidencing the 'un-Africanness' of both. At a time of increased divide with regards to this issue across the African continent, when successful campaigns for decriminalization in certain countries continue to coincide with pushes for further criminalization in others, calls to reject these misleading terms are urgent, and increasingly so.

Following Michel Foucault's genealogical method, Ruth Ramsden-Karelse perceptively eludes the temptation to search for the origins of the concept of 'moffie' in her essay. To search for origins, Foucault says, is to try to capture the exact essence of things, to look for foundations, to identify the supposedly hidden and unique trait of a phenomenon, value, or concept.[40] The search for origins stands in open opposition to the task of the critical genealogist. Friedrich Nietzsche had earlier characterized this distinction as the contrast between 'traditional history' and 'wirkliche Historie' (or 'effective history' for Foucault).[41] While the former goes back in time to restore the unbroken continuity of events, and assumes that, across time, 'words had kept their meaning, that desires still pointed in a single direction, and that ideas retained their logic', the latter is willing 'to discover, under the unique aspect of a trait or a concept, the myriad events through which they were formed'.[42]

To be sure, Ramsden-Karelse starts her chapter by introducing the etymological roots of the term *moffie*, which the authoritative voice of the OED situates in early twentieth-century nautical slang. However, this should not be read as an attempt to 'disclose an original identity' of the concept.[43] It motivates, instead, the development of an alternate genealogy that displays the plural, accidental, sometimes contradictory past of the attributions — and rather infrequent self-ascriptions — of the category of 'moffie' in their proper dispersion.[44]

Two scenes are selected and diagnosed here, which remarkably, but perhaps not surprisingly, are themselves attempts to historicize, to search for the roots of 'moffiedom', although in the sense rejected by Foucault. One scene comprises a pejorative narrative in mid-twentieth-

---

40   Foucault, 'Nietzsche, Genealogy, History', p. 142.

41   Ibid., p. 154.

42   Ibid., pp. 139, 146. For a more specific reflection on how philosophical discourse consists in a diagnosis of the present, starting from the integral archive of a culture, as opposed to a search for origins in the past, see Michel Foucault, *Le Discours Philosophique*, ed. by Daniele Lorenzini and Orazio Irrera (Paris: Éditions du Seuil, 2023). I thank Natascia Tosel for the reference and for her insight on this point.

43   Foucault, 'Nietzsche, Genealogy, History', p. 142.

44   Ibid., p. 146.

century South African print media, where communities classified as
'coloured' are portrayed as naturally open to sexual transgression. The
other scene can be described, following Bernard Williams, as a vindica-
tory or legitimizing search for origins.[45] Here 'moffie life' is pictured as
innately fluid, flourishing in the way it regards the relationship between
colouredness and queerness. It is then, in the context of 1990s human
rights discourse, a call to bring back and to celebrate a forgotten form
of tolerance.

Despite the disparities between the two scenes — in form, tone,
and value implications — what seems inescapable is that they share
an ingrained conception of colouredness as sexualized and racialized.
I therefore read Ramsden-Karelse's diagnosis of these scenes as reflecting what Amia Srinivasan calls 'genealogical anxiety': a fear, which
many of us share, of the unsettling effects that allowing episodes from
the past to show us the apparently inevitable entrenchment of certain values, despite their historical contingency, might have on our
present assessments and actions.[46] Here, the proposal to counteract
those unsettling effects is to take the pragmatist route. This is a route
that actively wants to take us from genealogical diagnosis to attempts
at worldmaking by changing our representational practices.[47] Appeals
to our agential power prompt us to reject pernicious categories, such as
the dichotomy built around what is 'un-African' (whether homosexuality or homophobia) in the contemporary academic debate, precisely
because it is impregnated by a sexualized and racialized understanding
of colouredness.

Yet, it would be worth considering a different route motivated by
the genealogical critique. For Srinivasan, it is not only the pragmatists who have the tools for transforming the world. It is often those
attempts that strike a fine balance between showing the world as we
know it is, and at the same time picturing it in a new light, as it has never
been so clearly pictured before, that are the most successful practices
of worldmaking.[48] In this case, merely exposing how, in different past

---

45   Bernard Williams, *Truth and Truthfulness: An Essay in Genealogy* (Princeton, NJ:
     Princeton University Press, 2002), p. 36.
46   Srinivasan, 'Genealogy, Epistemology and Worldmaking', p. 128.
47   Ibid., p. 145.
48   Ibid., p. 150.

and present episodes, there is a pervasive, seemingly inescapable identification of colouredness with queerness and race can be revealing on its own, as it shows, perhaps in a quiet but very powerful way, how the world we experience is constituted. And if the world we experience is one in which we don't seem to be able to evade damaging identifications, some creative spaces to imagine how we want the world to be might yet be opened.

References

Abad, Gémino, 'Our Scene so Fair: An Overview of Filipino English Poetry, 1905–2006', in Abad, *Our Scene so Fair: Filipino Poetry in English, 1905 to 1955* (Quezon City: University of the Philippines Press, 2008), pp. 1–20

Abći, Farah, *Never Arrive* (Malta: self-published, 2015)

Adamatzky, Andrew, *Physarum Machines: Computers from Slime Mould* (Singapore: World Scientific, 2010) <https://doi.org/10.1142/7968>

—— 'The World's Colonisation and Trade Routes Formation as Imitated by Slime Mould', *International Journal of Bifurcation and Chaos*, 22.8 (2012) <https://doi.org/10.1142/S0218127412300285>

—— ed., *Advances in Physarum Machines: Sensing and Computing with Slime Mould* (Cham, CH: Springer, 2016)

—— ed., *Bioevaluation of World Transport Networks* (Singapore: World Scientific, 2012) <https://doi.org/10.1142/8482>

Adamatzky, Andrew, and Genaro J. Martinez, 'Bio-Imitation of Mexican Migration Routes to the USA with Slime Mould on 3D Terrains', *Journal of Bionic Engineering*, 10 (2013), pp. 242–50 <https://doi.org/10.1016/S1672-6529(13)60220-6>

Adamatzky, Andrew, and Jeff Jones, 'Road Planning with Slime Mould: If *Physarum* Built Motorways It Would Route M6/M74 through Newcastle', *International Journal of Bifurcation and Chaos*, 20.10 (2010), pp. 3065–84 <https://doi.org/10.1142/S0218127410027568>

Adamatzky, Andrew, and others, 'On Creativity of Slime Mould', *International Journal of General Systems*, 42.5 (2013), pp. 441–57 <https://doi.org/10.1080/03081079.2013.776206>

—— 'Slime Mould Analogue Models of Space Exploration and Planet Colonisation', *Journal of the British Interplanetary Society*, 67 (2014), pp. 290–304

Adhikari, Mohamed, '"God Made the White Man, God Made the Black Man…": Popular Racial Stereotyping of Coloured People in Apartheid South Africa', *South African Historical Journal*, 55.1 (2006), pp. 142–64

—— *Not White Enough, Not Black Enough: Racial Identity in the South African Coloured Community* (Athens: Ohio University Press, 2005)

Afflerbach, Ian, 'On the Literary History of Selling Out: Craft, Identity, and Commercial Recognition', *PMLA*, 137.2 (2022), pp. 230–45 (p. 237) <https://doi.org/10.1632/S0030812922000098>

Aguilar, Maria Gloria, 'Appropriation and Resistance in Philippine Marian Devotion' (unpublished doctoral thesis, University of North London,

2001) <https://repository.londonmet.ac.uk/7291> [accessed 24 July 2024]

Aizura, Aren Z., 'The Persistence of Transgender Travel Narratives', in *Transgender Migrations: The Bodies, Borders, and Politics of Transition*, ed. by Trystan T. Cotten (New York: Routledge, 2012), pp. 139–56 <https://doi.org/10.4324/9780203808269>

Alcoba, Natalie, 'This Language Was Long Believed Extinct. Then One Man Spoke Up', *The New York Times*, 13 January 2024 <https://www.nytimes.com/2024/01/13/world/americas/indigenous-language-chana-blas-jaime.html> [accessed 19 January 2024]

Alejo, Anna, Robert Jenkins, and Haogen Yao, 'Learning Losses during the COVID-19 Pandemic: Understanding and Addressing Increased Learning Disparities', *Future in Educational Research*, 2.1 (2023) <https://doi.org/10.1002/fer3.21>

Aleksandrowicz, Marta, 'To Enter the Core of Death', in *Philosophy with Clarice Lispector*, ed. by Fernanda Negrete, special issue of *Angelaki*, 28.2 (2023), pp. 90–101 <https://doi.org/10.1080/0969725X.2023.2192068>

Almario, Virgilio S., 'Palabas at Paloob: Tambalang Mukha ng Pagtula', *Philippine Humanities Review*, 16.1 (2014), pp. 69–91 <https://journals.upd.edu.ph/index.php/phr/article/view/4971> [accessed 5 October 2023]

Althusser, Louis, 'Ideological State Apparatuses', in Althusser, *Lenin and Philosophy and Other Essays*, trans. by Ben Brewter (New York: Monthly Review Press, 1972)

Alvarez de Toledo, Sandra, 'Fernand Deligny: Repères cinèbiographiques', in Alvarez de Toledo, *Le Cinéma de Fernand Deligny* (Paris: Editions Montparnasse et les auteurs, 2007), pp. 3–8

Ambrosio, Chiara, and Julia Sánchez-Dorado, eds, *Abstraction in Science and Art: Philosophical Perspectives* (London: Routledge, 2024) <https://doi.org/10.4324/9781003380955>

Ames, Morgan, 'One Laptop per Child Can't Bridge the Digital Divide', *MIT Technology Review*, 27 October 2021 <https://www.technologyreview.com/2021/10/27/1037173/laptop-per-child-digital-divide/> [accessed 4 September 2024]

Amnesty International, 'Philippines: Deadly Practice of "Red-tagging" Continues Under Marcos Administration', 22 March 2023 <https://www.amnesty.org/en/documents/asa35/6582/2023/en/> [accessed 5 October 2023]

Andersen, Ross, 'How First Contact with Whale Civilization Could Unfold: If We Can Learn to Speak Their Language, What Should We Say?', *The Atlantic*, 24 February 2024 <https://www.theatlantic.com/science/archive/2024/02/talking-whales-project-ceti/677549/> [accessed 14 June 2024]

Anguiano, Dani, and Lois Beckett, 'How Hollywood Writers Triumphed over AI – and Why It Matters', *The Guardian*, 1 October 2023 <https://www.theguardian.com/culture/2023/oct/01/hollywood-writers-strike-artificial-intelligence> [accessed 1 July 2024]

Ankeny, Rachel A., and Sabina Leonelli, *Model Organisms* (Cambridge: Cambridge University Press, 2021) <https://doi.org/10.1017/9781108593014>

Anzaldúa, Gloria, *Borderlands / La Frontera: The New Mestiza*, 4th edn (San Francisco: Aunt Lute Books, 2012)

Apollon, Willy, 'The Limit: A Fundamental Question for the Subject in the Human Experience', in *Borderlines in Psychoanalysis*, ed. by Jeffrey Librett, special issue of *Konturen*, 3 (2010), pp. 103–18 <https://doi.org/10.5399/uo/konturen.3.1.1391>

—— 'Positions — 1: Writing and the Voice', trans. by Heidi Arsenault and Cynthia Mitchell, in *Beauty*, ed. by Marta Aleksandrowicz and Fernanda Negrete, special issue of Penumbr(*a*), 2 (2022), pp. 71–95 <https://www.penumbrajournal.org/no-2-beauty> [accessed 24 July 2024]

—— 'The Subject of the Quest', trans. by Daniel Wilson, in *Beauty*, ed. by Marta Aleksandrowicz and Fernanda Negrete, special issue of Penumbr(*a*), 2 (2022), pp. 1–14 <https://www.penumbrajournal.org/no-2-beauty> [accessed 22 July 2024]

Aristotle, *History of Animals*, 3 vols (Cambridge, MA: Harvard University Press, 1965–91), I, trans. by A. L. Peck (1965) <https://doi.org/10.4159/DLCL.aristotle-history_animals.1965>

artlaboratory-berlin.org, 'NONHUMAN AGENTS: Swarm | Cell | City', n.d. <https://artlaboratory-berlin.org/events/swarm-cell-city/> [accessed 26 July 2024]

Ashcroft, Bill, 'The Transformation of English in Postcolonial Literatures', *Language and Semiotic Studies*, 1.4 (2015), pp. 80–94 <https://doi.org/10.1515/lass-2015-010405>

Asimov, Isaac, 'The Fun They Had', in Asimov, *Earth Is Room Enough* (New York: Doubleday, 1957)

Ausserrer, Caroline, 'Portrait of Julius Kaggwa, Intersex Activist from Uganda', blog.lsvd.de, 24 February 2022 <https://blog.lsvd.de/portrait-of-julius-kaggwa-intersex-activist-from-uganda> [accessed 9 April 2024]

Austin, John L., *How to Do Things with Words* [1962] (Oxford: Oxford University Press, 1976) <https://doi.org/10.1093/acprof:oso/9780198245537.001.0001>

—— 'Performative Utterances', in Austin, *Philosophical Papers*, ed. by J. O. Urmson and G. J. Warnock (Oxford: Clarendon Press, 1961), pp. 233–52 <https://doi.org/10.1093/019283021X.003.0010>

Bach, Jhana, 'Assessing Transgender Asylum Claims', *Forced Migration Review*, 42 (2013), pp. 34–36

Baerg, Jason, 'Indigenous Abstraction: A Vehicle for Visioning', in *The Routledge Companion to Indigenous Art Histories in the United States and*

Canada, ed. by Heather Igloliorte and Carla Taunton (New York: Routledge, 2022) <https://doi.org/10.4324/9781003014256>

Bajohr, Hannes, 'Artificial and Post-Artificial Texts: On Machine Learning and the Reading Expectations Towards Literary and Non-Literary Writing', *Basel Media Culture and Cultural Techniques Working Papers*, 7 (2023) <https://doi.org/10.3929/ethz-b-000635926>

Bakhtin, Mikhail, 'Discourse in the Novel', in Bakhtin, *The Dialogic Imagination: Four Essays*, ed. by Michael Holquist, trans. by Caryl Emerson and Michael Holquist (Austin, TX: University of Texas Press, 1981), pp. 259–422

Balaguera, Martha, 'Trans-Migrations: Agency and Confinement at the Limits of Sovereignty', *Signs*, 43.4 (2018), pp. 641–64 <https://doi.org/10.1086/695302>

Baldacci, Cristina, Clio Nicastro, and Arianna Sforzini, eds, *Over and Over and Over Again: Reenactment Strategies in Contemporary Arts and Theory*, Cultural Inquiry, 21 (Berlin: ICI Berlin Press, 2022) <https://doi.org/10.37050/ci-21>

Barnett, Heather, 'Many-Headed: Co-Creating with the Collective', in *Slime Mould in Arts and Architecture*, ed. by Andrew Adamatzky (Gistrup, DK: River Publishers, 2019), pp. 13–37 <https://doi.org/10.1201/9781003339540-3>

Baterina, Margot, 'The "Dark Side" of Agoo', *Philippine Daily Inquirer*, 2 September 1993, pp. 1,8

Bender, Emily M., and others, 'On the Dangers of Stochastic Parrots: Can Language Models Be Too Big?', FAccT '21: Proceedings of the 2021 ACM Conference on Fairness, Accountability, and Transparency (New York: Association for Computing Machinery, 2021) <https://doi.org/10.1145/3442188.3445922>

Benjamin, Walter, *The Arcades Project*, trans. by Howard Eiland and Kevin McLaughlin (Cambridge, MA: Belknap Press, 1999)

—— 'The Author as Producer', trans. by Edmund Jephcott, in Benjamin, *Selected Writings*, ed. by Michael Jennings and others, 4 vols (Cambridge, MA: Harvard University Press, 2004–06), II.2: *1931–1934*, ed. by Michael W. Jennings, Howard Eiland, and Gary Smith (2005), pp. 768–82

Bennett, Jane, *Vibrant Matter: A Political Ecology of Things* (Durham, NC: Duke University Press, 2010) <https://doi.org/10.1215/9780822391623>

Benveniste, Émile, *Le Vocabulaire des institutions indo-européennes* (Paris: Éditions de Minuit, 1969)

Berg, Laurie, and Jenni Millbank, 'Constructing the Personal Narratives of Lesbian, Gay and Bisexual Asylum Claimants', *Journal of Refugee Studies*, 22.2 (2009), pp. 195–223 <https://doi.org/10.1093/jrs/fep010>

Bergthaller, Hannes, 'Cli-Fi and Petrofiction: Questioning Genre in the Anthropocene', *Amerikastudien/American Studies*, 62.1 (2017), pp.

120–25 <https://amst.winter-verlag.de/article/AMST/2017/1/10>
[accessed 4 August 2024]

Berlatsky, Noah, 'Why Sci-Fi Keeps Imagining the Subjugation of White
People', *The Atlantic*, 25 April 2014 <https://www.theatlantic.com/
entertainment/archive/2014/04/why-sci-fi-keeps-imagining-the-
enslavement-of-white-people/361173/> [accessed 14 April 2024]

Bersani, Leo, 'Gay Betrayals', in Bersani, *Is the Rectum a Grave? And Other
Essays* (Chicago: University of Chicago Press, 2009), pp. 36–44 <https:
//doi.org/10.7208/chicago/9780226043449.001.0001>

—— 'Preface', in Bersani, *Is the Rectum a Grave? And Other Essays* (Chicago:
University of Chicago Press, 2009), p. ix–x <https://doi.org/10.7208/
chicago/9780226043449.001.0001>

Bersani, Leo, Tim Dean, Hal Foster, and Kaja Silverman, 'A Conversation', in
Bersani, *Is the Rectum a Grave? And Other Essays* (Chicago: University of
Chicago Press, 2009), pp. 171–86 <https://doi.org/10.7208/chicago/
9780226043449.001.0001>

Bettcher, Talia Mae, 'Evil Deceivers and Make-Believers: On Transphobic
Violence and the Politics of Illusion', *Hypatia*, 22.3 (2007), pp. 43–65
<https://doi.org/10.1111/j.1527-2001.2007.tb01090.x>

—— 'Trapped in the Wrong Theory: Rethinking Trans Oppression and Resistance', *Signs*, 39.2 (2014), pp. 383–406 <https://doi.org/10.1086/
673088>

Bhabha, Jacqueline, 'Internationalist Gatekeepers?: The Tension between
Asylum Advocacy and Human Rights', *Harvard Human Rights Journal*, 15 (2002), pp. 155–81 <https://journals.law.harvard.edu/hrj/
wp-content/uploads/sites/83/2020/06/15HHRJ155-Bhabha.pdf>
[accessed 22 July 2024]

'Bicho', in *Linguee* (Cologne: DeepL SE, n.d.) <https://www.linguee.com/
english-portuguese/search?source=portuguese&query=bicho> [ac-
cessed 22 July 2024]

Birla, Ritu, 'Performativity between Logos and Nomos: Law, Temporality
and the Non-Economic Analysis of Power', *Columbia Journal of Gender
and Law*, 21.2 (2011) <https://doi.org/10.7916/cjgl.v21i2.2636>

Bishop, Elise, *Twee Lewens* (Hermanus, SA: Hemel & See, 2022)

Bivens, Hunter, 'Revisiting German Proletarian-Revolutionary Literature', in
Working-Class Literature(s): Historical and International Perspectives, ed.
by John Lennon and Magnus Nilsson, 2 vols (Stockholm: Stockholm
University Press, 2017–20), II, pp. 83–113 <https://doi.org/10.16993/
bbf>

Black, Fischer, 'Noise', *The Journal of Finance*, 41.3 (1986), pp. 529–43 <https:
//doi.org/10.1111/j.1540-6261.1986.tb04513.x>

Black, Fischer, and Myron Scholes, 'The Pricing of Options and Corporate
Liabilities', *The Journal of Political Economy*, 81.3 (1973), pp. 637–54
<https://doi.org/10.1086/260062>

Blackmore, Susan, *The Meme Machine* (Oxford: Oxford University Press, 1999)

Blichner, Lars C., and Anders Molander, 'Mapping Juridification', *European Law Journal*, 14.1 (2008), pp. 36–54 <https://doi.org/10.1111/j.1468-0386.2007.00405.x>

Boltzmann, Ludwig, 'Model', in *Theoretical Physics and Philosophical Problems*, ed. by Brian McGuinnes (Dordrecht: D. Reidel, 1974), pp. 213–20 <https://doi.org/10.1007/978-94-010-2091-6_16>

Borges, Jorge Luis, 'Of Exactitude in Science', in Borges, *A Universal History of Infamy*, trans. by Norman Thomas di Giovanni (New York: Dutton, 1972), p. 139

Bossuyt, Marc, 'Bossuyt waarschuwt voor "regering door rechters"', *Het Belang van Limburg*, 17 February 2011 <https://www.hbvl.be/cnt/aid1019380> [accessed 10 January 2024]

Bourdieu, Pierre, 'The Force of Law: Toward a Sociology of the Juridical Field', trans. by Richard Terdiman, *The Hastings Law Journal*, 38 (1987), pp. 805–53 <https://repository.uclawsf.edu/hastings_law_journal/vol38/iss5/3> [accessed 6 August 2024]

—— *Language and Symbolic Power* [1982], trans. by Gino Raymond and Matthew Adamson (Cambridge: Polity Press, 1991)

Bourdieu, Pierre, and Loïc Wacquant, *An Invitation to Reflexive Sociology* (Chicago: University of Chicago Press, 1992)

Boussard, Aurèle, and others, 'Adaptive Behaviour and Learning in Slime Moulds: The Role of Oscillations', *Philosophical Transactions of the Royal Society B*, 376 (2021) <https://doi.org/10.1098/rstb.2019.0757>

Bowen, Frank C., *Sea Slang: A Dictionary of the Old-Timers' Expressions and Epithets* (London: Sampson Low, Marston & Company, 1929)

Bowland, Lynn Edward, 'A Culture of Dissonance: Wassily Kandinsky, Atonality, and Abstraction' (unpublished doctoral thesis, University of Texas at Austin, 2014) <https://hdl.handle.net/2152/30323> [accessed 1 August 2024]

Bradley, James, 'It's Science over Capitalism: Kim Stanley Robinson and the Imperative of Hope', in *Tomorrow's Parties: Life in the Anthropocene*, ed. by Jonathan Strahan (Cambridge, MA: MIT Press, 2022), pp. 1–10 <https://doi.org/10.7551/mitpress/14384.003.0003>

Brandt, Bettina, '*Ein Wort, ein Ort*, or How Words Create Places: Interview with Yoko Tawada', *Women in German Yearbook*, 21 (2005), pp. 1–15

Bratton, Benjamin, and Blaise Agüera y Arcas, 'The Model Is the Message', in *The Model Is the Message*, ed. by Mohammed Salemy (Berlin: The New Centre for Research and Practice, 2023)

Bright, Liam Kofi, 'Du Bois' Democratic Defence of the Value Free Ideal', *Synthese*, 195.5 (2018), pp. 2227–45 <https://doi.org/10.1007/s11229-017-1333-z>

Brown, Tom B., and others, 'Language Models Are Few-Shot Learners', eprint arXiv:2005.14165v4 (May 2020) <https://doi.org/10.48550/arXiv.2005.14165>

Brown, Wendy, 'Suffering Rights as Paradoxes', *Constellations*, 7.2 (2000), pp. 230–41 <https://doi.org/10.1111/1467-8675.00183>

Burt, Stephanie, 'What Is This Thing Called Lyric?', *Modern Philology*, 113.3 (2016), pp. 422–40 <https://doi.org/10.1086/684097>

Butler, Cornelia H., and Luis Pérez-Oramas, eds, *Lygia Clark: The Abandonment of Art 1948–1988* (New York: Museum of Modern Art, 2014)

Butler, Judith, *Bodies that Matter: On the Discursive Limits of "Sex"* (New York: Routledge, 1993)

—— *Excitable Speech: A Politics of the Performative* (New York: Routledge, 1997)

—— 'Performative Agency', *Journal of Cultural Economy*, 3.2 (2010), pp. 147–61 <https://doi.org/10.1080/17530350.2010.494117>

—— 'Performativity's Social Magic', in *Bourdieu: A Critical Reader*, ed. by Richard Shusterman (Oxford: Blackwell, 1999), pp. 113–28

Callon, Michel, *The Laws of the Markets* (London: Blackwell, 1998)

Camminga, B, 'Competing Marginalities and Precarious Politics: A South African Case Study of NGO Representation of Transgender Refugees', *Gender, Place & Culture*, 31.9 (2024), pp. 1293–1310<https://doi.org/10.1080/0966369X.2022.2137473>

—— 'Ourbih's Legacy: Transgender Forced Displacement, Legal Boundaries, Lived Realities, and the Struggle for Recognition', in *Oxford Handbook of Intersectional Approaches to Migration, Gender, and Sexuality*, ed. by Gökce Yurdakul and others (Oxford: Oxford University Press, 2025)

—— *Transgender Refugees and the Imagined South Africa: Bodies Over Borders and Borders Over Bodies* (Cham, CH: Palgrave Macmillan, 2019) <https://doi.org/10.1007/978-3-319-92669-8>

—— 'What Is Private about "Private Parts"? On Navigating the Violence of the Digital African Trans Refugee Archive', in *Queer and Trans African Mobilities: Migration, Asylum and Diaspora*, ed. by B Camminga and John Marnell (London: Bloomsbury Academic, 2022), pp. 153–69 <https://doi.org/10.5040/9780755639021.ch-8>

—— 'When the Homo Deamon Went Digital: Writing Africa's Transgender Refugee Diaspora', *Communication, Culture and Critique*, 17.3 (2024), pp. 213–16 <https://doi.org/10.1093/ccc/tcae007>

—— 'Where's Your Umbrella? Decolonialisation and Transgender Studies in South Africa', *Postamble* 10.1 (2017), pp. 61–77

—— 'Withholding the Letter: Transgender Asylum Seekers, Legal Gender Recognition, and the UNHCR Mandate', *Journal of Refugee Studies*, published online 8 July 2024 <https://doi.org/10.1093/jrs/feae058>

Campbell, John L., and Ove K. Pederson, 'Knowledge Regimes and Comparative Political Economy', in *Ideas and Politics in Social Science Research*, ed. by Daniel Béland and Robert Henry Cox (Oxford: Oxford University

Press, 2010) <https://doi.org/10.1093/acprof:oso/9780199736430.003.0009>

Campolo, Alexander, and Katia Schwerzmann, 'From Rules to Examples: Machine Learning's Type of Authority', *Big Data & Society*, 10.2 (2023), pp. 1–13 <https://doi.org/10.1177/2053951723118>

Cantin, Lucie, 'The Drive, the Untreatable Quest of Desire', in *Constructing the Death Drive*, ed. by Tracy McNulty, special issue of *differences*, 28.2 (2017), pp. 24–45 <https://doi.org/10.1215/10407391-4151740>

Carrillo, Natalia, and Sergio Martínez, 'Scientific Inquiry: From Metaphors to Abstraction', Perspectives on Science, 31.2 (2023), pp. 233–61 <https://doi.org/10.1162/posc_a_00571>

Carroll, Lewis, *Sylvie and Bruno Concluded*, in *The Complete Works of Lewis Carroll* (New York: Vintage Books, 1976), pp. 509–749

Carter, Mia, 'The Politics of Pleasure: Cross-Cultural Autobiographic Performance in the Video Works of Sadie Benning', *Signs*, 23.3 (1998), pp. 745–76 <https://doi.org/10.1086/495287>

Cartwright, Nancy, *The Dappled World: A Study of the Boundaries of Science* (Cambridge: Cambridge University Press, 1999) <https://doi.org/10.1017/CBO9781139167093>

Cayanan, Mark Anthony, 'The Wilderness Was the Time Between Prophets', in *FE*, ed. by Jeff Alessandrelli and others (Portland, OR: Fonograf Editions), pp. 87–88

Ce gamin, là (Radeaux dans la montagne), dir. by Renaud Victor (France, 1975)

Cequina, Jeans, 'The Curious Case of Judiel Nieva', *POP!*, 7 January 2021 <https://pop.inquirer.net/103517/the-curious-case-of-judiel-nieva> [accessed 5 October 2023]

Chang, Hasok, *Inventing Temperature: Measurement and Scientific Progress* (Oxford: Oxford University Press, 2004) <https://doi.org/10.1093/0195171276.003.0006>

Chaput, Catherine, 'Rhetorical Circulation in Late Capitalism: Neoliberalism and the Overdetermination of Affective Energy', *Philosophy and Rhetoric*, 43.1 (2010), pp. 1–25

Chaput, Catherine, and Joshua S. Hanan, 'Economic Rhetoric as *Taxis*: Neoliberal Governmentality and the Dispositif of Freakonomics', *Journal of Cultural Economy*, 8.1 (2015), pp. 42–61 <https://doi.org/10.1080/17530350.2014.942349>

Cheah, Pheng, *What Is a World? On Postcolonial Literature as World Literature* (Durham, NC: Duke University Press, 2016) <https://doi.org/10.1515/9780822374534>

Chen, James, 'What Is Homo Economicus? Definition, Meaning, and Origins', *Investopedia*, 31 July 2021 <https://www.investopedia.com/terms/h/homoeconomicus.asp> [accessed 15 June 2024]

Cheruiyot, Kipkoech, 'Judicial Activism, Judicial Restraint and Constitutional Interpretation in Kenya: The Post-2010 Era', *SSRN*, published online 24 March 2022 <https://doi.org/10.2139/ssrn.4032620>

Chetty, Dhianaraj, 'A Drag at Madame Costello's: Cape Moffie Life and the Popular Press in the 1950s and 1960s', in *Defiant Desire: Gay and Lesbian Lives in South Africa*, ed. by Mark Gevisser and Edwin Cameron [1994] (Abingdon: Routledge, 2012), pp. 115–27 <https://doi.org/10.4324/9781315021782>

Choonoo, R. Neville, 'The Sophiatown Generation: Black Literary Journalism during the 1950s', in *South Africa's Alternative Press: Voices of Protest and Resistance, 1880s–1960s*, ed. by Les Switzer (Cambridge: Cambridge University Press, 1997), pp. 252–65

Chude-Sokei, Louis, *The Sound of Culture: Diaspora and Black Technopoetics* (Middletown, CT: Wesleyan University Press, 2016)

Clark, Lygia, 'The Bichos', in *Lygia Clark: The Abandonment of Art 1948–1988*, ed. by Cornelia H. Butler and Luis Pérez-Oramas (New York: Museum of Modern Art, 2014), p. 160

—— 'Caminhando', in *Lygia Clark: The Abandonment of Art 1948–1988*, ed. by Cornelia H. Butler and Luis Pérez-Oramas (New York: Museum of Modern Art, 2014), p. 160

—— 'To Capture a Fragment of Suspended Time', in *Lygia Clark*, ed. by Manuel J. Borja-Villel (Barcelona: Fundació Antoni Tàpies, 1998), p. 187

Clark, Timothy, 'Liberalism and Green Moralism', in Clark, *The Cambridge Introduction to Literature and the Environment* (Cambridge: Cambridge University Press, 2011), pp. 102–10 <https://doi.org/10.1017/CBO9780511976261>

Cobb, William Montague, 'Race and Runners', *The Journal of Health and Physical Education*, 7.1 (1936), n.p., published online as Department of Sociology and Anthropology Faculty Publications 13 (Washington, DC: Howard University) <https://dh.howard.edu/soci_fac/13/> [accessed 7 August 2024]

Cochoy, Franck, Martin Giraudeau, and Liz McFall, 'Performativity, Economics, and Politics: An Overview', *Journal of Cultural Economy*, 3.2 (2010) <https://doi.org/10.1080/17530350.2010.494116>

Coetzee, J. M., *Foe* (New York: Viking Press, 1986)

Comaroff, John L., and Simon Roberts, *Rules and Processes: The Cultural Logic of Dispute in an African Context* (Chicago: University of Chicago Press, 1981)

Consolo, Agostino, and António Dias da Silva, 'The Euro Area Labour Market through the Lens of the Beveridge Curve', *ECB Economic Bulletin*, 4 (2019) <https://www.ecb.europa.eu/pub/economic-bulletin/articles/2019/html/ecb.ebart201904_01~9070de27a0.en.html> [accessed 12 June 2023]

Costa, Albert, *The Bilingual Brain: And What It Tells Us About the Science of Language*, trans. by J. W. Schwieter [Spanish orig. *El Cerebro Bilingüe: La Neurosciencia del Lenguaje* (2017)] (London: Penguin, 2021)

Couture, Lise Anne, Hani Rashid, and Gregg Lynn, *Asymptote Architecture: NYSE Virtual Trading Floor; Oral History*, ed. by Greg Lynn (Montreal: Canadian Center for Architecture, 2015)

Cover, Robert, 'Nomos and Narrative', in *Narrative, Violence, and the Law: The Essays of Robert Cover*, ed. by Michael Ryan and Austin Sarat (Ann Arbor: University of Michigan Press, 1992), pp. 95–172

Coxon, Ann, Briony Fer, and Maria Müller-Schareck, *Anni Albers* (London: Yale University Press and Tate, 2018)

Crawford, Kate, *Atlas of AI: Power, Politics, and the Planetary Costs of Artificial Intelligence* (New Haven, CT: Yale University Press, 2021) <https://doi.org/10.12987/9780300252392>

Crawford, Lucas Cassidy, 'Transgender without Organs?: Mobilizing a Geo-Affective Theory of Gender Modification', *Womens Studies Quarterly*, 36.3–4 (2008), pp. 127–43 <https://doi.org/10.1353/wsq.0.0092>

Crawford, Margo Natalie, 'The Politics of Abstraction', in Crawford, *Black Post-Blackness: The Black Arts Movement and Twenty-First-Century Aesthetics* (Champaign: University of Illinois Press, 2017), pp. 42–81 <https://doi.org/10.5406/illinois/9780252041006.003.0003>

Croce, Mariano, *The Juridification of Politics* (London: Routledge, 2018)

Cruz, Isagani, 'English and Tagalog in Philippine Literature: A Study of Literary Bilingualism', *World Englishes*, 5.2–3 (1986), pp. 163–76 <https://doi.org/10.1111/j.1467-971x.1986.tb00723.x>

Cucu, Alina-Sandra, *Planning Labour: Time and the Foundations of Industrial Socialism in Romania* (Oxford and New York: Berghahn Books, 2019) <https://doi.org/10.3167/9781789201857>

Culler, Jonathan, 'Extending the *Theory of the Lyric*', *Diacritics*, 45.4 (2017), pp. 6–14 <https://doi.org/10.1353/dia.2017.0017>

—— *Theory of the Lyric* (Cambridge, MA: Harvard University Press, 2015) <https://doi.org/10.4159/9780674425781>

Dalziell, Jacqueline, 'Microbiology as Sociology: The Strange Sociality of Slime', in *What If Culture Was Nature All Along?*, ed. by Vicki Kirby (Edinburgh: Edinburgh University Press, 2017), pp. 153–78 <https://doi.org/10.1515/9781474419307-010>

Daniel, Jean-Pierre, 'Josée Manenti, la force de l'amitié. *Le Moindre Geste*, ou filmer l'enfant psychotique', *Le Coq-Héron*, 209 (2012), pp. 65–70 <https://doi.org/10.3917/cohe.209.0065>

Dasgupta, Sudeep, 'Sexual and Gender-Based Asylum and the Queering of Global Space: Reading Desire, Writing Identity and the Unconventionality of the Law', in *Refugee Imaginaries: Research Across the Humanities*, ed. by Emma Cox and others (Edinburgh: Edinburgh University Press, 2019), pp. 86–103 <https://doi.org/10.1515/9781474443210-009>

Davis, Heath Fogg, 'Sex-Classification Policies as Transgender Discrimination: An Intersectional Critique', *Perspectives on Politics*, 12.1 (2014), pp. 45–60 <https://doi.org/10.1017/S1537592713003708>

Davis, Lawrence-Minh Bùi, 'On Refugee Poetics and Exophony', *Poetry*, 1 April 2022 <https://www.poetryfoundation.org/poetrymagazine/articles/157568/on-refugee-poetics-and-exophony> [accessed 12 June 2023]

de la Cretaz, Frankie, 'Author Kai Cheng Thom on Writing a New Kind of Transgender Memoir', *Teen Vogue*, 5 April 2017 <https://www.teenvogue.com/story/author-kai-cheng-thom-on-writing-a-new-kind-of-transgender-memoir> [accessed 23 July 2024]

de Larch, Germaine, 'Transgender Identity: The Context and Intersectionality of Identity', *Gender Questions*, 5.1 (2017), pp. 1–4

de Oliveira, Guilherme Sanches, 'Representationalism Is a Dead End', *Synthese*, 198 (2018), pp. 209–35 <https://doi.org/10.1007/s11229-018-01995-9>

Deleuze, Gilles, 'Instincts and Institutions', in Deleuze, *Desert Islands and Other Texts 1953–1974* (New York: Semiotext(e), 2004), pp. 19–21

—— 'Seminar on Spinoza: The Velocities of Thought' (16 December 1980), trans. by Charles J. Stivale, *The Deleuze Seminars* (website) <https://deleuze.cla.purdue.edu/index.php/seminars/spinoza-velocities-thought/lecture-04-0> [accessed 12 August 2024]

Deleuze, Gilles, and Félix Guattari, *A Thousand Plateaus: Capitalism and Schizophrenia* [1980], trans. by Brian Massumi (Minneapolis: University of Minnesota Press, 2005)

Deligny, Fernand, 'Les Fossiles ont la vie dure', in *Fernand Deligny: Camérer. A propos d'images*, ed. by Sandra Alvarez de Toledo, Anaïs Masson, Marlon Miguel, and Marina Vidal-Naquet (Paris: L'Arachnéen, 2021), pp. 142–49

—— *Œuvres*, ed. by Sandra Alvarez de Toledo (Paris: L'Arachnéen, 2007)

Deligny, Fernand, Sandra Alvarez de Toledo, and Cyril Le Roy, *Cartes et lignes d'erre / Maps and Wander Lines: Traces du réseau de Fernand Deligny, 1969–1979* (Paris: L'Arachnéen, 2013)

Derrida, Jacques, 'Signature Événement Contexte', in Derrida, *Marges de la Philosophie* (Paris: Éditions de Minuit, 1972), pp. 365–93

Deuber-Mankowsky, Astrid, 'The Space of Appearance in Deep Underground: *A Film Is Being Made* and the Documentary Gesture', *MLN*, 137.3 (2022), pp. 443–65 <https://doi.org/10.1353/mln.2022.0034>

Dewey, John, *Human Nature and Conduct, 1922*, ed. by Jo Ann Boydston, The Middle Works, 1899–1924, 14 (Carbondale: Southern Illinois University Press, 1983)

Dhoest, Alexander, 'Learning to Be Gay: LGBTQ Forced Migrant Identities and Narratives in Belgium', *Journal of Ethnic and Migration Studies*, 45.7 (2019), pp. 1075–89 <https://doi.org/10.1080/1369183X.2017.1420466>

Dobrescu, Emilian, 'Double Conditioned Potential Output', paper delivered at the 28th General Conference of the International Association for Research in Income and Wealth (Cork, Ireland, 22–28 August 2004) <https://doi.org/10.2139/ssrn.1434909>

—— 'Unstable Processes and Macroeconomic Modelling', in *Macroeconomic Modelling*, ed. by Emilian Dobrescu (Bucharest: Centre for Economic Information and Documentation, 1996b), pp. 24–52

—— 'Unstable Processes and Macroeconomic Modelling', *Romanian Economic Review*, 41.1 (1996a), pp. 17–34

Dooms, Tessa, and Lynsey Ebony Chutel, *Coloured: How Classification Became Culture* (Johannesburg and Cape Town: Jonathan Ball, 2023)

Douglas, Heather, *Science, Policy, and the Value-Free Ideal* (Pittsburgh: University of Pittsburgh Press, 2009) <https://doi.org/10.2307/j.ctt6wrc78>

Dula, Rodolfo, 'Devil's Advocate in Agoo' (second of a series), *Malaya*, 18 February 1993, pp. 1,7

—— 'Devil's Advocate in Agoo' (fourth of a series), *Malaya*, 20 February 1993, pp. 1,3

—— 'Devil's Advocate in Agoo' (conclusion), *Malaya*, 21 February 1993, pp. 1,4

Dulley, Iracema, 'Naming Others: Translation and Subject Constitution in the Central Highlands of Angola (1926–1961)', *Comparative Studies in Society and History*, 64.2 (2022), pp. 363–93 <https://doi.org/10.1017/S0010417522000056>

Eckert, Julia, and others, eds, *Law Against the State: Ethnographic Forays into Law's Transformations* (Cambridge: Cambridge University Press, 2012) <https://doi.org/10.1017/CBO9781139043786>

Edmondson, George, and Klaus Mladek, eds, *Sovereignty in Ruins: A Politics of Crisis* (Durham, NC: Duke University Press, 2017) <https://doi.org/10.1215/9780822373391>

Elgin, Catherine, *True Enough* (Cambridge, MA: MIT Press, 2017) <https://doi.org/10.7551/mitpress/9780262036535.001.0001>

Emezi, Akwaeke, *Dear Senthuran: A Black Spirit Memoir* (London: Riverhead Books, 2021)

Endangered Language Alliance <https://www.elalliance.org/> [accessed 4 March 2024]

Erasmus, Zimitri, 'Introduction: Re-imagining Coloured Identities in Post-Apartheid South Africa', in *Coloured by History, Shaped by Place: New Perspectives on Coloured Identities in Cape Town*, ed. by Zimitri Erasmus (Cape Town and Maroelana, SA: Kwela Books and South African History Online, 2001), pp. 13–28

—— ed., *Coloured by History, Shaped by Place: New Perspectives on Coloured Identities in Cape Town* (Cape Town and Maroelana, SA: Kwela Books and South African History Online, 2001)

Erickson, Paul, and others, *How Reason Almost Lost its Mind: The Strange Career of Cold War Rationality* (Chicago: University of Chicago Press, 2015)

Esposito, Roberto, *Institution*, trans. by Zakiya Hanafi (Cambridge: Polity Press, 2022)

Faarax Xuseen Cabdi Ama Kim Abdi, dir. by sspamediacom, online video recording, YouTube, 25 March 2020 <https://www.youtube.com/watch?v=agjsTjRBTkg> [accessed 7 October 2023]

Fankhänel, Teresa, 'Analog World-Modelling: Anticipating a Post-War World Through Architectural Models', lecture, ICI Berlin, 8 January 2024, Models lecture series <https://doi.org/10.25620/e240108>

Farred, Grant, *Midfielder's Moment: Coloured Literature and Culture in Contemporary South Africa* [2000] (Abingdon: Routledge, 2018) <https://doi.org/10.4324/9780429040351>

Felt, Hali, *Soundings: The Story of the Remarkable Woman Who Mapped the Ocean Floor* (New York: Picador, 2012)

Fleck, Ludwik, *Genesis and Development of a Scientific Fact*, ed. by Thaddeus J. Trenn and Robert K. Merton, trans. by Fred Bradley and Thaddeus J. Trenn (Chicago: University of Chicago Press, 1979)

Fleig, Philipp, and others, 'Emergence of Behaviour in a Self-Organized Living Matter Network', *eLife*, published online 21 January 2022 <https://doi.org/10.7554/eLife.62863>

Flepp, Fabio, 'Reisegeschichten — Ein Leben voller Träume', *Schweizer Radio und Fernsehen* (*SRF*), 10 November 2015 <https://www.srf.ch/sendungen/reisegeschichten/reisegeschichten-ein-leben-voller-traeume> [accessed 7 October 2023]

Foote, Stephanie and Jeffrey Jerome Cohen, 'Introduction: Climate Change/Changing Climates', in *The Cambridge Companion to Environmental Humanities*, ed. by Jeffrey Jerome Cohen and Stephanie Foote (Cambridge, U.K.: Cambridge University Press, 2021), pp. 1–10 <https://doi.org/10.1017/9781009039369.002>

Foster, John Bellamy, *Marx's Ecology: Materialism and Nature* (New York: Monthly Review Press, 2000)

—— *The Return of Nature: Socialism and Ecology* (New York: Monthly Review Press, 2021)

Foucault, Michel, *Le Discours Philosophique*, ed. by Daniele Lorenzini and Orazio Irrera (Paris: Éditions du Seuil, 2023)

—— 'Nietzsche, Genealogy, History', in Foucault, *Language, Counter-Memory, Practice: Selected Essays and Interviews*, ed. by Donald F. Bouchard, trans. by Donald F. Bouchard and Sherry Simon (Ithaca, NY: Cornell University Press, 1980), pp. 139–64

—— 'What is Enlightenment?', in Foucault, *The Foucault Reader*, ed. by Paul Rabinow, trans. by Catherine Porter (New York: Pantheon Books, 1984), pp. 32–50

Fourcade, Marion, *Economists and Societies: Discipline and Profession in the United States, Britain, and France, 1890s to 1990s* (Princeton, NJ: Princeton University Press, 2010) <https://doi.org/10.1515/9781400833139>

Fraser, Nancy, *Cannibal Capitalism: How Our System Is Devouring Democracy, Care, and the Planet — and What We Can Do about It* (London: Verso, 2022)

Freud, Sigmund, *The Interpretation of Dreams*, ed. and trans. by James Strachey (London: Hogarth Press, 1953)

Frigg, Roman, and James Nguyen, 'The Fiction View of Models Reloaded', *The Monist*, 99.3 (2016), pp. 225–42 <https://doi.org/10.1093/monist/onw002>

Frigg, Roman, and Stephan Hartmann, 'Models in Science', *The Stanford Encyclopedia of Philosophy* (Fall 2024 edition), ed. by Edward N. Zalta and Uri Nodelman <https://plato.stanford.edu/archives/fall2024/entries/models-science/> [accessed 10 December 2024]

Fuchs, Christian, and Vincent Mosco, eds, *Marx in the Age of Digital Capitalism* (Leiden: Brill, 2015) <https://doi.org/10.1163/9789004291393>

Galison, Peter, 'The Ontology of the Enemy: Norbert Wiener and the Cybernetic Vision', *Critical Inquiry*, 21 (1994), pp. 228–66 <https://doi.org/10.1086/448747>

Galloway, Alexander, '"Black Box, Black Bloc"', lecture delivered at the New School, New York City, 12 April 2010 <http://cultureandcommunication.org/galloway/pdf/Galloway_Black_Box_Black_Bloc.pdf> [accessed 25 March 2024]

Garcia, J. Neil, 'Translational Poetics: Notes on Contemporary Philippine Poetry in English', *Likhaan: The Journal of Contemporary Philippine Literature*, 7 (2013), pp. 177–94 <https://www.journals.upd.edu.ph/index.php/lik/article/view/5062> [accessed 12 June 2023]

Geertz, Clifford, 'Religion as a Cultural System', in Geertz, *The Interpretation of Cultures: Selected Essays* (New York: Basic Books, 1973), pp. 87–125

Getsy, David J., *Abstract Bodies: Sixties Sculpture in the Expanded Field of Gender* (New Haven, CT: Yale University Press, 2015)

—— 'Reduction as Expansion: The Queer Capacities of Abstract Art', lecture, ICI Berlin, 1 February 2021 <https://doi.org/10.25620/e210201>

—— 'Ten Queer Theses on Abstraction', in *Queer Abstraction*, ed. by Jared Ledesma (Des Moines, IA: Des Moines Art Center, 2019), pp. 65–75

Gevisser, Mark, 'A Different Fight for Freedom', in *Defiant Desire: Gay and Lesbian Lives in South Africa*, ed. by Mark Gevisser and Edwin Cameron [1994] (Abingdon: Routledge, 2012), pp. 14–86 <https://doi.org/10.4324/9781315021782>

Gevisser, Mark, and Edwin Cameron, 'Defiant Desire: An Introduction', in *Defiant Desire: Gay and Lesbian Lives in South Africa*, ed. by Mark Gevisser and Edwin Cameron [1994] (Abingdon: Routledge, 2012), pp. 3–13 <https://doi.org/10.4324/9781315021782>

Ghosh, Amitav, *The Great Derangement: Climate Change and the Unthinkable* (Chicago: University of Chicago Press, 2016) <https://doi.org/10.7208/chicago/9780226323176.001.0001>

Giere, Ronald, *Explaining Science: A Cognitive Approach* (Chicago: University of Chicago Press, 1988) <https://doi.org/10.7208/chicago/9780226292038.001.0001>

Girl Power (Part 1), dir. by Sadie Benning (USA, 1992)

Gleeson, Jules Joanne, and Elle O'Rourke, 'Introduction', in *Transgender Marxism*, ed. by Jules Joanne Gleeson and Elle O'Rourke (London: Pluto Press, 2021), pp. 1–32 <https://doi.org/10.2307/j.ctv1n9dkjc.4>

Glissant, Édouard, *Caribbean Discourse*, trans. by J. Michael Dash [French orig. *Le Discours antillais* (1981)] (Charlottesville: University Press of Virginia, 1989)

—— 'For Opacity', in Glissant, *Poetics of Relation*, trans. by Betsy Wing (Ann Arbor, MI: University of Michigan Press, 1990), pp. 189–94

Godfrey-Smith, Peter, 'Abstractions, Idealizations, and Evolutionary Biology', in *Mapping the Future of Biology: Evolving Concepts and Theories*, ed. by Thomas Pradeu and others (Dordrecht: Springer Netherlands, 2009), pp. 47–56 <https://doi.org/10.1007/978-1-4020-9636-5>

Goh, Irving, 'Writing, Touching, and Eating in Clarice Lispector: *Água Viva* and a Breath of Life', *MLN*, 131.5 (2016), pp. 1347–69 <https://doi.org/10.1353/mln.2016.0093>

Goldie, Peter, *The Mess Inside: Narrative, Emotion, and the Mind* (Oxford: Oxford University Press, 2012) <https://doi.org/10.1093/acprof:oso/9780199230730.001.0001>

Gonzalez, N. V. M., 'Imaginative Writing in the Philippines', in *Philippine Writing: An Anthology*, ed. by T. D. Agcaoili (Westport, CT: Greenwood Press, 1971), pp. 321–28

Goodman, Nelson, *Languages of Art: An Approach to a Theory of Symbols* (Indianapolis: The Bobbs-Merrill Company, 1968)

—— *Ways of Worldmaking* (Hassocks: The Harvester Press, 1978) <https://doi.org/10.5040/9781350928558>

Goodwin, Paul, and Ming Tiampo, eds, *Worlding Concepts*, Worlding Public Cultures (Berlin: ICI Berlin Press, forthcoming)

Gorelick, Nathan, 'Why Sex Is Special: Psychoanalysis against New Materialism', in *Subject Lessons: Hegel, Lacan, and the Future of Materialism*, ed. by Russell Sbriglia and Slavoj Žižek (Evanston, IL: Northwestern University Press, 2020), pp. 171–89 <https://doi.org/10.2307/j.ctvw1d5dk.11>

Gossett, Reina, Eric A. Stanley, and Johanna Burton, eds, *Trap Door: Trans Cultural Production and the Politics of Visibility* (Cambridge, MA: MIT Press, 2017)

Gotinga, JC, 'Angel Locsin: Red-tagged Celebrity', *Rappler*, 18 December 2020 <https://www.rappler.com/newsbreak/in-depth/angel-locsin-

red-tagged-celebrity-faces-philippines-2020-series/> [accessed 5 October 2023]

Graham, Jorie, 'Vertigo', in *The End of Beauty* (New York: Ecco Press, 1987), pp. 66–67

Graziano, Michael S. A., 'The Brain Basis of Consciousness, and More...', Graziano Lab (website) <https://grazianolab.princeton.edu/> [accessed 10 August 2024]

Green, Huw, 'The Big Idea: Why Your Brain Needs Other People', *The Guardian*, 8 July 2024 <https://www.theguardian.com/books/article/2024/jul/08/the-big-idea-why-your-brain-needs-other-people> [accessed 9 July 2024]

Greimas, Algirdas Julien, 'The Interaction of Semiotic Constraints', in Greimas, *On Meaning: Selected Writings in Semiotic Theory*, trans. by Paul J. Perron and Frank H. Collins (Minneapolis: University of Minnesota Press, 1987), pp. 48–62

Grossman, Allen, 'Summa Lyrica: A Primer of the Commonplaces in Speculative Poetics', in *The Lyric Theory Reader: A Critical Anthology*, ed. by Virginia Jackson and Yopie Prins (Baltimore: Johns Hopkins University Press, 2014), pp. 419–30

Grove, Kevin, *Resilience* (New York: Routledge, 2018) <https://doi.org/10.4324/9781315661407>

Guéry, Alain, 'Institution: Histoire d'une notion et de ses utilisations dans l'histoire avant les institutionnalismes', *Cahiers d'économie politique*, 44.1 (2003), pp. 7–18 <https://doi.org/10.3917/cep.044.0007>

Gullar, Ferreira, and others, 'Neo-Concrete Manifesto' (Rio de Janeiro, March 1959) <https://391.org/manifestos/1959-neo-concrete-manifesto-ferreira-gullar/> [accessed 22 July 2024]

Habermas, Jürgen, *The Theory of Communicative Action*, trans. by Thomas McCarthy, 2 vols (Boston: Beacon Press, 1984–87), II: *Lifeworld and System: A Critique of Functionalist Reason* [1981] (1987)

Hacking, Ian, *The Taming of Chance* (Cambridge: Cambridge University Press, 1990) <https://doi.org/10.1017/CBO9780511819766>

von Hallberg, Robert, *Lyric Powers* (Chicago: University of Chicago Press, 2008) <https://doi.org/10.7208/chicago/9780226865027.001.0001>

Halpern, Orit, 'Dreams for Our Perceptual Present: Temporality, Storage, and Interactivity in Cybernetics', *Configurations* 13.2 (2005), p. 283–319 <https://doi.org/10.1353/con.2007.0016>

Hamblin, Robert, *Robert: A Queer and Crooked Memoir for the Not so Straight or Narrow* (Cape Town: Melinda Ferguson, 2021)

Hanan, Joshua S., Indradeep Ghosh, and Kaleb W. Brooks, 'Banking on the Present: The Ontological Rhetoric of Neo-Classical Economics and Its Relation to the 2008 Financial Crisis', *Quarterly Journal of Speech*, 100.2 (2014), pp. 139–62 <https://doi.org/10.1080/00335630.2014.961529>

Hancox-Li, Leif, 'Idealization and Abstraction in Models of Injustice', *Hypathia*, 32.2 (2017), pp. 329–46 <https://doi.org/10.1111/hypa. 12317>

Haraway, Donna, *Crystals, Fabrics, and Fields: Metaphors of Organicism in Twentieth-Century Developmental Biology* (London: Yale University Press, 1976)

Hau, Caroline S., 'The Filipino Novel in English', in *Philippine English: Linguistic and Literary Perspectives*, ed. by Maria Lourdes S. Bautista and Kingsley Bolton (Hong Kong: Hong Kong University Press, 2008), pp. 317–36

Hayek, Friedrich A., *The Sensory Order: An Inquiry into the Foundations of Theoretical Psychology* (Chicago: University of Chicago Press, 1952)

—— 'The Use of Knowledge in Society', *The American Economic Review*, 35.4 (1945), pp. 519–30 <https://doi.org/10.1142/9789812701275_ 0025>

Hebb, Donald O., *The Organization of Behavior: A Neuropsychological Theory* (New York: Wiley, 1949)

Heezen, Bruce, and Charles D. Hollister, *The Face of the Deep* (Oxford: Oxford University Press, 1971)

Heezen, Bruce, Marie Tharp, and Maurice Ewing, *The Floors of the Oceans: I. The North Atlantic; Text to Accompany the Physiographic Diagram of the North Atlantic*, Special Paper 65 (New York: The Geological Society of America, 1959) <https://doi.org/10.1130/SPE65-p1>

Heidegger, Martin, 'The Origin of the Work of Art' [1950], in Heidegger, *Poetry, Language, Thought*, trans. by Albert Hofstadter (New York: HarperCollins Modern Classics, 2001), pp. 15–86

Helmholtz, Hermann von, 'The Facts in Perception', in Helmholtz, *Science and Culture: Popular and Philosophical Essays*, ed. by David Cahan (Chicago: University of Chicago Press, 1995), pp. 342–80

—— 'Goethe's Presentiments of Coming Scientific Ideas', in Helmholtz, *Science and Culture: Popular and Philosophical Essays*, ed. by David Cahan (Chicago: University of Chicago Press, 1995), pp. 393–412

Hemmings, Clare, 'Telling Feminist Stories', *Feminist Theory*, 6.2 (2005), pp. 115–39 <https://doi.org/10.1177/1464700105053690>

Hermaszewska, Susannah, and others, 'Lived Experiences of Transgender Forced Migrants and Their Mental Health Outcomes: Systematic Review and Meta-Ethnography', *BJPsych Open*, 8.3 (2022) <https://doi. org/10.1192/bjo.2022.51>

Herr, Alex, 'Techscape: How Cheap Outsourced Labour in Africa Is Shaping AI Language', *The Guardian*, 16 April 2014 <https://www.theguardian. com/technology/2024/apr/16/techscape-ai-gadgest-humane-ai-pin-chatgpt> [accessed 23 June 2024]

Heyns, Jackie, 'The Moffie Manuscripts', *Drum*, July 1977

Hiller, Moritz, 'Es gibt keine Sprachmodelle', in *Noten zum Schreiben: Für Martin Stingelin zum 60. Geburtstag*, ed. by Davide Giuriato, Claas Morgenroth, and Sandro Zanetti (Paderborn: Brill | Fink, 2023), pp. 279–85 <https://doi.org/10.30965/9783846768433_037>

Hirschl, Ran, 'The Judicialization of Politics', in *The Oxford Handbook of Law and Politics*, ed. by Gregory A. Caldeira and others (Oxford: Oxford University Press, 2008), pp. 119–41 <https://doi.org/10.1093/oxfordhb/9780199208425.003.0008>

Hoad, Neville, 'Between the White Man's Burden and the White Man's Disease: Tracking Lesbian and Gay Human Rights in Southern Africa', *GLQ: A Journal of Lesbian and Gay Studies*, 5.4 (1999), pp. 559–84 <https://doi.org/10.1215/10642684-5-4-559>

Hogben, Lancelot, *Nature and Nurture* (London: Williams and Norgate, 1933)

—— *The Nature of Living Matter* (London: K. Paul, Trench, Trubner, 1930)

—— *Statistical Theory: The Relationship of Probability, Credibility, and Error* (New York: W. W. Norton & Company, 1968)

Holloway, John, 'Read Capital: The First Sentence: Or, Capital Starts with Wealth, not with the Commodity', *Historical Materialism*, 23.3 (2015), pp. 3–26 <https://doi.org/10.1163/1569206X-12341420>

Holmes, David, '"Cli-Fi": Could a Literary Genre Help Save the Planet?', *The Conversation*, 20 February 2014 <https://theconversation.com/cli-fi-could-a-literary-genre-help-save-the-planet-23478> [accessed 3 January 2024]

Holzhey, Christoph F. E., and Arnd Wedemeyer, eds, *Re-: An Errant Glossary*, Cultural Inquiry, 15 (Berlin: ICI Berlin Press, 2019) <https://doi.org/10.25620/ci-15>

Holzhey, Christoph F. E., and Jakob Schillinger, eds, *The Case for Reduction*, Cultural Inquiry, 25 (Berlin: ICI Berlin Press, 2022) <https://doi.org/10.37050/ci-25>

Holzhey, Christoph F. E., Marietta Kesting, and Claudia Peppel, 'Introduction', in *Breaking and Making Models*, ed. by Christoph F. E. Holzhey, Marietta Kesting, and Claudia Peppel, Cultural Inquiry, 33 (Berlin: ICI Berlin Press, 2025), pp. 1–17 <https:/ / doi.org/ 10.37050/ ci-33_00>

Hopfener, Birgit, and Ming Tiampo, 'Introduction', in *Worlding the Global: The Arts in the Age of Decolonization*, ed. by Birgit Hopfener and Ming Tiampo, Worlding Public Cultures (Berlin: ICI Berlin Press, forthcoming)

—— 'Worlding Global Art Histories', *Texte zur Kunst*, 128 (2022), pp. 146–51

Horning, Rob, 'Companionship without Companions', *Internal Exile* (blog), 3 August 2024 <https://robhorning.substack.com/p/companionship-without-companions> [accessed 12 August 2024]

Hsiao, Sissi, and Eli Collins, 'Try Bard and Share Your Feedback', *Google Tech* (blog), 21 March 2023 <https://blog.google/technology/ai/try-bard/> [accessed 7 July 2024]

Hsu, Sheryl, and Laura Schaposnik, 'Cell Fusion through Slime Mould Network Dynamics', *Journal of The Royal Society Interface*, 19 (2022) <https://doi.org/10.1098/rsif.2022.0054>

Hsu, Stephanie, 'Exotic Spectacle in *Tara's Crossing*, a Transgender Asylum Narrative', in *Queer Exoticism*, ed. by David Powell and Tamara Powell (Newcastle: Cambridge Scholars Publishing, 2010), pp. 81–91

Huggan, Graham, *The Postcolonial Exotic: Marketing the Margins* (London: Routledge, 2001) <https://doi.org/10.4324/9780203420102>

Hunt, Sarah, 'Ontologies of Indigeneity: The Politics of Embodying a Concept', *Cultural Geographies*, 21.1 (2014), pp. 27–34

İşcen, Özgün Eylül, 'Black Box Allegories of Gulf Futurism: The Irreducible Other of Computational Capital', in *The Case for Reduction*, ed. by Christoph F. E. Holzhey and Jakob Schillinger, Cultural Inquiry, 25 (Berlin: ICI Berlin Press, 2022), pp. 91–115 <https://doi.org/10.37050/ci-25_05>

Ingold, Tim, *Lines: A Brief History* (New York: Routledge, 2007) <https://doi.org/10.4324/9780203961155>

Jackson, Bernard, *Making Sense in Law* (Liverpool: Deborah Charles, 1995)

Jackson, Zakiyyah Iman, *Becoming Human: Matter and Meaning in an Anti-Black World* (New York: NYU Press, 2021) <https://doi.org/10.18574/nyu/9781479890040.001.0001>

Jacques, Juliet, 'Forms of Resistance: Uses of Memoir, Theory, and Fiction in Trans Life Writing', *Life Writing*, 14.3 (2017), pp. 357–70 <https://doi.org/10.1080/14484528.2017.1328301>

James, William, *Pragmatism* [1907] (Cambridge, MA: Harvard University Press, 1979)

Jameson, Fredric, *Allegory and Ideology* (London: Verso, 2019)

—— *Brecht and Method* (London: Verso, 1998)

—— foreword to Andre Jolles, *Simple Forms*, trans. by Peter J. Schwartz (London: Verso, 2017), pp. vii–xviii

—— *The Political Unconscious* (London: Routledge, 1981)

—— *Postmodernism, or, The Cultural Logic of Late Capitalism* (Durham, NC: Duke University Press, 1991) <https://doi.org/10.1215/9780822378419>

Jeppie, Shamil, 'Popular Culture and Carnival in Cape Town', in *The Struggle for District Six: Past and Present*, ed. by Shamil Jeppie and Crain Soudien (Cape Town: Buchu Books, 1990), pp. 67–87

Jolles, Andre, *Simple Forms*, trans. by Peter J. Schwartz (London: Verso, 2017)

Jones, Martin, 'Idealization and Abstraction: A Framework', in *Idealization XII: Correcting the Model; Idealization and Abstraction in the Sciences*, ed. by Nancy Cartwright and Martin Jones (Amsterdam: Rodopi, 2005), pp. 173–217 <https://doi.org/10.1163/9789401202732_010>

Kaggwa, Julius, *From Juliet to Julius: In Search of My True Identity* (Kampala: Fountain Publishers, 1998)

Kandinsky, Wassily, 'Inhalt und Form' [1910], in Kandinsky, *Gesammelte Schriften 1889–1916*, ed. by Helmut Friedel (Munich: Prestel, 2007), pp. 309–403

—— *On the Spiritual in Art* [1911], ed. and trans. by Hilla Rebay (New York: Solomon R. Guggenheim Foundation, 1946)

—— *Über das Geistige in der Kunst* [1911] (Bern: Benteli, 2009)

Kangaude, Godfrey Dalitso, ed., *Legal Grounds III: Reproductive and Sexual Rights in Sub-Saharan African Courts* (Pretoria: Pretoria University Law Press, 2017)

Katzir, Roni, 'Why Large Language Models Are Poor Theories of Human Linguistic Cognition: A Reply to Piantadosi', *Biolinguistics*, 17 (2023) <https://doi.org/10.5964/bioling.13153>

Kemp, Martin, 'The Impressionists' Bible', *Nature*, 453.37 (2008) <https://doi.org/10.1038/453037a>

Kennedy, Devin, 'The Machine in the Market: Computers and the Infrastructure of Price at the New York Stock Exchange, 1965–1975', *Social Studies of Science*, 47.6 (2017), pp. 888–917 <https://doi.org/10.1177/0306312717739367>

Kenya High Court, *Eric Gitari v. NGOs Co-ordination Board & 4 Others*, Petition No. 440 of 2013, Judgement of 24 April 2015

Kenya Supreme Court, *Eric Gitari v. NGOs Co-ordination Board & 3 Others*, Civil Appeal No. 16 of 2019, Judgement of 24 February 2023

Kesting, Marietta, 'Who Writes? Who Speaks? @Glissantbot: The More than Human Politics of Languaging in the Post-Colonies', in *Human after Man*, ed. by Marietta Kesting and Susanne Witzgall (Zurich and Berlin: diaphanes, 2022), pp. 129–42

Khan, Sal, 'How AI Could Save (Not Destroy) Education', *TED*, April 2023 <https://www.ted.com/talks/sal_khan_how_ai_could_save_not_destroy_education/transcript?language=en> [accessed 11 January 2024]

Khosrowi, Donal, 'Managing Performative Models', *Philosophy of the Social Sciences*, 53.5 (2023), pp. 371–95 <https://doi.org/10.1177/00483931231172455>

Kim, Soo Hwan, 'Sergei Tretyakov Revisited: The Cases of Walter Benjamin and Hito Steyerl', *e-flux*, 104 (2019) <https://www.e-flux.com/journal/104/298121/sergei-tretyakov-revisited-the-cases-of-walter-benjamin-and-hito-steyerl/> [accessed 3 January 2024]

Kirksey, Eben, and others, 'The Xenopus Pregnancy Test: A Performative Experiment', *Environmental Humanities* 8.1 (2016), pp. 37–56 <https://doi.org/10.1215/22011919-3527713>

Kisukidi, Nadia Yala, 'Dreams of Independence: Radical Imaginings in 1960s Africa', lecture, ICI Berlin, 27 May 2024, Models lecture series <https://doi.org/10.25620/e240527>

Kittler, Friedrich A., 'There Is No Software', *CTHEORY*, 18 October 1995 <https://journals.uvic.ca/index.php/ctheory/article/view/14655/ 5522> [accessed 12 August 2024]

Klee, Paul, 'Creative Confession' [1920], in Klee, *Creative Confession and Other Writings*, ed. by Matthew Gale, trans. by Norbert Guterman (London: Tate, 2013), pp. 7–14.

—— 'Klee', in *Schöpferische Konfession*, ed. by Kasimir Edschmid (Berlin: Erich Reiss, 1920), pp. 26–40

Knoll, Andrew K., *A Brief History of the Earth* (New York: Mariner, 2021)

Knuuttila, Tarja, 'Epistemic Artifacts and the Modal Dimension of Modeling', *European Journal for Philosophy of Science*, 11.65 (2021) <https://doi. org/10.1007/s13194-021-00374-5>

—— 'Modelling and Representing: An Artefactual Approach to Model-Based Representation', *Studies in History and Philosophy of Science Part A*, 42.2 (2011), pp. 262–71 <https://doi.org/10.1016/j.shpsa.2010. 11.034>

—— 'Surrogate Reasoning: An Artefactual Approach', lecture, ICI Berlin, 23 January 2023, Models lecture series <https://doi.org/10.25620/ e230123>

Krtolica, Igor, 'La "Tentative" des Cévennes. Deligny et la question de l'institution', *Chimères*, 72 (2010), pp. 73–97

Kruger, Sasha, and Sayantani DasGupta, 'Embodiment in [Critical] Auto|biography Studies', *a/b: Auto/Biography Studies*, 33.2 (2018), pp. 483–87 <https://doi.org/10.1080/08989575.2018.1445608>

Kugel, Seth, and Stephen Hiltner, 'A New Frontier for Travel Scammers: AI-Generated Guide Books', *The New York Times*, 23 August 2023 <https:// www.nytimes.com/2023/08/05/travel/amazon-guidebooks-artificial-intelligence.html> [accessed 10 March 2024]

Kuhn, Thomas S., *The Structure of Scientific Revolutions*, intro. by Ian Hacking (Chicago: University of Chicago Press, 2012)

Lacan, Jacques, *The Seminar of Jacques Lacan*, ed. by Jacques-Alain Miller (New York: Norton, 1988–), VII: *The Ethics of Psychoanalysis, 1959–1960*, trans. by Dennis Porter (1997)

Lampland, Martha, *The Value of Labor: The Science of Commodification in Hungary, 1920–1956* (Chicago: University of Chicago Press, 2016) <https: //doi.org/10.7208/chicago/9780226314747.001.0001>

Langford, Sasha J., 'The Psychotopology of Climate', in *Lacan and the Environment*, ed. by Clint Burnham and Paul Kingsbury (Cham, CH: Palgrave Macmillan, 2021), pp. 181–214 <https://doi.org/10.1007/978-3-030-67205-8>

Latour, Bruno, *Facing Gaia: Eight Lectures on the New Climatic Regime*, trans. by Catherine Porter (Cambridge: Polity Press, 2017)

—— 'From Realpolitik to Dingpolitik or How to Make Things Public', in *Making Things Public: Atmospheres of Democracy*, ed. by Bruno Latour and Peter Weibel (Cambridge, MA: MIT Press, 2005), pp. 14–41

—— 'No Transformation without Institution', online video recording, YouTube, 17 October 2015 <https://www.youtube.com/watch?v=2RCLTxUaWVo> [accessed 10 January 2024]

—— 'Why Has Critique Run out of Steam? From Matters of Fact to Matters of Concern', *Critical Inquiry*, 30.2 (2004), pp. 225–48 <https://doi.org/10.1086/421123>

Laugier, Sandra, 'Performativité, normativité et droit', *Archives de Philosophie*, 64.4 (2004), pp. 607–27 <https://doi.org/10.3917/aphi.674.0607>

Lawler, Steph, 'Rules of Engagement: Habitus, Power and Resistance', in *Feminism after Bourdieu*, ed. by Lisa Adkins and Beverley Skeggs (Oxford: Blackwell, 2004), pp. 110–28

Leap, William, 'Strangers on a Train: Sexual Citizenship and the Politics of Transportation in Apartheid Cape Town', in *Queer Globalizations: Citizenship and the Afterlife of Colonialism*, ed. by Arnaldo Cruz-Malavé and Martin Manalansan IV (New York: New York University Press, 2002), pp. 219–35 <https://doi.org/10.18574/nyu/9780814790182.003.0016>

Lease, Bryce, and Mark Gevisser, 'LGBTQI Rights in South Africa', *Safundi: The Journal of South African and American Studies*, 18.2 (2017), pp. 156–60 <https://doi.org/10.1080/17533171.2016.1270013>

LeMenager, Stephanie, 'Climate Change and the Struggle for Genre', in *Anthropocene Reading: Literary History in Geologic Times*, ed. by Tobias Menely and Jesse Oak Taylor (University Park: Penn State University Press, 2017), pp. 220–38 <https://doi.org/10.5325/jj.22247044.15>

Lemoine, Blake, 'Is LaMDA sentient? An Interview', *Medium*, 11 June 2022 <https://cajundiscordian.medium.com/is-lamda-sentient-an-interview-ea64d916d917> [accessed 3 March 2024]

Levy, Arnon, 'Idealization and Abstraction: Refining the Distinction', *Synthese*, 198 (2018), pp. 5855–72 <https://doi.org/10.1007/s11229-018-1721-z>

Lewis, Paul, 'The Emergence of "Emergence" in the Work of F. A. Hayek: A Historical Analysis', *History of Political Economy*, 48.1 (2016), pp. 111–50 <https://doi.org/10.1215/00182702-3452315>

Lezra, Jacques, *Defective Institutions: A Protocol for the Republic* (New York: Fordham University Press, 2024) <https://doi.org/10.5422/fordham/9781531506902.001.0001>

Librandi, Marília, *Writing by Ear: Lispector and the Aural Novel* (Toronto: Toronto University Press, 2018) <https://doi.org/10.3138/9781487514730>

Librett, Jeffrey, 'The Subject in the Age of World-Formation (*Mondialisation*): Advances in Lacanian Theory from the Québec Group', in *Innovations in Psychoanalysis: Originality, Development, Progress*, ed. by Aner Govrin and Jon Mills (New York: Routledge, 2020), pp. 75–100 <https://doi.org/10.4324/9780367809560-5>

Linao, Girlie, 'Church: Philippine Miracle a Hoax', *United Press International*, 6 September 1995 <https://www.upi.com/Archives/1995/09/06/Church-Philippine-miracle-a-hoax/5408810360000/> [accessed 12 June 2023]

Lispector, Clarice, *Água Viva*, trans. by Stefan Tobler (New York: New Directions, 2012)

—— *The Passion According to G.H.*, trans. by Idra Novey (New York: Penguin, 2014)

Longino, Helen, *Science as Social Knowledge* (Princeton, NJ: Princeton University Press, 1990)

—— *Studying Human Behavior: How Scientists Investigate Aggression and Sexuality* (Chicago: Chicago University Press, 2013) <https://doi.org/10.7208/chicago/9780226921822.001.0001>

Lorenzini, Daniele, 'On Possibilising Genealogy', *Inquiry: An Interdisciplinary Journal of Philosophy*, 67.7 (2020), pp. 2175–96 <https://doi.org/10.1080/0020174X.2020.1712227>

Lukács, Georg, 'Technology and Social Relations', *New Left Review*, 39 (1966), pp. 27–34

Lyon, Pamela, and others, 'Reframing Cognition: Getting Down to Biological Basics', *Philosophical Transactions of the Royal Society B*, 376 (2021) <https://doi.org/10.1098/rstb.2019.0750>

Mabenge, Landa, *Becoming Him: A Trans Memoir of Triumph* (Johannesburg: Jacana Media, 2019)

Macel, Christine, 'Lygia Clark: At the Border of Art', in *Lygia Clark: The Abandonment of Art 1948–1988*, ed. by Cornelia H. Butler and Luis Pérez-Oramas (New York: Museum of Modern Art, 2014), pp. 253–60

MacKenzie, Donald A., *An Engine, Not a Camera: How Financial Models Shape Markets* (Cambridge MA: MIT Press, 2006) <https://doi.org/10.7551/mitpress/9780262134606.001.0001>

MacKenzie, Donald A., and Yuval Millo, 'Constructing a Market, Performing Theory: The Historical Sociology of a Financial Derivatives Exchange', *American Journal of Sociology*, 109.1 (2003), pp. 107–45 <https://doi.org/10.1086/374404>

MacKenzie, Donald A., Fabian Muniesa, and Lucia Siu, eds, *Do Economists Make Markets? On the Performativity of Economics* (Princeton, NJ: Princeton University Press, 2008) <https://doi.org/10.1515/9780691214665>

Mäki, Uskali, 'Isolation, Idealization and Truth in Economics', in *Idealization VI: Idealization in Economics*, ed. by Bert Hamminga and Neil B. De Marchi, Poznań Studies in the Philosophy of the Sciences and the Humanities, 38 (Amsterdam: Rodopi, 1994), pp. 147–68 <https://doi.org/10.1163/9789004457379_010>

Mahari, Robert, and Pat Pataranutaporn, 'We Need to Prepare for "Addictive Intelligence"', *MIT Technology Review*, 5 August 2024 <https://www.

technologyreview.com/2024/08/05/1095600/we-need-to-prepare-for-addictive-intelligence/> [accessed 12 August 2024]

Malm, Andreas, *The Progress of This Storm: Nature and Society in a Warming World* (New York: Verso, 2017)

Mamdani, Mahmood, *When Victims Become Killers: Colonialism, Nativism, and the Genocide in Rwanda* (Princeton, NJ: Princeton University Press, 2014)

Maniglier, Patrice, 'La Parenté des autres. À propos de Maurice Godelier', *Critique*, 701 (2005), pp. 758–74 <https://doi.org/10.3917/criti.701.0758>

Manion, Anthony, 'Guide to the Gay and Lesbian Archives of South Africa', in *Sex and Politics in South Africa*, ed. by Neville Hoad, Karen Martin, and Graeme Reid (Cape Town: Double Storey Books, 2005), pp. 228–52

Mantaring, Jelo Ritzhie, 'PH Remains Worst Place for Land, Environmental Defenders in Asia — Watchdog', *CNN Philippines*, 30 September 2022 <https://www.cnnphilippines.com/news/2022/9/30/PH-remains-worst-place-for-land-and-environmental-defenders-in-Asia.html> [accessed 5 October 2023]

Martin, Isabel Pefianco, 'Colonial Education and the Shaping of Philippine Literature in English', in *Philippine English: Linguistic and Literary Perspectives*, ed. by Maria Lourdes S. Bautista and Kingsley Bolton (Hong Kong: Hong Kong University Press, 2008), pp. 245–59

Martin, Randy, 'What Difference Do Derivatives Make? From the Technical to the Political Conjuncture,' *Culture Unbound*, 6 (2014): 189–210 <https://doi.org/10.3384/cu.2000.1525.146189>

Marvin, Amy, 'A Brief History of Transphilosophy', *Contingent Magazine*, 21 September 2019 <https://contingentmagazine.org/2019/09/21/trans-philosophy/> [accessed 23 July 2024]

Massanat, Siwar, 'A Constellation of Transnational Poetics', *Jacket2*, 26 January 2023, <https://jacket2.org/article/constellation-transnational-poetics> [accessed 12 June 2023]

Masters, Kim, 'Auteur of Adolescence', *The Washington Post*, 17 October 1992 <https://www.washingtonpost.com/archive/lifestyle/1992/10/17/auteur-of-adolescence/bad908d9-02b0-4a56-a336-8d0cd1b78b31/> [accessed 20 August 2024]

Matsumoto, Kazuhito, '"Exophony" in the Midst of the Mother Tongue: Resources Between Languages', in *Doing English in Asia: Global Literature and Culture*, ed. by Patricia Haseltine and Sheng-mei Ma (Lanham, MD: Lexington Books, 2016), pp. 17–28

Matthyse, Liberty, *A Darling's Journey to Liberty* (Cape Town: self-published, 2016)

Mayne, Richard, Andrew Adamatzky, and Jeff Jones, 'On the Role of the Plasmodial Cytoskeleton in Facilitating Intelligent Behavior in Slime Mold *Physarum polycephalum*', *Communicative and Integrative Biology*, 8.4 (2015) <https://doi.org/10.1080/19420889.2015.1059007>

McCloskey, Deirdre, *The Rhetoric of Economics* (Brighton: Wheatsheaf, 1986)

McNulty, Tracy, 'The Traversal of the Fantasy as an Opening to Humanity', in *Psychoanalysis and Solidarity*, ed. by Michelle Rada, special issue of *differences*, 33.2–3 (2022), pp. 198–219 <https://doi.org/10.1215/10407391-10124760>

Metcalfe, Xandra, '"Why Are We Like This?": The Primacy of Transsexuality', in *Transgender Marxism*, ed. by Jules Joanne Gleeson and Elle O'Rourke (London: Pluto Press), pp. 219–29 <https://doi.org/10.2307/j.ctv1n9dkjc.17>

Meyer, Bernd, Cedrick Ansorge, and Toshiyoku Nakagaki, 'The Role of Noise in Self-Organized Decision Making by the True Slime Mold *Physarum polycephalum*', *PLoS ONE*, 12.3 (2017) <https://doi.org/10.1371/journal.pone.0172933>

Miguel, Marlon, *Camering: Fernand Deligny on Cinema and the Image* (Leiden: Leiden University Press, 2022) <https://doi.org/10.1017/9789400604308>

Mills, Charles W., 'Ideal Theory as Ideology', *Hypatia*, 20.3 (2005), pp. 165–83 <https://doi.org/10.1111/j.1527-2001.2005.tb00493.x>

Mills, Mara, 'On Disability and Cybernetics: Helen Keller, Norbert Wiener, and the Hearing Glove', *differences*, 22.2–3 (2011), pp. 74–111 <https://doi.org/10.1215/10407391-1428852>

Mirowski, Philip, *Machine Dreams: Economics Becomes a Cyborg Science* (Cambridge: Cambridge University Press, 2002) <https://doi.org/10.1017/CBO9780511613364>

—— 'Twelve Theses Concerning the History of Postwar Neoclassical Price Theory', *History of Political Economy*, 38 (2006), pp. 344–79 <https://doi.org/10.1215/00182702-2005-029>

Mitchell, Timothy, *Rule of Experts: Egypt, Techno-Politics, Modernity* (Berkeley, CA: University of California Press, 2002) <https://doi.org/10.1525/9780520928251>

—— 'The Work of Economics: How a Discipline Makes its World', *European Journal of Sociology*, 46.2 (2005), pp. 297–320 <https://doi.org/10.1017/S000397560500010X>

'Models: ICI Focus 2022–24 of the Core Project "Reduction"', ICI Berlin, 13 November 2021 <https://www.ici-berlin.org/projects/models/> [accessed 20 August 2024]

Mohyuddin, Fatima, 'United States Asylum Law in the Context of Sexual Orientation and Gender Identity: Justice of the Transgendered?' *Hastings Women's Law Journal* 12.2 (2001), pp. 387–410

'Montage', in *Larousse Bilingual Dictionary* (Paris: Larousse, n.d.) <https://www.larousse.fr/dictionnaires/francais-anglais/montage/52341> [accessed 30 March 2024]

'Montagem', in *Dicionário Houaiss* (Rio de Janeiro: Instituto Antônio Houaiss, n.d.) <https://houaiss.uol.com.br/> [accessed 22 July 2024]

Montagu, Ashley, *Man's Most Dangerous Myth: The Fallacy of Race* (Lanham, MD: Rowman & Littlefield, 1997)

Moore, Alfred, 'Hayek, Conspiracy, and Democracy', *Critical Review*, 28.1 (2016), pp. 44–62 <https://doi.org/10.1080/08913811.2016.1167405>

Moore, Jason W., *Capitalism in the Web of Life: Ecology and the Accumulation of Capital* (New York: Verso, 2015)

Morgan, Mary S., 'Model Narratives', lecture, ICI Berlin, 30 May 2023, Models lecture series <https://doi.org/10.25620/e230530>

—— *The World in the Model: How Economists Work and Think* (Cambridge: Cambridge University Press, 2012) <https://doi.org/10.1017/CBO9781139026185>

Morgan, Mary S., and Margaret Morrison, eds, *Models as Mediators* (Cambridge: Cambridge University Press, 1999) <https://doi.org/10.1017/CBO9780511660108>

—— *Models as Mediators: Perspectives on Natural and Social Sciences* (Cambridge: Cambridge University Press, 1999) <https://doi.org/10.1017/CBO9780511660108>

Morton, Timothy, *Hyperobjects: Philosophy and Ecology after the End of the World* (Minneapolis: University of Minnesota Press, 2013)

Moser, Benjamin, *Why This World: A Biography of Clarice Lispector* (Oxford: Oxford University Press, 2009)

Moszynska, Anna, *Abstract Art*, 2nd edn (London: Thames and Hudson, 2020)

Msibi, Thabo, 'The Lies We Have Been Told: On (Homo) Sexuality in Africa', *Africa Today*, 58.1 (2011), pp. 55–77 <https://doi.org/10.2979/africatoday.58.1.55>

Mudede, Charles Tonderai, 'Will AI Also Remember the Days of Slavery?', online video recording of lecture delivered at e-flux, New York, 9 January 2024, *e-flux* <https://www.e-flux.com/events/581284/will-ai-also-remember-the-days-of-slavery-a-lecture-by-charles-mudede/> [accessed 11 January 2024]

Muñoz, José Esteban, *Cruising Utopia: The Then and There of Queer Futurity* [2009], 10th anniversary edn (New York: New York University Press, 2019)

—— *Disidentifications: Queers of Color and the Performance of Politics* (Minneapolis: University of Minnesota Press, 1999)

Munro, Brenna M., *South Africa and the Dream of Love to Come: Queer Sexuality and the Struggle for Freedom* (Minneapolis: University of Minnesota Press, 2012)

Murray, David, 'The (Not so) Straight Story: Queering Migration Narratives of Sexual Orientation and Gendered Identity Refugee Claimants', *Sexualities*, 17.4 (2014), pp. 451–71 <https://doi.org/10.1177/1363460714524767>

Mwenda, Martin, 'The Context of Transformative Constitutionalism in Kenya', *SSRN*, published online 30 June 2015 <https://doi.org/10.2139/ssrn.2624928>

Nairobi Court of Appeal, *NGOs Co-ordination Board v. E. G. & 5 Others*, Civil Appeal No. 145 of 2015, Judgement of 22 March 2019

Nakagaki, Toshiyoku, Hiroyasu Yamada, and Ágota Tóth, 'Maze-Solving by an Amoeboid Organism', *Nature*, 407 (2000) <https://doi.org/10.1038/35035159>

Negrete, Fernanda, *The Aesthetic Clinic: Feminine Sublimation in Contemporary Writing, Psychoanalysis, and Art* (Albany: State University of New York Press, 2020) <https://doi.org/10.1515/9781438480220>

—— 'The Aesthetic Pass: Beauty and the End of Analysis', in *Psychoanalysis and Solidarity*, ed. by Michelle Rada, special issue of *differences*, 33.2–3 (2022), pp. 220–41 <https://doi.org/10.1215/10407391-10124774>

—— 'Approaching Impersonal Life with Clarice Lispector', in *New Encounters Between Philosophy and Literature II*, ed. by Krzysztof Ziarek, special issue of *Humanities*, 7.2 (2018) <https://doi.org/10.3390/h7020055>

Nersessian, Anahid, *The Calamity Form: Poetry and Social Life* (Chicago: University of Chicago Press, 2020) <https://doi.org/10.7208/chicago/9780226701455.001.0001>

A New Year, dir. by Sadie Benning (USA, 1989)

Newall, Michael, *What Is a Picture? Depiction, Realism, Abstraction* (Basingstoke: Palgrave Macmillan, 2011) <https://doi.org/10.1057/9780230297531>

Nyawa, Joshua Malidzo, 'The Kenyan Constitution 2010, Gay Sex (or Gay Rights?), and the Eric Gitari Ruling of 2019', *SSRN*, published online 16 June 2019 <http://dx.doi.org/10.2139/ssrn.3396306>

OECD, 'Concentration Pathways for the Four Outlook Scenarios Including All Climate Forcers, 2010–2100', in *OECD Environmental Outlook to 2050: The Consequences of Inaction* (Paris: OECD Publishing, 2012) <https://doi.org/10.1787/env_outlook-2012-graph38-en>

OED Online (Oxford: Oxford University Press, 2024) <https://www.oed.com/>

Oliva, Gabriel, 'The Road to Servomechanisms: The Influence of Cybernetics on Hayek from "The Sensory Order" to the Social Order', *Research in the History of Economic Thought and Methodology* 34 (2016), pp. 161–98 <https://doi.org/10.2139/ssrn.2670064>

O'Neill, Onora, 'Abstraction, Idealization and Ideology in Ethics', *Royal Institute of Philosophy Supplements*, 22 (1987), pp. 55–69 <https://doi.org/10.1017/S0957042X00003667>

Ordoñez, Elmer, 'An Overview of Philippine Literature', in Ordoñez, *Emergent Literature: Essays on Philippine Writing* (Quezon City: University of the Philippines Press, 2001), pp. 23–38

Ordorica Gallegos, Sergio Armando, 'The Explanatory Role of Abstraction Processes in Models: The Case of Aggregations', *Studies in History and*

Philosophy of Science Part A, 56 (2016), pp. 161–67 <https://doi.org/10.1016/j.shpsa.2015.10.002>

Pantoja-Hidalgo, Cristina, 'The Philippine Short Story in English: An Overview', in *Philippine English: Linguistic and Literary Perspectives*, ed. by Maria Lourdes S. Bautista and Kingsley Bolton (Hong Kong: Hong Kong University Press, 2008), pp. 299–316

Pardo, Melissa, 'Dialectal Diversity and Its Effect on the Language Model Landscape', *Appen*, 14 February 2024 <https://www.appen.com/blog/pulse-of-language-evolution> [accessed 4 June 2023]

Parisi, Luciana, 'Aimless Automata and Inhuman Techno-Materiality', in *Human after Man*, ed. by Marietta Kesting and Susanne Witzgall (Zurich and Berlin: diaphanes, 2022), pp. 143–50

Pastrano, Mozart, 'Apparition Star Judiel Nieva Is Now a Showbiz Star', *Philippine Daily Inquirer*, 5 September 2003, p. A29

—— 'The Virgin in Agoo', *Philippine Daily Inquirer*, 5 March 1993, pp. 1,10

Patke, Rajeev, and Philip Holden, *The Routledge Concise History of Southeast Asian Writing in English* (Abingdon: Routledge, 2010) <https://doi.org/10.4324/9780203874035>

Paul, Elliot Samuel, and Dustin Stokes, 'Creativity', *The Stanford Encyclopedia of Philosophy* (Spring 2024 edition), ed. by Edward N. Zalta and Uri Nodelman <https://plato.stanford.edu/archives/spr2024/entries/creativity/> [accessed 1 July 2024]

Pease, Donald E., 'Re-mapping the Transnational Turn', in *Re-framing the Transnational Turn in American Studies*, ed. by Winfried Fluck and others (Hanover, NH: Dartmouth College Press, 2011), pp. 1–46

Pendergrass, Drew, and Troy Vettese, *Half-Earth Socialism* (New York: Verso, 2022)

Peterson, Erik L., *The Life Organic: The Theoretical Biology Club and the Roots of Epigenetics* (Pittsburgh: University of Pittsburgh Press, 2017) <https://doi.org/10.2307/j.ctt1kc6hv4>

Pettman, Charles, *Africanderisms: A Glossary of South African Colloquial Words and Phrases and of Place and Other Names* (London: Longmans, Green and Co., 1913)

Piantadosi, Stephen T., and Felix Hill, 'Meaning without Reference in Large Language Models', eprint arXiv:2208.02957 (August 2022) <https://doi.org/10.48550/arXiv.2208.02957>

Poling, Clark V., *Kandinsky: Russian and Bauhaus Years, 1915–1933* (New York: Solomon R. Guggenheim Foundation, 1983)

Ponge, Francis, *Partisan of Things*, trans. by Joshua Corey and Jean-Luc Garneau (Berkeley, CA: Kenning Editions, 2016)

Potochnik, Angela, *Idealization and the Aims of Science* (Chicago: University of Chicago Press, 2017) <https://doi.org/10.7208/chicago/9780226507194.001.0001>

Prosser, Jay, *Second Skins: The Body Narratives of Transsexuality* (New York: Columbia University Press, 1998)

Qiu, Wen, 'Aristotle's Definition of Language', *International Journal of English Literature and Culture*, 2.8 (2014), pp. 194–202 <https://www.academicresearchjournals.org/IJELC/PDF/2014/August/Qiu.pdf> [accessed 4 September 2024]

Rabie, Francois, and Elmien Lesch, '"I Am Like A Woman": Constructions of Sexuality Among Gay Men in a Low-Income South African Community', *Culture, Health & Sexuality*, 11.7 (2009), pp. 717–29 <https://doi.org/10.1080/13691050902890344>

Radder, Hans, *The World Observed/The World Conceived* (Pittsburgh: Pittsburgh University Press, 2006) <https://doi.org/10.2307/j.ctt6wrcvz>

Raiford, Leigh, 'When Home is a Photograph: Kathleen Cleaver's Album of Exile', lecture, ICI Berlin, 27 March 2024, Model lecture series <https://doi.org/10.25620/e240327>

Ramazani, Jahan, *Poetry in a Global Age* (Chicago: University of Chicago Press, 2020) <https://doi.org/10.7208/chicago/9780226730288.001.0001>

Ramey, Joshua, 'Neoliberalism as a Political Theology of Chance: The Politics of Divination', *Palgrave Communications*, 1 (2015) <https://doi.org/10.1057/palcomms.2015.39>

Ramsden-Karelse, Ruth, 'Moving and Moved: Reading Kewpie's District Six', *GLQ: A Journal of Lesbian and Gay Studies*, 26.3 (2020), pp. 405–38 <https://doi.org/10.1215/10642684-8311772>

—— '"People Can't Say I'm A Man, They Can't Say I'm A Woman": Reality Expansion in the Kewpie Collection', in *The Routledge Handbook of Queer Rhetoric*, ed. by Jacqueline Rhodes and Jonathan Alexander (Abingdon: Routledge, 2022), pp. 207–14 <https://doi.org/10.4324/9781003144809>

Rancière, Jacques, *The Ignorant Schoolmaster: Five Lessons in Intellectual Emancipation*, trans. by Kristin Ross (Stanford, CA: Stanford University Press, 2007)

Rangøy, Øyvind, 'Train of Language: Notes on an Exophonic Anomaly', *Interlitteraria*, 26.1 (2021), pp. 235–48 <https://doi.org/10.12697/IL.2021.26.1.16>

Rashid, Hani, and Lise Anne Couture, *Asymptote: Architecture at the Interval* (New York: Rizzoli, 1995)

Reid, Graeme, 'Fragments from the Archives II', in *Sex and Politics in South Africa*, ed. by Neville Hoad, Karen Martin, and Graeme Reid (Cape Town: Double Storey Books, 2005), pp. 174–77

Republic of the Philippines, *Proclamation No. 1081* (Office of the President, 1972) <https://www.officialgazette.gov.ph/featured/declaration-of-martial-law/> [accessed 12 June 2023]

Rheinberger, Hans-Jörg, *Toward a History of Epistemic Things: Synthesizing Proteins in the Test Tube* (Stanford, CA: Stanford University Press, 1997)

Rice, Collin, *Leveraging Distortions: Explanation, Idealization, and Universality in Science* (Cambridge, MA: MIT Press, 2021) <https://doi.org/10.7551/mitpress/13784.001.0001>

Rich, Ruby, *New Queer Cinema: The Director's Cut* (Durham, NC: Duke University Press, 2013) <https://doi.org/10.1215/9780822399698>

Robinson, Kim Stanley, *The Ministry for the Future* (New York: Orbit, 2020)

Roden, David, 'Nature's Dark Domain: An Argument for a Naturalized Phenomenology', in *Phenomenology and Naturalism: Examining the Relationship Between Human Experience and Nature*, ed. by Havi Carel and Darian Meacham, special issue of *Royal Institute of Philosophy Supplement*, 72 (2013), pp. 169–88 <https://doi.org/10.1017/S135824611300009X>

Roen, Katrina, 'Transgender Theory and Embodiment: The Risk of Racial Marginalisation', *Journal of Gender Studies*, 10.3 (2001), pp. 253–63 <https://doi.org/10.1080/09589230120086467>

Rojas, Carlos, and Steven L. Stephenson, eds, *Myxomycetes: Biology, Systematics, Biogeography, and Ecology* (London: Elsevier, 2017)

Rolland, Angèle, and others, 'Behavioural Changes in Slime Moulds over Time', *Philosophical Transactions of the Royal Society B*, 378 (2023) <https://doi.org/10.1098/rstb.2022.0063>

Rondot, Sarah Ray, '"Bear Witness" and "Build Legacies": Twentieth- and Twenty-First-Century Trans* Autobiography', *a/b: Auto/Biography Studies*, 31.3 (2016), pp. 527–51 <https://doi.org/10.1080/08989575.2016.1183339>

Rosenberg, Jordy, 'Afterword: One Utopia, One Dystopia', in *Transgender Marxism*, ed. by Jules Joanne Gleeson and Elle O'Rourke (London: Pluto Press, 2021), pp. 259–95 <https://doi.org/10.2307/j.ctv1n9dkjc.19>

Rosenblatt, Frank, 'The Perceptron: A Probabilistic Model for Information Storage and Organization in the Brain', *Psychological Review*, 65.6 (1958), pp. 386–408 <https://doi.org/10.1037/h0042519>

—— *Principles of Neurodynamics: Perceptrons and the Theory of Brain Mechanisms* (Washington, DC: Spartan, 1962) <https://doi.org/10.21236/AD0256582>

Sabsay, Leticia, 'The Emergence of the Other Sexual Citizen: Orientalism and the Modernisation of Sexuality', *Citizenship Studies*, 16.5–6 (2012), pp. 605–23 <https://doi.org/10.1080/13621025.2012.698484>

'Sadie Benning, American, born 1973', Museum of Modern Art, n.d. <https://www.moma.org/artists/34902> [accessed 20 August 2024]

Saghieh, Hazem, *Mouzakarat Randa Al-Trans, or The Memoirs of Randa the Trans* (Beirut: Dar al-Saqi, 2010)

Saito, Kohei, *Marx in the Anthropocene: Towards the Idea of Degrowth Communism* (Cambridge: Cambridge University Press, 2023) <https://doi.org/10.1017/9781108933544>

Saleh, Fadi, 'Transgender as a Humanitarian Category: The Case of Syrian Queer and Gender-Variant Refugees in Turkey', *TSQ: Transgender Studies Quarterly*, 7.1 (2020), pp. 37–55 <https://doi.org/10.1215/23289252-7914500>

Salis, Fiora, 'The New Fiction View of Models', *British Journal for the Philosophy of Science*, 72.3 (2021), pp. 717–42 <https://doi.org/10.1093/bjps/axz015>

Sandja, Neo L., *Right Mind, Wrong Body: The Ultimate Trans Guide to Being Complete and Living a Fulfilled Life* (n.p.: Light Publishers, 2016)

Santos, Boaventura de Sousa, and César A. Rodríguez-Garavito, eds, *Law and Globalization from Below: Towards a Cosmopolitan Legality* (Cambridge: Cambridge University Press, 2005) <https://doi.org/10.1017/CBO9780511494093>

Schaus, Michael, 'Narrative & Value: Authorship in the Story of Money' (unpublished master's thesis, OCAD University, 2017) <https://openresearch.ocadu.ca/id/eprint/2719/> [accessed 27 September 2024]

Schneider-Mayerson, Matthew, 'Climate-Change Fiction', in *American Literature in Transition, 2000–2010*, ed. by Rachel Greenwald Smith (New York: Cambridge University Press, 2017), pp. 309–21 <https://doi.org/10.1017/9781316569290.021>

Schwartzman, Lisa H., 'Abstraction, Idealization, and Oppression', *Metaphilosophy*, 37.5 (2006), pp. 565–88 <https://doi.org/10.1111/j.1467-9973.2006.00457.x>

Scott, James C., *Seeing Like a State: How Certain Schemes to Improve the Human Condition Have Failed* (New Haven, CT: Yale University Press, 1999)

Searle, John, 'How Performatives Work', in Searle, *Consciousness and Language* (Cambridge: Cambridge University Press, 2002), pp. 156–79 <https://doi.org/10.1017/CBO9780511606366.011>

Sebastian, Rajani, Angela Laird, and Swathi Kiran, 'Meta-Analysis of the Neural Representation of First Language and Second Language', *Applied Psycholinguistics*, 32 (2011) <https://doi.org/10.1017/S0142716411000075>

Sedgwick, Eve Kosofsky, *Touching Feeling* (Durham, NC: Duke University Press, 2003) <https://doi.org/10.1215/9780822384786>

Shapiro, Martin, and Alec Stone Sweet, *On Law, Politics, and Judicialization* (Oxford: Oxford University Press, 2002) <https://doi.org/10.1093/0199256489.001.0001>

Shatz, Carla J., 'The Developing Brain', *Scientific American*, 267.3 (1992), pp. 60–67 <https://doi.org/10.1038/scientificamerican0992-60>

Shellhorse, Adam Joseph, 'Figurations of Immanence: Writing the Subaltern and the Feminine in Clarice Lispector', in *Anti-Literature: The Politics and Limits of Representation in Modern Brazil and Argentina* (Pittsburgh:

University of Pittsburgh Press, 2017), pp. 17–43 <https://doi.org/10.2307/j.ctt1r69xs2.5>

Shields, Ross, 'Hanging-Together: Goethe, Kant, and the Theory of Aesthetic Modernism' (unpublished doctoral thesis, Columbia University, 2019) <https://doi.org/10.7916/D8475TVQ>

Shleifer, Andrei, and Lawrence H. Summers, 'The Noise Trader Approach to Finance', *The Journal of Economic Perspectives*, 4.2 (1990), pp. 19–33 <https://doi.org/10.1257/jep.4.2.19>

Shumailov, Illia, and others, 'The Curse of Recursion: Training on Generated Data Makes Models Forget', eprint arXiv:2305.17493v2 (May 2023) <https://doi.org/10.48550/arXiv.2305.17493>

Sieder, Rachel, 'The Juridification of Politics', in *The Oxford Handbook of Law and Anthropology*, ed. by Marie-Claire Foblets and others (Oxford: Oxford University Press, 2020), pp. 701–15 <https://doi.org/10.1093/oxfordhb/9780198840534.013.41>

Silva, Hannah, *My Child, the Algorithm: An Alternatively Intelligent Book of Love* (London: Footnote Press, 2023)

Sison, José Maria, 'Literary Craft and Commitment', in Sison, *The Guerrilla Is Like a Poet / Ang Gerilya Ay Tulad ng Makata* (Santa Barbara, CA: Punctum Books, 2013), pp. 213–19 <https://doi.org/10.2307/j.ctv2sbm7n2.102>

Skidmore, Emily, 'Constructing the "Good Transsexual": Christine Jorgensen, Whiteness, and Heteronormativity in the Mid-Twentieth-Century Press', *Feminist Studies*, 37.2 (2011), pp. 270–300 <https://doi.org/10.1353/fem.2011.0043>

Smith, Adam, 'The History of Astronomy', in *The Glasgow Edition of the Works and Correspondence of Adam Smith*, 7 vols (Oxford: Oxford Scholarly Editions Online, 2014), III: *Essays on Philosophical Subjects with Dugald Stewart's Account of Adam Smith*, ed. by W. P. D. Wightman, J. C. Bryce, and I. S. Ross [1980], pp. 33–105 <https://doi.org/10.1093/actrade/9780198281870.book.1>

Solway, Diana, 'Transgender Artist Sadie Benning Is Not Afraid', *W*, 13 May 2016 <https://www.wmagazine.com/story/sadie-benning-artist-mary-boone-callicoon-fine-arts> [accessed 20 August 2024]

Sperling, Alison, 'Climate Fictions: Introduction', *Paradoxa*, 31 (2019), pp. 7–21 <https://paradoxa.com/no-30-climate-fictions-2020/> [accessed 4 August 2024]

Spivak, Gayatri Chakravorty, 'The Rani of Sirmur: An Essay in Reading the Archives', *History and Theory*, 24.3 (1985), pp. 247–72 <https://doi.org/10.2307/2505169>

Srinivasan, Amia, 'Genealogy, Epistemology and Worldmaking', *Proceedings of the Aristotelian Society*, 119.2 (2019), pp. 127–56 <https://doi.org/10.1093/arisoc/aoz009>

Stein, Gertrude, *Picasso* (New York: Dover, 1984)

Steinbock, Eliza, *Shimmering Images: Trans Cinema, Embodiment, and the Aesthetics of Change* (Durham, NC: Duke University Press, 2019) <https://doi.org/10.1515/9781478004509>

Stewart, Georgina Tuari, and others, 'Colonization of All Forms', *Educational Philosophy and Theory*, 56.11 (2024), pp. 1039–43 <https://doi.org/10.1080/00131857.2022.2040482>

Stierstorfer, Klaus, 'Models and/as/of Literature', *Anglia*, 138.4 (2020), pp. 673–98 <https://doi.org/10.1515/ang-2020-0053>

Stilling, Robert, 'Multicentric Modernism and Postcolonial Poetry', in *The Cambridge Companion to Postcolonial Poetry*, ed. by Jahan Ramazani (Cambridge: Cambridge University Press, 2017), pp. 127–38 <https://doi.org/10.1017/9781316111338.011>

Stoltzfus, Arlin, and Kele Cable, 'Mendelian-Mutationism: The Forgotten Evolutionary Synthesis', *Journal of the History of Biology*, 47 (2014), pp. 501–46 <https://doi.org/10.1007/s10739-014-9383-2>

Stone, Sandy, 'The *Empire* Strikes Back: A Posttranssexual Manifesto', *Camera Obscura: Feminism, Culture, and Media Studies*, 10.2 (1992), pp. 150–76 <https://doi.org/10.1215/02705346-10-2_29-150>

Stryker, Susan, '(De)Subjugated Knowledges: An Introduction to Transgender Studies', in *The Transgender Studies Reader*, ed. by Susan Stryker and Stephen Whittle (New York: Routledge, 2006), pp. 1–17

Stuart, Michael, and Anatolii Kozlov, 'Moving Targets and Models of Nothing: A New Sense of Abstraction for Philosophy of Science', in *Abstraction in Science and Art: Philosophical Perspectives*, ed. by Chiara Ambrosio and Julia Sánchez-Dorado (London: Routledge, 2024), pp. 118–42 <https://doi.org/10.4324/9781003380955-7>

Stychin, Carl, and Didi Herman, eds, *Sexuality in the Legal Arena* (London: The Athlone Press, 2000)

Suppes, Patrick, 'A Comparison of the Meaning and Uses of Models in Mathematics and the Empirical Sciences', *Synthese*, 12 (1960), pp. 287–301 <https://doi.org/10.1007/BF00485107>

Swarr, Amanda Lock, *Envisioning African Intersex: Challenging Colonial and Racist Legacies in South African Medicine* (Durham, NC: Duke University Press, 2023) <https://doi.org/10.1515/9781478093763>

Tabery, James, *Beyond Versus: The Struggle to Understand the Interaction of Nature and Nurture* (Cambridge, MA: MIT Press, 2014) <https://doi.org/10.7551/mitpress/9780262027373.001.0001>

—— 'R. A. Fisher, Lancelot Hogben, and the Origin(s) of Genotype–Environment Interaction', *Journal of the History of Biology*, 41.4 (2008), pp. 717–61 <https://doi.org/10.1007/s10739-008-9155-y>

Tate, C. Neal, and Torbjorn Vallinder, eds, *The Global Expansion of Judicial Power* (New York: New York University Press, 1995)

Ternois, Manon, and others, 'Slime Molds Response to Carbon Nanotubes Exposure: From Internalization to Behavior', *Nanotoxicology*,

15.4 (2021), pp. 511–26 <https://doi.org/10.1080/17435390.2021.1894615>

Tero, Atsushi, and others, 'Rules for Biologically Inspired Adaptive Network Design', *Science*, 327 (2010), pp. 439–42 <https://doi.org/10.1126/science.1177894>

Teubner, Gunther, 'Self-subversive Justice: Contingency or Transcendence Formula of Law?', *Modern Law Review*, 72 (2009), pp. 1–23 <https://doi.org/10.1111/j.1468-2230.2009.00731.x>

—— ed., *Juridification of Social Spheres: A Comparative Analysis in the Areas of Labor, Corporate, Antitrust and Social Welfare Law* (Berlin: De Gruyter, 1987) <https://doi.org/10.1515/9783110921472>

Tharp, Marie, 'Connect the Dots: Mapping the Seafloor and Discovering the Mid-Ocean Ridge', in *Lamont-Doherty Earth Observatory: Twelve Perspectives on the First Fifty Years, 1949–1999*, ed. by Laurence Lippsett (Palisades, NY: Lamont-Doherty Earth Observatory of Columbia University, 1999), pp. 31–37; reproduced as 'Marie Tharp's Adventures in Mapping the Seafloor, in her Own Words', 24 July 2020 <https://news.climate.columbia.edu/2020/07/24/marie-tharp-connecting-dots/> [accessed January 2024]

—— 'Mapping the Ocean Floor: 1947–1977', in *The Ocean Floor: Bruce Heezen Commemorative Volume*, ed. by R. A. Scrutton and M. Talwani (New York: Wiley, 1982), pp. 19–31

Thompson, Clive, 'The Gendered History of Human Computing', *Smithsonian Magazine*, June 2019 <https://www.smithsonianmag.com/science-nature/history-human-computers-180972202/> [accessed 4 December 2023]

Timane, Rizi Xavier, *An Unspoken Compromise: My Story of Gender and Spiritual Transition* (n.p.: self-published, 2017)

Todorov, Tzvetan, 'The Origin of Genres', trans. by Richard M. Berrong, *New Literary History*, 8.1 (1976), pp. 159–70 <https://doi.org/10.2307/468619>

Tomson, Anastacia, *Always Anastacia: A Transgender Life in South Africa* (Johannesburg: Jonathan Ball, 2016)

Toon, Adam, *Models as Make-Believe: Imagination, Fiction and Scientific Representation* (London: Palgrave Macmillian, 2012) <https://doi.org/10.1057/9781137292230>

Tosel, Natascia, 'State, Law, and Institutions: A Study on Juridification', *Soft Power: Revista euro-americana de teoría e historia de la política y del derecho*, 9.2 (2022), pp. 156–73 <https://www.softpowerjournal.com/state-law-and-institutions-a-study-on-juridification/> [accessed 6 August 2024]

Tournier, Michel, *Friday, or the Other Island* [French orig. *Vendredi ou les Limbes du Pacifique* (1967)], trans. by Norman Denny (Baltimore: Johns Hopkins University Press, 1997)

Tretyakov, Sergei, 'The Biography of the Object', *October*, 118 (2006), pp. 57–62 <https://doi.org/10.1162/octo.2006.118.1.57>

Tucker, Andrew, *Queer Visibilities: Space, Identity, and Interaction in Cape Town* (Oxford: Wiley Blackwell, 2009) <https://doi.org/10.1002/9781444306187>

Turing, Alan M., 'Computing Machinery and Intelligence', Mind, 59.236 (1950), pp. 433–60 <https://doi.org/10.1093/mind/LIX.236.433>

Ullrich, J. K., 'Climate Fiction: Can Books Save the Planet?', *The Atlantic*, 14 August 2015 <https://www.theatlantic.com/entertainment/archive/2015/08/climate-fiction-margaret-atwood-literature/400112/> [accessed 3 January 2024]

Umphrey, Martha Merrill, 'Law in Drag: Trials and Legal Performativity', *Columbia Journal of Gender and Law*, 21.2 (2011) <https://doi.org/10.7916/cjgl.v21i2.2638>

Vallejo, César, 'And What If After So Many Words…', trans. by Douglas Lawder and Robert Bly, in Robert Bly, *Leaping Poetry: An Idea with Poems and Translations* [1972] (Pittsburgh: University of Pittsburgh Press, 2008), pp. 36–39

van Fraassen, Bas C., *The Scientific Image* (Oxford: Oxford University Press, 1980) <https://doi.org/10.1093/0198244274.001.0001>

Vaswani, Ashish, and others, 'Attention Is All You Need', eprint arXiv:1706.03762 (June 2017) <https://doi.org/10.48550/arXiv.1706.03762>

Vidal-Ortiz, Salvador, 'Whiteness', *TSQ: Transgender Studies Quarterly*, 1.1–2 (2014), pp. 264–66 <https://doi.org/10.1215/23289252-2400217>

Villares, Lucia, *Examining Whiteness: Reading Clarice Lispector through Bessie Head and Toni Morrison* (New York: Legenda, 2011)

Vipond, Evan, 'Becoming Culturally (Un)Intelligible: Exploring the Terrain of Trans Life Writing', *a/b: Auto/Biography Studies*, 34.1 (2019), pp. 19–43 <https://doi.org/10.1080/08989575.2019.1542813>

Visser, Gustav, 'Gay Men, Leisure Space, and South African Cities: The Case of Cape Town', *Geoforum*, 34.1 (2003), pp. 123–37 <https://doi.org/10.1016/S0016-7185(02)00079-9>

Viveiros de Castro, Eduardo, *Cannibal Metaphysics: For a Post-Structuralist Anthropology* (Minneapolis: University of Minnesota Press, 2014)

Vogman, Elena, *Dance of Values: Sergei Eisenstein's Capital Project* (Zurich: Diaphanes, 2019)

Waal, Rodante van der, Kim Schoof, and Aukje van Rooden, 'When the Egg Breaks, the Chicken Bleeds', in *Philosophy with Clarice Lispector*, ed. by Fernanda Negrete, special issue of *Angelaki* 28.2 (2023), pp. 57–67 <https://doi.org/10.1080/0969725X.2023.2192064>

Wacquant, Loïc, 'Symbolic Power and Group-Making: On Pierre Bourdieu's Reframing of Class', *Journal of Classical Sociology*, 13.2 (2013), pp. 1–18 <https://doi.org/10.1177/1468795X12468737>

Walcott, Derek, *Pantomime*, in *Remembrance and Pantomime* (New York: Farrar Straus & Giroux, 1980)

Walker, Oliver, *K*****s Are Lively: Being Some Backstage Impressions of the South African Democracy* (London: V. Golancz, 1948)

Walton, Kendall, *Mimesis as Make-Believe: On the Foundations of the Representational Arts* (Cambridge, MA: Harvard University Press, 1990)

Wang, Angie, 'Is My Toddler a Stochastic Parrot?', *The New Yorker*, 15 November 2023 <https://www.newyorker.com/humor/sketchbook/is-my-toddler-a-stochastic-parrot> [accessed 4 December 2023]

Wang, Zian, 'When Bigger Isn't Always Better for Language Models', *Deepgram*, 2 August 2023 (updated 14 June 2024) <https://deepgram.com/learn/why-bigger-isnt-better-for-language-models> [accessed 15 August 2024]

Warner, Bernhard, 'How Alexa Was Taught Irish Brogue', *The New York Times*, 5 July 2023 <https://www.nytimes.com/2023/07/01/technology/amazon-alexa-irish.html> [accessed 4 December 2023]

Washington, Harriet A., *Medical Apartheid: The Dark History of Medical Experimentation on Black Americans from Colonial Times to the Present* (New York: Knopf Double Day, 2008)

Weare, Jessica, 'Anaphora', in *The Princeton Encyclopedia of Poetry & Poetics*, ed. by Roland Greene and others, 4th edn (Princeton, NJ: Princeton University Press, 2012), p. 50

Weber, Paul, 'Kandinskys Pädagogik aus der Perspektive seiner Theorie der Verschiebung', in *Wassily Kandinsky: Lehrer am Bauhaus*, ed. by Magdalena Droste (Berlin: Baushaus-Archiv, 2014), pp. 150–75

Wenzel, Jennifer, *The Disposition of Nature: Environmental Crisis and World Literature* (New York: Fordham University Press, 2020) <https://doi.org/10.1515/9780823286805>

Werskey, Gary, *The Visible College: The Collective Biography of British Scientific Socialists of the 1930s* (Boston: Holt, Rinehart, and Winston, 1979)

Whang, Oliver, 'From Baby Talk to Baby AI', *The New York Times*, 30 April 2024 (updated 6 May 2024) <https://www.nytimes.com/2024/04/30/science/ai-infants-language-learning.html> [accessed 7 July 2024]

Wharton, Annabel Jane, 'Defining Models', in *Modelwork: The Material Culture of Making and Knowing*, ed. by Martin Brückner, Sandy Isenstadt, and Sarah Wasserman (Minneapolis: University of Minnesota Press, 2021), pp. 3–20 <https://doi.org/10.5749/j.ctv1z9n20d.4>

Whitehead, Alfred North, *Process and Reality: An Essay in Cosmology* [1929] (New York: The Free Press, 1978)

—— *Science and the Modern World* [1925] (New York: The Free Press, 1967)

Wicomb, Zoë, 'Shame and Identity: The Case of the Coloured in South Africa', in *Writing South Africa*, ed. by Derek Attridge and Rosemary Jolly (Cambridge: Cambridge University Press, 1998), pp. 91–107 <https://doi.org/10.1017/CBO9780511586286.009>

Wiener, Norbert, *Cybernetics, or Control and Communication in the Animal and the Machine* (New York: MIT Press, 1961) <https://doi.org/10.1037/13140-000>

Williams, Bernard, *Truth and Truthfulness: An Essay in Genealogy* (Princeton, NJ: Princeton University Press, 2002)

Winther, Rasmus, 'James and Dewey on Abstraction', *The Pluralist*, 9.2 (2014), pp. 1–28 <https://doi.org/10.5406/pluralist.9.2.0001>

—— 'Mapping the Deep Blue Oceans', in *The Philosophy of GIS*, ed. by Timothy Tambassi (Cham, CH: Springer Geography, 2019), pp. 99–124 <https://doi.org/10.1007/978-3-030-16829-2>

Winther, Rasmus, and Marie Raffn, 'What If?', in *Abstraction in Science and Art: Philosophical Perspectives*, ed. by Chiara Ambrosio and Julia Sánchez-Dorado (London: Routledge, 2024), pp. 217–49 <https://doi.org/10.4324/9781003380955-11>

Wollheim, Richard, 'Seeing-as, Seeing-in, and Pictorial Representation', in Wollheim, *Art and its Objects*, 2nd edn [1980] (Cambridge: Cambridge University Press, 2015), pp. 137–51 <https://doi.org/10.1017/CBO9781316286777.009>

Wong, Cyril, 'A Conversation with Mark Anthony Cayanan', *Queer Southeast Asia: A Literary Journal of Transgressive Art*, June 2021 <http://queersoutheastasia.com/a-conversation-with-mark-anthony-cayanan-july-2021> [accessed 25 March 2024]

Woodard, Ben, *Slime Dynamics: Generation, Mutation, and the Creep of Life* (Winchester: Zero Books, 2012)

Woods, Derek, 'Genre at Earth Magnitude: A Theory of Climate Fiction', *New Literary History*, 54.2 (2023), pp. 1143–67 <https://doi.org/10.1353/nlh.2023.a907162>

Wright, Chantal, 'Writing in the "Grey Zone": Exophonic Literature in Contemporary Germany', *GFL: German as a Foreign Language*, 3 (2008), pp. 26–42 <http://gfl-journal.de/article/writing-in-the-grey-zone/> [accessed 24 July 2024]

Wynter, Sylvia, 'Unsettling the Coloniality of Being/Power/Truth/Freedom: Towards the Human, After Man, its Overrepresentation — An Argument', *CR: The New Centennial Review*, 3.3 (2003), pp. 257–337 <https://doi.org/10.1353/ncr.2004.0015>

Wynter, Sylvia, and Katherine McKittrick, *On Being Human as Praxis* (Durham, NC: Duke University Press, 2015)

Zamfir, Cătălin, *Romanian Wage System in the Transition to a Market Economy*, working paper 54 (Geneva: International Labour Organization, 1992)

Notes on the Contributors

Marta Aleksandrowicz is a researcher in the fields of psychoanalysis, comparative literature, and decolonial and feminist theory. She is also in formation as a psychoanalyst. She received her PhD in comparative literature from the State University of New York at Buffalo in 2022. Her research has appeared or is forthcoming in *Angelaki, Penumbr(a): A Journal of Psychoanalysis and Modernity, The Polish Review*, and *JCLA*. She is also the co-editor of the special issue of *Penumbr(a)* on beauty (2022).

B Camminga is a lecturer in the sociology of gender at the University of Bristol. They received their PhD from the University of Cape Town. They are the co-editor of *East African Queer and Trans Displacements* (Bloomsbury, 2025) and *Queer and Trans African Mobilities: Asylum, Migration and Diaspora* (Zed Books, 2022), and the author of *Transgender Refugees and the Imagined South Africa* (Palgrave Macmillan, 2018). They work on issues relating to gender identity and expression on the African continent.

Mark Anthony Cayanan is an associate professor at the University of the Philippines in Diliman. They have an MFA from the University of Wisconsin–Madison and a PhD from the University of Adelaide, where they received the 2021 Doctoral Research Medal. They are the author of the poetry books *Narcissus, Except You Enthrall Me*, and *Unanimal, Counterfeit, Scurrilous*, and they have received writing fellowships from Ventspils House and Art Omi. Poems from *Miracle Fever* have appeared in *Kenyon Review, Indiana Review*, and *Australian Poetry Journal*; the book project, written and completed at ICI Berlin, will be published in 2026 by Curbstone, an imprint of Northwestern University Press.

Alina-Sandra Cucu is a lecturer in the Department of Sociology and Social Anthropology at Central European University, Vienna. She is an interdisciplinary scholar in the field of global labour studies and the author of *Planning Labour: Time and the Foundations of Industrial Socialism in Romania* (Berghahn, 2020).

Maria Dębińska received her PhD in cultural anthropology from the University of Warsaw in 2015, for a thesis on trans politics in Poland (*Transgender in Poland: Production of a Category*, 2020, in Polish). Since 2019 she has been an assistant professor at the Institute of Archaeology and Ethnology of the Polish

Academy of Sciences, where in 2020–22 she was principal investigator of the research project 'Slime Mould as Method: Ethnography of Scientific Practice', funded by the National Science Centre.

Astrid Deuber-Mankowsky is Professor Emerita of Media Studies and Gender Studies at Ruhr-Universität Bochum. Her research focuses on topics in critical, feminist, and queer theory; media philosophy and epistemology; temporality and media aesthetics; media anthropology and theories of play; and Jewish philosophy. Her most recent monograph is *Queer Post-Cinema: Inventing a New Resistance* (ICI Berlin Press, 2025).

Orit Halpern is Full Professor and Chair of Digital Cultures and Societal Change at Technische Universität Dresden. Her work bridges the histories of science, computing, and cybernetics with design. Her first book, *Beautiful Data: A History of Vision and Reason since 1945* (Duke University Press, 2015), investigates histories of big data, design, and governmentality. Her second book, *The Smartness Mandate* (with Robert Mitchell, MIT Press, 2023), is a genealogy of the current obsession with smart technologies and artificial intelligence.

Christoph F. E. Holzhey is the founding director of the ICI Berlin Institute for Cultural Inquiry, which he has led since 2007. He holds PhDs in theoretical physics (1993) and German literature (2001). He has run several projects at the ICI Berlin and has (co-)edited several volumes, including *Tension/Spannung* (2010), *Multistable Figures* (2014), *De/Constituting Wholes* (2017), *Re-* (2019), *Weathering* (2020), *ERRANS* (2022), and *The Case for Reduction* (2022).

Marietta Kesting is a media and cultural theorist, currently working as research coordinator at the ICI Berlin and as leader of the FWF-funded project 'Future Dreaming in the Arts' in Vienna. From 2016 to 2022 she held a junior professorship at the Academy of Fine Arts Munich, and from 2022 to 2024 she taught at the University of Potsdam. She most recently co-edited the volumes *Human after Man* (with Susanne Witzgall, German in print 2022, English as e-book 2024) and *Landschaft, Wetter, Kraut und Kritter* (*FKW // Zeitschrift für Geschlechterforschung und visuelle Kultur*, 75, 2025, with Kerstin Brandes).

Claudia Peppel is in charge of academic coordination and communication at the ICI Berlin. She studied Italian and French literature at the Freie Universität Berlin and at La Sapienza in Rome and holds a PhD in philosophy from Technische Universität Darmstadt. Her publications focus on literary and cultural studies, as well as aesthetics, art history, and visual culture. She has taught at Berlin University of the Arts and has curated exhibitions of contemporary art. In 2019, she co-edited the volume *Die Kunst des Wartens* (with Brigitte Kölle), on the topic of waiting in the arts.

Ruth Ramsden-Karelse is the Martha LA McCain Postdoctoral Fellow at the University of Toronto's Mark S. Bonham Centre for Sexual Diversity Studies. Ruth received her DPhil in English from the University of Oxford and is currently completing her first monograph, *Gays and Girls Make Worlds*, showing how queers of colour in apartheid South Africa collaboratively created new realities, with a particular focus on the Kewpie Photographic Collection. Her writing has appeared in publications including *GLQ* and *Gender, Place & Culture*.

Julia Sánchez-Dorado is a philosopher and historian of science whose work explores how scientific models contribute to our understanding of complex phenomena in the world. Her research interests also include the problem of representation in science and art, creativity, and the history of analogical modelling in twentieth-century Earth science. She received a PhD from University College London in 2019 and was an Alexander von Humboldt Postdoctoral Fellow at Technische Universität Berlin from 2020 to 2022.

Ross Shields is a visiting assistant professor of German studies at Macalester College. He received his PhD in 2019 from Columbia University, for a dissertation on 'Kant, Goethe, and the Theory of Aesthetic Modernism'. His research is situated at the intersection of literature, philosophy, and the history of science, and focuses on the relation between aesthetics and ecology.

Natascia Tosel is a Marie Skłodowska-Curie Fellow at the University of Verona. She received her PhD in philosophy jointly from the University of Padua and the University of Paris 8, and is the author of *Gabriel Tarde* (DeriveApprodi, 2022) and *The Juridification of Politics* (Routledge, forthcoming). Her research explores the entanglement between law and politics in contemporary feminist and LGBTQIA+ movements, focusing mainly on the translation of political claims into demands for rights protection.

Ben Woodard is an affiliated fellow at the ICI Berlin. He received his PhD in theory and criticism from Western University in 2016. He regularly lectures at the Melbourne School of Continental Philosophy, the School of Materialist Research, and the New Centre for Research and Practice. He has two forthcoming books: *Uninhabited: Science Fiction and the Decolonial* (Zero Books) and *F. H. Bradley and the History of Philosophy: Animating a Lost Idealism* (Edinburgh University Press).

Index

Cultural Inquiry

EDITED BY CHRISTOPH F. E. HOLZHEY
AND MANUELE GRAGNOLATI